AA

Essential

explo

KU-052-646

PARIS

AA Publishing

Essential

Written by Fiona Dunlop
Series Adviser: Ingrid Morgan
Series Editor: Nia Williams
Design: Neil Roebuck Design

Edited, designed, produced and distributed by AA Publishing, Fanum House, Basingstoke, Hampshire RG21 2EA.
© The Automobile Association 1993.
Maps © The Automobile Association 1993.

A catalogue record for this book is available from the British Library.

ISBN 0 7495 0565 6

This book was produced using QuarkXPress ™, Aldus Freehand ™, and Microsoft Word ™ on Apple Macintosh ™ computers.

Colour origination by Fotographics Ltd
Printed and bound in Italy

Published by AA Publishing.

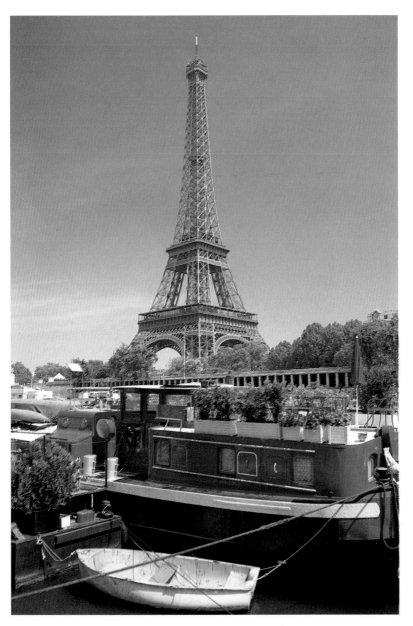

Fiona Dunlop lives in Paris and is the editor and author of the A&C Black *Paris Art Guide*. She is the Paris correspondent for *Arts Review* and *Artline* and has contributed to several travel guides to France and Paris, including the *Time Out Guide to Paris*. She is also a regular contributor to newspapers and magazines, including *Paris Passion*, *The Sunday Times*, *The European*, *France Today*, *Performance Magazine*, *Art International* and *Elle Décor*.

Gustave Eiffel's world-famous construction has become the emblem of Paris

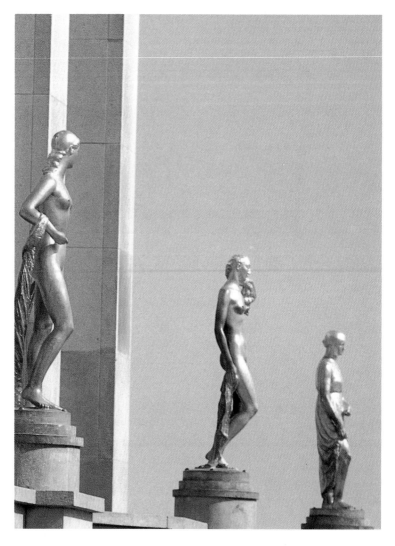

About this book

This book is divided into three principal sections.

The first part of the book discusses aspects of life today and in the past. Places to visit are then covered, along with Focus on... and Close-up features, which highlight areas and subjects in more detail. Drives and walks are also suggested in this section of the book. Finally, day-to-day practical information for the visitor is given in the Travel Facts chapter, along with a selected Directory of hotels and restaurants.

Elegant bronze statues guard the Palais de Chaillot

Some of the places described in this book have been given a special rating:

 Do not miss

 Highly recommended

 See if you can

General Contents

6

Walks

Drive

My Paris

by Annabel Buffet

Why is Paris still the city of everyone's dreams? What makes it the highlight of any itinerary? No-one can deny the city's beauty. Its sights and walks are overwhelming, whether you are strolling along the banks of the Seine, or admiring the perspective which follows a magnificent straight line from the Arc de Triomphe to the Louvre, or walking in Montmartre or St-Germain-des-Prés along streets which keep alive the shadows of the past. Then, of course, there is the world-famous Paris cuisine. And when you have satisfied your gastronomic desires you will face another temptation: window-shopping. The avenue Montaigne, the Faubourg St-Honoré, the delightful place des Victoires, all combine to form a stunning tableau of elegance and taste.

On the other hand, Paris can be something very different from haute-couture shopping or meals in three-star restaurants. I remember my emotions when, after the war which had exiled me to the South of France, I returned to Paris for the first time. I was 17 years old; in my purse I had scarcely enough for the bare necessities of life. I came out of the Gare de Lyon, deafened by the noise and disorientated by the soft Ile de France light, so different from the sun of Provence. The intense life of the capital gripped me, and scared me a little. A day or two later, that anxiety had disappeared. A week later, I had fallen in love with Paris for good. It was on foot and (when money permitted) by bus that I learned to love the city, area by area. Each quartier is a self-contained village; each has its churches, its cafés; and yet each breathes something which is the very essence of Paris: liberty.

Paris is, and will remain, a jewel-case in which one diamond will always sparkle: respect for the human being. Tender-hearted Paris, irrepressible Paris: this is where life is truly free and unconstrained.

Life in Montmartre: the place du Terte

Annabel Buffet has been a model, a singer and a writer. Her books include Daily Love, Good Manners, Beautiful Lies and St Tropez, Today and Yesterday. She married the artist , Bernard Buffet, in 1958; they have three children: Virginie, Danielle and Nicolas.

My Paris

by Maurice Raimbeaux

When I first arrived in Paris I stayed in a small hotel not far from the Etoile. Every morning I would walk to the metro, mesmerised by the giant Arc de Triomphe. Later, as I rose in the bank hierarchy, I didn't have to get up so early – but I still have fond memories of the morning light reflecting off the stone. Strangely enough, I've never been to the top of the Arc: I'm convinced it's only for tourists!

In the early days I also revelled in the Tuileries gardens; instead of having lunch in the bank cafeteria I'd buy a

Only for tourists? The towering Arc de Triomphe

sandwich and head for a sunny park bench.

Since then I've lived in five different arrondissements and discovered that Etoile was probably the most mundane. It's impossible to pick a favourite area: each quartier has its own personality. I loved Pigalle, where as a young bachelor I lived in an artist's atelier; many of my neighbours were painters and sculptors. Ther was a strong village atmosphere and on warm summer evenings we'd walk up the butte Montmartre looking for a cool breeze.

When I got married my wife and I moved to the rather bourgeois fifth arrondissement, right behind the Panthéon. Our apartment building had two entrances: on one side was a maze of narrow silent streets, on the other the rue Mouffetard, with its cheap restaurants, colourful market and crowds of students. On Sundays we'd often go for a walk in the Luxembourg gardens – later taking the baby – and watch the old men playing chess by the Orangerie. But that flat became too small for us so we moved to the Marais, where high-ceilinged flats in former aristocratic townhouses were still relatively cheap. It was the beginning of an enormous upheaval in that neighbourhoos, with gentrification transforming its character fast. We still live there, but we miss the early days, when there were fewer art galleries, restaurants and yuppies – although I suppose I must admit I'm one of them!

Maurice Raimbeaux is a banker who has lived in Paris for almost 20 years. He was born in a mountain village in the Pyrenees and went to university in Toulouse, before moving to Paris as a bank trainee.

PARIS

COURBEVOIE

N13

La Défense

PUTEAUX

N187

Ile de Puteaux

Parc de
Bagatelle

D1

N185

Bois

de

Boulogne

Hippodrome
d'Auteuil

Porte
d'Auteuil

A13

N307

Porte de
St-Cloud

N10

BOULOGNE-
BILLANCOURT

Ile St Germain

MEUDON

N187

D2

N308

Ile de la Grande Jatte

Seine

N187

N309

N310

N410

D1

CLICHY

Porte de
St-Ouen

Porte de
Clichy

Porte
d'Asnières

BOULEVARD

PERIPHERIQUE

BATIGNOLLES

WAGRAM

Cimetière de
Montmartre

CLICHY

LEVALLOIS-PERRET

Porte de
Champerret

NEUILLY-
SUR SEINE

Porte
Maillot

Jardin
d'Acclimatation

Porte
Dauphine

Porte de
la Muette

CHAILLOT

PASSY-
LA MUETTE

Maison de
Radio-France

Seine

AUTEUIL

GRENELLE

JAVEL

Héliport

Porte de
Sèvres

Plaine de
Vaugirard

Porte de
Versailles

ISSY-
LES-MOULINEAUX

TERNES

Palais des
Congrès

Arc de
Triomphe

PLACE CHARLES
DE GAULLE ETOILE

Palais
de Tokyo

Palais de
Chaillot

Tour Eiffel

Parc du
Champ
de Mars

Ecole
Militaire

UNESCO

MONCEAU

Parc
Monceau

Gare
St-Lazare

CHAMPS
ELYSEES

Palais
d'Elysée

Grand
Palais

Opéra

Ste-Marie
Madeleine

PLACE DE LA
CONCORDE

Jardin
des
Tuileries

Assemblée
Nationale

Musée
d'Orsay

Hôtel des
Invalides

FAUBOURG
ST-GERMAIN

ST
DES

INVALIDES

CHERCHE-
MIDI

Gare
Montparnasse

MONTPARNASSE

Cimetière de
Montparnasse

Palais des
Sports

VAUGIRARD

Parc des
Expositions

PLAISANCE

DENFERT-
ROCHEREAU

MALAKOFF

Porte de
Châtillon

Porte
d'Orléans

N306

MONTROUGE

N20

Cimitière
Parisien
de Bagneux

0   1   2 kilometres

0   1 mile

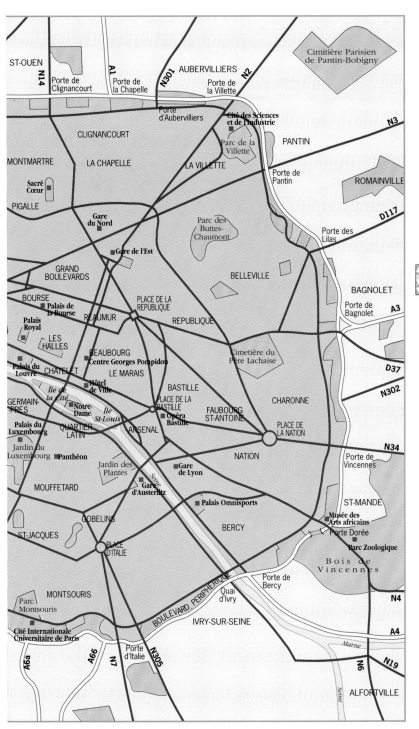

ST-OUEN

N14

A1

Porte de
Clignancourt

Porte de
la Chapelle

N301

AUBERVILLIERS

Porte de
la Villette

N2

Cimitière Parisien
de Pantin-Bobigny

Porte
d'Aubervilliers

Cité des Sciences
et de l'Industrie

N3

CLIGNANCOURT

Parc de la
Villette

PANTIN

MONTMARTRE

LA CHAPELLE

LA VILLETTE

Porte de
Pantin

ROMAINVILLE

Sacré
Cœur

Porte des
Lilas

D117

PIGALLE

Gare
du Nord

Parc des
Buttes-
Chaumont

Gare de l'Est

BAGNOLET

GRAND
BOULEVARDS

BELLEVILLE

Porte de
Bagnolet

A3

BOURSE

Palais de
la Bourse

RÉAUMUR

PLACE DE LA
RÉPUBLIQUE

REPUBLIQUE

Palais
Royal

LES
HALLES

BEAUBOURG

Centre Georges Pompidou

Cimetière du
Père Lachaise

D37

Palais du
Louvre

CHÂTELET

LE MARAIS

N302

Hôtel
de Ville

BASTILLE

Île de
la Cité

Notre-
Dame

PLACE DE LA
BASTILLE

FAUBOURG
ST-ANTOINE

CHARONNE

GERMAIN-
PRÈS

Île
St-Louis

Opéra
Bastille

PLACE DE
LA NATION

N34

Palais du
Luxembourg

QUARTIER
LATIN

ARSENAL

NATION

Porte de
Vincennes

Jardin du
Luxembourg

Panthéon

Jardin des
Plantes

Gare
de Lyon

ST-MANDE

MOUFFETARD

Seine

Gare
d'Austerlitz

Palais Omnisports

Musée des
Arts africains

GOBELINS

BERCY

Porte Dorée

ST-JACQUES

PLACE
D'ITALIE

Parc Zoologique

Bois de
Vincennes

MONTSOURIS

BOULEVARD PÉRIPHÉRIQUE

Porte de
Bercy

N4

Parc
Montsouris

Quai
d'Ivry

A4

Cité Internationale
Universitaire de Paris

IVRY-SUR-SEINE

Marne

A6a

A66

N7

Porte
d'Italie

N305

N6

N19

Seine

ALFORTVILLE

■ **Paris is one of the most densely populated cities in the world. Not only that: it is perhaps the capital most talked about, most written about, most hyped, most dreamed about. A holiday spent there leaves indelible memories – whether of the clear Spring light on the Seine, a gastronomic fantasy, an exhausting string of masterpieces at the Louvre or an unforgettably bolshy waiter serving a tray of delectable oysters. Full of contrasts, thick with history, it is also a city on the move, looking to the future. .....■**

Parisians themselves remain a mystery. Their general love of the good things in life – food, sex and fashion (not necessarily in that order) is accompanied by a strong intellectual streak. TV programmes regularly feature groups of writers chatting about their books, ideas and projects, while newspapers contain long columns written by philosophers. This interest in abstraction spins off into conversations in which heated arguments are commonplace and a necessary part of any friendship. For some, such a strong emphasis on abstract thought stops action, or at least postpones it, and the business world suffers directly.

Defining a typical Parisian means taking into account not only the many provincials who flock to the city but also a traditional foreign influx, whether from Central Africa, North Africa, Vietnam or Europe. Communities form rapidly, from the African and Arab quarters in Belleville to the Chinese and Vietnamese in the 13th *arrondissement*. Racism is disturbingly on the increase, particularly in the soulless suburbs bereft of social life and structure, and continues the traditional French xenophobia. In contrast, the prosperous and sacrosanct 16th *arrondissement* remains intact with its breed of bourgeoisie sprinkled with the odd Princess, Sheikh or retired Hollywood diva. In between the extremes lies the heart of French business and social trends.

Paris Style Ever since the heady days of the 1920s, Paris has harboured a hotbed of foreign artists, thinkers and political refugees, all of whom have contributed to the clichés of bohemianism. Glamour is never far: Paris is a city where enjoyment costs little, as it is always on display. Appearances are paramount, and the impeccably groomed businessman or woman, totally at ease drinking a champagne cocktail in the latest trendy restaurant, may well turn out to live in a minute studio-flat in a distant *arrondissement*. Money is worn on the back, or on the plate, and this can also be interpreted as a sheep-like trait. Fashion is not invented, it is followed; woe betide the pretender who misses the season's mark. Yet this apparent conformism is peppered with strong anarchistic qualitities, as traffic wardens and tourists well know. The notion of queueing (although originally from a French word) still seems to escape the Gallic consciousness; individualism wins hands down over any civic conscience or community sense.

Changing city The Paris of the 1990s has a radically different face to that of only 15 years ago. Ten years of a socialist President who, to some, seems to be moulding himself on predecessors such as Louis XIV or Napoleon III, have left their distinctive mark. *Grands projets* hit the skyline, new quartiers are created and Paris is gradually undergoing total gentrification. An obsession with history and one's role in the continuum is another characteristic of French rulers, and Mitterrand is no exception. Which other world capital has invested so much in cultural structures as a national trademark?

<< The population of Paris (intramuros, or within the ring road) stabilised in 1990 at 2,152,400 after 30 years of dropping. Each residence/flat/house has 1.92 inhabitants, compared with 2.35 in 1954. Ten per cent of lodgings are empty, rising to 18 per cent in the centre.   >>

Mind and body If the Parisians love culture and abstract ideals, they are equally preoccupied with sex, from the hot spots of Pigalle to advertisements whose blatancy make Anglo-Saxon feminists blanch. Parisian women somehow manage to retain an ambivalence: supremely elegant, they are increasingly prominent in French business and politics.

Thus a renovated Paris, its sense of pride (and sometimes superiority) intact, faces a new Europe. Times have changed and a non-French-speaking visitor is no longer ostracised. A new generation eagerly attempts to bridge the language barrier and remember, always, that however reserved a Parisian exterior may be, humour will always permeate it. The Parisian character lies somewhere in between Latin demonstrativeness (they would kiss their worst enemy on the cheek, left and right) and bourgeois restraint. Underneath is a *bon viveur* who, whatever his faults, helped coin the phrase *savoir vivre*.

All life is here: café society still flourishes in Paris, despite many other changes in the city

■ France has at last attained political stabililty and is now regarded as one of the most powerful Western democracies. In the last two centuries it has been ruled by no fewer than 16 constitutions, and only a few decades ago, in the immediate post-war period, government after government failed in their attempts to rule an ebullient nation undergoing profound socio-economic changes. Then came De Gaulle and the Fifth Republic. And then, after the dramatic events of 1968 and some intermediary Presidents, came 'the quiet strength' of Mitterrand. ..... ■

The longest surviving constitution was that of the Third Republic (1870–1940). Monarchies, republics, empires, all had their turn, ending, at the lowest ebb, with the national disgrace of Pétain's Vichy Régime. In 1945 the Fourth Republic was accepted by referendum and women were at last given the vote. But inherent constitutional weaknesses led to 30 successive governments, often rocky coalitions. The Algerian War of Independence finally brought down this Republic: under threat of a military *coup d'état*, the National Assembly admitted defeat in 1958 and called on De Gaulle to bail his country out.

Although a national referendum ratified the new constitution, many doubted that the Fifth Republic

The National Assembly, where Presidents dare not tread

ASSEMBLÉE NATIONALE

would survive the General's departure. Yet although severely shaken by the events of 1968 (student revolts and national strikes led to a three-week holiday, with the country at a standstill), it still survives today.

Political structure At the head of the government stands the President, elected every seven years by universal suffrage. Far from being a mere figurehead, as in many other European Republics, he is head of the army, responsible for nuclear defence, nominates the Prime Minister, can call referendums or dissolve Parliament. Based in the Elysée Palace, the President is not allowed to set foot in the National Assembly at the Palais Bourbon. He is answerable to the Conseil Constitutionnel, an independent body, and arbiter of the constitution. Nominated by the President and often changed at his whim, the Prime Minister heads the government and ensures execution of the laws. Based at the Hôtel Matignon, he nominates Ministers in collaboration with the President, but owes his authority to the confidence of the National Assembly. The government can be censured by parliament with a vote of absolute majority. Government's inner core, the cabinet, meets every Wednesday at the Elysée for a working meeting chaired by the President.

Parliament is composed of two chambers: the National Assembly, with 577 deputies elected every five years, and its upper body, the Senate, with 318 senators, elected by local representatives every nine years.
The differences in duration of power between the President (still seven years, despite various proposals to shorten the term) and the Assembly (five years) has led to potentially divisive situations. In 1986, for example, when Mitterrand was already five years into his first mandate, new legislative elections echoed a drop in popularity for the Socialists and produced a right-wing parliamentary majority. This led to the paradoxical situation of a Socialist President ruling with a right-wing (Gaullist) Prime Minister – Chirac – and the phrase 'cohabitation' was coined. Two years of thorny government followed.

Quick changes Chameleon-like, French political parties are constantly changing initials, allegiances and coalitions. Divided roughly equally between right-and left-wing, there are currently six main parties: the PS (Parti Socialiste), RPR (Gaullist), UDF (centre-right), PC (Communist), Les Verts (ecologist) and FN (Front National, extreme right). The latter, led by Le Pen, is enjoying an ominous increase in support, particularly in the south.
As a nation, the French are not strongly unionised and members are diminishing in number: only 13 per cent of the workforce are now registered. But the area where the French maintain overwhelming numbers is in the army of civil servants.
The traditionally heavyweight state administration dates back to the 17th century, was perfected by Napoleon and assured a legal and technical continuity throughout the turmoil of French political history.

> **<<** In all, 2,600,000 French men and women work for the state. **>>**

Exemplary in many fields, it has some of the best training-grounds for top-ranking administrators. Yet it is also stifling, encumbering the nation with an excessive bureaucracy. It also ensures that governmental power is far-reaching and all-encompassing: not always a healthy situation.
Above all, France is a technocracy in which civil servants play often dominant roles in economic or technical development. But when the traffic warden, one of the millions of civil servants, has handed out your parking ticket, remember that a new President always gives an amnesty for recalcitrants: so hold on!

■ 'Frenetic' is the only word to describe architectural activity in Paris over the last decade. Cranes groan on the horizon, while other machinery burrows away underground. Little remains untouched and, as a result, Paris has undergone a major face-lift, with entire quartiers like Le Marais restored to their former gleaming glory and countless sheets of glass lovingly installed into the façades of Paris' new landmarks.....■

The key building is the **Centre Pompidou**, more commonly known as **Beaubourg**, completed in 1977 and now attracting more visitors than the Eiffel Tower. Controversially high-tech, in marked contrast to the surrounding 18th- and 19th-century town houses, it set the tone for a new generation of architects and a new attitude towards public building. Although instigated by President Georges Pompidou, it was finished under Giscard d'Estaing – who had attempted to axe the plan – and was soon followed by more ambitious projects such as the **Parc de la Villette**, a kind of glorified urban playground, still under development, and the transformation of a former railway station and hotel into the **Musée d'Orsay**. Politics and architecture have always gone hand in hand (see pages 44–5) and the 1980s saw a particularly complex wrangle, with the Gaullist mayor of Paris, Jacques Chirac, countering the grandiose, some say megalomaniac projects of Socialist President Mitterrand. Many were bulldozed, and unimaginable budgets went out of the window, but quite a lot were built.

Grand finale With Mitterrand's 14 years of presidency drawing to an end in 1995, so his *grands projets* approach completion. The last one on the board is Dominique Perrault's national library, nicknamed the **TGB** (Très Grande Bibliothéque), whose four 100m-high glass towers are gradually emerging skywards. The cement- mixers will not leave when the TGB is completed, as the

<< The new Bibliothèque de France, being built at a cost of about 5.2 billion francs, will provide 400km of shelves to take some of the strain off the Bibliothèque Nationale. >>

Mairie de Paris has since instigated an ambitious plan to overhaul this rather neglected quarter in the east of Paris. Immediately north across the river, in Bercy, there has already been a transformation, with Chemetov's one-legged **Ministry of Finance** limping into the Seine and numerous office and apartment blocks jostling for a view over the newly landscaped **Parc de Bercy**.

New look Louvre Most close to the Parisian heart has been the creation of the *Grand Louvre* with IM Pei's metal and glass pyramid personally chosen by the President. When the whole project is completed in 1996 the Louvre will be the world's largest museum (although it seems like that anyway), at a cost of over $1 billion. The pyramid's symbolic position on the east-west axis marks a straight line from the **Opéra Bastille** in the east to the **Grande Arche**, far to the west at La Défense, with the **Tuileries, Concorde, Champs-Elysées** and **Arc de Triomphe** in between. Apart from pleasing a Cartesian sense of logic and geometry and bowing to a tradition of French rulers from Catherine de Médicis onwards, it also makes life easier for the landmark seeking visitor.

The Louvre: IM Pei's pyramid

La Grande Arche crowns the new business district of La Défense and has created a desperately needed focal point for what was previously a mass of tower blocks left over from the '60s and '70s. Von Spreckelsen's gateway design leaves the axis open for development, and the city without limits.

Completed just in time for the 1989 Bicentenary celebrations, the Grande Arche had a warmer reception than Mitterrand's other pet project, the 'people's' opera house at the Bastille. The design was by unknown Canadian architect Carlos Ott. Plans were radically modified, but it eventually opened in 1990. Although completely overpowering the rest of the *place*, the **Opéra Bastille** improves inside and seems to have overcome its teething problems.

Nouvel architecture Paris in the 1990s cannot be discussed without mentioning the *enfant terrible* of architecture, Jean Nouvel. His much praised **Institut du Monde Arabe**, completed in 1987, is a masterpiece of sculptural purity, but his next project for Paris, a 400m high cyclindrical tower for La Défense, is still on the drawing board.

The city's architectural renaissance has added to its unique style, not only in status-symbol monuments, but also in the far-flung *arrondissements* and the suburbs.

ORA GRAY DUNCAN

12 AVRIL 1922

■ **There are enough stars and 'would-bes' in Paris to launch another galaxy. Below is a check-list of prominent characters who have been part of Paris life during recent years – though not all have been worthy of gracing the cover of the gossip rag *Paris Match*. .....■**

Azzadine Alaïa Of Tunisian origin, Alaïa was adopted by the French fashion world when he worked from his living-room in the early 1980s, selling clinging dresses in black leather and slinky jerseys. He opened a boutique in the Marais and is now an international fashion name.

Isabelle Adjani Born in Paris of a German mother and Turkish father, Adjani started acting aged 14 and later joined the Comédie Française. She became famous with Truffaut's *Adèle H* in 1975. In 1981 she won the Cannes prize for best actress for her role in James Ivory's *Quartet*.

Pierre Boulez The great classical composer was born in 1925 and studied music at the Paris Conservatoire under Messïaen. He worked as a conductor in London and New York before directing acoustic research at IRCAM.

Daniel Buren France's most controversial contemporary artist, Buren was born in 1938 near Paris. Since the 1960s he has specialised in scandals and in taking intellectual stands in the art world. Stripes are a constant theme – see his columns in the Palais-Royal.

Henri Cartier-Bresson This world-famous globe-trotting photographer was a founding member of the Magnum photo-reporters' agency, and now lives on the rue de Rivoli. His images have become icons of the 20th century.

César A diminutive, bearded figure from the south of France, César's 'pop art' sculptures astonished the public in the early 1960s; he is particularly famous for his giant bronze thumbs. See his *Centaur* at the Carrefour de la Croix Rouge in St-Germain.

Patrice Chéreau Theatre and film director Chéreau first achieved international fame in the 1970s, with a revolutionary production of Wagner's *Ring* cycle in Bayreuth and Berg's *Lulu* in Paris. After successfully directing the Théâtre des Amandiers in Nanterre, Chéreau recently resigned to concentrate more on personal work.

Catherine Deneuve A blonde beauty propulsed to fame by director Roger Vadim in the 1960s. Jacques Démy's *Les Parapluies de Cherbourg* and Polanski's *Repulsion* sealed her destiny. Her face was a model for every town hall statue of *Marianne*.

Gérard Dépardieu His bulky muscular frame is now world-famous, following major roles in films by Wajda, Truffaut, Ferreri, Pialat and Resnais. Dépardieu recently turned to directing, with *Tartuffe*. He divides his time between tending his Burgundy vines and his Parisian apartment.

Marguerite Duras Author and film director Duras' entire output expresses the incommunicability of love in a tense, lonely world. She became famous in the 1950s, confirming her status with her film *India Song* and by writing the screenplay for Resnais' *Hiroshima mon amour*. Her bestseller *L'Amant* (1984) was based on her childhood in Indochina.

Serge Gainsbourg Although he died aged 62 in 1990, Gainsbourg's influence on French rock music and youth culture continues. Iconoclastic, with a sardonic humour inspired by

Face of France: Catherine Deneuve

Surrealism, he revolutionised French *chanson*, changing the writing and sonority of sung French. He was married to Jane Birkin and their daughter Charlotte Gainsbourg is now a talented young actress.

Jean-Paul Gaultier The ultimate French fashion designer of the 1980s, this recognised *enfant terrible* introduced the androgynous look, baroque caricatures and extraordinary fabrics. He started designing at Cardin's and created his own label in 1976.

Jean Nouvel One of a new generation of architects who put French design on the map. Nouvel's first major Parisian project was the Institut du Monde Arabe (1987). His designs make sophisticated use of high-tech materials and are often technical feats. His *Tour sans fin* design for La Défense, a 400m-high tower, is proving difficult. Nouvel is often spotted at Les Bains nightclub.

Christine Ockrent Came to fame in the 1980s as a TV newscaster, leading to clones on every other channel. Her 'superwoman' legend grew when she had her first child at the age of 40. She worked for CBS in the US and the BBC in the UK, and now presents debates and documentaries for Antenne 2.

Joël Robuchon This creator of everyone's dream cuisine is based in his 16th-*arrondissement* restaurant. A leading *nouvelle cuisine* chef, he started at the ovens aged 15 and worked his way up to cook under André Moreau at the age of 21.

Yves Saint-Laurent Born in Algeria in 1936, YSL divides his time between Marrakesh and Paris. He designed for Christian Dior from 1957 to 1960 and founded his own fashion house in 1962. The first couturier to introduce *prêt-à-porter*, he developed licensing for accessories, thus revolutionising the fashion business. He invented the trouser suit in the 1970s.

■ **When all is said and done, what remains of a civilisation is its culture and this the French understood long ago. The electricity of Parisian cultural life has always attracted foreign artists and today the capital is a stage for top international figures. Stimulated by a healthy rivalry between theatres and encouraged by generous state subsidies, the situation is enviable. .....■**

The all-powerful Minister of Culture does not only cover traditional forms; he is also Minister for rock music and comic-strips, while guiding the destiny of the fashion industry. But this paternalistic umbrella has its negative effects, creating a climate of dependency. The hard edge – a will to succeed and survive – is sometimes lacking.

Picture palace Living up to its role as nation-inventor of the cinema, France's capital offers over 300 different films weekly. Since the heyday of the *nouvelle vague*, new blood has appeared (**Beneix, Léo Carax, Bertrand Blier, Coline**

Théâtre des Champs Elysées

Serreau, Luc Besson, Chantal Akermann, Jean-Jacques Annaud, Alain Corneau**) while the older intimist generation of **Rivette, Chabrol, Rohmer, Resnais** or

<< In 1955 admissions to cinemas in France numbered 385 million. In 1989 they numbered 118 million. >>

Tavernier have not said their last word. The third largest producer of films in the world, much of France's cinema is filmed in the studios of Billancourt in west Paris, while once a year all eyes are on the Cannes Film Festival. Yet cinema audiences are dropping.

Music Whether jazz, rock or classical, sounds emerge from clubs, theatres, hotels, churches or concert halls all over the capital. Maintaining its pivotal role as the European jazz centre, Paris has attracted a stream of top American musicians since **Sydney Bechet's** days. Jazz clubs abound; traditionalists vye with experimentalists, **Miles Davis** would appear for a lightning set; and local musicians create their own syntheses.
Rock music, on the other hand, remains the black sheep of French culture – despite desperate state support. Exceptions such as the **Gypsy Kings** or **Les Négresses Vertes** bend the rule, but ultimately creative rock escapes the French character and language, possibly too analytical for such basic rhythms.

Cinema queues are on the decline

The recent explosion of 'world music' has given black Africans and North Africans (mainly Algerians) a chance to express new sounds, amalgamations of their native harmonies with westernised arrangements.

Opera and classical music are centralised fields in France: 75 per cent of French composers over 40 studied at the Paris Conservatoire, and the sophisticated new Conservatoire at La Villette will no doubt maintain this status quo. **Pierre Boulez, Henri Dutilleux, Edgar Varèse** and the Greek-born **Iannis Xenakis**, with **Olivier Messïaen** (who died in 1992) as a strong background influence, are France's contemporary masters who, although sometimes open to electro-acoustic innovation, avoid minimalist American models.

Dance has progressed by leaps and bounds throughout the 1980s and, unlike music, has found its place in the regions. Young choreographers such as **Jean-Claude Gallotta** (Grenoble), **Dominique Bagouet** (Montpellier), **Karine Saporta** (Caen) and **Angelin Prelocaj** (Chambéry) still have to perform in Paris, usually at the Théâtre de la Ville, to confront the capital's sophisticated audiences and critics. The Opéra de Paris ballet company, now directed by the brilliant young dancer **Patrick Dupond** after years of Rudolf Nureyev's vagaries, wavers between the classics and occasional avant garde choreography.

Theatre covers traditional boulevard farce, **Molière** or Racine, **Brecht, Beckett** or **Koltès** and includes that uniquely Parisian institution, café-théâtre. As in other fields, injections of foreign talent are welcome and the theatre scene would not be the same without **Ariane Mnouchkine's** theatre complex in Vincennes, La Cartoucherie, or **Peter Brook's** company based at Les Bouffes du Nord. Director **Patrice Chéreau** remains the *enfant chéri* of both public and critics and mounts his innovative productions all over Europe. A vital motor is the Festival d'Automne which, every autumn, invites foreign directors from **Luc Bondy** to **Heiner Müller** or **Bob Wilson**, thus providing Paris with an enviable and dynamic window on world theatre.

Art Parallel to the performing arts is an expanding visual art scene. Recovering from a low ebb, Paris now boasts hundreds of public and private galleries. But state aid does not create talent and French artists still tend to look too closely at their American and German contemporaries, although exceptions such as **Boltanski, César** or **Buren** have international status. Paris is still a magnet for creative talent and culture vultures alike; and with three weekly book programmes on TV, France is unlikely to lose touch with its literary roots.

■ **Despite repeated offensives from Milan, New York, London and Tokyo, the uncontested centre of fashion remains Paris. With an arrogant, relentless hold on women's wardrobes worldwide, its high fashion dictates are unashamedly copied in countless sweatshops from Hong Kong to Taiwan to Paris itself.** *Haute couture* **may be having a hard time but the new generation of** *prêt-à-porter* **designers are flourishing and keeping the tricolour flag flying. Fashion and its accessories are France's best ambassadresses.....■**

Paris quite simply breathes fashion. No central street is complete without its chic boutique and no woman rightfully self-assured without her designer accessory. Non-French designers, models and photographers flock to Paris for essential training and, more than anything else, sensitising to a general spirit of fashion awareness. It is a bitchy, back-biting business but it is also glamorous and/or outrageous: no self-respecting fashion professional can ignore it.

Big business In the 1990s **Haute Couture** and **Fashion Creators** together represent a several billion franc industry, 67 per cent of which is exported. It is hardly surprising that most of the 3,000 or so private *haute couture* clients are foreigners: prices range from 25,000 to 50,000 francs, a level more accessible to wives of sheikhs or Hollywood film moguls. Fashion Creators (Créateurs de Mode) is the name given to upmarket *prêt-à-porter* designers whose fame is often as great (**Chloé, Kenzo, Sonia Rykiel, Thierry Mugler** etc) as their elders, and who officially joined forces with the couturiers' federation in 1975. Strangely anachronistic, the *grands couturiers* have to follow a rigid set of rules in order to be allowed into the hallowed legally protected circle, currently numbering 21. These include presenting twice-yearly collections of at least 75 models to the press and at least 45 times to

clients inside the Couture house. January and July are the big months for, respectively, the Spring-Summer and the Autumn-Winter collections. Carefully juxtaposed, the fashion creators show their new designs in early October and March (when Parisian hotels are full to the brim). The Cour Carrée in the Louvre is a major venue for presenting these fashion shows but in late 1993 a new custom-designed area beneath the Tuileries will be functioning.

Invention and tradition Dreaming up innovative garments for a wide public has been a Parisian tradition since the first couturiers started up earlier this century. In the 1910s and '20s the master was **Paul Poiret**, the man who declared the corset undesirable and swathed his customers in Arabian Nights gear but later admitted 'I freed the bust but enslaved the legs'. **Chanel** first recognised a new direction for women after World War I and created soft, loose boyish-looking cuts as well as the famous 'little black dress'. Much to her annoyance the exuberant personality of **Elsa Schiaperelli** soon stepped in with humour, a clever antidote during the 1930s depression. She was the one to introduce the padded shoulders which remained fashionable until World War II. When **Dior** stunned the post-war world with his 'New Look' women were ready to return to a more feminine line and be extravagant with yards of cloth: this carried on throughout the 1950s. Since then couturiers like **Courrèges** (1960s space-age), **Saint- Laurent** (1970s retro influences) and the latest to be admitted to the inner circle with a flamenco flounce, **Christian Lacroix**, have influenced and reflected the spirit of the time. Rule-breaking is part and parcel of Parisian fashion extremism. Waists are clinched or forgotten, skirt lengths short or long, trousers baggy or drain-pipes, dresses clinging or billowing. Certain younger designers have led the way: **Thierry Mugler** (luxury Hollywood kitsch), **Jean-Paul Gaultier** (outrageous humorous designs) and **Claude Montana** (for moody science fiction heroines), while **Alaïa** was the man to bring back the feminine figure with a vengeance. Foreign designers such as **Karl Lagerfeld**, the Japanese contingent (from the precursor **Kenzo** to **Miyake**, **Yamamoto** and **Rei Kawakubo** of Comme les garçons) have all gravitated to Paris, naturally or forcibly, confirming the city's dual role as respected guardian and juvenile tearaway.

French fashion on show

■ **Of all the countries in the world France is the most closely associated with food, with gourmets and gourmandise. Food is a subject taken seriously, and has at least 15 national magazines devoted to it. Fortunes are spent on ingredients, let alone on restaurants. But food combines both science and pleasure, and so corresponds perfectly to the dual French psyche. .....** ■

Although this 'science' has been the nation's prerogative since the days of Rabelais, most French choose to forget that the dreaded Catherine de Médicis was responsible for bringing chefs from Italy to introduce new dishes in the 16th century. But the advent and spread of public restaurants and cafés in Paris did not happen till the Revolutionary period. Before the Revolution Paris boasted about 2,000 cafés; by the early 1800s they had doubled in number. *Ancien régime* cuisine was known for being elaborate, rich and heavy, with diners often struggling through twenty courses. In 1783 the first grandiose *dîner philosophique* was launched, creating that link between literature and gastronomy that is so much a part of France.

Change of diet World War I ended the gourmet golden age of the 19th

Simple and stylish: poulet à l'estragon *(chicken with tarragon), originally a Lyonnais dish*

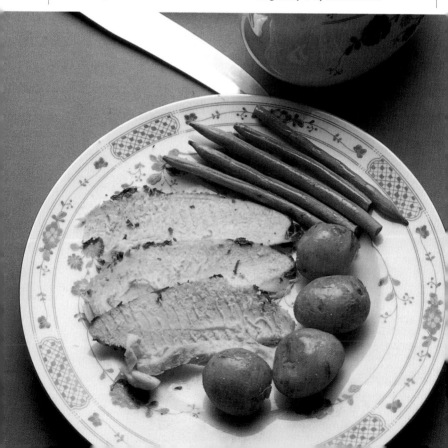

century, bringing a sense of measure and even in some cases frugality. With the spread of motoring a new accent was put on regional cuisine, echoed by the famous Guide Michelin, and when in 1936 annual paid holidays became law, restaurants were at last democraticised. The gastronomic variety of the provinces was soon discovered with a vengeance by crowds of foreign tourists armed, as always, with the little red book. Culinary dynasties in family inns scattered throughout France, from the Bocuse at Collognes to the Daguin at Auch, soon gained national and international status.

Culinary revolution A new consciousness of ecology, macrobiotics and dietary considerations influenced the cuisine of the 1960-70s, culminating in Michel Guérard's famous *cuisine minceur*. Its emphasis on balanced nutrition and adventurous experiments created the subversive *nouvelle cuisine*. A new generation of chefs looked beyond France for inspiration. Partly due to apprentice Japanese chefs in Paris kitchens, aesthetic presentation became paramount and classic table service disappeared.
However, by the late 1980s the tide was turning. Too many unworthy

> << The *crêpe suzette* was invented by mistake in Monte Carlo at the turn of the century. Chef Henri Charpentier was preparing some crêpes for the Prince of Wales and set fire to the alcohol he was imbibing them with. Delighted with the result, the Prince suggested naming them after his young companion. >>

chefs jumped on the two-carrot *nouvelle cuisine* bandwagon, leaving customers unsatisfied and hungry. As a result, wholesome, old-fashioned bourgeois cooking is back in fashion. Yet Guérard's techniques, applied to traditional recipes, now

inspire a lighter cuisine which satisfies both sophisticated and hungry appetites.

Great Chefs
Antoine Beauvilliers opened a famous restaurant in Palais-Royal in 1790. and wrote *L'Art du Cuisiner* in 1814, analysing cooking with a clear, scientific approach.

Paul Bocuse Descendant of a line of chefs since 1765 and an apprentice at Lucas-Carton and Lapérouse, Bocuse returned to his family restaurant outside Lyon in 1959, and very soon became known as France's unofficial gastronomic ambassador.

Auguste Escoffier The creator of the peach melba started in the kitchens aged 13 in 1859 and lived till 90, mainly working in London's Savoy and Carlton hotels.

Michel Guérard started as a pastry chef at the Crillon. In 1972 he opened his famous restaurant at Eugénie-le-Bains in the south west, where he created imaginative, light, aromatic food with the accent on fish, fowl and veal.

Joël Robuchon continues Guérard's tradition in his successful, ruinously expensive Neuilly restaurant, opened in 1981, with intensely flavoured combinations (cauliflower and caviar, lobster and artichoke).

Guy Savoy As unpredictable in his repertoire as Robuchon, Savoy experiments with textures and flavours and has a restaurant in the 17th *arrondissement*.

Taillevent Cook to 14th-century kings including Philippe VI, Taillevent wrote the oldest known treatise on cooking, Le Viandier.

François Vatel The 17th-century inventor of *crème chantilly* was chef to Fouquet, then the Prince de Condé. He committed suicide because the fish was not up to standard at a banquet in honour of Louis XIV.

25

■ Children's Paris is not all Punch and Judy shows. Specially designed facilities are installed all over the city and keep the whole range, from toddlers upwards, out of mischief. Every *arrondissement* has public squares equipped with sand-pits and/or swings and slides. Although you may think that this diminutive section of the population seems thin on the ground, it emerges visibly on no-school days Wednesdays, Saturdays and Sundays. Avoid most destinations mentioned below on these days. .....■

If museum-visiting is your priority the Atelier des Enfants at the **Centre Pompidou** is the ideal solution. Any child aged 6 to 12 can be booked in immediately prior to sessions (*open:* 14.00–18.00hrs except Sunday and Tuesday) and left in capable hands. Near by, in the heart of Les Halles, is another supervised playground, this one an open-air labyrinth full of slides, swings and tunnels. The **Jardin des Enfants** accepts children aged 7 to 11 daily but check exact opening hours (105 rue Rambuteau, tel: 45 08 07 18).

Puppets The infamous puppets (*guignols*), whose squeaky language won't mean much to a non-French child, are still good value. All function afternoons only on Wednesdays and at weekends. The following parks provide shows: **Montsouris, Rond-point des Champs-Elysées, Champ-de-Mars, Luxembourg, Buttes-Chaumont** and **Jardins du Ranelagh**. Best of all in the parks arena is the **Jardin d'Acclimatation** in the Bois de Boulogne (*open:* daily 10.00–18.00hrs, metro: Sablons), where Parisian children, revel in pleasure trains, donkey rides, boat trips or dodgems. A children's zoo, a hall of mirrors, a *guignol* theatre and an educational **Musée en Herbé** complete the package. At the eastern end of Paris the Bois de Vincennes has an equivalent area, the **Parc Floral,** which features a miniature train, a games area and a mini-golf course.

Museums Top of the list of museums catering for children comes the **Inventorium** at the Cité des Sciences et de l'Industrie (metro: Porte de la Villette) where children are encouraged to crack the mysteries of science: the computer games are as instructive as the keyboard experiments. (See pages 175 and 183.) In the same scientific vein but less high-tech is the **Palais**

de la Découverte, part of the Grand Palais (see page 124). Ardent stargazers shouldn't miss its planetarium.

Children with budding creative talents can participate in one of the sessions at the **Musée des Enfants,** downstairs at the Musée d'Art Moderne de la Ville de Paris (see pages 69–70). or a similar system at the **Musée des Arts Décoratifs.** And if all this instructive activity is losing favour, the waxworks at the Musée Grévin (see page 124) never fail to provoke thrilled squeals. .

Circuses For chilly or rainy days the heated **Cirque Diana Moreno** in the Jardin d'Acclimatation is ideal and boasts breath-taking acrobats. The famous national circus Alexis Gruss is now based near the Gare d'Austerlitz (145 qual de la Gare) and here children are thrilled by equestrian pantomimes and a team of clowns. Both circuses have sessions on Wednesday, Saturday and Sunday afternoons.

Outside Paris the field widens, from the **Parc Astérix** to **Thoiry** and the new mega **Euro Disney** (see pages 196–7). None is more than 40km away, and Thoiry can be reached by train from Montparnasse (go to Beynes, then a take a taxi). Astérix, of course, has more meaning if your children have spent time perusing the comic-strip hero's life. Whatever, the park makes a lively outing. Thoiry (*open:* daily 10.00–18.00hrs) is however the star here as between the 800 wild-ish animals, the Renaissance château and the Museum of Gastronomy, few tastes are neglected. The interest of the château and its gardens, landscaped by Le Nôtre, will fade into insignificance once your children know that this is the largest safari park in Europe. If in a car you'll be able to cruise through the hunting ground of tigers, bears and lions, while antelopes leap past the windscreen and zebras flash by. Good for picnics, too: it's a safe bet.

Concentration: being entertained is a serious business

27

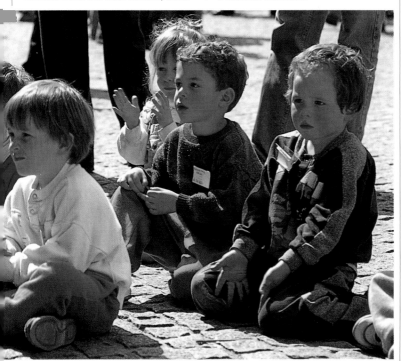

■ **Paris' first occupants were a Celtic tribe called the Parisii, who settled on the Ile de la Cité. Strategically located at the confluence of three rivers, the Seine, the Marne and the Oise, they flourished on trade until Caesar's Gallic Wars engulfed them in 52BC. .....**■

Renaming the settlement *Lutetia*, the Romans soon set about creating their own structures, which continued to thrive for almost 500 years. After rebuilding the Ile de la Cité the Romans moved across the Seine to the Left (south) Bank, where some monuments still stand today. The amphitheatre (now called les Arènes) on the Montagne Ste Geneviève could hold up to 15,000 people and became the backdrop for gladiator fights as well as more sober and less bloody entertainment.

Growing needs The rapidly expanding population demanded baths and of the three sites uncovered (Collège de France, rue Gay-Lussac and Cluny), the latter, built around 200AD, remains remarkably well preserved. In true Roman style, no fewer than 16km of richly decorated aqueduct were built to supply water to these establishments. The central forum was located in the rue Soufflot (now below ground), while the adjacent Montagne Ste Geneviève became the main residential quarter.

Roman roads Although nothing remains of the Imperial palace (apparently on the site of the present Palais de Justice) or the theatre (on boulevard Saint-Michel), the Romans left a network of firmly traced roads. Their north-south axes form the basis of Paris' main arteries, such as the rue St-Martin, which cuts straight as a die across the Seine to the rue St-Jacques, or the parallel boulevard Saint-Michel, the east-west rue des Ecoles or the rue de la Montagne Ste-Geneviève which steadfastly climbs the slope to become the rue Mouffetard.

End of an era River and road trade assured a peaceful prosperity until around 275AD, when increasingly frequent Barbarian attacks eventually destroyed most of the Left Bank, forcing the inhabitants to withdraw on to the Ile de la Cité. This soon became a walled enclave, its ramparts built with the ruins of the Left Bank. Although a fragile peace was restored and the population spread to the Right Bank, the northerners eventually won the day in 486 when Clovis, chief of the Franks, conquered the Roman ruler Syagrius at the battle of Soissons.

The frigidarium from the Roman baths, at the Musée de Cluny

■ **Although the courageous Geneviève had saved Paris from Attila's Huns in the 5th century, later becoming the city's patron saint, the Ile de France soon fell under the rule of a series of Frankish kings. Power fell into the hands of rulers with the exotic names of Clovis, Childebert and Dagobert, but when Charlemagne moved the capital of his powerful empire to Aix la Chapelle, Paris went into a dramatic decline. .....■**

Concentrated on the Ile de la Cité, the only signs of the city's former prosperity and importance were now at the neighbouring abbey of St-Denis, the royal graveyard since Dagobert. Only in the 10th century, with the rise to power of the Capetians, dukes of France and Counts of Paris, did the city regain its lustre. The development of agriculture and trade in the Middle Ages ensured new growth and wealth. For the first time, the Right Bank was settled and the swamp to the east, the Marais, was drained and cultivated. A port was established on **place de la Grève** (now l'Hôtel-de-Ville) opposite the Cité and a central market appeared at the end of the road from St-Denis, named after its wooden pavillions: **Les Halles**.

Financial pulse The Right Bank soon became the city's commercial heart. Its streets were still exceedingly narrow (the smallest a metre wide) and filthy. Muddy, badly lit, congested and a haven for nocturnal thieves, they remained the terror of the visitor well into the 19th century. The houses were plain and narrow, made of wood beams and plastered rubble, with high pitched gables. They took up every available space within the city walls and even piled up onto the town's four bridges, notable chiefly for the frequency with which they collapsed into the Seine.
A few buildings, like the royal palace (now the Palais de Justice), with its flamboyant Gothic chapel (**Sainte Chapelle**), the splendid new cathedral of **Notre Dame** or the fortress guarding the city's western gates, the **Louvre**, provided a note of distinction in this otherwise crowded, unplanned and smelly city.

Scholarly city In the late 12th century, under Philippe-Auguste, the **University of Paris** was founded and trades and crafts came under the control of tightly organised, prosperous guilds. The University, which gave its name to the Latin

France emerged from the Middle Ages under the reign of François I

Quarter on the Left Bank, soon became one of the most renowned in Europe, boasting scholars like Guillaume de Champeaux and Abélard.

Abélard and Héloïse Two of the most colourful and tragic figures of medieval Paris were the great scholar and theologian Abélard and his beloved Héloïse, daughter of a Notre Dame canon, Fulbert. After a passionate love affair they had a child and secretly married. Fulbert wrought a terrible revenge: tied up by three hired thugs Abélard was castrated. Further pursued by the Church for alleged heresy in his writings, Abélard wandered from monastery to monastery until he found refuge at the abbey of Cluny. Eight poignant letters survive, exchanged by Abélard and Héloïse after their separation. They are buried together in the Père Lachaise cemetery, and at no 9 Quai aux Fleurs you can see their sculpted heads.

Big city By the reign of Philippe Auguste's famous grandson, Saint Louis (1226–70), Paris was already a major European capital and, with its 200,000 inhabitants, the most populous city on the continent. A memorable moment for the city came in 1263, when the Parisian

Charles VII's reign saw the end of the Hundred Years' War: here he enters Paris in 1436

merchants elected their first representative, the Prévot des Marchands.

At war The Hundred Years' war (from the mid-14th to mid-15th centuries) plunged the city back into turbulence, bringing medieval peace and prosperity to a violent end. Paris was at times ruled by the English, who defended the city succesfully against Jeanne d'Arc. Violence also returned in the form of a rebellion in 1358 led by the Prévot, Etienne Marcel against the sovereign, the Dauphin Charles; unable to bear numerous humiliations, the Dauphin was forced to escape to the south of France to rally the nobles to his cause. Marcel was eventually murdered, enabling the Dauphin to return to Paris. Yet this first act of rebellion gave birth to the distrust which existed between the rulers of France and their capital city well into modern times. Abandoning the central Cité palace in favour of mansions closer to the city wall, the kings increasingly favoured provincial châteaux – a trend taken up to the full by the king who in many way characterised late medieval France: François I.

■ **Despotic and capricious, yet also a refined Renaissance gentleman, François I epitomised the contradictory aspects of French society in the 16th century. Still based on feudalism, this society nevertheless felt the increasing weight of royal authority as François I centralised power from his capital, Paris, seat of the Treasury, the Mint and the law courts. ....■**

The court diligently followed him from one splendid Loire château to the next, in Paris settling in the Louvre, re-built by the king in the brand new Renaissance style imported from Italy. Elaborate costumed balls, ballets and ceremonies kept the courtiers amused, and the title of 'Majesty', previously reserved for the Holy Roman emperor, was now applied to the French king.

Age of rebirth The breath of the Renaissance swept France in the wake of Italian artists imported to decorate Fontainebleau. The new passion for antiquity, poetry, literature and philosophy culminated in the founding of the Collège de France (1530), the kingdom's first secular educational institution. This was the age of Rabelais, Montaigne, the Humanist publisher Robert Estienne and of noble patrons of the arts and humanities, notably François I's sister, Marguerite de Navarre and Henri II's mistress, Diane de Poitiers.

Massacre and war This enlightenment was brought to an abrupt end by the Wars of Religion that swept through France in the latter half of the century (1562–98), a period dominated by the cunning Catherine de Médicis, wife of Henri II and domineering mother of the last three Valois kings (François II, Charles IX, Henri III). Its darkest episode occurred on Saint Bartholomew's day (24 August 1572) when, pressed by his mother, the vacillating Charles IX ordered the massacre of Protestant nobles gathered at the Louvre to celebrate the wedding of Henri de Bourbon (the future Henri IV) to the king's sister. Three thousand strangled and knifed Protestant corpses were thrown into the Seine on that fateful day and for over 20 years civil war raged throughout France.

'Paris is worth a mass' are the famous words uttered by Henri IV, the first Bourbon king, before abjuring his Protestant faith, last obstacle to his accession to the throne of France. His triumphal entry into a devastated and hungry Paris in 1594 spelt the temporary end to the wars of religion.

New era A pleasure-loving man, with as many mistresses as his predecessors, Henri IV was nevertheless the king who seriously set to re-organising the kingdom and notably its capital, Paris. Completing the great gallery of the Louvre, the Hôtel de Ville started by François I and endowing the city with new squares (place des Vosges, place Dauphine), bridges (Pont Neuf) and a hospital for plague victims (St-Louis), Henri began the process that would transform the still largely medieval city of the 16th century into the classical capital of the 17th and 18th centuries.

The first half of the 17th century (the Grand Siècle) was dominated by foreign and civil wars and the anxious personality of the chronically ill homosexual Louis XIII, sustained by the efforts of his brilliant but equally hypochondriac minister Cardinal Richelieu. This was the Paris of Alexandre Dumas' *Three Musketeers*, teeming with intrigue and the ongoing rivalry between the Cardinal and the Queen, the wilful and very Catholic Anne of Austria,

Henri IV pictured with his friend, Gabrielle d'Estrées

forever conspiring with the English and the Spanish against French interests.

Middle classes Amid court conspiracies and religious turmoil there emerged a Parisian class composed of the new civil servants, financiers and wealthy merchants, who provided the backbone of a great religious and cultural revival in the capital. Among the new churches and convents rose the sober, well proportioned mansions of the Marais, in which cultivated women of taste, the hostesses, presided over the first Parisian salons. The most celebrated of all was the Marquise de Rambouillet, in her rue St-Honoré house, who received all the great luminaries of her day from La Rochefoucauld to Corneille. Molière, whose theatre troupe settled in Paris in 1658, satirized the new manners in his great play, *Les Précieuses Ridicules*. The Fronde (1648–52) was the last great civil disturbance experienced

>> People of quality know everything without ever having been taught – Molière, *Les Précieuses Ridicules* >>

by Paris before the French Revolution. The victory of the regent, Anne of Austria and her wily prime minister, Cardinal Mazarin, over the rebellious Paris bourgeoisie and the nobility paved the way to the absolute power of Louis XIV.

■ When at the death of his mother's old prime minister, the Cardinal Mazarin, in 1661, Louis XIV announced he would govern on his own his ministers and the court were stupefied. Yet *l' Etat c'est Moi* perfectly describes the spirit of the later 17th century, a time when all the energies and resources of the kingdom were harnessed into the service and glorification of one single being and symbol: the Sun King. .....■

Though refusing to name a new prime minister, Louis XIV would have been unable to carry through his ambitious projects without the help and administrative talent of his finance minister, the dour, workaholic Colbert. Colbert's dream, a great palace for the king in Paris – the Louvre – was abandoned (literally without finishing the roof) in favour of Versailles, yet other of his projects were carried through. Royal Academies were established to control every facet of French cultural and intellectual life and a great Royal factory, the Gobelins, was set up to produce the furniture, silver and tapestries needed to fill Versailles.

Cultural capital By the end of the century, the talents of architects, painters, cabinet makers, musicians and playwrights trained to serve the king were already turning Paris and Versailles into the artistic and cultural centre of Europe. Nor did the removal of the court into the glittering and tightly controlled environment of Versailles mean that Paris was neglected. New squares, hospitals, bridges, churches and monumental avenues (Champs Elysées, the Grands Boulevards), better policing and lighting transformed the city more than ever before.

Much of the vitality of the Great King's reign was, however, extinguished long before his actual death (1715). The removal of the five-year-old Louis XV to the Tuileries palace by the regent signalled a renewal for the capital. Bored with the rigidity, etiquette and dusty grandeur of the Sun King, the court and nobility returned to Paris to throw themselves enthusiastically into a life entirely devoted to pleasure and dalliance.

Frivolity and flowers Thus sensual, frivolous rococo was born in the aristocratic mansions of the Faubourg St-Germain and the bankers' houses of the quartier St-Honoré. Watteau's flirting couples in romantic parks, Boucher's rosy mythological posteriors, shells, flowers and tendrils interpreted in chair legs and sofas, all provided the decorative background to the first half of Louis XV's reign.

Yet this is also the period of the revival of the literary salon. As the century wears on touches of intellectual curiosity, moralism and pedantry invade the witty, polished atmosphere of the salons of Mesdames du Deffand or Epinay. Beginning with Voltaire this libertarian spirit, alternately flirting with and defying royal authority, was enshrined in the circle of the new philosophers and encyclopédistes, the compilers of the world's first dictionary – Diderot, Buffon, Condorcet, Rousseau, D'Alembert, Helvétius.

<< 'You are going to be a great king. Do not copy me in my love of building or in my love of warfare; on the contrary, try to live peacefully with your neighbours.' – Louis XIV to the future Louis XV. >>

<< 'In an aristocracy, honours, pleasures, power and money are easily obtainable. Great discretion, however, is necessary. If abuse is flagrant, revolution will be the consequence' – Voltaire, *Philosophical Dictionary*. >>

Shift of focus Though the court returned to Versailles in 1724, it would never again be the focus of French life as it was under Louis XIV. It was to Paris that the aristocrats, even the King, now escaped for their fun, to the masked balls, the opera and, the latest rage, the first public art exhibitions, the salons held every other year in the Louvre.

This spirit of reform found its first visual outlet in the city's architecture. Though still elegant, from 1750 a sobriety and studious historical allusion pervaded the neo-classical style, with its Corinthian columns, swags and triangular pediments spreading across Paris from the place Louis XV (Concorde) to the Eglise Ste-Geneviève (Panthéon) and the new Royal Mint, La Monnaie. By the middle of the reign of Louis XVI (1774–93) and his beautiful, frivolous, unpopular Queen, Marie Antoinette, the still polite reformist mood of the earlier half of the century had turned into a flood of open sedition. Malicious printed jokes openly circulated at the Palais Royal and ended up beneath the Queen's plate at Versailles. The well intentioned but indecisive Louis XVI, unable to control the situation any longer, called for the representatives of all classes, *Les Etats Généraux,* to meet in Versailles in May 1789. No-one dreamed it, but that fateful spring was the end of the Ancien Régime.

The Water Gardens at Versailles: under Louis XIV's reign, Versailles became the focus of court life

■ **The Revolution signalled the end of royal excesses and the rise of popular democracy in a momentum that continued throughout the uprisings of the 19th century. Long before the gathering in Versailles of the *Etats Généraux*, which brought together the Clergy, Nobility and the Commons, trouble was afoot and the air rife with political agitation. Much of this was fermented at the Palais Royal, residence of the Dukes of Orléans, the rival branch of the royal family. .....■**

The Palais-Royal, though open to the public, was out of bounds to the police; so speechmaking and the distribution of anti-government pamphlets went on unhindered. It was here that in July 1789 a young journalist, Camille Desmoulins, gave the battlecry *aux armes!* to defend the city from a rumoured attack by the King's army. A great mob invaded the city hall and raided the Invalides barracks for muskets. Next morning, on 14 July, the same mob presented itself at a fortress on the eastern edge of the city, the Bastille. A four-hour battle, the first violent act of the Revolution, led to the fall of the fortress, the liberation of six prisoners (mostly counterfeiters) and the beheading of the governor. From here on events moved at a breath-taking pace until the Revolution finally ran out of steam in July 1794.

Royal prisoners A new mayor was nominated and the city organised its very own 'National' guard, headed by the Marquis de Lafayette. In October the Royal family was forcibly brought back from Versailles and installed in the Tuileries palace, virtual prisoners of the people and the new National Assembly. A period of relative calm, in which a Constitution and new laws were promulgated, came to an abrupt end with the King's failed attempt to escape on 21 June 1791. Now the anti-monarchist and left wing forces in the city, radicalised by the outbreak of war, gained the upper hand. On 10 August 1792, the Paris mob attacked the Tuileries palace, massacring 600 of the King's

Swiss guards and a few unlucky cooks and servants. A terrified royal family fled to the Assembly and the next day were locked up in the old medieval tower of the Temple. Soon the new Assembly, the Convention, abolished the monarchy and proclaimed the First Republic, along with a new calendar: 1792 became Year I of the new era. The King was tried, found guilty of high treason and guillotined on 21 January 1793. This was the year that opened the most violent period of the Revolution: the Reign of Terror. Nobles who had failed to emigrate, priests, the Queen and ordinary citizens were whisked to the Conciergerie prison on the Ile de la Cité. Judged by a mock court, they were then sent by the cartload, their hands tied and napes shaved, rattling along the rue St-Honoré to the guillotine on place de la Revolution (Concorde). As the stench of blood on the square led to complaints from the neighbours, the guillotine was transferred for a brief period to place de la Nation, but soon returned to

<< Originally a revolutionary song, next a chant for the Republicans confronting the monarchists, the *Marseillaise* became the national anthem in 1880. It was written in 1792 by Rouget de Lisle and became known as the *Marseillaise* when Parisians heard troops from the south of France singing it as they entered the capital. >>

the more central and convenient Concorde.

Political power was now concentrated in the hands of the misnamed Committee of Public Safety, led by a former lawyer, the calculating Robespierre. By now, the Revolution was devouring her own children. Beginning with the Mayor of Paris, a stream of moderate deputies was led to the blade. In March 1794 Robespierre eliminated the left wing and hit the Centre, including the revolutionary leaders, Desmoulins and Danton.

Robespierre now stood alone, But he had gone too far. The remaining deputies in the Convention, sensing their own short life expectancy, finally found the courage to gang up against him. In July Robespierre was arrested. He escaped and called the Paris citizens to his defence, but for the first time since 1789 the Paris mob, tired and dispirited, did not respond. Robespierre was guillotined on 28 July 1794. The Terror, and the Revolution, were over.

A social system on trial: Louis XVI comes before the people's court in 1792 (above) and (below) the march to Versailles, 1789

■ **Following the bloody days of the Terror and before France's first Emperor arrived on the scene with due pomp and ceremony, France was ruled by an intermediary government, the Directoire (1795–1799). This was a time of winding down of tensions and of gradual economic recovery, despite the continuing social and political instability. .....■**

With the old nobility and Church decimated by Revolutionary fervour, the bourgeoisie now controlled all political and financial power. The selling-off of confiscated religious and noble properties during the Revolution further ensured that the new class of profiteers and property owners, no matter how conservative, would never accept a return to the old status quo.

Defeat and caution The Paris municipality, last stronghold of the left wing and the working classes, the *sans-culottes* (meaning 'without breeches', ie not aristocratic) was suppressed in 1795. From Napoleon's era on, the city fell under the authority of the Prefect of the Seine, appointed by the government. So wary had the government become of the Parisians' seemingly endless potential for rebellion (borne out by the events of 1830, 1848, 1871, 1936 and 1968) that it took two centuries for Paris to be allowed a freely elected Mayor, in 1977.

Reaction and release Three years of revolutionary terror and patriotic fervour were succeeded by a mood of frivolity and unprecedented sexual liberation. Long-haired dandies and ladies in Greek hairdos and see-through dresses known as *incroyables* and *merveilleuses* danced the night away at the Café Frascati on the Grands Boulevards. Among the fashionable accessories of the day was a red ribbon round the neck, a discreet allusion to the past ravages and excitement of the guillotine.

One of the smartest Parisiennes of the period was the widow of a guillotined aristocrat, now mistress of the most powerful Directeur, **Joséphine de Beauharnais**. In 1796 she fell into the arms of an ardent,

Napoleon at the peak of his career: as the conquering general, portrayed by David...

rising young general, **Napoleon Bonaparte**. Eight years later, already owner of the most ravishing country house near Paris, Malmaison, she was crowned in Notre Dame as Empress of the French.

The Napoleonic age Napoleon's lightning rise and fall from power and glory, though brief (1800–14), left an indelible imprint on France and its capital city. Named First Consul of the Republic after the 1799 *coup d'état*, the ambitious young general soon proclaimed himself 'Emperor of the French'. A new nobility, composed of princes and barons (as opposed to the old dukes and counts) was invented. Most European territories conquered in the 1806–10 campaigns were carved out into kingdoms and principalities for the rest of the family and in-laws such as Murat, named 'King of Naples'. Paris was now capital of the greatest European Empire since Charlemagne.

Reconstruction A far-reaching programme of renovation and building was drawn up by the two official architects of the reign, **Percier** and **Fontaine**, whose object was to turn the city into a monumental New Rome. The result was an unprecedented proliferation of columns and 'temples' (the new **Assembly**, the **Bourse**, the **Madeleine**), Roman military monuments (**Colonne Vendôme, Arc du Carrousel, Arc de Triomphe**) and straight streets (**Castiglione, Rivoli**). Just as notable were the practical improvements in the city's infrastructure, the first signs in Paris of the dawning of an industrial age: the building of canals, the new stock exchange, an improved water supply and sewerage, modern cemeteries, a new meat market, even an iron bridge. The odd and even numbering system for the city's streets, with the low numbers beginning closest to the Seine, also dates from Napoleon I.
Napoleon's most permanent legacy to France and Paris were, however, the great national institutions in the

...and as self-styled Emperor Napoleon I of France, shown here wearing his Coronation robes in a tapestry by Gérard

fields of culture, education and law that he intitiated or reformed. The **Louvre Museum**, inaugurated during the Revolution, was greatly enriched by the artistic booty hauled in from all corners of the new Empire. The prestigious Grandes Ecoles, still the training ground for France's ruling élite today, the **Polytechnique, Ecole des Mines, Ponts et Chaussées, Ecole Normale Supérieure** and the **Natural History Museum** all date from Napoleon, as does the first national legal system in France, inspired by Roman Law, the Code Civil.

Capital city The concentration of the country's culture, government, education, financial and political power in the capital, begun by the Bourbons and pursued by the Revolution, was brought to a climax by Napoleon. His ambitious plans for France brought added status to the city. The pre-eminence of Paris in France would now remain unchallenged by every succeeding régime until the election in 1981 of François Mitterand.

■ **Nineteenth-century Paris can largely be characterised by a tapestry of weak rulers, violent social conflicts, rising liberal intellectualism and a new, monied bourgeoisie. Beyond the barricades and banks the arts flourished and foreign artists flocked to contribute to the capital's movements, but even greater designs were afoot. Symbolic of a will and need to change the fabric of society, Haussmann's mid-century urban transformations were a turning point for a new industrialised society. ....■**

Before Napoleon III manoeuvred into place, France underwent the last convulsions of its luckless monarchy during the Restoration. Under Louis XVIII and Charles X, a new romantic spirit developed in the arts (Delacroix, Géricault, Victor Hugo, Balzac, Berlioz, Baudelaire, Rimbaud), partly inspired by the philosophy of Rousseau and a nostalgia for the 'purity' of the Middle Ages – controversially practised by the architect Viollet-le-Duc.

Rebels and royalty The 1830 uprising, which rapidly turned to a bloody insurrection, ended the Bourbons' lineage and brought to power the 'citizen-king' Louis-Philippe of Orléans, more acceptable to the populace. But beneath a superficial self-satisfaction ('France is a nation which is bored' wrote Lamartine in 1839), the country was in ferment: strikes, spreading Republicanism, assassinations and a dropping standard of living, accompanied by the rising power of a corrupt monied class, all combined to make an explosive situation. The year 1848 signalled the end of the 'July Monarchy'. Blood and barricades soon heralded victory for the republicans and elections brought to power Louis-Napoléon, nephew of Bonaparte, described by de Toqueville as 'an enigmatic, sombre, insignificant numbskull'. Yet inspired by the parks of his London exile and determined to end the overcrowded conditions of the capital (as well as its potential for

revolution), Napoleon III immediately implemented an urban shake-up. And onto the stage now steps the Protestant administrator Baron Haussmann, who in 18 years managed to transform the face of the capital and prepare it for the 20th century.

<< 'Paris is the heart of France. Let's put all our efforts into embellishing this big city. Let's open new roads, make the populous neighbourhoods which lack air and daylight healthy, and may charitable light penetrate everywhere in our walls.'– Napoleon III >>

City facelift Between 1800 and 1850 the population of Paris had doubled to over a million; in 1832 a cholera epidemic claimed 19,000 victims. Housing and proper sanitation were thus desperately needed. Conscious of the imbalance in activities between the east and west, north and south of the capital, as well as the imminent asphyxiation of its narrow, overcrowded streets, Haussmann traced an urban web of wide boulevards and avenues. Against a backdrop of sparkling social gatherings, operettas by Offenbach and *haute couture* by Worth, he set about tearing down 20,000 houses, building 40,000, constructing 90km of roads, 560km of sewers, and two reservoirs and landscaping two woods, three parks, two gardens and 19 squares. The final jewel in Napoleon III's crown was Charles Garnier's ostentatious Opera House, the only real symbol of Second Empire architecture.

Wholesale clearance The Emperor's approach was romantic, that of Haussmann more inclined to straight lines. For 15 years Paris was one gigantic building site, as Haussmann, with little consideration for preservation, swept away entire quartiers such as the Ile de la Cité, where only Notre Dame, its immediate vicinity and the western tip were spared. Many of the Faubourg St-Germain's finest mansions crumbled to make way for the rue de Rennes and the boulevard Saint-Germain and much of the picturesque medieval Latin Quarter succumbed to demolition.

New conflict Modern sewerage, abattoirs (La Villette), a hygienic central market place (Les Halles), a public bus company, squares and parks completed this metamorphosis. However, the drums were rolling again with the Franco-Prussian War of 1870, the ensuing siege of Paris, when Parisians ate anything from rats to inmates of the zoo, and finally the last of the great revolutionary movements of the 19th century, the Paris Commune. Parisian radicals, disgusted with the peace treaty negotiated with Bismarck, had taken up arms and controlled the city, declaring it a free Commune. After a week of desperate fighting, when the Hôtel de Ville and the Tuileries Palace went up in smoke, Communards massacred priests and government troops shot on sight, the last stand took place at the Père Lachaise cemetery. In that one week over 20,000 people died. It was the 19th century's last lesson in civil uprising.

Charles Garnier's Opera House, a Second Empire symbol

■ **The shaky régime installed in France after the humiliating defeat inflicted by Bismarck's Prussia proved in the end to be the longest lasting since the Revolution. Paris hosted three Universal Exhibitions (1878, 1889 and 1900), which helped restore French morale and promote the prestige of the Third Republic. .....■**

The Eiffel Tower illuminated, 1889

As well as boosting morale, the Universal Exhibitions left several new landmarks on the horizon: the Palais de Chaillot (later rebuilt); the Eiffel Tower, built for the first centenary of the Revolution, and the Pont Alexandre III. The Grand and Petit Palais appeared in 1900, the year when Paris was consecrated as 'World Capital' and France recognised as one of the great industrial and colonial Empires.

Nostalgia The 'Belle Epoque' refers to the period between 1885 and the outbreak of the Great War in 1914. Industrial squalor, labour strikes and anarchist assassinations (like that in 1894 of the President Sadi Carnot) were forgotten in favour of the good life at the Opera, new boulevard cafés, music and dance halls (Folies-Bergère, Moulin Rouge).
Middle class weekends spent boating and picnicking in the country or the suburbs (now accessible by train) became the subject matter for a new generation of painters, the Impressionists: Monet, Renoir, Degas, Caillebotte, Sisley. The artists themselves lived in the new Batignolles district, north of Saint-Lazare station, and met in the cafés of Pigalle and Clichy.

Change of mood By the 1880s the sunny insouciance of '70s Impressionism gave way to a more imaginative, but also pessimistic mood. In poetry this was expounded by the Decadents, later the Symbolists, inspired by the writings of the explosive lovers, Verlaine and Rimbaud. The leading *fin de siècle* Symbolist was undoubtedly Mallarmé, whose enigmatic verses best convey the melancholy that overcame his generation.
The late 1880s were marked by modern art's first martyrs: Gauguin and Van Gogh, the latter's style having developed in the bohemian atmosphere of the still, half rural Montmartre. By the '90s a new intricate decorative style, art nouveau, blossomed on the apartment buildings of Guimard, the new Métro and department stores (Galeries Lafayette). This was also the city of Proust and Toulouse-Lautrec – a teeming cosmopolitan Paris, where an over-indulged high society rubbed shoulders in a frisson of pleasure with the alcoholics,

42

A dance capturing the exuberance of the Belle Epoque: the can-can

morphine addicts, prostitutes, can-can dancers and singers at the Moulin Rouge and the new 'artistic' cabarets of Montmartre. The Bohemian life, epitomised by low dives like Montmartre's *Lapin Agile*, gradually shifted into a more sophisticated gear as artists and poets moved to the new Montparnasse cafés, the Dôme and the Rotonde. This was when Derain, Matisse, Picasso, Braque, Delaunay and Léger laid the foundations of 20th-century art.

The Banquet In 1908, Picasso threw a dinner party at his Montmartre studio that later became one of the legends of early Modernism. Guest of honour was Henri Rousseau, the great 'naïve' painter. Other guests included the poets Max Jacob, André Salmon and Apollinaire, the American collectors Leo and Gertrude Stein and the painters Vlaminck, Braque and Marie Laurencin. Marie Laurencin danced, while her lover Apollinaire, unperturbed, caught up with his correspondence in a corner of the room. Frédé, owner of the *Lapin Agile*, wandered in with his donkey Lolo, who consumed the last of the food. To crown the evening two of the poets faked an attack of delirium, frothing (chewed soap) at the mouth, which sent the smartly dressed American guests scurrying home. This mix of exaltation and buffoonery perfectly conveys the atmosphere of Parisian Bohemia before the Great War – a certain innocence and *joie de vivre* later lost in the more worldly ambience of 1920s Montparnasse. In the same years Eric Satie, Stravinsky, Alfred Jarry, Proust and Diaghilev revolutionised modern music, theatre, literature and ballet. Rarely had so much innovative talent gathered in the same place at the same time as in the Paris of 1900 to 1914.

>> The Bateau Lavoir was a ramshackle wooden piano factory below the Moulin de la Galette, used as a studio by Picasso and his contemporaries – the city's poorest painters and poets. It was so named because of its resemblance to the laundry boats on the Seine, adorned with sheets and trousers hanging out to dry. >>

■ **Paris between the wars was described as 'a magnificent and well-equipped showcase'. Its frenetic cultural pleasures attracted a stream of foreign artists, firstly political refugees from Eastern Europe and then, as the 1920s gained momentum and became *les années folles*, an influx of Americans living high on their dollars. Jazz was the rhythm, Chanel the fashion, Charleston the step, art deco the style, Surrealism the art, and Montparnasse the quartier that epitomised the cultural climate of this period. .....■**

Profoundly marked by World War I, in which 1.4 million Frenchmen had died and over a million were disabled, the nation licked her wounds and embarked on an energetic and creative commitment. Victory celebrations were held in an attempt to wipe out memories of Big Bertha, the huge German cannon that had bombarded Paris, and national pride was restored by the return of Alsace Lorraine from German annexation. But could France after 1914 ever know another Belle Epoque?

Shock value Although Apollinaire, the inventor of the term 'Surrealism', died in 1918, it was only after the war that Tristan Tzara brought the Dada movement from Zürich to Paris. 'Art is nonsense' cried its protagonists, the poets Breton, Eluard and Aragon, rejecting traditional values and aiming to shock, as did Duchamp by exhibiting his 'ready-made' urinal. However, they soon realised the limitations of negativity and by the time art students ceremonially drowned a Dada effigy in the Seine in 1921 the movement was dead.
Drawn to Freud's discoveries, Breton and his band, joined by the German Max Ernst, turned to free association, to the power of the subconscious and to images generated by dreams. In 1924 their influential Surrealist Manifesto announced a Parisian movement that was to infiltrate much of European creativity (art, literature, film) right up to World War II and beyond. Although their political affiliations were largely pro-Communist, it was on this point that the group eventually broke up. Nevertheless, artists such as Dali, de Chirico and

> << 'Pure automatism' – André Breton, describing Surrealist movement >>

the film maker Buñuel, despite disputes with the authoritarian leader Breton, spread its images throughout the world. Magazines were used to spread Surrealist ideas, starting with *La Révolution Surréaliste* in 1924. Other magazines brought the gospel to Belgium, England and New York.

Kiki and co Alongside these purveyors of fantasy, other creative individuals gathered around the tables of the famous Montparnasse cafés, Le Dôme, La Rotonde and La Coupole. These included Russian and Polish émigrés (Chagall, Lempicka), Léger, Soutine, the

> << 'Hand-painted dream photographs' – Salvador Dali, describing his own work >>

stylish Foujita and the vivacious Kiki de Montparnasse, dancer and model, who lived with photographer Man

Ray. Montparnasse meant cheap accommodation and meals, freedom and congenial company, but this foreign influx sometimes encountered French xenophobia from supporters of the fascist *Action Française*, steadily gaining popularity.

The US factor Less integrated was a growing American community, steeped in dreams of Paris and busily penning some of the 20th century's most innovative literature. At the centre of this web was Sylvia Beach's bookshop in the rue de l'Odéon, Shakespeare and Company, which attracted expatriate scribes such as Hemingway, Ezra Pound, Henry Miller, Scott Fitzgerald and Gertrude Stein. Her devotion to James Joyce stretched to typing his illegible manuscripts and actually publishing *Ulysses*, a feat that nearly bankrupted her bookshop but left the world with a masterpiece. The Wall Street crash in 1929 announced the end of high living for many of the American expats, although the economy of France itself had a delayed reaction.

With the advent of 'talkies', American films dominated Paris – but there was soon another, hotter import: that of jazz and black culture. The Bal Nègre, in the 5th *arrondissement*, was packed nightly with elegant women shaking to the new dance rhythms in the arms of West Indians or Africans. But the climax came in 1925, when the *Revue Nègre* hit town. Josephine Baker, attired in Poiret, Sonia Delaunay or Schiaparelli, outshone homegrown star Mistinguette. Meanwhile, three World Fairs proved to the world that native French culture was far from dead. In 1925 the Exposition des Arts Décoratifs marked, in Le Corbusier's words, 'the decisive turning point in the quarrel between the old and the new'. Art deco was acknowledged king, with the modernist designs of Ruhlmann, Dunand, Mallet-Stevens and Chareau reinforcing Le Corbusier's *Esprit Nouveau*. The 1931 Exposition Coloniale, symbolising France's strong colonial power, bequeathed the city with the striking Musée des Arts Africains; but it was the 1937 Universal Exhibition that left the strongest architectural mark, in Trocadéro's Palais de Chaillot and the Palais de Tokyo. It also exhibited Picasso's *Guernica* – a sign of what was to come.

The Palais de Chaillot, built for the Exposition Universelle in 1937

■ **When the bells of liberation finally tolled at Notre Dame on 26 August 1944, Paris emerged from 50 months of German occupation. Humiliated by the all powerful German army which had taken over the capital, some Parisians had escaped, others turned a blind eye, some collaborated and some resisted. Hundreds of thousands died. But miraculously the city itself survived and even General Von Cholitz disobeyed Hitler's final desperate orders to blow it up. .....■**

At the outbreak of war in September 1939 little changed for Paris but by May 1940, when the German army crossed the French borders, the capital woke up. Traumatised by memories of the Great War, the French army was by then in disarray: 100,000 escaped via Dunkirk but thousands more were taken prisoner, and others fled to the south of France. Refugees poured in, including herds of abandoned cattle, and a frenzied exodus southwards from the capital saw Ministries, the press, the civil service and the contents of the Louvre taking to the road. When the German tanks finally rolled in on 14 June they were greeted with an eerie, deserted city; only a quarter of its inhabitants remained.

France divided Soon Paris adopted a different rhythm. Four days after de Gaulle's impassioned though unheeded radio message from London an armistice was signed between the ageing French President, Marshal Pétain, and Hitler, allowing the Germans to occupy and use Paris 'temporarily' as its military headquarters for the occupied zone. Free France kept 40 per cent of the country, with its government based in Vichy. For many, relieved to see the end of war and disorder, Pétain was seen as a saviour despite disastrously unfavourable peace clauses and the reality that France had become a colonised country.

Occupied city In Paris clocks were changed to central European time, all luxury hotels and public buildings were requisitioned, swastikas fluttered from their roofs, road signs appeared in German, and the changing of the guard goose-stepped down the Champs-Elysées daily at 12.30pm. Commerce was stimulated by the big-spending habits of the occupiers, who could pay in Deutschemarks.

For the average Parisian shortages and rationing became part of daily life as the cost of living rose dramatically along with the mortality rate. Soon a flourishing black market was controlled by criminal gangs making vast fortunes. Petrol was unobtainable and Paris fell silent. Meanwhile Jews had to wear yellow stars, 30,000 Communists were arrested, trade unions were

German troops in Paris

abolished and the left wing banned. In July 1942 13,000 Jews were rounded up in abominable conditions at a sports stadium before being deported to concentration camps. This was the turning point and the silent majority began to form an underground resistance movement. From all classes and ages, their only common purpose was a desire to rid France of its invaders.

Initially operating through individual acts of sabotage, the Resistancea achieved a unity when **Jean Moulin**

<< At the Mémorial de la Déportation, 200,000 quartz pebbles line the tunnel of a crypt which commemorates the same number of French who died during the Holocaust. Buried at the eastern tip of the Ile de la Cité, this monument was built in 1962 to a stark and effective design by GH Pingusson. >>

was parachuted in to co-ordinate all regional networks. Perturbed by Resistance activities, the Germans and the Vichy police reacted violently, arresting, assassinating and deporting. Moulin himself was arrested and executed in June 1943 but by then the *maquis* were riding high on de Gaulle's growing momentum from Algiers, where he was preparing for government.

The tide turns Strikes and demonstrations grew, clandestine newspapers boosted morale and by the time the Allies disembarked in June 1944, posters and tracts called for an insurrection. Between 19 and 24 August Paris resumed its street-fighting. Trees were felled, paving-stones dug up, barricades erected, ambushes laid and sharp-shooters installed. When General Leclerc's tanks rolled in it was to an accompaniment of ringing bells, ecstatic crowds and the refrain of the Marseillaise. The next day Von Cholitz capitulated and on 26 August de Gaulle led the emotional liberation celebrations down the Champs-Elysées to Notre-Dame.

■ **A city is characterised by its architecture and monuments, but a less definable spirit is created by its culture, a product of personalities from all epochs. Below are some of the Parisians who have left their mark.** .....■

Apollinaire (1880–1918) Of Polish descent; one of the early 20th-century intelligentsia who led the schools of the Cubism and Futurism, and France's first modern poet. *Alcools* and *Calligrammes* abandoned punctuation and experimented with typographical patterns.

Baudelaire (1821–67) Poet, critic, translator of Edgar Allan Poe. Introduced a modern sensibility and explored the musicality of French language. With his mulatto mistress, he led a debauched life of opium and alcohol, haunted by a sense of his own damnation. Many poems in *Les Fleurs du Mal* were banned for offending against public morals. Died of syphilis.

Simone de Beauvoir (1908–86) Sartre's lifelong companion, and a novelist and essayist in her own right. *Le Deuxième Sexe* (1949) and *Les Mandarins* (1954) became handbooks for French feminists. Contributed to the existentialist review *Les Temps Modernes*.

Brassai (1899–1984) Of Hungarian origin but Parisian by adoption, Brassai was a photographer who became 'the eye of Paris', chronicling the nightlife and street-life of the city in the 1920s and '30s.

André Breton (1896–1966) Founder and theorist of Surrealism, an art collector and mentor for many painters. Breton was a poet and writer; *Nadja* was his semi-autobiographical novel.

Coco Chanel (1883–1971) The first truly modern couturier introduced jersey, short skirts, simple box jackets and 'the little black dress' in the 1920s. She started a vogue for costume jewellery and aimed to democratise fashion.

>> **'**Each frill discarded makes one look younger' – Coco Chanel. >>

Colette (1873–1954) The first woman to preside over the Académie Goncourt. Her writing was supple, sensuous and intuitive, often

Colette poses for a 1909 magazine

exploring more perverse sides of human nature.

Le Corbusier (1887–1965) Of Swiss origin, Le Corbusier settled in Paris in 1917 as a painter, and then an architect who propagated the use of reinforced concrete. His rigid style that revolutionised architecture.

Claude Debussy (1862–1918) Debussy entered the Paris Conservatoire aged 10. His music used mood and suggestion in works such as *Prélude à l'après-midi d'un faune* (1894) and *Pelléas et Mélisande* (1902).

Anatole France (1844–1924) Parisian novelist, critic and essayist. France was elected to the Académie Française, and won the Nobel Prize for literature in 1921. He confessed to finding Proust unreadable. His erudite work emulated 18th-century Classicism with an ironic style.

Léon Gambetta (1838–82) Gambetta was a barrister before entering politics, a brilliant orator who opposed the Second Empire. He became a Deputy but left Paris by balloon during the 1870 Prussian siege to organise resistance from Tours. With Thiers, he was instrumental in forming the Third Republic in 1875.

André Gide (1869–1951) Critic, essayist, novelist and founder of the influential *Nouvelle Revue Française* in 1908. *La Porte Etroite* was his first major public success. Gide's questioning of moral dilemmas included his own homosexuality.

Victor Hugo (1802-85) Champion of Romanticism in poetry, drama and novels, famous for *Notre Dame de Paris*. Hugo was politically active as a Royalist and then a Republican, and exiled himself in Guernsey after Napoleon III's *coup d'état*. After his death, his body lay in state under the Arc de Triomphe before being transported to the Panthéon.

André Malraux (1901–1976) A charismatic idealist, aesthete,

Debussy, master of mood music

novelist, essayist, traveller and Minister of Culture. He wrote La Condition Humaine, based on his days in Indo-China. During the Spanish Civil War Malraux organised Republican volunteers. Called upon by de Gaulle to 'change the colour of Paris', he renovated the centre and took culture to the suburbs.

Jean-Paul Sartre (1905–80) Paris-born philosopher, novelist, dramatist and exponent of Existentialism, starting with the novel *La Nausée*. He wrote prolifically during the war and in the 1950s, and was active in the Communist Party. Sartre refused to accept the Nobel Prize for Literature in 1964.

François Truffaut (1932–84) Film director of the post-war *Nouvelle Vague* movement, who started as a critic in the influential *Cahiers du Cinéma*. In a series of five films, starting with *Les Quatre Cent Coups*, (1959), Truffaut explored the dreamy personality of Antoine Doinel.

Emile Zola (1840–1902) A novelist of the Realist school, conveying the tumultuous life of Paris and grim details of a growing industrial society. He defended Dreyfus with a celebrated open letter *J'accuse*, accusing the government of a miscarriage of justice.

PARIS

Basilique du Sacré-Cœur

18

BOULEVARD BARBÈS

ROCHECHOUART

BOULEVARD DE LA CHAPELLE

RUE MARX DORMOY

RUE DE FLANDRE

QUAI DE LA SEINE

Bassin de la Villette

Gare du Nord

RUE DU FAUBOURG ST-DENIS

BLVD DE LA VILLETTE

AVENUE JEAN JAURES

DU MAUBEUGE

BOULEVARD DE MAGENTA

RUE LA FAYETTE

RUE LA FAYETTE

RUE DU FAUBOURG ST-MARTIN

AUBOURG SAINT-MARTIN

19

Parc des Buttes Chaumont

Gare de l'Est

Canal Saint-Martin

Folies Bergère

ée vin

10

RUE DU

BLVD DE STRASBOURG

BOULEVARD DE MAGENTA

Hôpital St-Louis

BLVD DE LA VILLETTE

20

BLVD DE BELLEVILLE

BLVD BONNE NOUVELLE

BOULEVARD BONNE NOUVELLE

SONNIÈRE

2

BLVD ST-MARTIN

PLACE DE LA RÉPUBLIQUE

RUE RÉAUMUR

RUE ST-MARTIN

BLVD DE SÉBASTOPOL

BLVD ST-MARTIN

Conservatoire National des Arts et Métiers

AVENUE DE LA RÉPUBLIQUE

otel des Postes St-Eustache

RUE RÉAUMUR

RUE RÉAUMUR

RUE BEAUBOURG

BLVD DE SÉBASTOPOL

3

BOULEVARD DU TEMPLE

BLVD BEAUMARCHAIS

BOULEVARD VOLTAIRE

11

Les Halles

Beaubourg/Centre Georges Pompidou - Centre National d'Art et de Culture

Forum

Archives Nationales

RUE DE RENARD

RUE DU TEMPLE

BOULEVARD RICHARD LENOIR

Tour St-Jacques

héâtre usical

Théâtre de la Ville

RUE DE RIVOLI

Musée Picasso

RUE DE LA

OO DE GESVRES

SSERIE

Musée Carnavalet

Hôtel de Ville

PLACE DES VOSGES

Ile

VOIE GEORGES POMPIDOU

QUAI DE L'

RUE ST-ANTOINE

de la

Hôtel Dieu

HÔTEL DE VILLE

4

QUAI DES CÉLESTINS

PLACE DE LA BASTILLE

RUE DU FAUBOURG ST-ANTOINE

BLVD DU PALAIS

Préf de Police **Cité**

Cathédrale Notre-Dame

QUAI DES

BLVD HENRI IV

QUAI DE LA

Ile

St-Louis

Opéra Bastille

MONTEBELLO

QUAI

QUAI DE LA TOURNELLE

PONT DE SULLY

12

QUAI HENRI IV

AVENUE LEDRU-ROLLIN

ssée de ny

BLVD SAINT-GERMAIN

Seine

BLVD MORLAND

AVE LYON

BOULEVARD DIDEROT

rbonne

Institut de Monde Arabe

QUAI ST-BERNARD

PONT D'AUSTERLITZ

QUAI DE LYON

Gare de Lyon

AVENUE DAUMESNIL

Panthéon

Jardin des Plantes

QUAI DE LA RAPÉE

Mosquée

QUAI D'AUSTERLITZ

BLVD DE BERCY

ital de Grâce

Muséum National d'Histoire Naturelle

BOULEVARD DE L'HÔPITAL

Gare d'Austerlitz

PONT DE BERCY

Palais Omnisports de Bercy

RT-ROYAL

BLVD ST-MARCEL

QUAI DE LA GARE

QUAI DE BERCY

Manufacture des Gobelins

AVE DES GOBELINS

13

BOULEVARD VINCENT AURIOL

QUAI DE BERCY

BLVD AUGUSTE BLANQUI

PLACE D'ITALIE

0   1/2   1 km

0   1/2 mile

LE CAFÉ DU COMMERCE

The Left Bank

It is impossible to tire of Paris' central Left Bank area. Its narrow streets, lined with shops and restaurants, combine with breathtaking monuments and Parisian chic to create a unique atmosphere. However the city may develop, nothing can change the historic streets and buildings of the **Quartier Latin**, the **Montagne Ste-Geneviève** and **St-Germain-des-Prés**.

Transformations There have, however, been changes further afield. **Montparnasse**, the quarter famous for its literary and artistic connotations in pre-war Paris, is a flagrant example. Today the main boulevard presents a rather artificial, plastic face. The architectural *faux pas* of the 209m-high **Tour Montparnasse**, part of Pompidou's heritage, is so extraordinarily out of place that it almost assumes a perverted monumental glory. The urban developments behind the city's most confusing station (Montparnasse) are best ignored. Many Left Bank residents claim that they hardly ever cross the Seine. They have their Roman ruins, their cinemas, galleries, literary cafés and halls of learning. They also have France's government, concentrated in the **Faubourg St-Germain**, once the height of bourgeois fashion. Between the **rue du Bac** and **Les Invalides** is yet another world: hidden ministry gardens and embassies housed in superb 18th-century mansions. Immediately to the west are the stately residential avenues of the 7th *arrondissement* leading south to the heavily populated 15th. Apart from the **Eiffel Tower** and **Les Invalides** this area is devoid of 'tourist attractions': all the more reason to give it some attention.

In the southern 13th *arrondissement,* southeast Asian immigrants have created a firmly identifiable **Chinatown**. Here you can celebrate Chinese New Year or sample ethnic cuisine. Towering over you are high-rise blocks, a far cry from the historic townhouses and middle-class apartments near by, and proof that even the Left Bank of Paris is still evolving.

A huge redevelopment project in the 13th *arrondissement* will have as its skyline symbol four glass towers – part of the new Bibliothèque de France (National Library), a vast and ambitious operation which will close President Mitterrand's 14-year reign of *grands projets* in 1995. Meanwhile the entire surrounding *quartier* of Tolbiac, which runs east along the Seine from the Gare d'Austerlitz will be restructured at a projected cost of 25 billion francs: all part of a massive boost for the Left Bank image

52

Walk **Exploring the Rive Gauche**

Starting at the 12th-century church of St-Germain des Prés, walk down the rue Bonaparte and turn immediately right after the corner garden into the rue de l'Abbaye. Turn left into the rue de Furstenberg. Here you cross the delightful square once inhabited by the painter Delacroix, before coming to the rue Jacob.

Follow rue Jacob to the left. This street has numerous antique and interior decoration shops.

At the rue Bonaparte, follow this fascinating shopping street to the right. On your left you will pass the grand entrance to the **Beaux Arts.**

Having reached the Seine, walk along the Quai Malaquais, which leads directly into the Quai Voltaire and the Quai Anatole France. From here there is a good view of the Louvre across the Seine. The quais themselves are lined with up-market antique shops and the odd restaurant. At **no 19 Quai Malaquais** stands a literary landmark; Anatole France was born here, and it was previously the home of George Sand, who was deeply involved with Alfred de Musset.

Cross the rue du Bac. Pass the courtyard of the **Caisse des Dépôts**, dominated by a sculpture by Dubuffet, before coming to the almighty Musée d'Orsay.

Circle round to the left, following the chic rue de Bellechasse to the rue de l'Université Turn left. The route continues past more antique shops and galleries.

At the rue des Saints-Pères, turn right to rejoin the boulevard St-Germain, with the church along to the left.

The Right Bank

A horseman looks out over the 17th-century place des Victoires, now a focus for 20th-century fashions

Look at a map of Paris. Notice how the Seine gently curves around the Left Bank, almost enclosing it, leaving the Right Bank more open and more extensive. Covering a much greater area, it governs the north, east and west of Paris and over the centuries has suffered for it. The Baron Haussmann created his wide arteries here; kings built their palaces here; and every ruler left at least one monument. Less intimate in scale, more disparate in style, its atmosphere can be stately or decidedly tacky, and is certainly less easy to define. This is also the banking and business centre, and its rhythm is fast: those notorious long Paris lunches are here generally replaced by a quick sandwich.

Changing pace This is contemporary Paris. It also boasts two opera houses, two museums of contemporary art, the Louvre, countless other monuments and museums and a dense concentration of gastronomic halts and nocturnal haunts. Cushioning the grandeur are burgeoning new *quartiers*, rebuilt or redeveloped. The most obvious is the **Marais** which over the last 15 years has undergone intensive renovation and is now a hive of avant-garde art galleries and trendy restaurants. Historic buildings have become museums, like the **Musée Picasso**, while at the eastern end the **Bastille** is developing along similar lines. Towering over the central square is a mammoth and prestigious new opera house, while in the back streets flourish a mass of tiny boutiques, shady bars and experimental galleries.

Les Halles The central area of the Right Bank is monopolised by another renovated area, **Les Halles**, the hub of Paris which kicks off the *arrondissement* system (this curls outwards snail-like from here). The **Centre Pompidou** remains a controversial landmark, offering hot culture and panoramic views, while just a few streets away is the infamous **rue St-Denis**, thick with sex shops and prostitutes. Unfortunate in the spectacular and protracted bulldozering of its past, Les Halles has taken on a peculiar identity, closely linked with a vast underground shopping centre and the RER station which speeds in suburban teenagers for their nights on the town.

Once again, things change radically only a few streets away. Here you enter the realm of fashion victims and ultra-chic designer clothes shops which revolve around the superb 17th-century **place des Victoires**. Continuing the paradox, this area skates round the **Banque de France** and the **Bourse** before, deep in the 2nd *arrondissement*, becoming a maze of wholesale rag-traders and basement sweat-shops. Punctuating all the above are the main press offices and agencies of the capital.

Nightlife For the visitor the Right Bank also means glamour and glitter. While the avenue **Montaigne** and the **Faubourg St-Honoré** maintain their monopoly on haute couture and related boutiques, the **Champs-Elysées** has seen better days. However, many of Paris' luxury hotels and exclusive nightclubs cluster around this major axis, and the temples of its top chefs are generously sprinkled between the 8th and adjoining 17th *arrondissements*.

Meanwhile the 16th *arrondissement* maintains its discreetly chic residential atmosphere, at the same time displaying some of France's most avant-garde architecture from the turn of the century, as well as monumental relics from various Expositions Universelles.

Montmartre Few come to Paris without the obligatory pilgrimage to Montmartre which, although still attracting residents from the world of film and media, has turned over many of its charms to the tourist masses. At the bottom of the hill in **Pigalle** tourist buses line the boulevard, while sex shops and clubs ply their trade, but in the streets running downhill through the 9th *arrondissement* you will find some of the city's more genuine nightlife. This village-like area runs down to the *grands boulevards,* once a social hub, now following the same fate as the Champs-Elysées.

New developments are legion on this side of the Seine, from the mega-development of **La Défense**, on-going since 1958, to (marginally) more modest projects such as **La Villette** and **Bercy**, both of which should be complete by the mid-'90s. This policy of injecting life and facilities into neglected outlying areas attempts to combine the latest architectural styles harmoniously with historical features and structures. But traditionally working-class districts such as **Belleville** or the **Bastille** are both suffering at the hands of property developers. Nothing is built without controversy: all the more fuel for Parisian polemics; all the more coffees to accompany the endless debate and discussion. At least those essential Parisian characteristics are saved.

A view across the Seine of the 8th **arrondissement** *on the Right Bank*

The Islands

Happily floating mid-stream in the Seine, the Ile de la Cité and the Ile St-Louis are as different in character as the two banks they separate. One is the site of the first (pre-Roman) settlement of the Parisii tribe; the other is the symbol of a successful 17th-century property development. Linked by a fragile footbridge, both are surrounded by extensive water-level *quais*, favourites with anglers, sun-bathers, young couples, book-readers and a cross-section of the Parisian gay community.

Ile St-Louis Densely inhabited by successful literati and a cosmopolitan breed of wealthy business people, the Ile St-Louis has become an exclusive residential area inevitably frequented by tourists. One long street which runs from end to end is a mass of restaurants and shops more geared to foreigners than to locals, although many residents swear by the quality of the food shops. Locally produced, world-famous ice cream is a strong attraction, but the architectural unity and beauty of Le Vau's 17th-century town-houses and the elegant comfort they exude make neck- craning the favourite pastime here. One of Paris' best views is from the western tip along the Seine.

Ile de la Cité Historically the heart of Paris, the Ile de la Cité boasts three major monuments: Notre-Dame, **Sainte-Chapelle** and the **Conciergerie**. Also strong on government buildings such as the **Palais de Justice**, the **Hôtel Dieu** (a hospital) and the **Préfecture**, the result is a bizarre mixture of the sublime and the banal. Some residents manage to squeeze in between the medieval monuments, living along the *quais* or on the delightful **place Dauphine**, while the flower market occupies a square behind the Préfecture, constantly passed by police cars and ambulances which, sirens wailing, tear past the Gothic towers of Notre Dame. This relaxed eclecticism is perhaps symbolic of the entire city: nothing is sacred, but every area eventually has its monument.

56

Sainte-Chapelle and the gates to the Palais de Justice, Ile de la Cité

Walk Exploring the Rive Droite

From the Concorde cross to the Tuileries gardens beside the Jeu de Paume.
From here you can either walk along the **Terrasse des Feuillants**, set up by Le Nôtre in the 1660s, and enjoy the view across the garden or follow the arcaded **rue de Rivoli** and its tourist shops.

After an underpass, walk beside the Musée des Arts de la Mode, soon followed by the Musée des Arts Décoratifs, before the Louvre itself. At the place du Palais Royal turn sharp left, cross the rue St-Honoré to the Comédie Française and enter the Palais Royal through a discreet arch.
Here you confront the controversial art installation by Daniel Buren, before entering the gardens proper. Walk to the end, leaving on the left side past the historic restaurant Le **Grand Véfour**.

Go up to the rue des Petits Champs. Turn left here, passing the Bibliothèque Nationale on your right, and go on to the avenue de l'Opéra. Japanese restaurants in the side-streets indicate the proximity of Paris' 'Little Tokyo'.

Turn right towards the opera house, cross the avenue, then turn left and walk down the rue de la Paix, This is Paris' high-class jewellery street, which leads to the no less classy **place Vendôme**. The legendary **Ritz Hotel** occupies the right half of the square.

Go straight on down the rue de Castiglione, until you reach the rue de Rivoli and the Concorde.

■ **As dawn breaks over Les Halles, clusters of bleary-eyed, home-bound nighthawks cross paths with the first wave of workmen. The rue Montorgueil, one of the main market streets when Les Halles was really Les Halles, still has many classic suppliers and services intact. .....■**

Six kilometres of streets around the rue Montorgueil will be repaved by 1994, to create Europe's largest pedestrian area.

Little has changed here, except that in 1992 most of this lengthy street was transformed into a pedestrian precinct. The first café to open its doors, at 5.30am – the **Pointe Sainte-Eustache** – is also the first in the street at the Les Halles end. Not overly boisterous when they arrive, local workers in their *bleus* (traditional blue overalls) soon warm up with *un petit coup de blanc sec* or even manage to slip down a quick cognac. Employed in the market or on local building sites, they face a long day, generally out of doors; hence their winter alcoholic requirements.

Early risers Also starting the day early are the municipal workers, emptying dustbins into their poison-green dustcarts. When Paris regained its first mayor since the Revolution, in 1976, it also gained an army of street-cleaning machinery, including motorised 'poopscoopers'. Streets are cleaned in the early mornings by streams of water gushing through the gutters, chanelled by strategically positioned lumpy rags. In the wake of the dustcart, *concierges* soon emerge to pull in their bins and restore order to the building in their care. Their net-curtained *loges* still exist and *concierges* continue to fulfil an important social role in Parisian residential life. By 8am a few white-collar workers start appearing, some hurrying straight to the metro, others taking time to stop for a coffee and croissant as they peruse the morning paper. By now the market is getting into its swing, although officially most stalls and shops open at 9am. Boulangeries are an exception, opening at around 7.30, when the baguette is often at its optimum. Queen of the pâtissiers in the rue Montorgueil is **Stohrer,** founded by Louis XV's chef pâtissier at no 51 in 1730.

Cosmopolitan tastes Montorgueil literally means 'proud mount', a poetic way of describing the road's gentle slope upwards towards the *Grands Boulevards*. The southern end was once the central oyster and seafood market where produce from the northern ports ended up. This explains the proximity of the all-night seafood counters on the adjoining **rue de la Coquillière.** Today, cosmopolitan tastes have moved in and the choice is more eclectic: an oriental grocer sells manioc, lychees and sweet potatoes; a North African wholesaler displays buckets and barrels piled high with olives, grains, dates and nuts; further up a pungent Greek grocery offers houmous or stuffed vine leaves, while the windows of two Italian delicatessens are full of fresh pasta of all shapes and sizes and strings of salamis. As you wander through the market crowds you will hear Spanish, Arabic or even English and German. The fresh, colourful fruit and vegetable stalls attract every nationality, generation and status, as do the prices, which are a fraction of neighbourhood grocery stores.

Lunch break By midday it is lunchtime for numerous office and street workers. Bistros abound in this street, from the traditional **Estivals Montorgueil** at no 50, where you can eat a wholesome dish of pork and lentils, to the trendier **Centre Ville** which serves salads. Shoppers gradually disappear as 1pm approaches: this is closing time for the fish, meat, fruit and vegetable shops which take a rest till 4pm.

The afternoon session closes again at around 7.30pm, though some late-opening stores benefit from the last few dedicated office workers hurrying home with a baguette and a bottle of wine to catch the 8pm TV news.

Twilight zone Although ostensibly quiet in the evenings, the rue Montorgueil is far from dead. There are several popular restaurants and, at its southern end, a relaxed young bar, **Alex**, stays open till the early hours. But the side streets are where it is all happening: the rue **Tiquetonne** boasts Thai transvestite bars or an all-night African restaurant, and the **rue Marie-Stuart** an equally eccentric selection, covering ethnic flavours from Spain to the Cameroons, all of which keeps the locals going until the 24-hour cycle starts again.

59

Business as usual in the rue Montorgueil

The Institut de France, home of the Académie Française

▶ ▷ ▷   Académie Française

Institut de France, 23 Quai de Conti, 75006
metro: Pont-Neuf

This venerable institution, although somewhat dusty at the edges, remains a heeded voice in certain French circles, its 40 members occasionally emitting dictums that just have to be obeyed. Founded by Richelieu in 1635, the Académie's rule over the standards of the French language, which includes a high level of protectionism, is embodied in the *Dictionnaire de la Langue Française*, a 10-tome affair which is periodically revised and published, volume by hefty volume.

The Académie's weekly meetings, which once a year become solemn occasions in the famous domed hall, are held at the **Institut de France**, an edifice which you cannot fail to spot in its prime Left Bank position overlooking the Pont des Arts. The building itself was designed in 1663 by Le Vau, one of the architects of the Louvre, and was financed by a generous donation from Cardinal Mazarin to found a college for choice provincial students. By 1790 it had lost this function to the vagaries of the Directoire, and five years later the five academies of the Institut de France were moved in.

Elected only when a seat is liberated by a member's death, the average age of *académicien* is consequently elevated. Today the Académie Française is a concerted voice of historians, writers, doctors and representatives of the church, army and diplomatic circles.

Although the Institut is not open to individual visits, which means nobody can pay homage to Mazarin's tomb, you can enter the courtyard to have a closer look.

▶ ▷ ▷   Angleterre, Hôtel d'

44 rue Jacob, 6e

This elegant 18th-century townhouse in the heart of the antique district once housed the British Embassy, whence its name. This generated a diplomatic incident when Benjamin Franklin refused to set foot on 'British soil' to sign the US Declaration of Independence. More recently Hemingway lived here (modestly) and it is now a charming and discreet hotel preserving many of its historic features, including a flowery courtyard.

▷ ▷ ▷   Aquariums

Apart from the small aquariums squeezed between cages of rabbits in the shops along the Quai de la Mégisserie, underwater enthusiasts can also see no fewer than 12 aquariums at the **Institut Océanographique**, 195 rue Saint-Jacques, 5e (tel:46 33 08 61). Set up by Jacques Cousteau, it explains his ambitious underwater projects undertaken since the 1960s. However Paris' largest liquid universe and the second in Europe is housed downstairs at the **Musée des Arts Africains et Océaniens** (see page 63).

▶ ▶ ▶   Arc de Triomphe

Along with the Eiffel Tower, the Arc de Triomphe remains the great Paris landmark, dominating the axis leading east down the Champs Elysées and west down the avenue de la Grande Armée towards Porte Maillot and La Défense. The central point of a web of 12 avenues constantly swirling with traffic, this major cross-roads is known as the Etoile (star). The Arc's conception goes back to Napoleon, who in 1806 commissioned an awesome memorial to be built for the French army, but it was not until 1836, under Louis-Philippe, that the monument was completed. By the time Haussmann had finished with redesigning Paris the Etoile had assumed the form it has today, and its symbolic role was confirmed after World War I with parades of victorious troops marching through and the burial of the unknown soldier beneath. Over 70 years later, a ceremony takes place every 11 November (Armistice Day), the flame is lit daily at 18.30hrs.

The sculpted façade is actually the work of three different sculptors, and the 30 shields studding the crown of the arch each bear the name of a Revolutionary or Imperial victory (Waterloo does not figure...). The Arc stands 50m high, and it is worth braving the queues to take the lift or labouring up the steps – the view is superb and gives a clear vision of Haussmann's urban lay-out. Access is via the underpasses beneath the chaos of the traffic.

Open: daily 10.00–17.00hrs; till 17.30 in summer.

Symbol of military victory and power, and a long-lasting landmark: the Arc de Triomphe

▶▶▶ **Archives Nationales**
The bureaucratic personality of France is well symbolised by its Archives Nationales, which fill 350km of shelves in the Marais. Napoleon was responsible for housing them in the remarkable Hôtel de Soubise (see page 126) but they have since spilled over into adjacent mansions and in 1988 a new centre was built in the rue des Quatre Fils.

Open: Wednesday to Monday 14.00–17.00hrs.

Walk From the Etoile and along the avenues

Start at the Etoile metro and walk down the Champs Elysées.
Stop at the famous **Fouquets** at no 99, an exclusive restaurant recently declared a historic monument.

Continue to Rond Point and turn right into the avenue Montaigne.
This is the mecca of French *haute couture.* You will pass Louis Vuitton, Chanel, Cartier, Givenchy *et al,* as well as the luxurious Plaza-Athénée hotel, and, at no 15, the **Théâtre des Champs Elysées**. Designed in 1911–3 by Auguste Perret, it saw the first scandalous performance of Stravinsky's *Le Sacré du Printemps,* danced by Nijinsky. The marble façade and the interior were recently restored and crowned by a controversial restaurant.

Cross the place de l'Alma and take the avenue du Président Wilson.

Pass the mammoth colonnaded 1937 buildings of the **Musée d'Art Moderne** and the **Palais de Tokyo,** both important exhibition centres. On the other side of the avenue rises the imposing **Palais Galliera**.

Turn right on to the avenue Pierre 1er de Serbie, from the place d'Iéna.
The entrance to the Palais Galliera is on this avenue.

Walk straight on, crossing the avenue Marceau with the church of St-Pierre-de-Chaillot on your left, until you come to the avenue George V.
A short detour to the right takes you to the neo-gothic **American Cathedral**.

Turn left and pass the prestigious hotels George V and Prince de Galles before returning to the Champs Elysées.

▶▶ **Arts Africains et Océaniens, Musée des**

293 avenue Dausmesnil, 12e
metro: Porte Dorée

This museum is a perennial favourite for children. The basement aquariums are a constant draw: leopard sharks swim in the company of a fish named Grace Kelly, yellow-tailed Picasso balistas, bewhiskered catfish or a mound of slow-motion turtles all circulate eternally. Apart from this aspect, the museum is yet

another Parisian monument to the aesthetics of art deco. Built for the 1931 Exposition Coloniale in reinforced concrete, its colonnaded façade is backed by an extraordinary stone bas-relief by Alfred Janniot depicting the glories of the French colonies. Inside, two floors of galleries open on to an enormous ballroom with a superb 'pagoda' ceiling, mosaic floors and murals by Ducos de la Haille. More astonishing examples of art deco are found in two circular rooms leading off the main entrance hall: both boast murals, this time by Lemaître and Louis Bouquet, and are respectively decorated by Printz and by Ruhlmann.

The actual collections cover parts of the Pacific (Melanesia, New Hebrides, Australia), Central and West Africa and finally, on the top floor, the arts of the Maghreb (Algeria, Tunisia and Morocco). The latter displays silver jewellery, ceramics, Koranic tablets, arms and textiles as well as architectural features. However the main riches of the museum lie in the African department on the first floor: Here the tone is set by Dogon masks, rings and statues, reflecting a fascination for the coexistence of life and death. Other tribes such as the Bambaras, Lobi, Akan, Benin or Kongo are represented by items ranging from basic to sacred.

The Pacific islands are represented on the ground floor by masks, carved wooden statues and a large collection of Australian aboriginal art. Bark painting represent the aborigines' approach to their natural world.

Open: Wednesday to Monday 10.00–noon, 13.30–17.30hrs; weekends 12.30–18.00hrs.

The popular Musée des Arts Africains et Océaniens, set in splendid isolation on the edge of the Bois de Vincennes

63

► ► ► **Arts Décoratifs, Musée des**

107 rue de Rivoli, 1e
metro: Palais-Royal

For art nouveau and art deco fanatics, this is the place to go. The museum was founded by the Union Centrale des Arts Décoratifs in a wing of the Louvre at the beginning of this century to collect and exhibit 'beauty in function'. Its didactic role reached its zenith in the '20s and '30s with designers such as Le Corbusier, Charlotte Perriand and Mallet-Stevens contributing to its influence. The museum itself still possesses the charm and drawbacks of its early years: despite some renovation it remains a labyrinth, awaiting expansion into an adjoining wing of the Louvre, scheduled for 1995. In the meantime its tricky access and itinerary make it a tranquil haven of reconstructed salons of the 18th century or ornate oak panelled halls, thick with tapestries. Pick up a plan of the four floors when you buy your ticket; the museum is lacking in signs or logic.

Floor by floor On the top floor (Level 5) you can see two precious collections only open to the public on Thursday afternoons. One is a collection of glass that skips through the centuries and countries, from Roman times through ornate Dutch and Bohemian pieces of the 17th and 18th centuries to the inventive finesse of Murano, along with the sober forms and clear colours of Chinese pieces. Gallé, Daum and Tiffany are well represented. The other treasure here is a collection of wallpaper from its handpainted 17th-century origins to early 20th-century samples.

The lower floors are organised according to periods, so here you can make your choice between medieval/Gothic and Renaissance (Level 2) or the fabulously rich 1900–25 gallery (Level 1), which includes a room entirely faced in art nouveau woodwork (Georges Hoentschell) with furniture by Hector Guimard (famous for his metro entrances). Much of the 1920s collection was donated by the couturier Jeanne Lanvin. Of the many stunning reconstructed interiors from her 7th *arrondissement* apartment, don't miss Rateau's remarkable bathroom design.

Levels 3 and 4 are devoted to the 17th- to early 19th-century collections and here you can focus on porcelain, vast panels of wallpaper depicting exotic landscapes or marquetry masterpieces by Boulle. Again, entire rooms are reconstructed in the style of different periods, while the corridors are lined with water-colours.

State of the art Finally, don't miss the contemporary design section back on Level 1, which displays furniture and objects by today's stars: designers such as Jean-Michel Wilmotte, Philippe Starck or Andrée Putman. After a quiet period, French decorative arts have come back into their own, and this is a good place to get a quick overview of what the last decade has produced. On the same level, apparently an anomaly in this museum, is the Dubuffet donation which the painter gave the museum in 1967 in thanks for arranging his first retrospective. Jean Dubuffet, the master of *art brut*, died in Paris in 1985. Temporary exhibitions of crafts or design complete the cycle.

There is a bookshop on the ground floor and a gift-shop opposite which sells copies and a good range of contemporary design – glass, jewellery, ceramics etc.

Open: Wednesday to Saturday, 12.30–18.00hrs; Sunday 11.00–18.00hrs.

▶▶▷ **Arts de la Mode, Musée des**
109 rue de Rivoli, 1e

Part of the same umbrella structure as the above, the Musée des Arts de la Mode was opened in 1986 in the far corner of the Musée des Arts Décoratifs. Following the same fate, it awaits a major extension so that it will at last be able to accommodate its permanent collections. For the moment, after a dynamic programme of temporary exhibitions ranging from St Laurent to theatre designs by Tirelli or the history of French perfume, it is a museum keeping a low profile, open only during exhibitions. Despite spectacular renovation which gives some fabulous vistas east over the Tuileries, administrative problems have left it unfinished.

In 1991 the government finally earmarked 175 million francs for the entire restructuring and modernisation of both these museums, which now also incorporate the **Musée de la Publicité**. In 1995 this exceptional Parisian showcase spanning the history of design, advertising and fashion will present a refreshed face to the public.

Open: Wednesday to Monday, 12.30–18.00hrs; Sunday 11.00–18.00hrs during exhibitions only.

■ **Revelling in its historic reputation, the Paris art scene is, in the 1990s, still alive and well. After experiencing a rather low ebb with international attention firmly focussed on New York throughout the 1960s and 1970s, Paris has recently re-emerged as a contemporary art cross-roads......■**

The late 1980s saw an unprecedented boom in the art market worldwide, and Paris reaped the rewards with galleries monopolising areas such as the Marais, their scale often directly proportional to the conceptual nature of the work shown. The Bastille too had its renaissance and many younger gallery-owners have turned to this booming quarter as an alternative to the high-flying rents now common in the Marais.

Left Bank But what about the traditional hotbed of art in St-Germain des Prés? The rue de Seine, rue Mazarine and adjoining characteristic streets have put their avant-garde days behind them. Today this area has its own distinct flavour, nothing to do with what is going on across the Seine. Antiques, art deco furniture, prints, ethnographical wonders and 1950s abstract paintings are the mainstay of hundreds of small galleries lining a well defined territory between the rue Bonaparte, rue Guénégaud and the rue de Seine. High quality antiques shops are concentrated further west in what is known as the *Carré Rive Gauche*, a grid of streets running between the Quai Voltaire, the rue du Bac, the rue de l'Université and the rue des Saints Péres, including the famous rue de Beaune.

Back in the epicentre of the Left Bank galleries, head for the eclectic atmosphere of the rue des Beaux Arts. Beautiful objects abound while galleries such as **Albert Loeb** and **Claude Bernard** still promote the figurative style that made their reputations a few decades ago. The rue de Seine offers anything from floral prints to Jean Cocteau originals, while the **Galerie Isy Brachot** on the corner of the rue Guénégaud and the rue Mazarine, has two galleries showing relatively avant-garde work. The **Galerie Montenay** at 31 rue Mazarine, concentrates on young European and American artists and is worth checking out. For contemporary sculpture go to **JGM** in the short but sweet rue Jacques-Callot. Meanwhile there is no shortage of prospective painters in the area: the Ecole des Beaux Arts in the rue Bonaparte regorges flocks of portfolio-lugging students and the eternal café meeting-point, La Palette, remains a favourite for gallery-owners and artists alike.

Right Bank chic For strictly high price brackets, head for another traditional gallery agglomeration over on the Right Bank. Here, between the avenue Matignon, the Faubourg St-Honoré and (further north) the boulevard Haussmann, you can track down works by artists, dead or alive, who have hit the heights. The **Galerie Lelong** at 13/14 rue de Téhéran, founded by the illustrious art

For anyone unconcerned with the latest volatile trends of the art world, Paris has an unbeatable selection of back-street galleries showing classical paintings and drawings, both old and new. If you like the object, you can buy it; but unless you have real flair, don't think you're making an investment — only dealers govern that domain and the last few years have proved how wrong even they can be.

A spacious converted workshop is the setting for European and American art in the Galerie Yvon Lambert's collection (see page 68)

dealer Aimé Maeght, still shows artists such as Magnelli, Alechinsky, Francis Bacon or Tapiès, as well as younger names such as James Brown or Garcià-Sevilla. Near by, the prestigious **Galerie Louis Carré** could be exhibiting anything from Delaunay to Hartung or a French contemporary such as Jean-Pierre Raynaud. For more accessible purchases go to Artcurial, the art department store at 9 avenue Matignon, which specialises in multiples (prints, jewellery, carpets) and boasts one of the best art bookshops in town.

On a very different note, clustered around Beaubourg and spreading east through the Marais are hundreds of contemporary galleries promoting today's avant-garde. From the narrow rue Quincampoix parallel to the boulevard Sébastopol to the labyrinth circling around the Musée Picasso and over towards the place des Vosges, galleries exhibit installations, large format paintings or photographs and occasionally words. To find your way in this circuit, pick up one of the specialised listing-maps *Rive Gauche Rive Droite* which are distributed free throughout the galleries. This itinerary is strictly for the initiated, the state of art today often being generally inaccessible.

Architecturally speaking, it is an opportunity to look at some remarkable renovations of mansions or factories – ceilings are high and often sky-lit, courtyards are commonplace and floors are bleached wood or painted concrete. The well established **Galerie Beaubourg**, opposite the Centre Pompidou, has an airy annexe behind which, in the rue St-Merri, the **Galerie Maeght** now occupies a generous 2,000sq m inside 17th-century walls. The **Galerie Yvon Lambert** in the rue Vieille du Temple (showing top European and American names from Kiefer to Barcelo or Richard Serra) glows in the natural light of a converted workshop while underneath, around and above it a Greek dealer, Renos Xippas, has designed a labyrinthine gallery space.

The youthful Bastille For unknown talent, the Bastille is perhaps the best bet. Although the area between the rue de Charonne, rue de Lappe and rue Keller has experienced a gallery invasion lately, quality is not always the common denominator, so don't be fooled. An exception is the impressive **Galerie Durand-Dessert** at 28 rue de Lappe, which occupies four floors of former factory space and exhibits highly regarded international work by the likes of Mario Merz, Kounellis, William Wegman as well as Gérard Garouste and Bertrand Lavier. However, you're unlikely to find a bargain here.

Juggling hard to become Europe's art capital, Paris thus covers the gamut of periods, prices and styles with specialised geographical concentrations. And outside the gallery circuit there still exist numerous 'salons', a hark-back to the 19th-century tradition, although their participants are aunlikely to cause ripples, as did their forerunners the Impressionists. The **Grand Palais** hosts many of these salons but the art affair of the year is the **FIAC**, a contemporary art fair which attracts galleries and collectors from all over the world every October. Its opening *(vernissage)* is the epitome of the Parisian art world: international, elegant and pretentious.

68

The Galerie Maeght, owned by the family of artistic talent-scout Adrien Maeght

Art Moderne de la Ville de Paris, Musée d'
11 avenue du Président Wilson, 75016
metro: léna

This monumental, colonnaded construction standing high above the Seine was designed by Aubert, Dondel and Viard for the 1937 International Exhibition. It was intended to celebrate the progress of technology, but labour disputes meant that on the day of its official opening little was complete and the President was rushed around an unfinished site. However, one brilliant survivor of this harrowed period is Dufy's 60m by 10m mural dedicated to *La Fée électricité*, colourfully intact and covering the walls of a mezzanine room. Another great mural, Matisse's *La Danse* (1932), together with four major paintings, *Rhythmes* (1938) by Robert Delaunay, dynamise the lofty main hall downstairs.

After years of neglect the museum has now come into its own, guided by a new team of curators. The permanent collection built up over the years from private donations gives the flavour of a museum of 20th-century *Ecole de Paris*, yet a lively contemporary department consistently produces temporary exhibitions of outstanding quality and ambition which help keep this museum within an international sphere.

The core collection Start your visit downstairs, where the permanent collection kicks off with Utrillo, Rouault, Valadon, Bonnard and Vuillard. Don't miss the latter's exquisite portraits of his contemporaries, Bonnard, Maurice Denis, Roussel and Maillol. The next step is

Modern art is still a going concern: a display at the Musée d'Art Moderne (left) and on the gates of a Paris school (above)

Both the museum bookshop (limited in space but well stocked) and the snack bar on the lower floor are worth investigation. The latter is particularly enticing in the summer months, when tables move outside on to the terrace dotted with Bourdelle's statues overlooking the river – but as always, avoid peak lunch hours when the queues are long.

The oldest house in Paris is at 51 rue de Montmorency, 3e and was built by Nicolas Flamel in 1407. The house in nearby rue du Volta, reputed to be older, is in fact a 16th-century reconstruction. The smallest house is at 38 rue du Château d'Eau, has a façade measuring 1.10m wide and is 5m high.

Fauvism (Matisse, Derain), Cubism (Braque, Picasso) and related contemporaries Metzinger, Lhote, Léger, Gromaire, Robert and Sonia Delaunay. Two works by R Delaunay in particular are worth stopping at: his *Ville de Paris* (1911) and his *Rugby Players*. This burgeoning pre-war period, when Paris was an international hub, also encompasses Modigliani, Szenes, Foujita, Chagall, Soutine, all immigrant artists who contributed to creating the first *Ecole de Paris*. Less strong on surrealism, the collection moves into abstraction (Arp, Domela, Magnelli, Fautrier) and *nouveau réalisme*, a 1960s return to figuration and France's version of Pop Art.

Also exhibited here is an exceptional collection of art deco furniture (1920–37) which includes pieces by Ruhlmann, Chareau and Jean Dunand.

The Musée des Enfants, situated behind the art deco room, aims to stimulate children's budding creative urges, organising exhibitions and workshops around contemporary artists accessible to young minds.

The spacious galleries on the street level and first floor are reserved for temporary exhibitions, usually keeping a historical 20th-century figure parallel with avant-garde work by young artists of today.

Open: Tuesday to Sunday, 10.00–17.40hrs (Wednesday to 20.30hrs).

Astérix, Parc see pages 26–7

Avaux, Hôtel d'

71 rue du Temple, 3e
metro: Arts et Métiers

Built by Le Muet in 1650 for the Comte d'Avaux, this mansion in the heart of the Marias is immediately memorable for its imaginative façade. Pushing open its imposing gate decorated with sculpted heads, you enter a vast, ordered courtyard of massive Corinthian pilasters. The left wing façade is actually a *trompe-l'oeil* designed to hide part of Philippe Auguste's peripheral wall. The mansion now belongs to the government and is partly used for stocking archives.

Bac, rue du

This mainly 18th-century street winds south from the Pont-Royal and crosses the boulevard St Germain before narrowing into a classy shopping street, ending at the almighty department store **Au Bon Marché** – Paris' oldest. The name Bac goes back to the days when the Louvre palace was under construction and a boat (bac) ferried stone across the river to the site.

As you wander southwards from the bridge you pass some of Paris' most prestigious antique shops, as well as the **Galerie Maeght** which, at no 46, occupies the former Hôtel de Boulogne, built in 1744 for a gentleman who died nine years later, completely bankrupt from fast living. One of his financial victims was Voltaire. Another literary association with the rue du Bac is the memory of Alexandre Dumas' three celebtrated sword-thrusting musketeers, who were based in barracks in this street.

South of St-Germain, the rue du Bac boasts anything from shoes to fine wines, furniture or a branch of

Hédiard. Its houses once sheltered literary salons and members of the 19th-century intelligentsia such as Chateaubriand (at no 118–120), who was buried a few doors away from his home at the chapel of the **Missions Etrangères.**

After making a nice little profit selling a painting to the French government in 1893, the American painter James Whistler installed himself at no 110. Cohorts such as Degas, Toulouse-Lautrec, Manet and the writers Mallarmé and Henry James dropped by for no doubt animated discussions, while his child-models scandalised the concierge by frolicking naked in the garden.

At no 136–140 the **Hôtel de la Vallière** houses the Chapel of the Filles de la Charité where, in 1830, repeated visions of the Virgin Mary finally led a nun named Catherine Labouré to glorious canonisation. One million or so pilgrims come by every year to see her relics.

The garden of the Maison de Balzac (left), where Honoré de Balzac (below) went into hiding from his debtors

▶▶▶ **Balzac, Maison de**
47 rue Raynouard, 16e
metro: Passy
Pursued by debtors, the writer Honoré de Balzac laid low in this pretty Passy house from 1840 until 1847, using an assumed name but nevertheless managing to pen *La Cousine Bette* and *Le Cousin Pons* in a creative flow which happened from midnight onwards. This intimate museum contains portraits and caricatures of the writer and of his favourite mistress alongside other memorabilia. A library devoted to his works and critical reviews of them completes the Balzacien picture.
Open: Tuesday to Sunday, 10.00–17.40hrs.

▷▷▷ **Banque de France**
rue Croix-des-Petits-Champs, 2e
A Napoleonic initiative, the Bank of France was founded in 1800 and soon moved to its present imposing quarters, conveniently down the road from the Bourse (stock exchange). Although the mansion was built in 1635 by François Mansart, much was rebuilt in the 19th century. It is not open to visits.

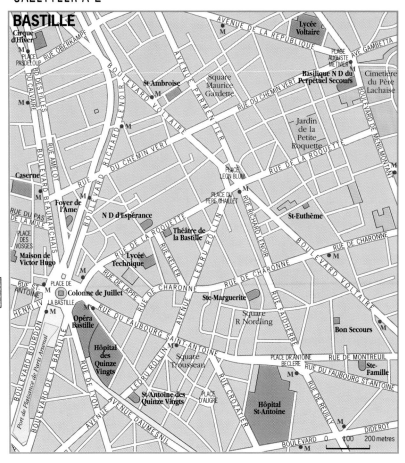

▶▶▷ Bastille

metro: Bastille

Forever linked with the storming of its prison in 1789 – the first violent uprising of the French Revolution – today's Bastille area is just as lively, though more dedicated to a hedonistic way of life. Designer bars, night clubs, white-walled art galleries, a marina and ethnic restaurants create its 1990s character while its new symbol, the 'people's' opera house, towers over the main square.

A new look Only 10 years ago this was still a resolutely working-class district, full of specialised craftsmen's workshops often located in verdant courtyards or hidden passages. Artists were the first to move in, transforming derelict industrial spaces into spacious studios and homes. And where artists go, galleries follow, soon chased by appropriate watering-holes. The **marina** terminating the Canal St-Martin was redeveloped in the early 1980s, and soon after that the **opera house** rose from the ground, vying for attention with the central column, the **Colonne de Juillet**, erected in 1840 to commemorate victims of the 1830 uprising. Beneath the

Looking to the future and commemorating the past: the Opéra de la Bastille (left) and the Colonne de Juillet (below)

traffic circulating wildly around it are buried hundreds of citizens.

Unique streets Today's main artery running northeast from the square is the **rue de la Roquette**: here you have your choice of hip bars, trendy clothes shops and the adventurous **Théâtre de la Bastille**. The perpendicular **rue de Lappe** has maintained a nocturnal reputation since the 1930s when the Balajo dance-hall attracted the likes of Mistinguett, Arletty and Piaf. This street also has traditional connections with the Auvergne: a specialised grocery shop and a restaurant roofed with wooden clogs remain – but who knows for how long?.

Other lively streets worth investigating are the **rue Amelot, rue de Charonne** and **rue Keller**, while the **Faubourg St-Antoine** is traditionally lined with furniture shops, from kitsch to contemporary, part of its long-standing crafts tradition. To alleviate the tedium of this stretch, go into no 56, the **Cour du Bel Air,** where you will discover a paradisical ivy-clad courtyard with a rare charm.

Meeting of worlds North of the Faubourg you feel the strangely schizophrenic character of this area, still undergoing transformation. Street water pumps used by African immigrants stand in front of art galleries selling paintings for thousands of francs. Carpenters knock back their breakfast stimulants at a bar next to sleek young advertising executives. Many worlds meet at the Bastille but their universe is still without definition.

■ **The Seine and its banks give as much flavour to the city as any monument. It runs a 776km course from Burgundy to the Channel and joins both the Oise and the Marne just outside Paris. Named by Julius Caesar, it was described in 1862 by Verlaine as a 'muddy old snake', with its cargoes of 'wood, coal and corpses'. Today the river boasts cleaner water (much appreciated by local anglers), new cargoes of sightseers, houseboats and riverside expressways speeding traffic along this essential artery. .....■**

The *bateaux-mouches*, which sail along the Seine night and day, can be boarded at the Pont d'Alma and during summer run every half-hour from 10.00 to 21.00hrs (tel: 42 25 96 10). At the Pont d'Iéna, you can catch a *bateau parisien* (tel: 47 05 50 00), traveling east to the Ile St-Louis and west as far as the scaled down version of the Statue of Liberty. All trips provide a multi-lingual commentary and last about an hour. For smaller rivercraft, go to the tip of the Ile de la Cité at Pont-Neuf for the Vedettes du Pont-Neuf (tel: 46 33 98 38).

With the city divided between Rive Gauche (Left Bank) and Rive Droite (Right Bank) and monuments lining both banks, the Seine can never be ignored. Sensitive to winter rain, it often reaches menacing levels, leading to the closure of its lower banks (*berges*) and creating ensuing havoc in the Parisian traffic flow. However, the Seine blossoms into its own in the warmer months, sprouting contented anglers, rows of *bouquinistes*, idle students, snoozing tramps, star-struck lovers and various forms of sun-worshippers. When you tire of retracing Parisian history, chasing the latest architectural feats or fox-trotting traffic, this should be your destination.

River history Until the 14th century the banks of the Seine remained a web of tow-paths and specialised ports. The first *quai* to be structured was the **Quai des Grands Augustins** in 1313, but it was the Rive Droite which developed fastest under Henri IV, soon becoming a continuous stretch from the **Tuileries** to the **Quai des Célestins**. Louis XVI was the saviour of the Rive Gauche and built up the embankment leading from the **Quai St Bernard** through **St-Michel** and the **Quai des Grands Augustins** as far as the **Invalides**. Following the pattern set by the construction of the **Pont-Neuf** in 1607 (now the oldest bridge in Paris), other bridges were gradually cleared of houses and shops, and under Napoleon the last water-mills disappeared, leaving an unimpeded view along the river. Haussmann is once again to be thanked for the trees which line long stretches of the *quais* and provide essential summer shade.

River road Scandal broke out in the 1960s when part of the precious Rive Droite was developed into an expressway; public outcry was such that the equivalent Rive Gauche project was abandoned. However, one of the great Parisian nocturnal experiences is speeding through the Rive Droite tunnel from Concorde and emerging at river level with a glittering view across to the **Ile de la Cité** and the floodlit turrets of the **Conciergerie**.

River walks For a historic riverside promenade, you could do a lot worse than choose the central Rive Droite stretch, accessible from beside the **Pont des Arts,** which runs as far as the **Pont Alexandre** next to the **Grand Palais.** A leisurely walk here will take you past a string of monuments across the river (**Institut de France, Beaux-Arts, Musée d'Orsay, Assemblée Nationale**), as well some imaginatively decked out houseboats and, in summer, an army of bronzing bodies.

For pure romanticism nothing can beat the *quais* of the **Ile St-Louis,** while, on the Rive Gauche, you can now walk unimpeded from the **Pont-Royal** (beside the Musée d'Orsay) right through the centre as far as the **Pont d'Austerlitz** in the east, emerging at the **Jardin des Plantes.** At St-Michel there is a section frequented by down-and-outs.

Down by the river again, in front of **Notre Dame,** the route moves into a more up-market stretch with houseboats and a contemporary sculpture garden. This part is also characterised by joggers and amateur painters having a go at the backview of Notre Dame: it provides a superb view of the elegant mansions lining the **Ile St-Louis** opposite.

Riverside reading If you want to dig out obscure magazines, second-hand and antiquarian books, prints or postcards, don't forget to investigate the *bouquinistes.* Most are concentrated on the Rive Gauche between the **Quai de la Tournelle** and the **Quai Malaquais** (opposite the islands); their wooden stalls are an inimitable fixture of the riverside landscape.

Two ways to see the river: by bateau-mouche *or just by sitting on the banks*

■ **Thirty-five bridges span the Seine along its 13km flow through Paris; the oldest, dating back to 1607, is the Pont-Neuf . Tramps sleep below them, lovers are entwined atop them, suicides throw themselves off them and poetry is written about them. From the two-tiered Pont du Bir-Hakeim, with its art nouveau pillars and metros rattling across the top, to the idyllic planked footbridge, the Pont des Arts, idolised in the songs of Georges Brassens, the bridges of Paris are all part of the city's cultural and physical landscape. .....■**

76

For centuries the city only had two bridges: the **Grand Pont** and the **Petit Pont**, which linked the Ile de la Cité with both banks. It was only in the late Middle Ages that three more wooden bridges appeared, the **Pont Notre Dame**, the **Pont au Change** and the **Pont St-Michel**, none of which were solid constructions, and so frequently bowed to high waters, ice, fires or collisions by rivercraft. However, their commercial viability was underlined in 1414 by a letter from Charles VI which authorised the building of houses on the Pont Notre-Dame 'for the good, the decoration and the increased revenue of the town'. **The Pont au Change** (opposite Châtelet) was so named for its continuous rows of money-changers' shops, and when the **Pont-Marie** was built in 1635 it still carried an overload of real estate.

Bridges boom Things changed with the far-sighted minister Colbert who, in 1716, created an official institution, the **Ponts et Chaussées**, which led to the feverish construction of 21 new bridges and the consolidation of existing ones. Bridges were gradually being cleared of their cumbersome houses, and by the time Napoleon came along new materials such as cast iron created the uncluttered spans that we see today. Paris' 36th bridge, the **Pont Charles-de-Gaulle**, will grow into place by 1994 to link the banks of the fast-developing 12th and 13th *arrondissements* in eastern Paris.

Pont-Neuf Paris' oldest bridge, the Pont-Neuf, is also its most famous. Built to facilitate the King's journey between the Louvre Palace and the abbey of St-Germain-des- Prés, its innovative, houseless design was controversial. Flamboyant as ever, Henri IV inaugurated it in 1607 by galloping across on his charger; and today his equestrian statue still dominates the stretch (a 1818 replacement of an earlier statue, melted down during the Revolution). For years this was the site of a permanent funfair, attracting jugglers, acrobats and street sellers; painted by Turner, the Pont-Neuf was also ceremoniously wrapped up by the land- artist Christo in 1985.

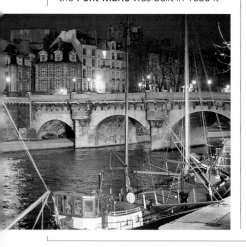

Pont-Neuf, the city's oldest bridge

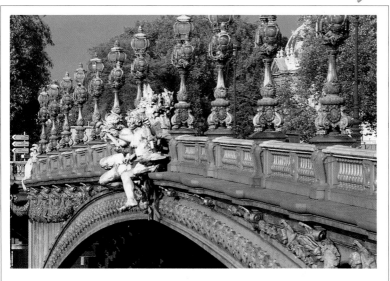

Belle Epoque architecture at its most ornate: Pont Alexandre III

Pont-Marie The 1635 Pont-Marie joins the Ile St-Louis with the Right Bank. Named after the property developer of the Ile St-Louis, a certain Mr Marie, this bridge nearly had a very short 20-year life. It was top-heavy with four-storey houses (all the more *écus* to the developer), until the spring thaw of 1658 caused a powerful flood, and half of these homes, shops and their occupants toppled into the Seine.

Pont Royal Slightly more youthful, the Pont Royal, which joins the Tuileries to the rue du Bac, was entirely financed by Louis XIV and built in 1689 by Gabriel after Mansart's design. This time the object was to make life easier for

<< A bridge you may not discover easily is the romantically curved footbridge from which Arletty murmured *Atmosphères, atmosphères* in Marcel Carné's classic film, *Hôtel du Nord*. This is no figment of cinematographic imagination but actually spans the Canal St-Martin, a 4 1/2 km canal running from the Bastille to the Canal de l'Ourcq. **>>**

nobles visiting the Palace from the exclusive Faubourg St-Germain. The pure classical style of its graceful stone arches has never been modified, and on each end pillar there is a hydrographic scale showing historic high water levels.

Pont Alexandre III In complete contrast, the wildly ornate Pont Alexandre III flashes its gilt and bronzed cupids in the setting sun. Symbolic of the optimism of the Belle Epoque, it was built for the 1900 Exposition Universelle and dedicated to a new alliance between Russia and France. The first stone was laid by the Tsar in 1896, and the façades bear coats of arms of the two countries. Over 15 artists worked on this wedding-cake bridge to create winged horses, gilded cupids, garlands and various other Greco-Roman artifices on every available ramp, balustrade or corner.

Pont de l'Alma Commemorating a victory over the Russians by the Franco-British alliance in the Crimean War, the Pont de l'Alma was originally built in 1856 and replaced in 1974. Of the four symbolic statues of the participating armies only the Zouave soldier remains, acting as an official high-water marker.

Walk Exploring the city's islands

Start at Pont-Neuf. Cross to the statue of Henri IV where steps lead down to the island tip.
Here you can circle round the island tip, or take a boat trip.

Back up on the bridge cross to enter the place Dauphine.
The **place Dauphine** is where Yves Montand and Simone Signoret both used to live.

In front of the Palais de Justice, turn right, then left along the Quai des Orfèvres to the Pont St-Michel. Turn left here.
The route now takes you past the courtyard of the **Palais de Justice.**

Immediately after the Préfecture, turn right into the rue de Lutèce
The **rue de Lutèce** leads through the flower market to the **rue de la Cité.**

Go left at the rue de la Cité and turn right along the Quai de la Corse.
The **Quai de la Corse** continues into the **Quai aux Fleurs** and has a view north of the **Hôtel de Ville** and east towards the **Ile St-Louis.**

Circle round back to Notre Dame.
At this point you are walking among Paris' oldest medieval streets.

Walk round Notre Dame and through the gardens on the south side; cross the little bridge onto the Ile St-Louis.
Once the home of wealthy financiers and magistrates, the island remains remarkably conserved; keep an eye open for superb courtyards, wrought-iron details and sculpted heads.

Follow the Quai d'Orléans past some magnificent 17th-century town-houses to the rue des Deux Ponts. Turn left here then right into the rue St-Louis-en-l'Ile.
Pass Paris' best ice cream maker, **Berthillon**, and the island's richly decorated church. The corner **Hôtel Lambert**, at no 2, is reputed to be the finest mansion of this period in Paris, designed by Le Vau in 1640.

Turn left along the Quai d'Anjou.
At **no17 Quai d'Anjou** a town-house with an exceptional balcony, both Baudelaire and Théophile Gauthier once lived here. Straight on at **no19** is the magnificent mansion where Camille Claudel lived and worked.

Cross the Pont Louis-Philippe, with its stunning view along the Seine.

▶▷▷ Baccarat, Musée

30 bis rue de Paradis, 10e
metro: Gare de l'Est, Poissonnière

A visit to this glass museum and showroom means a dive into a street packed with porcelain and crystal outlets, the best example being the 1900s ceramic façade of no 18. Baccarat, however, has remained the king ever since 1828, when he became supplier to royalty and heads of state and moved his company to the present site. The museum exhibits anything from chandeliers to perfume bottles as well as personalised crystal sets made for various VIPs.

Open: Monday to Friday, 09.00–18.00hrs, Saturday 10.00–12.00/14.00–17.00hrs.

Beaubourg see pages 80–1

▷▷▷ Beaux Arts, Ecole Nationale Supérieure

17 Quai Malaquais, 6e
metro: St Germain

Once a convent, now Paris' art school, built between 1820 and 1862, this imposing façade glowering across the river at the Louvre is the hub for Parisian art students. Its entrance at 14 rue Bonaparte leads into the main courtyard, which still contains a selection of architectural features salvaged by the archaeologist Lenoir from destructive Revolutionary fervour. Look inside at the rather delapidated central hall and galleries, feel the dust, then compare the recently restored Chapelle des Petits-Augustins (1608), in which plaster casts, Renaissance reproductions and the real thing nonchalantly rub shoulders. The exhibition halls opening on to the quai sometimes hold interesting shows.

Open: daily, 08.00–20.00hrs; library 13.00–18.00hrs.

▶▶▷ Belleville

metros: Belleville, Ménilmontant

Rising almost as high above central Paris as Montmartre, and with corresponding panoramic views, the northeastern quarter of Belleville is a colourful, eclectic mixture. Its traditional working-class character combines with an immigrant population and errant artists to animate its streets, bars and restaurants, though real estate promoters have already wrought patchy havoc.

Throwing the light on glassware: the Musée Baccarat

If you explore the side-streets leading off the rue de Belleville, rue de Ménilmontant and the rue des Pyrénées you'll come across some surprises: look for the Passage de la Duée (1m wide) or the atmospheric Passage des Soupirs. And if you yearn for a vast choice of Asiatic or North African cuisine, this is where to head for.

MUSEE NATIONAL D'ART MODERNE

KEY TO EXHIBITORS

1 Tinguely
2 Matisse
3 Duchamp-Villon
4 Picasso
5 Braque
6 Picasso after 1918
7 Braque after 1918
8 Léger
9 Kandinski
10 Klee
11 Malevitch
12 Brancusi
13 Pevsner
14 Kupka
15 Delaunay
16 Mondrian
17 Arp
18 Soutine
19 Rouault
20 Chagall
21 Masson
22 Calder
23 Magritte
24 Dali
25 Miró
26 Giacometti
27 Dubuffet
28 Cobra
29 Appel
30 Jorn
31 Kemeny
32 Bazaine
33 Hartung
34 Poliakoff
35 De Staël
36 Calder
37 Pollock
38 Arman
39 Christo
40 César
41 Rauschenberg
42 Warhol
43 Miró
44 Ernst
45 Laurens

▶ ▶ ▶ **Beaubourg**

Centre Georges Pompidou, plateau Beaubourg, 75004 Paris

metros: Rambuteau, Hôtel de Ville

This factory-like museum and free-wheeling cultural centre stands out as a landmark of high-tech style in the middle of historic Paris, as well as being a symbol of democratised culture.

Decried by many, Beaubourg's worst failing is in fact its great popularity, unimagined by architects Piano and Rogers when it opened in 1977. In its first 14 years of existence over 90 million visitors crossed the threshold – so expect long queues in the summer.

MNAM For many visitors the priority is the national collection of modern art (MNAM) on the fourth floor. Inside the glass walls major movements and/or artists are displayed chronologically in partitioned spaces. The collection continues on the third floor, where works covering the last 25 years are exhibited. Starting with the **Fauves** (1905), a remarkable itinerary leads you through **cubism, dada, surrealism, abstraction, pop art, minimalism** and today's **conceptualism. Matisse** is extremely well represented; cubist works by **Picasso, Braque** and **Juan Gris** are shown with **Picabia**, followed by **Léger's** visions of the mechanised world. One of the most successful rooms combines **Calder's** ethereal mobiles with paintings by **Miro**, including the vast, luminous *Bleu II*. The most striking piece as you leave this floor is an early example of conceptual art, **Beuys'** *Infiltration homogène* (1966), a grand piano neatly encased in felt with its empty double (*La Peau*) hanging on a wall nearby.

Grandes Galeries Above the museum, on the fifth floor, is the Grandes Galeries, where major temporary exhibitions of 20th-century art are held. Next door is a cinema showing films relevant to these blockbuster exhibitions and a large, uninspiring cafeteria which has seen better days, as has its notion of 'cuisine'. The panoramic view from the terrace is nevertheless the destination for a daily average of 25,000 visitors.

The show goes on, inside and outside the Beaubourg

Other attractions Part of the second floor is occupied by an enormous, well equipped and very popular **reference library**. Back on the ground floor activities start buzzing again around the **Forum**, a central hole used for unusually scaled exhibitions. The spaces tucked below the surrounding mezzanine structures include a cinema, the **Salle Garance,** which has daily programmes of rarely shown films in thematic festivals, and a **packed bookshop**. Another active department is the **CCI** (industrial design), with a documentation centre and two galleries used for temporary exhibitions ranging from architecture to furniture design. The mezzanine **Galeries contemporaines** are used for works by contemporary artists.

Children's choice If you have children in tow you could drop them off at the **Atelier des Enfants** while you check the programme of concerts and/ or dance, held in the basement halls, which concentrate on international avant-garde performers. Related debates and lectures are often worth following here.

Open: Wednesday to Monday 12.00–22.00hrs. Weekends 10.00–22.00hrs.

■ **As the city's face changes with the transience of the seasons, so does its fun. Numerous events are held year in, year out at the same date, the most famous being Bastille Day on 14 July, a great opportunity to witness boisterous street partying. The Office de Tourisme (127 Champs Elysées, 8e; tel: 47 23 61 72) publishes an annual guide every January; below are some of the regular highlights......■**

Winter

Epiphany: the Russian Orthodox version of Christmas on 6 and 7 January is celebrated at the **Saint Alexandre Nievsky Cathedral** (12 rue Daru, 8e). For the French, 6 January becomes the **Fête des Rois**, memorable for its pâtisserie, an almond cake ring containing a hidden bean. The cruncher of the bean dons a gold foil crown and chooses his consort.

Chinese New Year: between late January and early February Chinatown comes into its own. Make sure you are in the 13th *arrondissement* between the avenue d'Ivry and the avenue de Choisy for this colourful event. (for information tel: 45 20 74 09).

Spring

Foire du Trône: France's largest fun-fair sets up from March to May at the **Porte Dorée**, next to the Bois de Vincennes. Candy-floss and dodgems replace what was orignally a medieval fair selling rye bread during Holy Week.

May Day: 1 May is Labour Day, still taken very seriously, with marches organised by most trade unions, shops and museums closed, and no newspapers. Buy a posy of symbolic lily-of-the-valley from a street-seller and

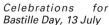

Celebrations for Bastille Day, 13 July

join in the crowds. **Ascension** and **Whitsun** add two further opportunities to *faire le pont* (ie join midweek holiday to a weekend for four or five days' break).

Roland-Garros: the French Tennis Open is held late May to early June and is now a fashionable place to be seen. Theoretically, tickets for outside courts can be bought on the day but black marketeers have wrapped up this trade. Otherwise apply in writing to Stade Roland-Garros, 2 avenue Gordon Bennett, 75016 Paris (tel: 47 43 48 00).

Summer

Exposition de roses: against the bucolic background of the **Jardin de Bagatelle** in the Bois de Boulogne, an international rose competition is held on 21 June and the rose garden remains open till October. The Trianon also hosts the **Chopin Festival** from late June to July (tel: 45 01 20 10).

Féte de la Musique: mid-summer is now loudly celebrated all over Paris with free concerts. Key sites (the **Palais-Royal**, the **Bastille**, **République** etc) resound to amplified rock or world music into the small hours.

Course des Garçons de café: over 500 professional waiters and waitresses career around the streets of Paris, each bearing aloft a tray laden with bottle and glasses. The fastest non-spilling participant wins. Starting and finishing at the **Hôtel de Ville,** it takes place in late June.

Bastille Day: the action really takes place on the evening of 13 July with *bals populaires* pulling in pulsating crowds to every square or fire station. Beware of firecrackers, which are freely chucked around. Fireworks and the ubiquitous *merguez* (barbecued spicy sausages) complete the ambience. On 14 July a surprisingly pompous military parade passes down the **Champs Elysées.**

Tour de France: the grand finale of this wildly popular bike race pedals manically along the quais of the Rive Droite before crossing the finishing line in the **Champs Elysées.** Third week in June.

Autumn

Festival d'Automne: the city's most avant-garde cultural festival sets the ball rolling after the long summer break. Held in various venues over Paris, its dance, theatre and music programme is always worth investigating (tel: 42 96 12 27).

Fête des Vendanges à Montmartre: Montmartre's biggest yearly splash takes place for the harvesting of its tiny vineyard on the first Saturday in October.

Prix de l'Arc de Triomphe: This is *the* equestrian event of the year opening the racing season in early October at the **Hippodrome de Longchamp.**

FIAC: a social event disguised as an international art fair, the FIAC (Faire International d'Art Contemporain) opens the art season in late October under the spectacular webbed iron domes of the **Grand Palais.**

Festival de Jazz de Paris: after spending the summer in the south of France, jazz comes to Paris in the second half of October. A subscription ticket opens the doors of clubs and concert halls (tel: 40 56 07 17).

On the third Thursday in November the race is on to get the first bottles of the year's Beaujolais Nouveau to Paris. Never regarded as a serious wine, it can be over-acid or fruity, but the tradition of who gets there first has spread all over the world. On that revered Thursday afternoon, Paris stops work, bars spill out into the street and endless vociferous opinions on this year's vintage float away into the night air.

83

The Bibliothèque Nationale contains 11 million printed books, 15 million prints and photos, 1 million records, 600,000 maps, 800,000 coins and medals, 350,000 periodicals. Every year a further 80,000 books are added.

▶▷▷   Bercy
metro: Bercy

Once nostalgically known for its wine warehouses, which formed a self-sufficient village of their own in eastern Paris, Bercy is now an area undergoing intensive development. Already the site for the **Palais Omnisports** (which plays a double act of accommodating sports activities and rock concerts) and the mammoth **Ministry of Finance**, Bercy spreads east from the **Gare de Lyon** through a maze of new office and apartment blocks. Another new arrival, the **American Center**, daringly designed by Frank Gehry, opens in 1993 as a lively pole for American culture, counterbalancing the Mickey Mouses of Euro Disney outside Paris. However, not all is concrete in Bercy. At the heart of these sites lies a freshly landscaped park, the **Parc de Bercy**, which has preserved some of the old wine warehouses from the bulldozers, so allowing some remnants of its past to linger on.

▶▷▷   Berryer, Cité
25 rue Royale, 75008
metro: Madeleine

Once an open-air market, this alleyway leading off the rue Royale recently attained the distinction of 'historical monument'. In fact more a lunch- time haunt for local businessmen, it is at its best in the summer months when restaurants and wine-bars invade the pavement.

▶▷▷   Bibliothèque Nationale
58 rue de Richelieu, 75002
metros: Bourse, Quatre-Septembre

Nearly 12 million books are stored in this sprawling symbol of French literacy, which has evolved since the 17th century as a combination of the royal library with that of Cardinal Mazarin. By law a copy of every publication made in France has to be deposited here. The original Hôtel Tubeuf gradually accumulated adjacent annexes, culminating in the Galerie Colbert, across the rue Vivienne, which exhibits prints and photographs. In the main building take a look at the soaring glass domed reading-room, designed by Labrouste (1873), and go to the sumptuous Galerie Mazarine, designed by François Mansart, on the first floor: here Romanelli's mythological ceiling paintings vie with Grimaldi's landscapes for splendour.

The **Cabinet des Médailles et Antiques**, (*open*: daily, 13.00–17.00hrs) has a remarkable display built up from royal collections and confiscations made during the Revolution. From Greek and Roman antiques to thousands of medals and coins or Dagobert's throne, it makes a curious mixture.

The Bibliothèque Nationale

▶▶▷   Bois de Boulogne
metros: Pointe Dauphine, Maillot, d'Auteuil

Over 800 hectares of park and playground make up western Paris' lungs, well frequented at weekends by the better heeled inhabitants from nearby Neuilly and the 16th arrondissement. A favourite medieval hunting-ground, in the 18th century it became an aristocratic leisure ground. Finally Napoleon III and Baron

Haussmann gave the park the form it has today and made it public. It is awash with lakes, waterfalls, follies, winding paths and open spaces, with two racetracks: Auteuil and Longchamp. Its nocturnal users (transvestites, prostitutes) are a very different race from the jogging businessmen of the morning hours.

Make for one of the high spots, the **Jardin de Bagatelle**, where a small château (built in 1775) overlooks a romantic park originally laid out by the landscape gardener Thomas Blaikie. Rose bushes abound (over 700 varieties) and a restaurant with open terrace overflows on summer nights. Further south, the **Pré Catalan** is another well laid-out garden, with a gigantic copper beech as its main feature. However far into the woods you go, you'll never starve and here there is another up-market gastronomic halt overlooking a small lake. Adjoining it is the **Jardin Shakespeare**, so-called because of its open-air theatre and vegetation inspired by the bard's botanical references.

Children's pursuits If your children-in-tow are tiring, head for the **Jardin d'Acclimatation** on the far north edge (metro: Les Sablons) where amusements await them – from toy trains to puppet- shows, an 'enchanted river' and a small zoo. This section of the park is open 10.00 to 18.00hrs daily, with special events on Wednesdays and at weekends.

● **Stroll** *For a dream and a stroll, go to the **Serres d'Auteuil** at the southern point of the Bois (metro Porte d'Auteuil). Here the tropics await you in some superb 19th-century greenhouses. If you are here in late May walk a little further and you'll come to **Roland-Garros**, where the famous French Tennis Open takes place.*

The best jogging track in the Bois de Boulogne surrounds the Lac Inférieur, an idyllic expanse of water punctuated by two islands, where you can hire rowing-boats or bicycles.

At no 93 place Edmond-Rostand, next to the Luxembourg metro station, is the house which sheltered the American bookshop owner Sylvia Beach (founder of Shakespeare & Co, an American literary landmark in pre-war Paris) from the Nazis for two years.

A tour of the Palais Bourbon includes the sumptuous library ceiling painted by Delacroix in 1838–47 with his version of the history of civilisation. Tours take place every Saturday at 10.00, 14.00 and 15.00hrs. The first 10 visitors to arrive each day are allowed in to watch debates.

▶▶▶ Boulevard Saint-Michel

Traditionally thick with students and tourists, the boulevard Saint-Michel had its heyday during the 1968 student riots, when barricades outnumbered cafés and confrontations with the forces of order carried on deep into the night. In Roman times it was one of the two roads leading south from the Ile de la Cité, lined with baths, a theatre and the forum.

Today its bookshops and cinemas are interjected with an increasing number of cheap clothes stores and fast-food joints. Although it is the symbolic heart of the Latin Quarter, the boulevard is really only of passing interest, as the architectural and historical high points lie in its side streets.

Nightlife At its northern starting-point by the Seine, the Fontaine St-Michel, designed by Davioud in 1860, is a favourite nocturnal gathering-point for street artists, buskers and other hangers-out. The nearby metro entrance is one of the few remaining Hector Guimard art nouveau originals. Cafés and cinemas are buzzing into the early hours and if you're short of reading-matter or cigarettes at this time, here is where to go. In the daytime you are more likely to see students escaping to the cafés from long lectures at the Sorbonne or the Ecole de Médecine.

● **Stroll** *If you take a stroll starting on the corner of the boulevard St-Germain you cannot miss the superb* **Musée de Cluny**, *floodlit at night, a forceful presence by day. As you head uphill you pass the* **place de la Sorbonne**, *a small square lined with trees and café-terrasses, even at chillier times of the year. The* **place Edmond-Rostand**, *crowned by an inevitable fountain, ends the slope and the animated section of the boulevard, opening out on to the* **Jardin du Luxembourg** *to the west and with an impressive vista of the* **Panthéon** *to the east.*

▶▶▶ Bourbon, Palais

33 Quai d'Orsay, 75007
metro: Assemblée Nationale

Hiding behind the imposing façade of this 18th-century mansion are the halls of French power: its central parliament, the Assemblée Nationale. Elected every four years, its 577 deputies come and go, and are usually more absent than politically present, a habit which has led to some scolding in recent times by the powers above.

The mansion's history Originally constructed for the Duchess of Bourbon in 1722, the building passed through the hands of the Condé family and Louis XV before Revolutionary confiscation. In 1807 Napoleon, with an astute eye for aesthetics, insisted on a new neo-classical façade (by Poyet) to mirror that of the Madeleine, directly opposite across the Seine and the place de la Concorde.

Today visitors (in limited numbers) can observe heated debates from the gallery overlooking the vast crimson and gold embellished chamber.

▶▶▶ Bourse du Commerce

Place de la Bourse, 75002
metro: Bourse

Every major city has its money-spinning hub and in Paris it all happens at the Bourse, another neo-classical Napoleonic invention. Once the Corn Exchange, the circular building is the only relic left from Les Halles. Built on the site of a convent in 1826, it was remodelled in 1888, and is now the meeting-point for commodity traders, setting the tone for the surrounding streets, full of money-changers and restaurants called *L'Ecu* or the *Stock Exchange Luncheon Bar* (1878).

Inside the Bourse you can watch brokers haggle and bonds change hands at a frenetic pace from the visitors' gallery overlooking the den.

The fluted column adjoining the building was once part of Catherine de'Médicis' Hôtel de la Reine, built in 1572, and apparently the home of her personal astrologer, Ruggieri.

Open: Monday to Friday, 11.00–13.00hrs, for guided tours lasting one and a half hours.

▶▶▶ Bricard de la Serrure, Musée

1 rue Perle, 75003
metro: St Sébastien-Froissart

An eccentric collection of door decorations – locks, keys, knockers, handles and plaques – is housed in a magnificent 1685 mansion, built by the architect of the Hôtel des Invalides, Libéral Bruant, for his own personal use.

Eugène Bricard was the 19th man hell-bent on gathering these unusual objects from all periods and countries, displayed in six lofty rooms. Bricard still exists as a lock manufacturer.

Open: Tuesday to Saturday, 10.00–noon, 14.00–17.00hrs.

Money and security: the Bourse du Commerce (above) and the Musée Bricard de la Serrure (below)

■ **Paris has for a century rested on the green laurels of Haussmann's two woods (Vincennes and Boulogne), three parks (Montsouris, Monceau and Buttes Chaumont) and two gardens. There are few other real breathing spaces. .....■**

The architectural renaissance of the 1980s has, however, woken up to arboreal needs and seen a renewal of the garden tradition, previously buried under a will to kill anything green in the urban mosaic. The **Parc de la Villette**, on the northeastern perimeter, whatever its overall design shortcomings, provides canals and vast lawns – good for local frisbee experts – as well as 'conceptual' gardens.

But gone are the 19th-century days of romantic artificial lakes and hills, exemplified by the Buttes Chaumont, a fantastic project which transformed a city rubbish dump into a hillocked mini-paradise complete with grotto, waterfall and colonnaded temple. Today architects and landscape gardeners have to impose their abstract concepts on available structures, missing out completely on escapist naturalism.

Of the new park projects the Parc **Citroën** is perhaps the most ambitious. On the site of the old Citroën factories in southwestern Paris, nearly 14 hectares of land have been landscaped to lead directly down to the river, burying embankment traffic in their wake. Two gigantic high-tech greenhouses reign over a garden with more geometric precision than a Swiss watch. If this Cartesian approach touches your soul, don't miss the still emerging **Parc de Bercy** (see page 84), which follows a more classical pattern to match the lay-out of its former village of warehouses. A lucky bonus here is the existence of centennial trees – otherwise parks take decades to assume any form.

Parks of the past Step back a century or so and you can rest in relative bucolic peace in any one of Paris' classic parks. The **Jardin du Luxembourg**, saved from Haussmann's ambitions by a petition of 12,000 signatures, remains a symbolic expanse. Creating a natural northern limit to the Latin Quarter and its itinerant students, it is also a favourite haunt for chic Montparnasse residents and their offspring. Its fountains, statues, kiosks, tennis courts, chess or card-players and book-reading habitués give it an unchanging atmosphere, strengthened by endless literary and celluloid links. Remember the struggling Hemingway who at low points would drop by to pick up a pigeon for dinner or numerous *Nouvelle Vague* scenes with existentially oriented actors staring morosely into the pond.

Arty park Further to the south, the **Parc Montsouris** belies its granite quarry past and instead lives up to its 1920/30s arty character, the days when the nearby artists' studios were actually inhabited by brush or pen-

The Jardin du Luxembourg

Developers were presented with a gaping hole when the 19th-century Baltard pavilions, site of the central fruit and vegetable market, were demolished. The hole remained for years, until one bright spark thought of filling it with a shopping centre. Thus the Forum des Halles was born and an adjacent garden laid out. Today locals cower under a sparse sprinkling of trees, trip over concrete steps or squeeze on to one of the few triangles of grass to fight with litter or tramps.

wielding luminaries (Braque, Derain, Salvador Dali and Henry Miller were all neighbours). Today swans, joggers and child-minders are the chief park-users, joined by a brass band in the summer months (see page 151).

Back on the Right Bank, the over-populated though convenient **Tuileries** are destined for relandscaping in a major overhaul which will not be completed until 1995. Otherwise a great park classic is the **Parc Monceau**, originally planted in English style by Thomas Blaikie in 1783. Picturesque ruins of columns, a pyramid, tombs, Ledoux's rotunda and statues complete a peaceful setting perfect for local nannies and their wards.

Over in Boulogne (metro: Porte de St-Cloud) a curious and little known garden gives an overview of different botanical styles, from a Japanese garden to a Vosges-type forest. The **Jardins Albert-Kahn** were laid out at the beginning of the century by a horticulturally obsessed philanthropist who also founded a rare documentation centre about nature all over the planet. Ultimately, though, you cannot beat the **Bois de Boulogne** or the **Bois de Vincennes** for bucolic escapism.

Relaxation among the flowers in the Parc Monceau

*José-Maria Sert's
1925 ballroom in the
Musée Carnavalet*

▶ ▶ ▶ **Carnavalet, Musée**
23 rue de Sévigné, 75003
metro: St Paul

Two adjoining mansions in the Marais house the
museum of the history of Paris from prehistory through
to the 20th century. Exemplary in its presentation, it
juxtaposes visions of Paris through the eyes of painters,
documents, the decorative arts and period rooms.
Descriptive panels are in French only.

Entrance is through a beautifully sculpted courtyard of
the 16th-century Hôtel Carnavalet, much transformed in
1660 by François Mansart before the arrival of its most
celebrated resident, the writer Madame de Sévigné. The
collections exhibited here take you from the origins of
Paris through to the Middle Ages. The splendours of the
Renaissance are evoked in four vast ground floor rooms,
while Madame de Sévigné's possessions and
furnishings on the first floor give a rounded view of
Louis XIV's era. Sizzling heights of decoration from
under Louis XV's and XVI's reigns are displayed in
panelled interiors, while the richly painted and gilded
woodwork (1656) from the Hôtel Colbert de Villacerf is a
superb example of Louis XIV ornateness.

Next door, the collections installed in the sleekly
renovated Hôtel Le Peletier de Saint-Fargeau (1690) take
you on through the Revolution to the 19th century and
finish in the early 20th century. Look out for the keys of
the Bastille prison, Hubert Robert's paintings, made in
and out of prison in the 1790s, and Le Sueur's unusual
comic-strip account of this period. Anything and
everything was decorated with revolutionary slogans –
fans, plates, clocks, furniture. Napoleon's favourite
campaign picnic-case (110 pieces) introduces you to the
Empire and the elaborate cradle of the Imperial prince
(1856) to the Second Empire. Reconstructed interiors
include Proust's corklined bedroom and brass bed,
Henri Sauvage's Café de Paris and the ballroom from the
Hôtel de Wendel, painted by José-Maria Sert in 1925.
Open: Tuesday to Sunday, 10.00–17.40hrs.

▶ ▶ ▶ Catacombes

1 place Denfert-Rochereau, 75014
metro: Denfert-Rochereau

Over 6 million slumbering skeletons hide out here in the world's largest deposit of human bones. The sign at the entrance, 'Stop. Beyond is the empire of death', sets the tone for this underground network of 165km of tunnels, although only 65km are 'peopled'. During World War II the Catacombes were used as a secret meeting- place for Resistance fighters. Today urban potholers regularly slip into them from points all over Paris for chilly and chilling explorations. Visitors tour in groups to view macabre remains, neatly aligned against the walls of the tunnels. Remember a torch and pullover, even if it's mid-summer, and be prepared to climb hundreds of steps.
Open: Tuesday to Friday, 14.00–16.00hrs, Saturday/Sunday, 09.00–11.00/14.00–16.00hrs.

▶ ▶ ▶ Chaillot, Palais de

Place du Trocadéro, 75016
metro: Trocadéro

No fewer than four museums, a theatre and a cinema are housed in this colonnaded mammoth, which commands a stunning perspective of the Eiffel Tower and the Champ de Mars, directly across the Seine. Built for the Exposition Universelle in 1937, its curved wings are dotted with glittering bronze statues and the wide terraces overlook a fountain-ridden garden.

In the basement is the **TNP** (Théâtre National Populaire), whose post-war director, Jean Vilar, democratised theatre and later founded the Festival D'Avignon. On the same level, but with access from behind in the avenue Albert de Mun, is the **Cinémathèque Française**, founded in 1936 by Henri Langlois, which shows a fantastic programme of film classics, changing daily – a cinephile's paradise.

Continued on page 94

The Catacombes were originally channelled out in Roman times to provide stone and plaster; it was only after a campaign orchestrated by Voltaire in 1785 that the occupants of the pestilential cemeteries above ground were moved below.

The 1937 Palais de Chaillot, framing the Eiffel Tower

■ **Mountains of fruit and veg, hundreds of varieties of cheese, strings of saucisson, clouds of perfumed herbs...food markets are part and parcel of Paris life. Then there are books, stamps, flowers, birds; and antiques and bric-à-brac change hands as if industrialisation had never existed......■**

The Paris flea-market was first set up in a no-man's land in northeastern Paris around 1880. In 1920 Romain Vernaison, a property owner, installed stalls and let them to antique dealers (Marché Vernaison) and the Marché Biron soon followed suit, in 1925. Today the flea market at the Porte de Clignancourt covers 30 hectares and has over 1,500 shops and 1,400 licensed stalls.

A stroll around a French food market is a gastronomical education in itself. When you see a stall-holder squeezing camemberts, pressing avocados or pinching melons you'll be witnessing a precise and incontestable philosophy in action. Parisians shop daily, as produce is fresh and the timing of its consumption must be perfect. Keep that camembert too long and it will walk off the table; eat it too soon and you miss out on its very essence.

Apart from the circulating markets, which set up on sites and days all over the city, there are permanent daily street markets such as the **Marché d'Aligre**, the **rue Poncelet, rue Montorgueil, rue Mouffetard** or the **rue de Buci**. These unveil their wares around nine in the morning and pack up towards seven, not forgetting a very provincial lunch-break between one and four. Sunday afternoons and Mondays finally give market workers time to recuperate from the weekend onslaught, when even the most ardent restaurant-goers indulge in a serious return to their culinary sources.

The art of shopping Every market has its historic boulangerie or cheese shop – often with fantastically ornate interiors worthy of a château – that proves the level of attention and pride bestowed on mere foodstuff. Amid the sea of outdoor stalls, these five-star landmarks can usually be spotted by their lengthy queues – Parisians are tremendously faithful, gastronomically at

The daily market at rue Mouffetard

least. Cafés are, of course, another integral part of market-shopping. The market operation being a lengthy and concentrated business (each purchase requires at least five minutes, depending on the stall's popularity or the holder's garrulousness), it merits a drink and quick exchange of wit at half-time.

One of the most picturesque street markets, the **rue Mouffetard**, has also, unfortunately, become one of the most well known to tourists. It still has its charm however, as does the **rue de Buci** in St-Germain-des-Prés, another crowd-puller, due to its conventient central location.

But make sure you go to a typical local market such as the **rue Poncelet** (17th *arrondissement*), the **place d'Aligre** (12th), which doubles up as a bric-à-brac market and is also strong on North African specialities, or the **rue du Poteau** (18th), high on the slopes of Montmartre, with its inimitable 'old Paris' character.

Famous fleas Flea markets (*marché aux puces*), are judiciously sited around the city perimeter. Their eclectic and often dusty and/or exotic goods never lose their pull, whether for well heeled tourists and residents or for the poorer inhabitants.

The world famous **Porte de Clignacourt** flea market is rightly known as a tourist trap, yet its alleyways, covered markets and stalls always come up with something for everyone – the sheer bulk of goods plus the laws of probability see to that. From old buttons to recycled clothes to Louis XV mirrors to 1950s coffee-pots – it's very difficult not to find your own particular joy among these offerings.

Diametrically opposite the Porte de Clignancourt on the Paris map, the flea market at the **Porte de Vanves** has recently become a favourite with young trendies; there is little of great value but plenty of eccentricities, art deco and 1950s furniture, a smattering of exotica and quite a wide selection of old prints.

Not as popular nor as interesting as it used to be, the **Marché de Montreuil** in the east of Paris is gradually being taken over by bargain household goods stalls, leaving little space for the junk; however, second-hand clothes remain a speciality and St Laurent jackets have been known to be found in perfect condition, so...keep looking.

For second-hand books, if the *bouquinistes* (dealers) don't suffice, spend your weekend at the **Parc Georges Brassens** (15th), where you will find an unrivalled array of antiquarian and second-hand books.

For a market with colour, go to the Marché aux fleurs (held daily on the Ile de la Cité in front of the Préfecture), replaced on Sundays by a bird market. Or try the stamp market held on Thursdays and weekends in the Cour Marigny, off the Champs Elysées.

GAZETTEER A-Z

There is an excellent bookshop in the Musée del'Homme, as well as the ultimate restaurant-with-a-view, the Totem.

In the basement below the palace, the Musée du Cinéma displays over 3,000 relevant items going back to the origins of photography. The Lumière brothers' photorama and Edison's kinetoscope of 1894 are included alongside set models by Eisenstein, photographs, costumes (worn by the likes of Valentino and Garbo) and actual sets from Metropolis. Entrance is only with guided tours (10.00, 11.00, 14.00, 15.00 and 16.00hrs, closed Tuesday).

94

Continued from page 91

The east wing of Chaillot houses a rather extraordinary museum, created in 1882 by the architect Viollet-le-Duc. The **Musée des Monuments Français** (closed Tuesday) is a museum of full-scale copies of French architectural features from pre-Roman times to the 19th century. It is a good opportunity to see a succinct panorama of this field in one fell swoop. Reproductions of frescos, church façades, fountains and sarcophagi all create an unreal atmosphere in a much neglected museum.

Back above ground in Chaillot's west wing you have the choice of two valiant museums, the **Musée de l'Homme** or the **Musée de la Marine** (both closed Tuesday). Predictably, the Musée de la Marine concentrates on French naval history and is packed with ship models, marine instruments, paintings (including 13 of Vernet's *Ports de France*, executed between 1754 and 1765) and sculpture. Don't miss the Emperor's barge (built in 1811 for Napoleon) or a cross-section model of the glittering transatlantic liner *Normandie*, the floating 1932 palace of decorative arts destroyed by fire during World War II.

The **Musée de l'Homme**, although a little shabby round the edges and in dire need of a window-cleaner, houses fascinating anthropological and ethnographical displays. Mental travel is possible from the Pacific to Africa with detours around Asia and, particularly strong, South America. Watch out for the life-sized 'shark-man', King Béhanzin and the medieval frescos from Abyssinia, both in the very rich African section. On the top floor, in the Salon de la Musique, 500 or so world instruments are displayed with background sound. Live concerts are a regular feature.

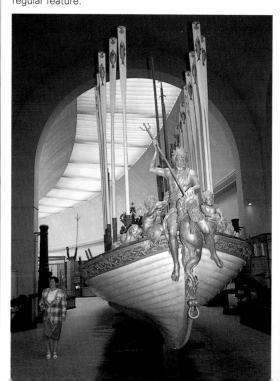

An exhibit from the Palais de Chaillot's Musée de la Marine

▶▶▷ Champs Elysées

The broad pavements and wide expanse of this avenue, which sweeps majestically down from the Arc de Triomphe to the place de la Concorde, no longer exude the glamour of times gone by. Although one of the places dreamed about by visitors to Paris, it proves a disappointment in today's age of fast-food and shopping malls. Its best feature remains a string of large-scale cinemas showing the latest releases, hard to beat for their comfort (or their queues).

You can thank Marie de Médicis, wife of Henri IV, for turning it into a fashionable driveway in 1616. Then thank the landscape designer, Le Nôtre, for the gracious alleys of trees and gardens leading from the Concorde which by 1707 had earned the avenue its name: Elysian Fields. It was in 1824 that the avenue became structured with pavements and fountains, soon crowded with cafés and restaurants and a very swish clientele. Various Universal Exhibitions helped to increase its popularity, particularly in 1900, when the **Grand Palais** and **Petit Palais** sidled up together.

Centre of ceremony Despite its tackiness, the Champs Elysées remains the central Parisian stretch for official processions and celebrations. Catch it on 14 July (Bastille Day) and most of the French army rolls past with a jet accompaniment flying exceedingly low overhead. Later in July you may find yourself here for the last leg of the Tour de France bicycle race, an event deeply rooted in the French psyche which pulls in thousands of spectators. You can catch the setting at its best around Christmas, when every tree glitters with festoons of elegant white lights – then try New Year's Eve for size.

The lower half of the avenue boasts a few select restaurants nestling in the chestnut trees: **Ledoyen, Jardins de Lenôtre** or **Le Pavillon Elysée** – all have astronomical prices but make a nice indulgence with their garden terraces. Otherwise avoid any eating establishment on this avenue – everything is geared towards unsuspecting tourists.

In 1989 the Bicentenary celebrations culminated in Jean-Paul Goude's spectacular procession moving and dancing down to the Concorde, with Jessye Norman singing at its head. De Gaulle's triumphal Liberation march took place here in 1944, as did the silent procession in 1970 paying tribute to him after his death; and Victor Hugo's funeral parade made its way along the avenue in 1885.

■ **Where else did Lenin, Sartre, Picasso, Modigliani, Apollinaire, James Joyce and Trotsky cultivate their genius but in Parisian cafés? Not to speak of the intellectuals of the Revolution, who plotted France's future in the watering holes of the Palais Royal. The café tradition lives on, and Parisian thinkers still hatch ideas or chew the cultural cud in public rather than in their often miniscule abodes. Time was when cafés were part of the Great French Pick-up tradition, but lone women are nowadays as much at ease here as they are at home. .....■**

The Parisian habit of people-watching includes fashion comparisons, or attention to *le look*. Where better to indulge it than from a shady café-terrasse in the summer months, or a warm, noisy, smoky interior during winter? Unfortunately the majority of Paris' 12,000 or so cafés reek of *croque-monsieurs* (grilled ham and cheese sandwiches) and resound to sounds of pin-ball machines, so shrewd selection is essential.

Many of the favourites are in up-market Saint-Germain, number one being the **Café de Flore**, which rose to fame when Sartre and Simone de Beauvoir set up literary shop there during World War II. Its 19th-century wood-panelled interior is as inviting as the terrace, which is glassed in during the winter, and if you get tired of the constant visual appraisal, go upstairs, where you can read *Le Monde* in peace. Clientele still includes philosophers, writers, artists, and a smattering of chic tourists. But, as in every historic café beware the prices!

Historic haunts A few doors along is the equally famous **Aux Deux Magots**, named after the statues of two corpulent Chinamen astride their money-boxes. *Magot* also means a hoard of money, and this is what you'll spend if you succumb to the menu of 25 different brands of whisky. But think of the ghosts of Mallarmé, André Breton, Hemingway, André Gide and Sartre and stick to a pot of their excellent expresso coffee. Tourists and Middle Eastern businessmen abound, and the odd native publisher or movie star still slips in.

For a more down-to-earth café, head down to the corner of the rue de Seine and the rue Jacques-Callot. Here you can plunge into the less monied and eccentric **La Palette**, with its comfortable and noisy back room. La Palette is a favourite with art students, artists and gallery owners. Its walls are plastered with good and bad art, and its head-waiter-cum-proprietor is a classic: quick-witted or scowling, he's unforgettable.

Back in an increasingly tacky Montparnasse, an institution not to miss is **La Coupole**. Built in 1926 by an astute waiter working at Le Dôme across the street, its majestic art deco splendour is hard to rival, despite recent remodelling. The main hall is a world-famous

Sartre and Simone de Beauvoir were regulars at the Café de Flore

brasserie frequented by the rich and famous, and again, ghosts abound. They include pre-war Americans in Paris such as Hemingway (he got everywhere), Man Ray and Henry Miller, backed up by locals Matisse and Kiki de Montparnasse. Across the road, the rival **Le Sélect** dates from the same period and still attracts a heterogeneous crowd late into the night.

Right Bank landmarks In the heart of the Rive Droite's commercial quarter, Opéra, stands another Parisian landmark café, the **Café de la Paix.** Although lacking the atmosphere of the previous establishments and mainly frequented by exhausted tourists, its interior demands a visit. Designed by Charles Garnier, responsible for the neighbouring opera-house, its murals, mouldings and chandeliers are a shrine to the glorious excesses of mid-19th-century décor.

However many famous cafés litter the centre of Paris, you will doubtless come across your own finds, rich in local characters and decorative idiosyncrasies. And don't miss out on the latest *fin de siècle* cafés, the **Café Costes** and the **Café Beaubourg.** Both are in Les Halles, both owned by the same family, both designed by 'star' architects, but there familiarity ends. The Costes, which opens on to the place des Innocents, has become a favourite hangout for suburban teenagers. The superb design and furniture by Philippe Starck are pure 1980s, and the innovatory downstairs toilets demand a detour. More inviting, however, is the Café Beaubourg on the square outside the Centre Pompidou. Here, in Christian de Portzamparc's post-modernist setting, you can watch Rive Droite intellectuals go by.

The first café to open its doors in Paris was Le Procope (which still exists but as a restaurant), in 1686, run by a Sicilian who soon attracted most of the political and literary élite to his tables. Voltaire had a daily habit of drinking 40 cups of mixed coffee and chocolate there, and the young artillery officer Napoleon Bonaparte once had to leave his hat as a deposit while he went off to search for funds.

A teenage favourite: the Café Costes

■ **In the early days, brasseries only sold beer. Today, high ceilings echo with clattering plates and chattering voices, mirrors double the people-watching scope, carved wood and etched glass partitions protect your privacy and waiters in full-length white aprons swing trays of oysters or *choucroute* between the tables. .....■**

An invention which arrived from Alsace in eastern France, wholesome brasserie fare usually includes sausages piled high on *choucroute* (sauerkraut), ham, cassoulet and anything else that can be concocted from a pig – all drowned in litres of beer. Many specialise in seafood, so if you're in Paris during the 'r' months (September to April) when oysters are at their optimum, indulge. Brasseries are mostly open on Sundays and last orders carry on well after midnight, making them ideal for late eaters.

The world-famous brasserie **Flo** chain, which includes **Flo, Julien** and **Terminus Nord** in the 10th, the **Vaudeville** in the 2nd and most recently **La Coupole** in the 14th, is hard to beat for atmosphere, value and spectacular settings. The **Brasserie Flo** itself remains a Parisian favourite, tucked away in a courtyard and inevitably packed, out whereas Julien, more visible on the Faubourg, has a higher tourist concentration. Bang opposite the Stock Exchange, the patronising

La Coupole, one of the celebrated Flo chain of brasseries

Vaudeville waiters serve traders sweating over the *Financial Times* at lunchtime and a mixed glamorous bunch in the evening. The elegant **Terminus Nord**, the only jewel in the ambivalent quartier of the Gare du Nord, has an easy-going atmosphere.

.**La Coupole** is, of course, La Coupole. Josephine Baker and her pet lion-cub are not the only celebrities to have sat on its red velvet seats under its soaring art deco ceiling. Despite its recent, much criticised renovation, the famous pillars painted by artists (in exchange for meals) such as Chagall, Léger, Juan Gris, Delaunay and Soutine remain. Othon Friesz's dynamic murals have been restored and 600 seats are still available. Actors, artists, models, businessmen and plain ordinary people all mix in to this non-stop party.

Paris' star brasserie, the **Lipp**, is centrally situated on the boulevard St-Germain, where all celebrities seem to tread. Once ruled by a man with an iron glove, Roger Cazes, who was quick to decide whether you were worthy of a ground-floor table or were to be relegated upstairs, it now has a less disdainful management. Long a favourite with politicians (from De Gaulle to Pompidou and Mitterrand) it is also a great haunt for authors. Idiosyncrasies prevail: no soup on Sundays, roast pork on Monday, cassoulet on Thursday...and non-stop *choucroute*. No bookings; pot-luck and the shape of your face decide your destiny.

First draughts One of Paris' oldest brasseries (1864), and apparently the first to serve draught beer, the **Bofinger** thrives in a side street off the Bastille. Blessed with an elaborate glass dome, extensive marquetry and gracefully framed mirrors, it is a delight to dine in.

Less opulent but serving the same basic fare minus the shellfish, the **Brasserie de l'Ile Saint-Louis** boasts the best brasserie terrace in Paris. A south-facing view over the Seine, Notre-Dame a few metres away and Berthillon ice creams: its credentials are impeccable. Inside, the stuffed stork perched on the bar is about the same age as the 1913 expresso machine, and the barman has pulled draught beer here since the 1950s. Crowded and cramped, its backroom restaurant remains a firm favourite with tourists and eccentric locals.

Pigalle, too, has its *choucroute* institution, namely the venerable **Brasserie Wepler** on the place Clichy. Better value than the central establishments and just as accommodating in size, its oyster bar is outstanding. The vast, brassy décor is not the most discreet, but its eclectic clientele fills out the corners comfortably.

A sign of good taste: the still flamboyant Bofinger

Gabriel's imposing Ecole Militaire in the Champ de Mars

Champ de Mars

Originally laid out for army manoeuvres, whence the name, which refers to Mars, the Roman god of war, the green lawns of the Champ de Mars stretch from the Eiffel Tower down to the Ecole Militaire. It was the site where the Roman invaders battled it out with the Parisii in 52BC to obtain supremacy over Paris and where the Parisians later beat off the Vikings. The Champ de Mars has witnessed many an official celebration, horse-races and ballooning experiments by the Montgolfier brothers. It is a favourite with children of chic local residents.

Dominating the area is the Ecole Militaire, designed as a military academy by Gabriel, (also responsible for Versailles' Petit Trianon), who was commissioned by Louis XV and his mistress, Madame de Pompadour.

Chartres see pages 194–5

Chasse et Nature, Musée de la

60 rue des Archives, 75003
metros: Arts et Métiers, Hôtel de Ville
Definitely one of Paris' more curious museums, this is also a great favourite with children, enthralled by rooms of hunting weapons and stuffed animals. Housed in a Marais mansion, the Hôtel Guénégaud, which was built in 1650 by François Mansart, it possesses a tiny yet perfectly manicured garden at the back, visible from the rue des Quatre Fils. The museum collection itself covers hunting arms used from prehistory until the 19th century (knives, cross-bows, swords, air- guns, rifles). On the second floor big-game hunting comes to the fore (with souvenirs of the museum's founder, Monsieur Sommer). A rich collection of relevant paintings and decorative arts include hunting and animal scenes depicted by François Desportes, the court artist employed by Louis XIV at Versailles, alongside Chardin, Oudry and Carle Vernet. *Open*:Wednesday to Monday, 10.00–12.30/ 13.30–17.30hrs.

Thanks to a new tax on playing-cards and the lottery, funds were found for the colonnaded and domed Ecole Militaire, completed in 1773 and considered to be Gabriel's masterpiece. Thus the 18th-century gamblers inadvertently financed the grooming of France's military cadets, one of whom was none other than Napoleon who entered the academy aged 15, in 1784, considered fit 'to be an excellent sailor'.

■ **Since 1895, when Louis Lumière held his first cinematographic projections in a basement room of Le Grand Café, at no 14 boulevard des Capucines, Paris has remained the world capital of cinema. Nearly a century later, there are over 300 films showing at any time of the day or evening, from old Hollywood classics to recently released European avant garde efforts – and many foreign language films are shown in their original version (labelled VO). .....■**

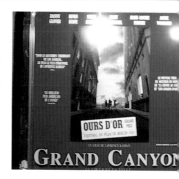

City images Many French film-makers are inextricably linked with the atmosphere of Paris, not least being the directors of the 1930s and '40s. Born in Les Halles and a pupil of the famous Lycée Louis-Le-Grand, René Clair showed Paris for the first time on screen in *Paris qui dort* (1923) and soon after in *Sous les toits de Paris*. Yet however authentic they look, his charming, animated old streets, rattling omnibuses and smoking chimney-pots were all studio-built.

A decade later, Marcel Carné, another Parisian born and bred in Batignolles, focused on the rough, industrial life of the faubourgs, encapsulating Montmartre and Jean Gabin in the *Quai des Brumes* and the Canal St Martin in *Hôtel du Nord*, which starred the legendary Arletty and Louis Jouvet. *Les Enfants du Paradis* poetically interpreted the street underworld around the Cour des Miracles in a classic Parisian fresco. The other side of the Parisian coin was reflected in Jean Renoir's *La Règle du Jeu* (1939). Here was the elegant, muted, bourgeois world of Proust and the 16th *arrondissement*, rife with barely disguised jealousies.

Classic venues To see such Parisian classics go to the **Vidéothèque** (see page 183), the **Cinémathèque** (see page 91), the **Salle Garance** at Beaubourg (see pages 80–1) or the **Palais de Tokyo** (see page 163); all specialise in re-runs, as do certain Rive Gauche cinemas. For these

programmes, which often change daily, check one of the three weekly listings magazines (*Pariscope, 7 à Paris* and *L'Officiel des Spectacles*), all published on Wednesdays. But for real audience comfort go to any of the following: **Kinopanorama** (15th), **Max Linder** (9th), **Forum Horizon THX** (1st), or **Rex** (2nd). Strangest of all is **La Pagode** (7th), built in 1896 as a private ballroom in the form of a pagoda, and a lavishly decorated 'Chinoiserie' cinema since 1931.

Mass-release films are shown in a string of Champs Elysées cinemas

At the crossroads: place du Châtelet

The best time of the year to visit Chinatown is during Chinese New Year (late January), when dragons take to the streets.

▶▶▶ Châtelet, place du

A hectic central crossroads, the place du Châtelet lies between the Pont au Change, which crosses to the Ile de la Cité, and the boulevard de Sébastopol. Once the site of an imposing fortress, Châtelet is known today for its vast underground metro station, where all lines and all buskers seem to meet. Two important theatres flank the square and in its centre the sphinx-endowed fountain, erected in 1808, commemorates yet another Napoleonic victory, the Egyptian campaign.

Both identical theatres were built by Davioud in 1862 but now lead separate and even rival existences. The **Châtelet** concentrates mainly on opera and classical music, with occasional ballet, and usually has a rich programme of international performers. It recently acquired an annexe in Les Halles, the Auditorium, where more unusual or obscure music is performed.

The modernised interior of the **Théâtre de la Ville,** previously named the Sarah Bernhardt, has preserved for posterity the diva's dressing-room. Audiences flock here to see the top names of contemporary dance or innovative French theatre. Early evening concerts of jazz or world music have recently been programmed to give homebound office workers a chance to unwind.

▶▶▶ Chinatown

Following world tradition, Paris now has its very own Chinatown in the 13th *arrondissement*, spreading south from the place d'Italie through the rue de Tolbiac to the Porte de Choisy. Asiatics are now said to constitute 10 per cent of the population of this *arrondissement*, and China is by no means the only country of origin. Squeezed between high-rises, pagoda-like shopfronts crammed with Chinese curios jostle with a fantastic variety of eateries on all scales, from Hong Kong-style canteens to more intimate Laotian, Cambodian or Vietnamese places. Clubs, dance-halls and gambling dens also contribute to the atmosphere but these are usually out of bounds to westerners, as the fortunes changing hands are illegal.

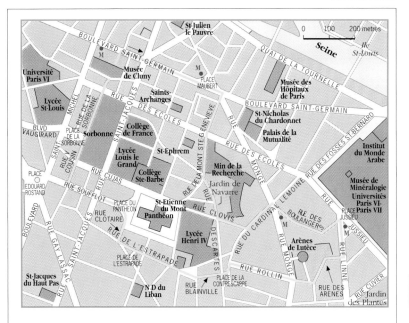

Walk **A circular walk from the Musée de Cluny**

Start in front of the Musée de Cluny. Walk east along boulevard St-Germain to the place Maubert. Turn right behind the vast police station and walk up the steep rue de la Montagne Ste-Geneviève.
Named after the patroness of Paris, the **rue de la Montagne Ste-Geneviève** was part of the Roman road linking Lutetia with Italy, and for centuries was lined with colleges and schools. Some remain today.

At a fork, turn up the rue Descartes. The route now passes what was once the famous **Ecole Polytechnique** and is now a ministry (its delightful gardens are open to the public).

Turn left into the short rue Clovis. The **rue Clovis** was named after the king of the Franks who defeated the Romans and founded France. Near **no 5** is a section of Philippe-Auguste's medieval city wall.

Walk downhill towards the place du Cardinal Lemoine and take the

second narrow turning on your right down the rue des Boulangers, right up the rue Linné and right again into the rue des Arènes.
Here, you enter the ruined **Roman amphitheatre**, now used for *boules*.

Exit onto the rue Monge, and take the rue Rollin opposite, which crosses the animated place de la Contrescarpe and becomes the rue Blainville.
The **rue Blainville** was the site of Paris' first public library.

Follow this street into the rue de l'Estrapade, turning right down the rue Clotaire to confront the illustrious Panthéon. Walk down the gracious rue Soufflot.
Below the **rue Soufflot** are the ruins of a Roman forum.

Turn right down rue V Cousin, which leads to the rue de la Sorbonne, symbolic heart of French learning.
Pass **Ste-Ursule-de-la-Sorbonne** (1642), where Richelieu is buried, before returning to the Cluny.

103

Between 1500 and 1844, when it became a museum of the Middle Ages, the Hôtel de Cluny housed the likes of Mary Tudor, widowed at 16 after a three-month marriage to Louis XII; James V of Scotland, before his marriage to François I's daughter; and, in the 17th century, various cardinals including Mazarin.

▶ ▶ ▶ **Cluny, Musée de**

6 place Paul-Painlevé, 75005

metros: St Michel, Maubert-Mutualité

Once a pied-à-terre for a wealthy order of Benedictine monks from Cluny in Burgundy, the Hôtel de Cluny stands on and beside Paris' oldest Roman ruins. Rebuilt in 1500, the mansion is one of France's finest examples of domestic Gothic architecture. Sold off after the Revolution to replenish government coffers, in 1833 it entered the hands of art collector Alexandre de Sommerard, whose rich finds form the basis of the museum today.

Although 8,000 Renaissance works were recently transferred to the museum at the Château d'Ecouen, the Cluny vaults contain another 20,000 objects, rarely displayed. However, those that are visible are superb. From the mutilated heads of statues from Notre-Dame (more Revolutionary decapitation) unearthed in 1977 in a bank vault, to an incomparable series of 15th-century tapestries, to dazzling displays of jewellery, manuscripts and stained glass, this is a collection of unfailing inspiration.

Roman baths On the lower floor the late 2nd century

La famille Jouvenel des Ursins *(1445–9), one of the tapestries in the Musée de Cluny*

baths are a reminder of the strength of Roman architecture. The vaulted ceiling of the Frigidarium (cold bath) rises over 14m with 2m-thick walls. In one corner stands the *Pilier des nautes*, Paris' oldest sculpture. Leading off from here, a vast network of Roman vaults has recently been restored and can be toured.

Back on the ground floor, you enter the museum via displays of medieval costume and accessories (including 14th-century winklepickers), Byzantine, Coptic and European textiles and a series of tapestries. One series, *La Vie Seigneuriale*, shows the life of a noble household. On the first floor a rotunda-shaped room houses one of the museum's great splendours, the six allegorical tapestries of *La Dame à la Licorne*. Exquisitely woven, probably in the southern Netherlands for the Lyonnais family of Le Viste, their delicate tones represent flora and fauna as a graceful background to the central feminine figure. Each tapestry shows her acting out a sense – sight, touch, smell, taste, sound – while the enigmatic sixth work presents her in front of the motto A *mon seul désir* (to my only desire). Is this freedom from the senses or mastery of all five? Your guess is as good as anybody's over the last five centuries.

Jewels and crowns Room XVI presents a treasure trove of goldwork and jewellery: Gallic, Barbarian, Merovingian examples include belts, buckles, bracelets, the sublimely fashioned 'Rose d'Or', six Visigoth crowns and two 13th-century double gold crosses.

Apart from the stained-glass windows removed from Ste Chapelle and St Denis, the most striking church relic is the glittering gold altar frontal (1015) from Basel cathedral, made for the Emperor Heinrich II.

At the back of the top floor don't miss the Abbot's Chapel with its flamboyant vaulting fanning out from a central pillar. Twelve niches contain statues of the Amboise family (Jacques Amboise rebuilt the mansion in 1500) and tapestries depicting the life of St Stephen carry on into adjoining rooms.

Open: Wednesday to Monday, 09.45–12.30, 14.00–17.15hrs.

The 21 mutilated heads from Notre Dame, displayed in Room VIII, actually represented kings of Judea and Israel, but were assumed by the stampeding revolutionary mob to be kings of France – hence their sorry fate.

Home base of the Comédie Française: the Théâtre Français

The guillotine is not such an anachronism: it was only abolished in 1961, after nearly 200 years of loyal service.

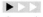

Collections Historiques de la Préfecture de Police, Musée des

1 bis rue des Carmes, 75005
metro: Maubert-Mutualité

If you feel like checking Charlotte Corday's statement about murdering Marat in his bathtub, this is where to go. Situated at the back of the 5th *arrondissement* commissariat (police station), this macabre little collection covers many of Paris' great criminal moments from the 16th century to the present. A particularly graphic representation shows the punishment meted out to the murderer of the Duc de Guise in 1563: he was tied to four horses and quartered. Other niceties include orders for the arrest of Docteur Guillotin in 1795 and a book splattered with the bloodstains of the assassinated President Paul Doumer. An array of weapons runs the gamut of knuckledusters, garrottes (strangling cords), variously concealed knives (one in a lady's fan), and a guillotine blade.

Open: Monday to Thursday, 09.00–17.00hrs, Friday, 10.00–16.30hrs.

Comédie Française

2 rue de Richelieu, 75001
metro: Palais-Royal

A monument to French classical theatre, the building named the Théâtre Français is actually a 1900 remodelling job of the original 1790 Doric- style edifice, mostly destroyed in a fire. It has been home since 1799 to the Comédie Française company, founded by Louis XIV with members of Molière's troupe. The playwright himself died on stage seven years earlier while performing in *Le Malade Imaginaire*; the armchair which cushioned his fall when illness struck can still be seen in the foyer along with busts and statues of dramatists: Carpeaux's Dumas, Rodin's Mirabeau, Clésinger's Georges Sand and Houdon's sedentary Voltaire.

Although the basic repertoire of the Comédie Française remains a string of Molière, Racine, Corneille and Marivaux classics, a recently appointed director has opened up the field. And nobody will forget the spirit of Sarah Bernhardt, the great tragic actress who played many of her finest roles here.

Phone 42 96 10 24 for information on the rare guided tours.

Design

■ **French furniture and *objets d'art* design is well illustrated by the collection at the Musée des Arts Décoratifs, where much emphasis is put on the early 20th century. From the organic curves of art nouveau, French design moved effortlessly into a more sober art deco style exemplified by the Exposition Internationale des Arts Décoratifs in 1925. .....■**

The great couturier **Poiret** bankrupted himself with his three converted barges decorated by Dufy; Parisian design moved resolutely into geometric modernism. After **Dunand, Chareau, Ruhlmann** and **Le Corbusier** the next French designer to open up a new style was **Jean Prouvé**, master of the 1950s curves.

New life After decades of remaining dormant, French design underwent a minor renaissance in the 1980s. Stimulation came from the **Mobilier National,** which since 1964 had acted as an inspiring go-between for designers and furniture manufacturers and the government agency **VIA,** which supported and promoted young designers. The **VIA** showroom, now in the Cour du Commerce St-André, displays prototypes and manufactured items, all for sale, some more functional than others. Temporary exhibitions upstairs are also a good window on the creative whims of individual designers.

State style Design has become such a cultural symbol that even the President has commissioned new furnishings for the Elysées, and some Ministries have adopted a distinctly futuristic image. **Philippe Starck, Jean-Michel Wilmotte, Andrée Putman** and **Garouste et Bonetti** are favourites in the official field, and their status is now international.
Another wave carries with it the names of **Sylvain Dubuisson, Martin Szekely, Pucci de Rossi** and **Marie-Christine Dorner.** A precursor in this field is the **Galerie Néotu** (25

rue du Renard, 4e; tel: 42 78 96 97), which regularly exhibits the latest in French avant-garde design.
The **Galerie Yves Gastou** (12 rue Bonaparte, 6e; tel: 46 34 72 17) exhibits designs by **Ettore Sottsass, Ron Arad** and **Kuramata** while **En attendant les barbares** (50 rue Etienne-Marcel, 2e; tel:42 33 37 87) is a hive of weird objects.

Décor of the day If you prefer to see examples of French design *in situ*, probably the most obvious relics of the 1980s in Paris are the interiors of the **Café Costes, Café Beaubourg** (see page 97) and **La Villa** (a hotel with a public bar and a

Accessible design at the Café Coste – does it mark the end of an era, or simply a pause for thought?

jazz-club at no 29 rue Jacob, designed by **Dorner**).

Designs on the future? So far the 1990s have not left a visible mark on any public interior. Is French design going into another decline or is everyone just waiting for the year 2000?

LA CONCIERGERIE

Rue de Harlay

Vestibule de Harlay

Chambre Civile

Police Judiciaire

Cour des Appels Correctionels

Cour d'Assises

Galerie Lamoignon

Cour de Cassation

Jardin

Galerie de la Première Présidence

Parquet du Procureur Général

Cour du Dépôt

Cour du Dépôt

Tour Bonbec

Cour Saint-Martin

Galerie St-Louis

Cour du Premier Président

Cour d'Appel

1ere Chambre

Galerie Duc

Galerie Duc

Tour d'Argent

Cour de la Sainte-Chapelle

Galerie des Prisonniers

Tribunal

Mont de Berryer

1ère Chambre Civile

Chambres

de

Galerie Marchande

Salle des Pas-Perdus

Cour de Conciergerie

Tour de César

Vestibule René Parodi

Grand Instance

Gal de la Ste-Chapelle

Tribunal de G Instance

Correctionelles

Sainte-Chapelle

Escalier Louis XVI

Tour de l'Horloge

Couloir du Procureur de la République

Cour du Mai

Boulevard du Palais

Quai des Orfèvres

Quai de l'Horloge

108

▶▷▷ **Conciergerie, La**
1 Quai de l'Horloge, 75001
metros: Cité, Châtelet

Rising above the roofs of the Quai de l'Horloge on the Ile de la Cité, the twin towers of the Conciergerie struck horror into the hearts of thousands for over five centuries. Originally built to house Philippe-le-Bel's caretaker (concierge) and palace guards, by 1391 it was functioning as a prison and continued as such until 1914. Before entering, stop at the corner to look at the **Tour de l'Horloge**, which incorporates Paris' first public clock. Commissioned by Charles V in 1371, it is set against a constellation of gold fleur-de-lys; the surrounding sculptures of law and justice were added in the 16th century. A bell that rang for three days following the birth of any royal babe could not really toll for the Revolutionaries, so in 1793 a new silver bell was installed.

Grim history The prisons of the Conciergerie are best known for their hospitable role during the Revolution, although they had already housed and tortured thousands, including Ravaillac, murderer of Henri IV. During the Terror 4,164 citizens were held here, 2,278 of whom finished under the guillotine. The best remembered inmate is Marie-Antoinette, the extravagant Austrian wife of Louis XVI. Other guests included Charlotte Corday, Marat's assassin; Madame du Barry, mistress of Louis XV; and, when the tide turned, Danton and Robespierre.

Entrance is through the Salles des Gardes, a vaulted stone chamber plunged into shadow by the construction of the embankment outside the windows. This opens on to the equally gloomy Salle des Gens d'Arme, an astonishing hall measuring 70m by 27m. Said to be Europe's oldest surviving medieval hall, it was restored the 19th century by Viollet-le-Duc. A spiral staircase at the back leads to the original kitchens. Four walk-in fireplaces big enough to roast a couple of sheep indicate the scale of medieval appetites.

Star-rated cells Back at the entrance to the Salle des Gens d'Arme, follow the rue de Paris, where less monied prisoners (*les pailleux*) snoozed on straw bedding. Three types of accommodation were available: the communal straw-strewn floor; a shared cell with beds; and for those with real pull and funds, a private cell complete with table for memoir-writing. From this corridor you reach what was once the prison's most animated cross-roads, the Galerie des Prisonniers, where lawyers, visitors and prisoners came and went. On the left was the barber's cell, where inmates were shorn before their trip to the guillotine.

A narrow staircase leads up to displays of objects related to the Conciergerie's bloody history. The first musty room is the most striking: wall panels list all the 2,780 guillotined victims of the Revolution.

Downstairs you reach the Chapelle des Girondins, named after the 22 condemned Girondins (left-wing members of the 1791 Legislative Assembly) who celebrated their last night with true revelry here. What is now the altar was the site of Marie-Antoinette's cell.

At the far end of the Galerie des Prisonniers, her cell has been re-created. None of its contents is authentic but the spartan furniture, peeling wallpaper and models of card-playing guards behind a screen give the sorry feel of Marie-Antoinette's last sojourn.

Open: June to August, 09.30–18.30hrs, September, April and May 09.30–18.00hrs, October to March, 10.00–16.30hrs.

Floodlights now shine on to the grim façade of the Conciergerie

The city's first public clock, on the Tour de l'Horloge

Dr Guillotin perfected his 'philanthropic beheading machine' by trying it out on a miserable bunch of sheep.

▶ ▶ ▶   Concorde, place de la

Once a swamp, now Paris' largest square, throbbing with traffic and fumes, the Concorde was designed in 1775 chiefly to accommodate an equestrian statue of the reigning king, Louis XV. It soon changed name and function when the guillotine was trundled out. As the place de la Revolution it saw over 1,300 heads roll, including Louis XVI, Marie-Antoinette, Danton and Robespierre. The architect, Jacques-Ange Gabriel, also designed the two properties flanking the rue Royale, one of which survived the Revolution in the hands of the Comte de Crillon, and is now the **Hôtel Crillon.**

With the cooling of revolutionary passions in 1795 the square was renamed Concorde and soon acquired Coustou's *Chevaux de Marly* at the entrance to the Champs Elysées. The next transformation came in 1833 under Louis-Philippe, when he was presented with a 23m-high, 3,000-year-old obelisk by Mohammed Ali, viceroy of Egypt (see page 158). Gabriel's eight stone pavilions, each topped by a statue depicting a French town in human guise, still remain.

▶ ▶ ▷   Cour du Commerce St-André (Cour de Rohan)

59/61 rue St-André-des-Arts, 75006
metro: Odéon

A shopping-mall with atmosphere and history: it seems to be a contradiction in terms. However, Paris has 17 such places (see page 181) and the Cour du Commerce was the first. Built in 1776 on the site of a tennis-court, it became a hive of revolutionary activity, with Marat printing his pamphlet *L'Ami du Peuple* at no 8, Danton installed at no 20 and the anatomy professor Dr Guillotin at no 9. At no 4 you can see the remains of a 13th-century tower, part of the city wall, and the Renaissance courtyards of the Cour de Rohan are still picturesque. Today the passage houses a string of restaurants and tea-shops, and, at no 4/8, the official window on French contemporary design, **VIA** (see page 107).

A great Parisian crossroads: the place de la Concorde

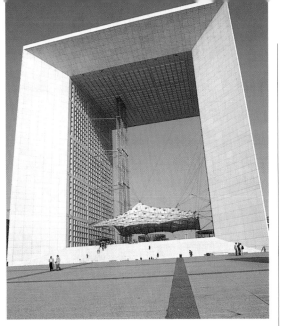

La Grande Arche, a window on new development in Paris

111

▶▶▷ **La Défense**

RER: La Défense

Paris' new 305,000-tonne white marble symbol, La Grande Arche, is the western gateway to the capital and reigns over an urban development first mooted in the 1930s. World War II put a brake on all urbanist projects, but by 1958 an astonishing edifice, the CNIT, had risen from the ground. Throughout the 1960s, wondrous and hideous architectural experiments sprouted in all directions, symbols of France's postwar mutation. Catastrophic in many cases, utopic in others, La Défense was intended as a new business and residential centre. The oil crisis in 1973 slowed its momentum but had a positive effect too, forcing architects and developers to look more closely at what was fast becoming a nightmare knot of viaducts, tunnels and unrelated forms.

Three successive Presidents examined three successive projects to complete *La Tête Défense* (head) and finally provide this labyrinth with a focal point. An unknown Danish architect, Otto Von Spreckelsen, was finally selected by Mitterrand to build his marble 'window on the world', the disembowelled cube that has become La Grande Arche. Its symbolic measurements (100m by 100m) echo those of the Cour Carrée in the Louvre. Completed in time (just) for the Bicentenary celebrations in 1989, its unfortunate architect had by then abandoned the whole project in a huff and died before its inauguration.

The wide esplanade of La Défense has now assumed its own identity, with office-workers happily lunching by the fountains or on café terrasses. Numerous contemporary sculptures punctuate this concrete landscape, one of the most striking being François Morellet's *La Défonce*, a fine geometric construction which topples into the recently opened underground store-rooms of the national contemporary art collection.

Fast becoming a must on the tourist trail for its fantastic open-air panoramic views over Paris, La Grande Arche offers a ride to the roof in transparent shaftless lifts – vertigo sufferers beware! Beautifully designed galleries on the top floor house temporary exhibitions, as do the EPAD galleries buried beneath the forecourt outside (access to roof Monday to Friday 09.00–17.00hrs and weekends 10.00–19.00hrs).

Self-portrait, *by*
Eugène Delacroix

Although he yearned to be a pure classicist, Delacroix was the embodiment of romanticism. His wide knowledge of literature and his contact with the old masters of the Louvre gave him a rare imaginative breadth. The influence of classical legends and history is apparent in his early works: *Dante and Virgil crossing the Styx*, *Death of Sardanapalus*, *The Capture of Constantinople* (all at the Louvre). But is was a trip to Morocco in 1832 that left an indelible mark on his style, foreshadowing Impressionism. Prolific and talented in every field, from portraits to wild beasts, Delacroix was also an accomplished decorator; you can see his vigorous style in the Chapelle des Anges of St-Sulpice or the royal salon and library at the Palais Bourbon.

▶▶▷ **Delacroix, Musée**
6 place Furstemberg, 75006
metro: St-Germain des Prés
The apartment and studio where the great Romantic painter Eugène Delacroix (1798–1863) spent the last six years of his life is now a small but charming museum, freshly restored in 1991. The place Furstemberg itself has hardly changed over the last century or so and still has a provincial atmosphere, with its flowering trees and decorative street-lamps. Visiting this museum is more a chance to experience the calm and character of Delacroix's environment than to see his works, most of which are happily housed in the Louvre.

Personal effects The first of the three rooms was his bedroom and still contains some furniture, as well as his treasured tobacco-pot. The dining-room displays his intricate painting table and the central salon his desk. Other memorabilia, etchings, sketches, watercolours and letters are displayed throughout, but look out particularly for a recently acquired painting, *La Madeleine au désert*. Delacroix manages in this compelling image to convey the enigmatic strength and aura of the saint with a typically luminous yet ambiguous treatment.
Continue outside down a wrought-iron staircase across a tiny garden to Delacroix's studio, which he had built himself. The studio is a fairly ordinary building, though decorated with neo-classical bas-reliefs, and contains more studies, sketches and a portrait of his redoubtable mistress, Jenny Le Guillou, who scared many a friend from his door in his later years. Lithography stones used to print his edition of Hamlet are presented, along with paintings by his disciples Riesener and Andrieu.
Open: Wednesday to Monday, 09.45–12.30, 14.00–17.15hrs.

■ **There are signs that the high-flying days of 'Gay Paris' are, if not over, at least dropping in altitude – despite a more liberal state approach in recent years. Encouraged by a governmental decision in 1981 to destroy secret service files on homosexuals, and by the lowering of the legal age for homosexual activity to 16 (as for heterosexuals), the gay population of Paris acquired a new identity virtually overnight. .....■**

The headquarters of the gay community moved from the rather sleazy rue Ste-Anne to the gentrified Marais, where certain locals still claim that 'they've taken over'. Yet today the Senate is attempting to raise the legal age to 18 again, and the influential *Fréquence Gai*, Europe's only gay radio station, has disappeared: tell-tale signs, perhaps, of the end of an era.

Changing attitudes AIDS has had an enormous influence on attitudes to gay and heterosexual life. Greater Paris has a population roughly equivalent to that of Greater London but twice as many AIDS cases. Unlike the US, where cruising areas, saunas and sex clubs were closed down, Paris has reacted more moderately, trying instead to change sexual behaviour slowly, without putting a stop to it. However, the closing in early 1992 of the Bois de Boulogne, known for its nocturnal sexual activities, may be seen as a sign of major changes to come. Areas known as gay meeting-places include the Tuileries esplanade, overlooking the Seine, the riverbank opposite the Musée d'Orsay in the summer months or the shady tranquillity of the Père Lachaise cemetery. Sunday afternoon dancing at **Le Palace**, a decade-old tradition, attracts hundreds of men (8 rue du Faubourg Montmartre, 17.00–22.00hrs); while for other days of the week the hotspot is **BOYS**, a predominantly gay disco accepting women and specialising in house music (6 rue Caumartin, from 23.00hrs nightly). For a more low-key evening, **Le Central**'s bar and coffee-house in the Marais have become the epicentre (corner of rue Vieille-du-Temple and rue Ste-Croix-de-la-Brétonnerie). From here it is a stone's throw to popular bars such as the **Subway** (35 Ste-Croix-de-la-Brétonnerie), **Le Swing** (42 rue Vieille-du-Temple) and the very fashionable **Le Quetzal** (10 rue de la Verrerie).

For more addresses the weekly gay magazine *Gai-Pied* abounds with listings and even features a digest in English.

The gay community in Paris may be facing a more restrictive era

The 'Queen of Paris'

The Eiffel Tower has inspired much idiosyncratic behaviour. Those who have plummeted from its peak include a moustachioed Icarus who, in 1912, plunged to his death when his wings failed to open. He turned out to be a bankrupt tailor escaping from his debtors. In 1928 a watchmaker tried out a new parachute – too innovative: it didn't open either and he rapidly met his maker. A luckier performer cycled down the steps from top to bottom to win a bet, survived, but was arrested for provocative behaviour.

▶ ▶ ▶   Eiffel, Tour

metro: Bir-Hakeim
RER: Champ de Mars

A 'hollow chandelier', 'staircase to infinity', 'tower of Babel' or 'aviary of the world', monstrosity or hallowed symbol of Paris, the Eiffel Tower has run the gamut of descriptions in its 100 odd years of existence. Built in a record two years by Gustave Eiffel for the 1889 Universal Exhibition, celebrating the French Revolution centenary, it was intended for demolition 20 years later. But by then it had as many artistic and intellectual fans as it had opponents when built, and it was saved for the utilitarian purposes of its broadcasting antennae. Thus the instincts of writers and artists such as Apollinaire, Dufy, Delaunay, Utrillo and Pissarro were vindicated and the scandalised agonies of Garnier, Verlaine, Leconte de Lisle, Maupassant and Zola relegated to history.

Standing a regal 300m high, weighing over 7,000 tonnes and composed of 15,000 iron parts, the 'Queen of Paris' (*dixit* Cocteau) sways no more than 12cm in high winds and shrinks or grows 15cm according to temperature. For 40 years it remained the highest structure in the world until it was usurped by New York's Chrysler building, although it acquired a further 20m in height in 1957 when television antennae were added to existing radio, telegraph and meteorological apparatus. Mountaineers have scaled it, pilots have tried to fly through its pillars and in 1909 the Comte de Lambert circled 100m above it in a flying machine.

Public spectacle About four million people visit this extraordinary construction annually, so be prepared for a long wait at the lifts. Go to the third floor (at 276m) for Paris' most spectacular view which, on a clear day, extends 67km. Hardier folk can attempt the steps in the south pillar which lead up to the first and second platforms (respectively at 57m and 115m). Above all don't dismiss its nocturnal transformation. Even if you are not dining in one of the Tower's two restaurants, go to the top for a glittering visual feast or at least pass close by for an unforgettable vision of the 292,000-watt interior lighting system, illuminating the intricate structure against the night sky.

Towering figure The engineer Gustave Eiffel kept an office in his Tower until his death in 1923. Although this was the ultimate symbol of his skill and imagination, Eiffel left hundreds of other constructions all over the world. Born in 1832 in Burgundy of German stock, he was already working on the famous Bordeaux bridge at the age of 26. Bridges soon became his speciality: iron and the hydraulic methods he used for installing their supports helped to build his reputation. Factories, churches, a synagogue (rue des Tournelles), shops (Le Bon Marché), banks and, over a period of 18 years, 31 railway viaducts and 17 major bridges all came within his creative sphere. Egypt, Peru, Portugal, Hungary, Bolivia and Indo-China all have their Eiffel monuments, while the US has its 46m tall Statue of Liberty – a mere stripling beside the Tower.

Constructive contributions When his wife died at a young age in 1877 Eiffel threw himself heart and soul into his work, never remarrying. Shortly before the tower commission he was involved in an embroglio over the Suez Canal and was sued for not respecting a deadline. He untied himself from these potentially uncomfortable knots with the help of fellow Freemasons, a powerful pressure group in those days. After his masterwork was built he continued to produce marvels of engineering and contributed constructions to the 1900 Universal Exhibition. With the saving of the Tower from demolition in 1910, Gustave Eiffel must have been a satisfied man when he died at 91.

Open: daily, 10.00–23.00hrs (July and August, 09.30–24.00hrs).

Gustave Eiffel

Three hundred and seventy suicide victims chose this edifice to end their days. Protective shields, finally installed in 1971 on every outdoor platform, put an end to this tragic spin-off.

Le Général
A caricaturist's delight, with his towering height and unmistakable nose, Charles de Gaulle was to some a hero, to others a tyrant: without doubt he was a unique and outspoken French President. His escape to London in World War II and organisation of the free French movement made him a symbol of liberty, but after the war he fell from political favour. De Gaulle's comeback in 1958 led to a new constitution and strengthened presidency. Age and narrowmindedness brought his downfall; three years after the student riots and general strikes of 1968 he died at his home in Colombey-les-Deux-Eglises.

Palais de l'Elysée

l'Elysée, Palais de
55–7 rue du Faubourg St-Honoré, 75008
metro: Miromesnil

This sumptuous residence has housed French presidents for over a century. Built in 1718, it was greatly altered in 1753 to suit the extravagant tastes of Madame de Pompadour. A radical volte-face came with the Revolution, when the Elysée turned into a public entertainment park, but under Napoleon it reverted to being a private residence – first for his sister, then for his wife Joséphine. Various other notables, including Wellington, Napoléon III (before becoming Emperor) and Queen Victoria, passed through its courtyard, garden and grand staircase before 1873 when it assumed its role as the President's official residence.

Already greatly modified, modernised and enlarged, the Elysée continues to undergo the decorative whims of each President. Agam's op-art works, commissioned by Pompidou, have since been moved to the Musée d'Art Moderne. Valéry Giscard d'Estaing left his mark above all for inviting in the local street-cleaners for a chat on his return from a radical night out. Mitterrand has had many of the salon ceilings painted in a neo-classical style by Gérard Garouste. So who's next?
Not open to the public.

A hidden corner in one of the courtyards of the Faubourg St-Honoré

Faubourgs

Inextricably linked with the urban development of Paris, the 'faubourgs' still possess an identity of their own. The word itself means 'fake borough' and refers to the extension of inner streets beyond specific city boundaries. Paris' first suburbs have since the 14th century been integrated into the fabric of the city centre. Yet the word still has a pejorative ring: 'he was born in the faubourgs' implies that someone's origins are not the most sophisticated. The queen of the faubourgs, Edith Piaf, nevertheless built her career on her modest beginnings in **Belleville**, making the faubourg accent chic in itself. Ironically, the first faubourg to exist, the **Faubourg St-Honoré**, which extended the central rue St-Honoré, is now the hub of Parisian wealth, power and elegance. Similarly, the **Faubourg St-Germain** area is a haven for the discreet residences of the bourgeoisie and more obvious government buildings.

Historically the **Faubourg St-Antoine** which runs east from the Bastille to the place de la Nation, is the most eventful. By the late 18th century it was a thriving centre for artisans, and this concentration of workers made the faubourg 'the crater from which revolutionary lava escaped most often'. June 1789 proved this reputation: revolutionary zeal led to pillaging and arson before the famous march on the Bastille. In 1848 29 barricades were set up along the faubourg. Today, more peaceful in spirit, its identity is still linked with the traditions and crafts of furniture manufacturing.

However, the real atmosphere of the faubourgs can still be found in the area between the **Faubourgs Montmartre** and **Poissonière** in the ninth arrondissement. Starting at the Grands Boulevards, the Faubourg Montmartre winds uphill towards Pigalle and Montmartre, carrying in its wake a colourful string of bars, cheap restaurants and original 18th-century shops. Peppered with picturesque cul-de-sacs and some fine mansions but lacking in major sites, it is mistakenly overlooked by many visitors to Paris.

Poseurs' Paris

■ **There's no better place than Paris to play at being a jet-setter. Steeped in a tradition of ostentation, its temples of pretension and luxury are legion. An important feature of the Parisian psyche is the ability to flaunt style, often but not always linked with wealth. A fine line divides the BCBG (traditional chic) from the flashier and sometimes more imaginative displays of new money, but for outsiders this is not an essential factor. A thick wad of 500FF notes or a collection of credit cards is. .....■**

Although a recently coined term, BCBG (*bon chic, bon genre*) has firmly stuck as a label for the Parisian equivalent of London's 'Sloane Rangers'. Its subjects hide out in the prosperous 16th *arrondissement*. Passy and Neuilly shelter hordes of this well-groomed species clad in finely cut grey or navy suits (both sexes) and a touch of flamboyance symbolised by a Hermès scarf. Sleek discretion is the key. Weekend golf is the pastime.

Eating Glamorous gastronomy is no mean affair in Paris and the moment you enter the three- and four-*toque* category of the Frenchman's bible, the *Gault Millau*, you are guaranteed not only an elegant setting and sublime victuals, but also a sophisticated array of dining companions. Try the historic monuments, such as Lucas-Carton, Le Grand Véfour, La Tour d'Argent, Taillevent or Ledoyen. Allow yourself to be pampered by sycophantic waiters and relax in sensual comfort. And for the grand panacea of Parisian cuisine, book a table (months ahead) at Robuchon, where the lobster with artichoke will guarantee your elitist election to paradise.

Drinking Whatever your liquid tastes, Paris will provide the appropriate watering-niche, from discreet *salons de thé* to shadowy nocturnal haunts. For the most elegant of breakfasts or teas, head for Ladurée in the rue Royale, where you'll wade through carrier-bags marked Lanvin or Chanel to get to a table. Savour the coffee while enjoying the ceiling fresco of a cherubic pastry-chef. In the nearby rue de Rivoli reigns the historic Angélina's, also straight out of the Belle Epoque, as are some of its regulars. As day turns to night head for Le Forum in the boulevard Malesherbes, where one of their 150 cocktails should put you in the right mood, failing which carry on to the bar of the Hôtel George V, where the champagne concoctions make up for the height of the bar stools. Still thirsty after midnight and on the Left Bank? Then go to Montparnasse's media mecca, La Closerie des Lilas, where tinkling piano music, polished wood and a long history of illustrious drinkers generate a special aura.

Shopping For chic shopping stick to the Faubourg St-Honoré, rue Royale, place Vendôme and rue de la Paix. Have a shirt made to measure at Charvet, shoes at Hermès (by London bootmaker John Lobb), pick up a watch at Van Cleef & Arpels, indulge in a new hair-cut at Carita's, then stop for a snack at Caviar Kaspia. Short on household goods? Lalique in the rue Royale will supply a nice range of frosted crystal and Christofle, across the street, has the lobster forks. Need some new

Hermès is an essential part of the BCBG look

asparagus dishes? Then head round the corner to **Au Bain Marie**, a haven for more imaginative BCBGs.

Sleeping For one of the world's best siestas go to the sparkling **Crillon** and stretch out in a spacious suite with its terraced view over the Concorde. Or book in at Paris' first 'grand hotel', the gilded and chandeliered **Meurice,** which dates from 1815. Try the **Raphaël** on the avenue Kléber for a quick transposition to a country château atmosphere, increasingly appreciated by the film world. Or join the *crème de la crème* and ghosts of Proust and Chanel at the eternal **Ritz**.

Walking For a glamorous stroll you can definitely strike off the Champs Elysées. Instead, keep to the streets of stylish shopping (above) or, for more bucolic surroundings, the shady paths of the **Parc Monceau**.

Dancing If you can talk your way in (no mean achievement), **Castel's** and **Régine's** remain Paris' glossiest nightspots, where a monied international set rubs shoulders on the dance-floors. Or join the jet-setting businessmen and top models at **Olivia Valère** in the rue du Colisée.

Fashionable drinking at Angélina's

■ **Paris is not solely reserved for the rich and famous, as many an impoverished writer or artist has found out. Its easy-going cafés make ideal focal points for struggling creators of all sorts and visitors on extra-low budgets. And you don't have to sleep under the bridges to survive. .....■**

For drinks and snacks remember that prices are almost 50 per cent cheaper if you stand at the bar. Beer drinkers should ask for *une pression* or *un demi*, signifying draught beer, as opposed to the pricier bottled variety. *Café au lait*, or *café crème* and tea are big money spinners – try and convert to black coffee, *un café*, the cheapest possible beverage.

Locomotion Much of central Paris can be covered on foot but there are moments when a metro or bus ride is unavoidable – and welcome. Make sure you use either a carnet of 10 tickets (valid for all central Paris transport) or a weekly coupon jaune, a better deal than the tourist-oriented Paris Visite, which provides unlimited transport for three or five days. If you're really dug in, buy a *carte orange*, which whisks you around for a month. All season tickets are available at metro stations and are pretty reasonable for a reliable and efficient service.

Accommodation Give the faubourgs a go! Enjoy the colourful life of a less central quartier, hang out in local cafés, sample its bistros and markets and you'll save yourself the price of a few more nights. One- and two-star hotels beyond the Bastille, around République, the Faubourg Montmartre or the Gare de l'Est, deep in Montparnasse or as far south as Chinatown, will come up with some surprisingly acceptable accommodation at (relatively) low prices.

It is possible to eat well in Paris on a low budget...

Gastronomic survival If you're not developing the baguette-saucisson-and-cheap-plonk-in-the-hotel-bedroom technique, there are plenty of bistros that will supply you with a copious feed for 60FF or so. Lunchtime fixed menus, even in smarter areas, are invariably excellent value, as are the *plats du jour* in cafés and brasseries. Forget mineral water and order a free *carafe d'eau* or drink wine by the *pichet*.

Evening feeds prove more difficult, but not insoluble. Although much frequented by tourists, **Chartier** and its lesser known sibling, **Drouot**, still provide good basic fare in extraordinary settings – but get there early. In the fifth *arrondissement* a multitude of Greek, Italian, Vietnamese and even French restaurants cater for a vast and hungry student population. Head up the steep rue des Boulangers where, if **Aux Savoyards** is full, you can take your pick from a handful of similarly bustling bistros. Alternatively, continue uphill to the rue Mouffetard, still a favourite despite being under touristic siege for a decade or so, and stop at **Le Pavé aux Herbes** for taramasalata and brochette.

In the sixth there is no shortage either: at the **Polidor** you eat with the spirits of Verlaine and James Joyce, while **Le Petit Benoît** offers bland but ancient décor and solid French cuisine. The popular **Restaurant des Beaux Arts**, is substantial and always fun. Off St-Germain, the narrow rue Grégoire de Tours has a string of low-priced Greek and Italian haunts close to the action and you can't go wrong for atmosphere and budget if you dive into the hub of streets surrounding rue de la Huchette: the odours of shish kebab announce an irresistible menu.

Don't forget Chinatown, in the 13th *arrondissement*, which feeds millions at low rates, while Belleville and La Goutte d'Or, although far from the madding crowd, have an insurpassable mixture of Oriental, Arab and African restaurants, all very reasonable. Couscous makes an excellent cheap and balanced diet wherever you are in Paris.

Culture Entrance fees to museums mount up, so it may be worth investing in a *carte musée*, valid for one, three or five consecutive days and providing unlimited entry to all monuments and museums, as well as avoiding the queues.

Otherwise Sundays, although sometimes crowded, are often half-price and in some cases free. Don't forget that private art galleries cost nothing (see pages 66–8), Parisian architecture and views are free and street artists provide itinerant amusement.

Shopping Apart from the flea markets, Paris has a good line in cheap supermarkets and stores such as **Prisunic** and **Monoprix**, where you can pick up household gadgets or fashion accessories for unbeatable prices. Fashion victims should seek out the *dépôt-vente* shops, where little-worn designer and couture gear is sold at a fraction of its original price. Then there are the ubiquitous **TATI** branches (boulevard Rochechouart, rue de Rennes, République), where, if you fight through the crowds of concierges, you can kit yourself out for derisory amounts, although no one's guaranteeing the quality.

121

...even if it means a snack on the hoof

The Folies Bergère, still going after all these years...

Over 5,000 tapestries have been woven at the Manufacture des Gobelins, using a palette of almost 15,000 colours and including designs by Poussin, Boucher, Gromaire, Picasso and Matisse.

Ferronerie, rue de la

With a name that has not changed since 1229, the 'ironmongers' street remains firmly engraved in history books as the site of Henri IV's assassination in 1610. The determined Ravaillac, who had walked from Angoulême to accomplish his dastardly deed, was subsequently quartered. Today, only a marble plaque at no 11 reminds us of its blood-stained history.

Folies Bergère

32 rue Richer, 75009
metro: Cadet, Le Peletier
Tacky it may be, but the Folies Bergère still stands after 125 years. Its bar has been immortalised on canvas by Manet, and this was where the likes of Mistinguett and Josephine Baker thrilled the audiences of les *années folles*, while the acrobatic Tiller Girls swung along astride their merry-go-round horses under its dome. The Folies Bergère has today lost much of its sparkle and daring. Feathers, bare breasts, sequins and plastic smiles seem a little systematic, as the army of dancers goes through its repertoire of *Bal à Versailles* or the Eiffel Tower can-can. Whatever, it is still the least pretentious of the Parisian cabarets and won't cost you an arm and a leg.

Fontaine des Innocents

square des Innocents, 75001
metro: Châtelet, Les Halles
Sheets of water have gushed down three sides of this superb Renaissance fountain designed by Pierre Lescot and sculpted by Jean Goujon since it was erected in 1550. Now the focus of attention for the cruisers and bruisers of Les Halles, for centuries this square was the site of a cemetery, as well as being a meeting place for the food merchants of Les Halles. In 1786, when not much available soil was left, it was decided to transfer the two million or so stinking skeletons to the

fountain, originally on the corner of the rue St-Denis, which was then shifted to its present central site and acquired its fourth side.

▶▶▶ Fontaine des Quatre Saisons
57–9 rue de Grenelle, 75007
metro: rue du Bac
Barely visible on a side street off the rue du Bac, this magnificent fountain seems wasted. Designed and sculpted by Bouchardon in 1739, it was the response to complaints from illustrious inhabitants of the Faubourg St-Germain about a severe water shortage. The sculptures represent the City of Paris with the Seine and the Marne prostrate at her feet.

Fontainebleau see pages 198–9

▶▶▶ Furstemberg, place
metro: St-Germain
Once the *cour d'honneur* of the abbot of St Germain's palace and named after Cardinal Furstemberg, who rebuilt it in 1699, this little square embodies everyone's dreams of Paris in the spring. Blessed with four generous, perfumed magnolia trees and an unaffected architectural harmony, it makes a balmy evening's favourite for musicians and promenading couples. The corner houses at nos 6 and 8, which include Delacroix's former apartment and studio, were once the palace stables.

Giverny see pages 200–1

▶▶▶ Gobelins, Manufacture des
42 avenue des Gobelins, 75013
metro: Gobelins
Not a factory churning out little creatures, but the official tapestry factory since the heyday of Louis XIV. Originally a dyeworks set up by the Gobelin brothers, then taken over by Flemish weavers, it soon attracted royal attention through the eyes of Colbert, Louis XIV's astute minister. By 1662 it became the royal tapestry centre and rapidly expanded to include furniture and carpet workshops. Much of the interior decoration of Versailles was woven, carved or inlaid here and even Marie-Antoinette deigned to visit the workshops. You can still see the centuries-old looms clicking away today, guided by expert weavers, who start training aged 16. The one-and-a-half hour guided tour also takes in the famous Savonnerie carpet workshops.
Open: Tuesday, Wednesday, Thursday at 14.15 and 14.45hrs.

▶▶▶ Goutte d'Or
metro: Barbès-Rochechouart
Immediately east of Pigalle, the poetic-sounding Goutte d'Or (Drop of Gold) is a hive of cosmopolitan activity, where Arabs and Africans live, shop, lunch, dine and hang out in an atmosphere straight out of Algiers or Abidjan. As with Belleville, the property developers are moving in fast, while the city council is working hard at 'cleaning up' an area also notorious for drug-dealers and

Jean Goujon's 16th-century Fontaine des Innocents

Shedding its light across the river: the Grand Palais

One permanent exhibition exists in the Grand Palais: the Jacques-Henri Lartigue donation, displaying the photographer's whimsical images of early 20th-century society.

squatters. If you're seeking a friendly, low-priced couscous joint, go there on a summer evening when the locals congregate on doorsteps. This is not chic Paris – and unfortunately it won't last.

 Grand Palais
avenue Winston-Churchill, 75008.
metro: Champs Elysées–Clémenceau
Its soaring iron and glass domes visible from far along the river, the Grand Palais is another example of ambitious turn-of-the-century architecture. Built, together with the Petit Palais opposite, for the 1900 Universal Exhibition, it has since hosted hundreds of temporary fairs and art salons. Its west wing, which opens on to the avenue Franklin-Roosevelt, houses the Palais de la Découverte (*open*: Tuesday to Sunday, 10.00–18.00hrs), an accessible, well organised science museum with a superb planetarium. The main halls on the east side exhibit art retrospectives and salons such as the FIAC, Paris' annual contemporary art extravaganza. *Open*: Wednesday 10.00–22.00hrs; Thursday to Monday, 10.00–20.00hrs.

Grand Véfour, Le
17 rue de Beaujolais, 75001
metro: Palais-Royal, Pyramides
Ornately mirrored, gilded and painted, the restaurant Le Grand Véfour is a living historic monument. Peep through the windows at its Restoration painted ceiling and glass-protected dancing walls: it is a seductive delight. Nestling in a neo-classical colonnade since the late 18th century, when the Palais-Royal was the heart of Parisian intellectual life, Le Grand Véfour has seen diners such as Napoleon, Victor Hugo and Colette (who lived upstairs).

Grévin, Musée
10 boulevard Montmartre, 75009
metro: rue Montmartre
Over a century old, the Musée Grévin is the Parisian answer to London's Madame Tussaud's. Throngs of immobile figures beckon you through the city's history and blood and gore is assured in the Revolution section. Elsewhere, rock and film stars are aligned with Presidents, and a recently opened annexe in the Forum des Halles displays scenes from the Belle Epoque, highlighted by a rather tacky son-et-lumière.
Open: daily, 13.00–19.00hrs.

▶ ▶ ▶ Guimet, Musée (Musée Nationale d'Arts Asiatiques Guimet)

6 place d'Iéna, 75016
metro: Iéna

This superb museum exhibits a remarkable display of Oriental antiquities, built up from the industrialist Emile Guimet's 1879 collection. Much of the Louvre's Asiatic department has been transferred here to widen the panorama of sculptures, carvings, paintings and artefacts from Indo-China, China, Japan, Tibet, Afghanistan, Pakistan and India.

Particularly stunning, the ground-floor halls contain Khmer art, which includes serene stone buddhas and Hindu gods (6th- to 12th-century). In colourful contrast, the adjoining rooms display richly painted Tibetan and Nepalese tankas and intricate inlaid silverwork.

On the first floor the Indian department includes early Mathura and Amarâvati carvings, south-Indian bronze deities and Moghul and Rajput miniatures. A rich Chinese department includes the Calmann collection, a wide-ranging display of porcelain. Both China and Japan are also represented in a separate collection at the museum annexe (19 avenue d'Iéna), Le Panthéon Bouddhique, where buddhas of all periods, media and sizes meditate for eternity.

Open: Wednesday to Monday, 09.45–17.15hrs.

125

▶ ▶ ▷ Les Halles

metro: Les Halles
RER: Châtelet–Les Halles

The 'belly of Paris' (*dixit* Victor Hugo) has undergone multiple transformations since the great days of the food market which started around 1100. Neatly delineated by the rue Beaubourg in the east, the rue du Louvre in the west, the northern rue Réaumur and southern rue de Rivoli, Les Halles functioned as a market until 1969. The grocers and butchers were then moved out to the suburb of Rungis and their superb 1860s Baltard pavilions were demolished (only one was preserved, now installed at Nogent-sur-Marne).

It took the city council and government 10 years of wrangling to decide how to fill the gaping hole: although the result is aesthetically disastrous, Les Halles has recovered its role as a central commercial and social hub. Venture below ground into the **Forum** for shopping, cinemas, swimming, billiards, videos or concerts. Stay above ground for basic food and drink, hustlers, street-artists *et al*. The traditional 5am onion soup can still be consumed at **Au Pied de Cochon** but your fellow-suppers will be tourists, not market vendors. Yet a wander through the surrounding streets throws up atmospheric bars and restaurants which haven't changed for a century.

▶ ▷ ▷ Hammam

La Mosquée, 19/39 rue Geoffroy-St-Hilaire, 75005
metro: Censier–Daubenton

Sick of Parisian chic or lowlife? Then go to the Turkish baths at La Mosquée where, around a marble fountain sheltered by a tiled dome, you can mentally waft yourself to Marrakesh. The steam of the 90°C sauna

Les Halles in its 20th-century guise

The Musée de l'Histoire de France

126

At the Musée de l'Histoire de France, look out for Louis XVI's classic diary entry for 14 July 1789, the day the Revolution broke out: he quite simply inscribed *Rien* ('nothing').

helps...allow three to four hours for the full relaxing benefit. Finish with a mint tea.
Open: for women: Monday, Wednesday, Thursday, Saturday; for men: Friday, Sunday.

▶ ▶ ▶ l'Histoire de France, Musée de
Hôtel de Soubise, 60 rue des Francs-Bourgeois, 75003
metro: Rambuteau, Hôtel de Ville
Although some of the historic documents displayed here are fascinating, the principal interest lies in the museum's sumptuous architecture. It was mostly built by Delamair in 1709 for the Princesse de Soubise, by extending a 14th-century manor (whose double-towered entrance on the rue des Archives remains intact), and the interiors were decorated in the 1730s by Boffrand. The richness of this period accompanies you from the majestic Cour d'Honneur into the ground floor palace apartments, where Boffrand employed the talents of painters such as Boucher, Van Loo and Natoire. The ornate decoration continues throughout the Princess' first-floor apartments, where the museum documents are now displayed. Letters written by Charlemagne and Joan of Arc, the wills of Louis XIV and Napoleon and Marie-Antoinette's last missive before the chop are worth a read.
Open: Wednesday to Monday, 13.45–17.45hrs.

▶ ▷ ▷ Holographie, Musée de
Level 1, Forum-des-Halles, 75001; enter from the Porte Lescot
metro, RER: Châtelet–Les Halles
Buried in this central labyrinth is a museum favourite for children. Although invented in 1947, holography has only recently become known to the general public, mainly through images on credit cards and beer taps. This small museum shows the use of laser technology for creating 3D images of antiquities. Some of the holograms are fun, others less inspiring.
Open: Monday to Saturday, 10.00–19.00hrs, Sunday 13.00–19.00hrs.

▶ ▷ ▷ Huchette, rue de la
metro, RER: St-Michel
One of Paris' oldest streets, dating back to 1284, the rue de la Huchette is known today for its unadventurous gastronomy: it's souvlaki or souvlaki. At the heart of the Latin Quarter, students and tourists pile in here thinking they have discovered authentic Paris along its cobbled, narrow length. Two symbols remain of the 1950s, when this street experienced a real high: a minute theatre and a basement jazz bar. Still running at the theatre since the days when Ionesco first staged them are his plays *La Cantatrice Chauve* and *La Leçon*. Downstairs in the crowded caveau at no 5 be-bop has hardly missed a note.

▶ ▶ ▶ Institut du Monde Arabe
1 rue des Fossés St Bernard, 75005
metro: Jussieu
Difficult to miss as you cross the Seine from the Ile St-Louis, the Institut du Monde Arabe benefits both from

its strategic location on the Quai St-Bernard and its sleek contemporary architecture. Founded in 1980, it moved into these custom-built premises in 1987, partly financed by the government and partly by 20 Arab states anxious to encourage cultural exchanges between Islam and the West. This aim is achieved through temporary exhibitions, a permanent museum collection, concerts, lectures, a library and research facilities. Although budgets remain a thorny point – recent upheavals in the Middle East having stemmed the financial flow – and the museum is still sparsely filled, the Institute is an attraction for anyone interested in the Arab world.

Before looking at anything else, notice the powerful aluminium and glass building designed by Jean Nouvel and the Architecture Studio. Apart from the light-sensitive diaphragm windows on the south façade, the transparent lift shaft alone justifies the visit. Spirit yourself to the ninth floor terrace, which provides magnificent views west along the river and north towards the Bastille. In the elegant, pricey restaurant you can enjoy the same views, along with baklava or shish kebab, seated in a Philippe Starck chair.

Design priorities continue on the three floors of the museum, where astrolabs vie for attention with display systems. From Spain to India, spanning the 9th to 19th centuries, the ceramics, bronzes, ivories and carpets of this collection reflect the brilliance of this civilisation.

Open: daily (except Monday), 13.00–20.00hrs.

Number 10 rue de la Huchette reeks of Napoleonic lore. This was where Bonaparte languished for long months, despairing of his future, having fallen out with the authorities. In October 1795 he re-entered the political spotlight by dint of gunning down an insurgent mob; five years later he was gloriously installed at the Tuileries Palace across the river.

127

The Institut du Monde Arabe

■ **Giving a definitive opinion about the best features in Paris is a hazardous enterprise. Seasons change, as do quality and popularity, all decisive factors in the enjoyment of certain places. Luckily, however, there are always unchangeables and these include the places which are listed below. .....■**

Café bests The best café with a view is an outdoor terrace in central Paris, 70m up on the 10th floor of the department store **La Samaritaine**, overlooking Pont-Neuf. Open only during the warmer months (generally May to October), it is a popular lunch spot for local office-workers, but always has room at other times. The view due south and either way along the Seine of monuments within spitting distance is spectacular. A look-out point above displays an enamelled 'artist's impression' of Paris in 1900, good for comparing with today's horizon. A similarly central but more chic terrace with a view concentrating on the Ile St-Louis and the Bastille, is on the ninth floor of the **Institut du**

Best for refreshments with a panoramic view – La Samaritaine department store

Monde Arabe. More a glorified tea-room it is open 15.00–19.00hrs throughout spring and summer.

Antique bests If you are looking for top class antiques, don't go to the **Marché de Vanves**, Paris' best junk market *(brocante* in French). Open Saturday and Sunday mornings at the Porte de Vanves, it has now established itself among young couples as the place to go for finding the ultimate item of battered yet stylish furniture. Stall- holders are full of witty banter and always ready to 'discuss' a price. Rainy days, although not the most enjoyable, do lead to the best bargains.

Oyster bar bests Although difficult to pronounce the best oyster bar, Le Bar à Huîtres (112 boulevard du Montparnasse) is without a doubt the most convenient. Oysters can be eaten in any quantity you like: on the pavement outside, or with more attention, seated at a bar-stool inside. *Belons, fines de claires* or *Marennes* are all superbly fresh and immaculately opened by friendly Bretons, and are best washed down with a pitcher of Sauvignon or a bottle of young Muscadet. **Montparnasse** is traditionally the seafood centre of Paris because of its proximity to trains arriving directly from Brittany and Normandy. Remember that oysters are best consumed during the 'r' months (September to April).

Tea break bests In winter months *salons de thé* are easily the most accessible and comfortable places to recover from weary pavement- and museum-bashing, often graced with deep armchairs, reading matter and classical music: they are an alternative to the bright, noisy atmosphere of bistros and cafés. A favourite in the Marais is **Les Enfants Gatés** (43 rue des Francs-Bourgeois). Convenient for the Musée Picasso, the Carnavalet or the place des Vosges, it is a long-standing, unpretentious tea-room, which serves delicious cakes, savoury tarts and salads throughout the day (open 12.30–20.00hrs).

Water bests In the heat of summer, you may want to escape in a different way from the tourist circuit and finally hit some water. The best and snobbiest swimming pool, without a doubt, is the **Piscine Déligny**. Located on the Quai Anatole-France, close to the Musée d'Orsay, this floating, barge-like structure has attracted chic swimmers since 1840. Today it is even more fashionable, as it belongs to the owners of Paris top night club, Les Bains, and poseurs frustrated by daylight spend most of their afternoons preening themselves on the sundecks here.

Studio bests For a fascinating view of how a late 19th-century artist lived, go to the best artist's studio-museum in Paris, the **Musée Gustave Moreau** (14 rue de La Rochefoucauld, 9e; tel: 48 74 38 50). Although the lower floors (his studio) have been open to the public for years, the upstairs apartment was only reconstructed and renovated in late 1991 and presents his rooms with the objects and decoration he chose. Moreau himself (1826–98) prepared the museum for posterity shortly before his death, and over 6,000 of his eery symbolist works are exhibited in this elegant town-house. At last the artist's wish has been fully accomplished.

Bakery bests Parisians have been lamenting for several years the gradual disappearance of the good old baguette, with its crispy golden crust and soft white interior. Many boulangeries have turned to industrial baking methods, and that inimitable chewiness has given way to a bland, anonymous sponginess. But all is not lost. What has really taken Paris by storm over the last few years is a type of bread called **Pain Poilâne,** (named after Lionel Poilâne), now airlifted to New York and Tokyo and sold all over Paris. For your first experience go to the family bakery, 8 rue du Cherche-Midi, 6e, to savour this bread, which is made only with hand-ground French flour, yeast and sea-salt and cooked in a wood-oven.

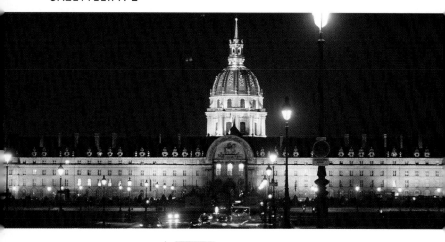

The Sun King's wounded soldiers were given a home at Les Invalides

The tomb of Marshall Foch in Les Invalides. Foch was overall commander of French, British and American armies towards the end of World War I

▶ ▶ ▷ Les Invalides

metros: Latour–Maubourg, Invalides, Varenne

Pompous, severe, authoritarian, the 196m façade of the Hôtel des Invalides masks a masterpiece of French classical architecture. Designed by Libéral Bruand, it was completed in 1676 by Hardouin-Mansart, who later incorporated the impressive Eglise du Dôme (1705), a commission by Louis XIV to reflect the greatness of his reign. For once the Sun King was thinking of others, as Les Invalides was designed to house old soldiers, many invalided (hence the name) and reduced in their old age to dire straits. Six thousand once resided there; today under a hundred remain.

The main attraction for time-limited visitors is **Napoleon's tomb**, which presides gloriously over the crypt of the Dôme. Twenty years after his death on the distant island of St Helena, Napoleon's body was returned to France and in 1861, like a Russian doll, it was encased in six layers of coffins crowning an immense granite base. Other military tombs fill the chapels of this superb baroque church, rich in painted cupolas, graceful arches, columns, sculptures, bas-reliefs and inlaid marble floors. An ornate gilded, garlanded and ribbed dome completes these glories.

Not to be confused with the Eglise du Dôme, the adjacent Eglise St-Louis also concentrates on military memorabilia. Here numerous generals are buried but more visible are the tattered remains of captured regimental banners which hang from the upper galleries. On entering Les Invalides through its Cour d'Honneur you will be following in the footsteps of many a military hero, including de Gaulle and Churchill. To examine the ins and outs of military history head straight for the **Musée de l'Armée**. One of the world's largest in this field, its extensive collections of weapons, armour, flags, uniforms and paintings trace the evolution of warfare from prehistoric days to World War II. Inevitably Napoleonic relics abound (including his stuffed horse, 'Vizier') but other periods such as the Second Empire and both World Wars are equally well displayed. Nor is the Orient forgotten: one section specialises in the superbly crafted arms of the Middle and Far East.

In the **Musée des Plans-Reliefs**, scale models of fortresses in France and near her borders form a collection which originated under Louis XIV in 1668 and for years remained a military secret.
Open: daily, 10.00–17.45hrs (winter till 16.45hrs).

▷▷▷ IRCAM

31 rue St-Merri, 75004
metro: Hôtel-de-Ville
Behind the dancing, clanking sculptures of the Fontaine Stravinsky, in the shadow of Beaubourg, stands an understated entrance. It leads to one of France's most important cultural laboratories: below ground lies a high-technology musical research center. The founder of IRCAM was composer and conductor Pierre Boulez; here, a team of electronic engineers and composers has unrivalled facilities for acoustic invention and experiment. Concerts and workshops are held in a futuristic auditorium, and visiting composers can try out the 4X, a digital sound processor which performs 220 million operations per second.

▶▶▷ Jacob, rue

metro: St-Germain-des-Prés
Reeking of what everyone expects the Rive Gauche to be, the picturesque rue Jacob is crammed with galleries, antique shops, bookshops and interior decoration shops. Stroll along this street watching out for the shadows of former residents Racine, Wagner, Mérimée and Stendhal but keeping an eye open for ethnic jewellery, astrolabs, art deco curios, Chinese porcelain, architectural prints or swathes of sumptuous fabric. The choice is wide and quality generally reliable. Walk east and you'll end up in the Left Bank gallery mecca; go west and you'll eventually arrive at Les Invalides.

▶▷▷ Jacquemart-André, Musée

158 boulevard Haussmann, 75008
metro: St-Phillipe-du-Roule
Once a prestigious private collection of 17th- to 18th-century European art and Italian Renaissance works, subsequently bequeathed to the nation, the Musée Jacquemart-André recently disappeared in a cloud of scandal when its curator was accused of appropriating funds. Result: the museum closed, but should reopen by summer 1992. If all is well this elegant 1870 mansion will still display paintings and drawings by Rubens, Rembrandt, Frans Hals, Van Dyck, Chardin, Boucher, Watteau and Lancret, alongside Savonnerie carpets and Gobelins tapestries.
Open: Wednesday to Sunday 13.00–17.30hrs.

▶▶▷ Jeu de Paume, Galerie Nationale du

place de la Concorde, 75001
metro: Concorde
Reopened in 1991 after five years of renovation and internal transformation, the Jeu de Paume now turns a rejuvenated face to the public. This is just another in a long string of mutations since its 1878 origins as an indoor tennis-court. The Jeu de Paume saw its first exhibition in 1909 and by 1922 became a fully fledged

'Listen to your century' – slogan of the Ensemble InterContemporain, a group of contemporary instrumentalists based at IRCAM.

Galerie Nationale du Jeu de Paume

museum, housing a number of outstanding exhibitions. Under the Occupation it was requisitioned by German troops for stocking works seized from Jewish art collectors and intended for transfer to German museums. Immediately after the war it took on the cloak for which it is still remembered: that of the museum of the Impressionists. For 40 years it attracted millions of visitors (the highest density of any museum in the world) before closing its doors in 1986, after the exodus of its rich collection to the Musée d'Orsay.

Today its successfully modernised interior contains several spacious galleries used for temporary exhibitions of international contemporary art.

Open: Wednesday to Friday, 12.00–19.00hrs (Tuesday till 21.00hrs), Saturday to Sunday 10.00–19.00hrs.

 Justice, Palais de
2 boulevard du Palais, 75001
metro: Cité

'Liberté, Egalité, Fraternité' are the words inscribed above the entrance at the top of the grand marble steps leading into France's symbol of civil authority. It is only since the Revolution that the palace took on its present function. Before that it played royal palace, with many architectural transformations, from Roman times until 1358, when Charles V abandoned it completely. Turned over to the Parliament, it acquired a different aspect during the Revolution, when summary judgements were passed and prisoners left the Cour du Mai by the cartload, destined for the guillotine. The May trees have gone from the courtyard, as have the knitting gossips, but the main lobby (the 17th-century Salle des Pas-Perdus) is still thick with black-robed barristers, judges and plaintiffs. Don't miss the stunningly decorated blue and gold Première Chambre Civile, once possibly Louis IX's bedroom and later used by the Revolutionary Tribunal. It is possible to watch the action in most of the courts, but your French may not be up to the animated repartees.

Open: Monday to Friday, 09.00–18.00hrs.

► ► ► Louvre

rue de Rivoli, 75001.
metros: Palais-Royal, Louvre

The Louvre represents an astonishing historical continuum of French rulers from the Middle Ages to the present — and it is not over yet. Since 1981 this palatial museum has been in constant mutation, undergoing restoration and underground extension. Guiding these radical changes is the American architect IM Pei, whose transparent pyramid now crowns the Cour Napoleon. Nor have these transformations been without their archaeological surprises: medieval fortifications have been thrown up in the wake of the bulldozers along with thousands of other disparate objects, mundane or royal.

How to visit To do the museum and your intellect any kind of justice, several visits should be planned, bearing in mind the late opening hours on Mondays and Wednesdays when queues are distinctly shorter. High points of the collections are well signposted and regularly revised plans are available at the entrance. Between 1992 and autumn 1993 (bicentenary of the museum opening) 10,000 works will be shuffled around; by 1996 at least the same number again will change place as renovations are gradually completed. For this reason you may find certain sections closed.

History Its eventful background first took palatial form under Charles V who, in the late 14th century, transformed Philippe Auguste's fortress into a turreted medieval castle. It was not until the wily Renaissance king François I that the Louvre again hosted a royal presence. Considerable rebuilding was instigated, mostly designed by Pierre Lescot in 1546. François I, a man of taste, initiated the Louvre collection by looting Titians and Raphaels from Italy, and also brought the Mona Lisa and its creator, Da Vinci, to France.

Consolation prize Strong-willed as ever, Catherine de Médicis had a completely new palace built in 1578 to compensate for her husband's accidental death in their Marais palace. It was here that she extorted from her hapless son the order for the St Bartholomew's Day massacre in 1572. The new royal residence, the Palais des Tuileries, was at the far end of the present Louvre, looking out across the Tuileries gardens.

Louis XIII set about extending the Cour Carrée but abruptly stopped for financial reasons. Not so his son, Louis XIV, who brought in his pet architect Le Vau (conceiver of Versailles) to complete his father's project before the court transferred lock stock and barrel to Versailles. The Louvre's golden days were almost over, as the last king to live in the palace was Louis XV, and this was only while the Palais des Tuileries was being cleaned.

New role Meanwhile other purposes were found for this vast building: concert hall, art gallery and theatre, it was also invaded by tenants, in particular a colony of artists, including Bouchardon and Boucher. Less socially acceptable were the squatters, 'cabaret' artists, and

133

Louis XIV used the Salle des Caryatides for an unusual ceremony, when he annually washed the feet of 13 paupers.

When the Louvre was opened to the public the royal collection numbered over 2,500 works. Today there are over 30,000 exhibited.

The Louvre's glass pyramid is cleaned monthly by eight professional mountaineers using 800 litres of detergent.

PLACE DU PALAIS ROYAL

RUE SAINT-HONORE

RUE DE MARENGO

RUE DE L'ORATOIRE

RUE DU LOUVRE

RUE DE RIVOLI

Cour du ...istre

Cour des Caisses

Cour de la Poste

Pavillon Richelieu

Pavillon Colbert

Pavillon de Marengo

Pavillon de L'Oratoire

Oriental Antiquities

...ramide

Cour

Napoléon

Pavillon Sully

Salle des Caryatides

Cour Carrée

Place du Louvre

RUE DE L'AMIRAL DE COLIGNY

Egyptian Antiquities

Dungeon of Phillippe Auguste

Porte Denon

Pavillon Denon

Pavillon Daru

Greek, Roman and Etruscan Antiquities

Pavillon du Petit Bourbon

Pavillon des Arts

Cour ...efuel

Cour Visconti

Cour du Sphinx

Jardin de L'Infante

QUAI DU LOUVRE

PONT DES ARTS

Seine

The Louvre – its old and new aspects

By 1996, the Louvre will be the largest museum in the world, covering a mere 240,000 square metres (almost doubling its area).

whores who set up in and outside its walls, creating such a slum that in 1750 it narrowly escaped demolition. Another close shave came during the Revolution, when the Louvre was a tempting candidate for mob arson, but in 1793 a museum was opened to the public in the Grande Galerie — the Musée de la République.

Revival came with Napoleon, who moved into the Palais des Tuileries — severely ransacked by the mob — and celebrated his marriage to Marie-Louise in the Louvre. Always ready to leave his mark, Napoleon set about creating a central courtyard dominated by the Arc du Carrousel, building a northern wing and adding floors. Equally important was Napoleon's contribution to the wealth of the museum, as at every one of his numerous victories ransoms and looting increased the Louvre stock. Under Napoleon III considerable extension finally united the Louvre and the Palais des Tuileries, although this union was short-lived: in 1871 the Tuileries palace was burnt to the ground by the Commune.

The Museum Entrance to the Louvre is through the unmistakable glass pyramid, which leads down into a gleaming marble underworld of further entrances for each wing. A gigantic bookshop, the *chalcographie* (print) department, a café and restaurant all contribute to the animation of this crossroads, which by 1996 will be accessible from an underground car park under the Carrousel. The newly built area will also contain the **Centre de la Mode** for professional fashion shows. On the east side of the Hall Napoléon, follow the Sully entrance to visit the impressive medieval remains of

Philippe Auguste's dungeons (c 1200) and galleries exhibiting pottery and royal artefacts found during excavations.

On the ground and first floor of the Sully wing are exhibited, at the far end, Egyptian antiquities, while the extensive Greek, Roman and Etruscan collections are immediately to the right of the entrance. Here you will find the eternally serene *Venus de Milo* and, in the corner staircase of the Denon wing, the soaring *Victory of Samothrace*, one of whose mutilated hands is exhibited in a case nearby (it was excavated nearly a century later). In the southeastern corner of this wing is the **Salle des Caryatides**. This is the oldest surviving room of the palace built for Henri II and is named after the four monumental statues by Jean Goujon which support the end gallery.

The Orient On the north side, galleries of Oriental antiquities are slowly being moved into place. A highlight of this section, partly created by moving out the Ministry of Finances, will be the Cour Khorsabad, a skylit courtyard displaying the massive sculptural façades of crowned and winged bulls from the Assyrian Palace of Khorsabad (c 713BC).

The paintings For many visitors the Louvre means painting. Take the Denon entrance to the first floor, allowing a quick detour through the Italian sculpture

section on the ground floor to look at, among the Bellinis, Della Robbias and Donatellos, Michelangelo's two formidable Slaves. Above is the Grande Galerie, where large scale paintings by David, Gros, Géricault and Delacroix still hang alongside Italian Renaissance masterpieces (Vinci, Raphaël, Titian) onwards; here too is the *Mona Lisa*, usually hidden by crowds of admirers.

French painting of the 18th and 19th centuries (Watteau, Boucher, Chardin, Fragonard, Robert, Ingres, Corot) will be concentrated, as of 1993, on the second floor of the Cour Carrée, linking the Sully and Richelieu wings. Flemish, Dutch and Northern schools complete the galleries of the recuperated Richelieu wing on this floor while below, on the first floor, are exhibited the fabulous Trésor de St-Denis and *objets d'art*.

Open: Thursday to Sunday, 09.00–18.00hrs, Monday and Wednesday until 21.45hrs.

On either side of the entrance leading into the Louvre from the Palais-Royal, two immense covered courtyards will display monumental French Sculpture, including the original *Chevaux de Marly*.

137

Some intensive appreciation in the Louvre galleries

▶ ▷▷▷ **Luxembourg, Palais du**
15 rue de Vaugirard, 75006
metro/RER: Luxembourg

Yet another symbol of the vagaries of French history, the Palais du Luxembourg and its famous gardens were originally commissioned by Marie de Médicis, the widow of the assassinated Henri IV. Bored with the Louvre, her idea was to build a palace that would remind her of her native Florence. The architect Salmon de Brosse was given plans of the Pitti Palace for inspiration and work started in 1615. However, by the time it was completed in 1631 she had twice been forced into exile: once by her own son, Louis XIII, and (following a reconciliation with the king) again by the powerful Cardinal Richelieu. She died in Cologne, penniless.

Many of the fabulous works of art commissioned for its interior have since been moved. The series of 24 allegorical paintings by Rubens depicting Marie de Médicis' life now hang in the Louvre's Galerie Médicis. Major renovation undertaken by Chalgrin (who later designed the Arc de Triomphe) was rudely interrupted by the Revolution when the palace took on the role of prison (keeping out of trouble, among others, Danton, the De Noailles family and Camille Desmoulins), before passing into the hands of the Directoire. Chalgrin's work resumed and by 1804 the palace was ready to receive the newly created Senate, which still meets here today. Delacroix added to the rich interior in 1847 by painting the Library ceiling with homages to Virgil, Homer and Dante, while the architect Alphonse de Gisors made major additions, including the fabulously decorated Salle des Conférences.

War and peace After almost a century of relative calm,

The Palais du Luxembourg

during World War II the Palais du Luxembourg was occupied by the head of the Luftwaffe for the western front, and its gardens were soon riddled with underground air-raid shelters. Today its political role and promenading popularity have regained the upper hand. Don't forget to pay homage to the instigator of this palace at the shady Fontaine Médicis. Set in one of the few original Italianate features, the fountain sculptures (added later) depict a bronze cyclops, Polyphemus, glaring downwards at the innocent marble lovers, Acis and Galatea. Leaving no stone untouched, the reverse side, facing the rue de Médicis, boasts a bas-relief of Leda and the swan (1807).

Open: only by appointment on the first Sunday of each month (tel: 44 61 21 66).

▶▶▶ Lycée Henri IV
23 rue Clovis, 75005
metro/RER: Luxembourg

In the heart of the intellectual fifth *arrondissement*, the Lycée Henri IV is one of France's most prestigious high schools and claims Jean-Paul Sartre among its former teachers. It was built in 1796 on the site of an abbey devoted to Ste Geneviève, the patron saint of Paris, and a former basilica founded by Clovis, the man who beat the Romans in 497AD. Once the Revolution had swept by only the Gothic Tour de Clovis, the refectory and some kitchens remained.

Closed to the public.

▶▶▶ Madeleine
place de la Madeleine, 75008
metro: Madeleine

Something of a white elephant, the Madeleine has had a checkered career, narrowly avoiding being transformed into a railway station, a stock exchange, a bank, a theatre and yet another temple to Napoleon. Although building started on it in 1764, many ups and downs ensued before it at last regained its original function in 1842 and was completed as a church. Its unmistakable Greek temple form, supported by 52 corinthian pillars, commands a spectacular perspective down the rue Royale towards the Concorde and beyond. A classic site for society weddings and funerals, the rose marble interior has seen the coffins of Chopin, Josephine Baker and, more recently, Marlene Dietrich.

Open: Monday to Sunday, 07.00–19.00hrs. Closed over lunch at weekends.

A church disguised as a Greek temple: the Madeleine

▶▶▷ Maison de Verre
31 rue St Guillaume, 75007
metro: rue du Bac

A temple to the purity of modernism, this extraordinary house was built between 1928 and 1931 by the art deco architect Pierre Chareau, contemporary of Le Corbusier. Walls of glass bricks with steel frames and an airy geometric interior are the innovations which replaced a 17th-century townhouse. Only one thing remained: a stubborn tenant in her top-floor flat.

Malmaison see pages 202–3.

The exterior of Pierre Chareau's Maison de Verre (1932) is visible from the courtyard, but written applications are necessary to tour inside (31 rue St-Guillaume 75007).

Places of Worship

■ 'Paris is well worth a mass' stated Henri IV before rapidly converting to Catholicism and bringing to an end the bloody Wars of Religion. Since then the Catholic faith has dominated Paris and the main concentration of Protestants lies in the south of France. As a mere visitor to Paris you may think the same as Henri IV and want to witness French church traditions. Or you may want to participate in the ceremonies of another faith. All is possible: Paris contains over a hundred parish churches and many a synagogue, temple or mosque. .....■

Catholic Most churches are open from about 08.00hrs to 19.00hrs and hold morning, midday and evening masses, stepped up on Sundays to at least five throughout the day. For an atmospheric Catholic mass, number one priority is **Notre-Dame**. Despite the hordes of fellow tourists it's hard to find a more inspiring setting (see pages 154–7). **St-Germain-des-Prés**, an ancient Benedictine abbey, makes a similarly historic context, while the nearby church of **St-Sulpice** (see page 174) has the sounds of France's largest organ, as well as murals by Delacroix.

For diehards **Sacré-Coeur** in Montmartre (see page 171) is a monumental basilica and has hourly services every morning, evening mass at 22.15hrs and sung mass at 11.00hrs on Sundays.

St Etienne du Mont's arched rood screen

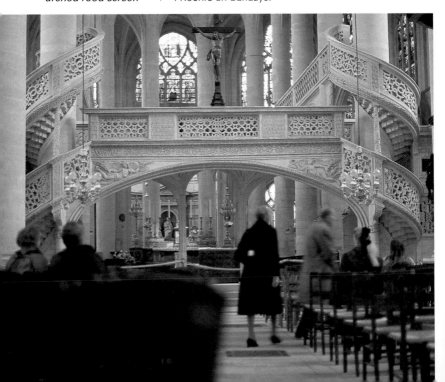

Other options Although slightly off the main tourist beat, a handful of other Parisian churches will supply rare historic settings. Instead of Sacré-Coeur, for example, go round the corner to one of Paris' oldest churches, **St Pierre de Montmartre** which has preserved much of its original 12th-century architecture. In central Paris, near Beaubourg, the **Eglise Saint Merri** is a superb example of Flamboyant Gothic, although it was not actually completed until 1612. A 1331 bell remains from the medieval chapel which previously occupied the site and, if you attend a midday service here, admire the superb 16th-century stained-glass windows and remarkable carved woodwork. The massive 17th-century organ was once played by Saint-Saëns and concerts are still held here (tel: 42 74 42 96 for details).

Another historic organ, one century older and particularly ornamental, remains in the church of **St Etienne du Mont**. The bizarre architectural mixture (Gothic, Renaissance, classical) is due to a long construction period stretching from 1492 to 1626. Don't miss the delicately fretted rood screen, unique in Paris, which forms an arch between the nave and the choir. Both Pascal and Racine were buried here and Ste Geneviève's relics lie in the crypt.

Protestant There is a reasonable though more limited choice of Protestant churches. The neo-gothic **American Church** on the Quai d'Orsay is a classic, particularly for the expatriate American community, which organises all sorts of fund-raising activities. Services are at 11.00hrs on Sundays. Not to be confused with this is the **American Cathedral** in the avenue Georges V, of Anglican leaning, which holds two Sunday morning services, one with a choir at 11.00hrs. Paris' best reputed voices can be heard at **St George's English Church** near the Etoile in their 10.30hrs Sunday service. Presbyterians should make for the **Church of Scotland** in the rue Bayard or the Scots **Kirk Manse** in the rue Thimonnier.

Jewish At the heart of the Jewish quarter around the **rue des Rosiers**, there is a synagogue designed in 1913 by the art nouveau architect Hector Guimard, although its façade is hard to see in the narrow rue Pavée. Further north in the Marais, near another traditionally Jewish area, the Temple, is the synagogue in the **rue Notre Dame de Nazareth** while the ninth *arrondissement*, which bristles with kosher restaurants, has a large religious centre in the rue St Georges and another synagogue, which can be found in the **rue de la Victoire**.

Islamic Despite the large percentage of Muslims in France, their worshipping needs are not the best catered for. The imposing central Mosque's minaret rises over the **rue Geoffroy St Hilaire** opposite the Jardin des Plantes; (Friday prayers at 12.30hrs are reserved for Muslims.

See also **Travel Facts** page 264.

Creatively minded worshippers can head for the Eglise Saint-Roch, which holds a special Sunday midday mass in honour of artists and musicians. Some artists even have studios in the upper reaches of the church, and Corneille's tomb honours all writers. As with many of Paris' central historic churches, concerts are held regularly here.

The winding streets of Le Marais boast what is considered to be the oldest house in Paris (c1300), as well as a lively Jewish quarter dating from the 13th century.

▶ ▶ ▶   Le Marais

Only 15 years ago, the Marais was a dilapidated, neglected corner of central Paris, a far cry from the fashionable quartier it has now become. Its Cinderella-like transformation was mostly due to André Malraux who, in 1962, pointed out the historic value of numerous crumbling monuments, and a restoration programme was embarked upon, soon followed by an invasion of smart boutiques, restaurants and art galleries.

The background Stretching west to east between Les Halles and the Bastille and north to south from the République to the Seine, the heart of the Marais remains immediately west of its lung, the place des Vosges. Before Henri IV commissioned this symmetrical 'place Royale' in 1605, the nearby rue St-Antoine was already a

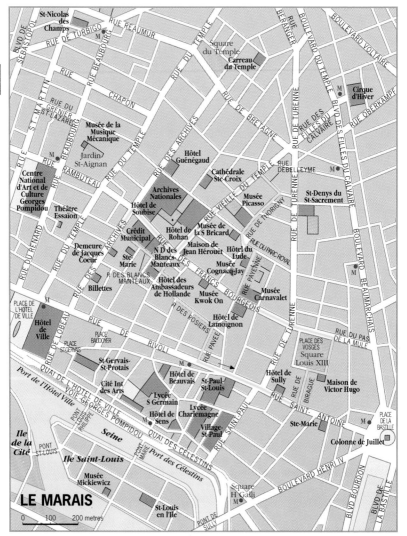

LE MARAIS

popular axis for royal festivities, while for two centuries the northern section had been controlled by the powerful religious and military Ordre des Templiers (Knights Templar) until its brutal suppression in 1313. Even in Roman times this low-lying area was called Le Marais (the marsh).

But it was the 17th and, to a lesser extent, the 18th centuries that propelled the Marais to its zenith, with aristocrats vying to create the most elegant mansion, the most imposing courtyard or the most precious interior. Literary salons, philosophical debates, duels, love affairs, power struggles: the Marais rapidly became a hotbed for the likes of Madame de Sévigné, Voltaire, Molière, Racine and Richelieu. With the Revolution, its aristocratic sun set and its glorious mansions were sold off to merchants and craftsmen.

Masterpieces It's impossible to wander around the Marais without stumbling across architectural masterpieces, even if you can only admire them from their courtyards. Don't miss the following: **Hôtel de Lamoignon**, 24 rue Pavée; **Hôtel de Sully,** 62 rue St-Antoine (see page 178); **Hôtel de Rohan,** 87 rue Vieille du Temple; **Hôtel du Lude**, 13 rue Payenne; **Hôtel de Sens**, 1 rue du Figuier (see page 175); **Hôtel des Ambassadeurs de Hollande**, 47 rue Vieille du Temple; and the **Hôtel Salé,** housing the **Musée Picasso,** the Hôtel Guénégaud and its **Musée de la Chasse,** and the **Hôtel Libéral Bruand,** which houses the **Musée Bricard** (see pages 163, 100 and 87).

Between the restored façades you'll also find plenty of 20th-century temptations, in the form of hundreds of contemporary art galleries, restaurants, bars, clothes and antique shops. Yuppies have moved in with a

Henri IV, founder of the place Royale, missed its inauguration ceremony: he had been assassinated two years earlier.

143

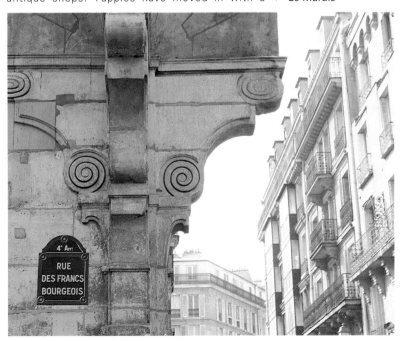

Architectural detail in Le Marais

Taking a break in the graceful place des Vosges

vengeance, yet there's a small **Chinatown** around the rue Chapon, where crowded backroom workshops churn out goods. The wholesale costume jewellery and rag trades still monopolise much of the **rue du Temple** and its side-streets. A unique combination of history, function and trendy chic makes this one of Paris' favourite strolling areas.

Place des Vosges Since 10,000 spectators watched the spectacular celebrations to inaugurate the 'place Royale' in 1612, a string of famous characters has inhabited its mansions and apartments. Princesses, duchesses, official mistresses, Richelieu, Sully, Victor Hugo, Gautier, Daudet, Bossuet and, more recently, the painter Francis Bacon and the architect Richard Rodgers (of Centre Pompidou fame) have all gazed at its perfect symmetry. Thirty-six red brick- and stone-faced houses with arcaded ground floors and steep pitched roofs create the harmonious form of this square, which encloses a garden of fountains, plane-trees and gravel paths. Before the square was built it was the site of a royal palace, the Palais des Tournelles, abandoned and demolished by Catherine de Médicis when her husband Henri II was killed in a tournament here. The north and south façades retained the royal touch, as each has a larger, central house, respectively the queen and the king's pavilion. In 1800 the name 'place Royale' was replaced by 'place des Vosges' in honour of the first French district to pay its new taxes.

Literary echo Although restaurants, chic clothes shops, antique dealers and art galleries now line the place des Vosges, there remains one remnant of the square's literary past in the **Maison de Victor Hugo** at no 6. Between 1832 and 1848 the great French writer penned many a manuscript here (see page 182). Maybe he witnessed one of the many duels which took place on the square, despite Richelieu's ban on them in the 17th century. This argumentative habit continued well into the 19th century although the favourite dawn meeting place was transferred to the Bois de Boulogne.

Walk **A tour of Le Marais**

See map page 142.

Starting from the metro St-Paul, walk east along the rue St-Antoine.
Pass the **church**, built in 1634, and on your left, at no 62, the magnificent **Hôtel de Sully**.

Turn left into the rue de Birague which leads into the spectacular place des Vosges.
Notice that the façades are painted in *trompe l'oeil* to resemble brick. Commissioned by Henri IV, the square was completed in 1612 and became home to luminaries such as Richelieu, Moliére and, at no 6, Victor Hugo, in a house now devoted to his museum. Continue around the square past restaurants, galleries and some eccentric shops, look into the garden entrance of no 28, the discreet hotel **Pavillon de la Reine,** and stop for a drink at no 19, **Ma Bourgogne,** which in summer spreads its tables under the arcades.

Continue to the rue des Francs Bourgeois.
Pass the **Musée Carnavalet**, built in 1540 and later home to the writer Madame de Sévigné.

Turn right along the rue Payenne.
The gardens on the right and courtyards on the left are typical of the 17th-century Marais style.

Follow the rue du Parc Royal to the left and turn right into the rue de Thorigny.
Here you pass the **Hôtel Salé**, built in 1659, now the **Musée Picasso**.

At the end turn left along the rue Debelleyme, past some contemporary art galleries and left again down the rue Vieille du Temple.
Halfway down on your right at no 87, you pass the carved gates of the **Hôtel Rohan** and, on the corner of the rue des Francs Bourgeois, the picturesque 1510 turret of the

A boutique in Le Marais

Maison de Jean Hérouët.

Turn right here, past more elegant mansions and the Crédit Municipal (municipal pawnshop) at no 55 on your left.
On the right is the impressive 1709 courtyard of the **Hôtel de Soubise,** now the national archives.

A short distance down the rue des Archives turn left again into the rue des Blancs-Manteaux, which takes you back to the rue Vieille- du- Temple. Cut across to follow the rue des Rosiers.
This is the central Jewish quarter, full of specialist shops as far as the rue Pavée.

Turn right at the rue Pavée, past the synagogue designed by Guimard, to return to your starting point.

▶▶▶ Marly, Chevaux de

Sculpted by Nicolas and Guillaume Coustou, these two groups of rearing white marble horses were salvaged from the Château de Marly (destroyed during the Revolution) and brought in 1795 to guard the entrance to the Champs Elysées. Sixteen live horses were needed to pull their weighty mass. The originals are now preserved from pollution in the Louvre and copies stand in their place on the corner of the place de la Concorde.

▶▶▶ Marmottan, Musée

2 rue Louis Boilly, 75016
metro: Muette

Located opposite the discreet charm of the Ranelagh gardens, which still boast a hand-cranked merry-go-round, the Musée Marmottan is another of the 16th *arrondissement*'s hidden treasures. Although Paris' main concentration of Impressionist works is at the Musée d'Orsay, the Marmottan follows closely in the quality stakes.

The 19th-century townhouse originally contained a Renaissance and Empire collection bequeathed to the state by the historian Paul Marmottan, later extended by a generous Wildenstein donation of medieval manuscripts and finally by the magnificent Michel Monet donation. Son of the Impressionist Claude Monet, he left a collection essentially composed of 65 of his father's works executed towards the end of his life at Giverny. Thus clouds of irises, wisteria and water-lilies fill much of an underground gallery, backed up with works by Monet's contemporaries such as Renoir, Pissarro, Sisley, Berthe Morisot and Caillebotte. Another

A fine collection of Monet's work is displayed at the Musée Marmottan

donation, made in 1987, extended this remarkable collection to include Gauguin and Corot. Don't miss Monet's seminal painting *Impression – soleil levant*, which gave the movement its name and was also one of a booty of nine paintings stolen from this museum in 1985 and recovered five years later in Corsica.
Open: Tuesday to Sunday, 10.00–17.30hrs.

▶▶▶ Marronniers, Hôtel des
21 rue Jacob, 75006
metro: Mabillon
Nature-lovers should try to stay at this hotel in the heart of St-Germain – its obsessive decorating style is nearly entirely based on vegetation, fruit, birds and flowers, while two superb chestnut trees dominate the garden. Declared a national monument, the oak-beamed rooms, views over St-Germain and superb vaulted cellars (converted into lounges) all combine to create an atmosphere of special charm. Obviously advance booking is essential.

▶▶▶ Meurice, Hôtel
228 rue de Rivoli, 75001
metro: Tuileries
Once a favourite with Spaniards as diverse as King Alphonse XIII and the moustachioed Salvador Dali, who made the Royal Suite his Paris base for 30 odd years, the Meurice still claims a good percentage of the world's rich and famous. Opened in 1816, it was Paris' first 'grand hotel' and immediately saw a string of multinational royalty pass through its period suites and chandeliered reception rooms. During World War II it had the doubtful honour of becoming Nazi headquarters and in August 1944 witnessed the surrender of Von Cholitz to the Allies. Bought by the Italian Ciga hotels group in 1988, it has undergone a few discreet transformations, while retaining its aristocratic, old world atmosphere. Opposite the Tuileries, the Meurice makes an elegant setting for tea or cocktails.

▶▶▶ Monnaie, Hôtel et Musée de la
11 Quai de Conti, 75006
metro: Pont-Neuf
Another of the dignified façades lining the Left Bank of the Seine, La Monnaie was once the national mint, before these activities were transferred to southwest France. This elegant building was designed by Antoine in 1770 (he lived in his creation until his death in 1801), replacing the 17th-century Hôtel de Conti. Today the workshops (*ateliers*) still churn out special commemorative coins and guided tours will explain the techniques (Tuesday and Friday only, 14.15–15.00hrs).
At the front of the Hôtel, a series of lofty salons overlooking the Seine are used for temporary exhibitions; the main museum is situated at the back of the courtyard. Here the history of coins and medals is traced from 300BC to the present. A museum shop opening on to the rue Guénégaud sells a wide selection of items in this field.
Open: Tuesday to Sunday, 13.00–18.00hrs, Wednesday 13.00–21.00hrs.

The rue de Nevers, which runs parallel to the rue Guénégaud off the Quai de Conti, is one of Paris' oldest streets, and hasn't changed its skinny width since the 13th century. Once marking the boundary between a convent and a townhouse, it contains a section of the Philippe-Auguste city wall. The arch over the entrance (constructed at a later date) is engraved with part of Claude le Petit's 17th-century poem satirising the Pont Neuf (directly opposite) and its imminent collapse; the author finished at the stake.

147

MONTMARTRE

Le Moulin Rouge

▶ ▶ ▶ Montmartre

High on its northern hill overlooking Paris, Montmartre was long linked with the artistic community that scraped a living there. Toulouse Lautrec immortalised the can-can kicking Jane Avril, the Moulin Rouge and singer-poet Aristide Bruant, and no doubt frequented the local hot cabaret, *Au Lapin Agile*. Meanwhile, Cubism was born in the draughty Bateau-Lavoir studios, which housed no lesser figures than Picasso, Juan Gris and Braque. Today little is left of this burgeoning creative community: the 'painters' on the place du Tertre can hardly swing a brush and real estate values are high enough to keep any impoverished artist at bay. Yet as you wander through its backstreets you can't help but be affected by the charm of this neighbourhood, perfectly revealed in its romantic tree-lined steps, squares, gardens and individually designed houses.

The Mill The landmark most associated with Montmartre is, of course, **Le Moulin Rouge**, located on the tacky boulevard de Clichy at the bottom of the hill in Pigalle, best known for its sex shops and hustlers. But why a mill? In fact there were once over 30 windmills in Montmartre, which ground silex from the underground gypsum quarries riddling the hill, but by the early 19th century the quarrying and mills were abandoned to save the hill from collapse.

Following closely in the symbol stakes is **Sacré-Coeur,** the white marble wedding-cake basilica crowning the hill. When it was completed in 1910 (it took 35 years to build) its architect was heavily criticised for its Romanesque-Byzantine style, but no one realised how many millions would flood to see it. One good reason for its popularity is the view across Paris: on clear days it stretches a spectacular 30km.

Presenting the past To get a better idea of the history of this area, go to the **Musée de Montmartre** at 12 rue Cortot (*open*: Tuesday to Sunday 14.30–18.00hrs). This 17th-century house and its pretty garden once belonged to a member of Molière's theatre troupe and was later inhabited by Renoir, Utrillo and Dufy. Locally made porcelain, a reconstructed interior of a 19th-century bistro, caricatures of local eccentrics by Daumier, drawings by Toulouse Lautrec...it is an interesting if not extensive collection.

Fruit of the vine Back in the land of the living, don't miss Montmartre's **vineyard** (opposite the historical cabaret) on the rue des Saules. Every October the grapes are harvested and 500 or so bottles of *Clos Montmartre* are filled. Lastly, whichever street you take you can't miss the **place du Tertre**: at least you can truthfully say what a tourist trap it is.

Paris at dusk, from Montmartre

Walk **circuit of Montmartre**

See map page 148.

Start at Abbesses metro station.
This station boasts one of the
original 1900s Guimard entrances.

*Follow the rue des Abbesses, west
till the road branches. Turn right up
the rue Lepic.*
Number 54 is where Van Gogh and
his brother Theo once lived.

*Follow the curve until you see the
Moulin de la Galette on your left.*
The **Moulin de la Galette** was once
a dance hall, frequented by Renoir.

*Turn left and left again into the
avenue Junot.*
At no 13 lived the artist Poulbot,
inventor of the ubiquitous wide-eyed
urchin image. Next door at no 15 is
the Dadaist Tristan Tzara's house,
designed by Adolf Loos.

*Turn right along the rue S Dereure
and on to the Allée des Brouillards.*
The Allée leads to an 18th-century
mansion, once a dance hall and
home to the poet Nerval.

*Follow the raised path beside the
gardens to the rue Girardon, where
you can either turn left down the
steps to visit the Cimetière St
Vincent or go along the rue de
l'Abreuvoir to the rue des Saules.*

The **Maison Rose** restaurant on the
corner was painted by Utrillo and
today provides an ideal terrace for
lunch. Opposite is Montmartre's
vineyard, harvested annually on the
first Saturday in October.

*Follow the rue St Vincent, passing
the famous Au Lapin Agile. At the
rue du Mont Cenis, turn right and
climb the steps.*
En route, pass Berlioz' former
apartment and the pretty **rue Cortot,**
which contains the local museum.

Go straight on to the place du Tertre.
Patachon is a tea-room with a
superb view; walk round the back of
it to the **place du Calvaire.**

*Returning to the entrance to the
place du Tertre, follow the rue Azaïs
to the front of Sacré-Coeur.*
Here you can climb to the top of the
bell tower or take the Montmartre
funiculaire, recently modernised.

*At the bottom go straight on down
the rue de Steinkerque, past a lively
string of shops selling cheap fabrics,
then turn right into the rue d'Orsel.*
On your left you pass the charming
Théâtre de l'Atelier (1822).

Return to the place des Abbesses.

Place des Abbesses metro station

▶▶▶ Montsouris, Parc

metro: Cité Universitaire

Another of the Baron Haussmann's creations, the site of the Parc Montsouris was once peppered with windmills, relics of its granite quarry past. By the turn of the century this pocket of landscaped green had become a favourite hideaway for artists and literati escaping the intellectual overkill in nearby Montparnasse. The Belle Epoque restaurant suitably called Jardin de la Paresse (Garden of Laziness) on the rue Gazan is a superb example of architecture of the period, and claims such illustrious diners as Trotsky, Mata Hari and Sartre. At the top of the hill is a replica of the Tunisian palace of Beys built in 1867 and recently extensively restored.

Open: sunrise to sunset.

▶▶▶ Mosquée, la

place du Puits-de-l'Ermite, 75005

metro: Monge

One of the Left Bank's best surprises, the Paris Mosque was built in 1926 with French funds as thanks for North African military support during World War I. Strongly faithful to ornate Moorish architecture, its roofs are green tiled, fountains pink marbled and doors carved, while the *salon de thé* whisks you to Cairo. The worshipping area can be visited with a guided tour.

Open: Saturday to Thursday, 09.00–12.00hrs, 14.00–18.00hrs.

For a little exoticism, the African section of the Marché Mouffetard, near the rue de l'Arbalète, has a bright array of smoked fish, hand-woven baskets and sandals.

▶▶▶ Mouffetard, Marché

metro: Monge

Thronging with tourists, the Marché Mouffetard is

nevertheless one of Paris' most picturesque central markets. This is the land of gastronomic fantasies, where the products available probably outstrip any mental invention. Go late morning, when shoppers elbow past piles of vegetables and stall-holders' desire to sell is peaking volubly. Stop for a coffee and succulent home-made croissants at the **Café Mouffetard** at no 116 and don't miss the colourful murals at the Italian grocer **Chez Facchetti** (no 134).

Open: Tuesday to Saturday, 08.00–13.00hrs, 16.00–19.00hrs and Sunday morning.

Fruits de mer *at the Marché Mouffetard*

MONTPARNASSE

0   200   400 metres

Notable former residents of the area lie in the Montparnasse cemetery, accessible from the boulevard Edgar Quinet, where you can pay homage to Sartre, de Beauvoir, Baudelaire, Maupassant, Saint-Saëns and, car-lovers' hero, André Citroën.

 Montparnasse

Although its sun set long ago, Montparnasse is so evocative of early 20th-century cultural history that it is hard to miss out. Legendary meeting places still exist, haunted by shadows of literary and artistic gurus of the 1920s and '30s, yet its main boulevards have lost much of their charm, sacrificed to the whims of consumerism.

Tour Montparnasse Symbolic of this transformation, the heart of the area is towered over by the 210m-high **Tour Montparnasse**, an architectural *faux pas* erected in 1973 to crown a vast commercial centre. It does, however, offer unbeatable panoramic views from its 59th floor. Near by, building continues on the **TGV Atlantique** terminus, but the modernised station remains confusing and badly designed. Behind this gigantic structure is a quartier that has undergone 20 years of redevelopment, replacing atmospheric narrow streets with uninspired apartment blocks. Ricardo Bofill's neo-classical designs are perhaps the most interesting.

High points But despair not! Some corners are worth searching out such as no 16 rue Antoine Bourdelle, where you can visit the **Musée Bourdelle**, (open: Tuesday to Sunday, 10.00–17.40hrs); the picturesque garden, house and overflowing studios of this sculptor, student of Rodin, are fascinating. Near by, at 15 rue Falgère, stand the newly built offices of France's most respected daily newspaper, *Le Monde*, while further south is another institutional landmark, the **Institut Pasteur**.

Pursuit of pleasure Back to the east of the Tower, follow the boulevard Edgar Quinet to the **rue de la Gaîté**, Montparnasse's answer to the rue St-Denis. Its traditional pleasure-seeking character survives among the sex shops and a number of small theatres and cabarets; here, too, floats the ghost of the modernist dancer Isadora Duncan, who performed at no 26 and lived at no 4.

Heart of the matter The pulse of Montparnasse remains centred along the stretch between the boulevard Raspail (reigned over by Rodin's statue of Balzac) and the rue du Montparnasse. Between fascinating specialist shops, restaurants, the architecture of the rue Vavin and, finally, Montparnasse's living symbol, **La Coupole**, visitors may at last experience something of the area's past ebullience.

Paris mapped out from the Tour Montparnasse

Cabarets and theatres can be found among the sex shops on the rue de la Gaîté

NOTRE-DAME

1 Entrance to Tower
2 Portail de la Vierge
3 Portail du Jugement Dernier
4 Portail de Sainte-Anne
5 Baptistery
6 Pulpit
7 Portail du Cloître
8 N rose window
9 S rose window
10 Portail de Saint-Etienne
11 Notre-Dame de Paris
12 Saint Denis
13 Choir Stalls
14 High altar
15 Pietà
16 Statue of Louis XIII
17 Statue of Louis XIV
18 Porte Rouge
19 Tomb of Mgr de Beaumont
20 Tomb of Mgr de Juigné
21 St-Louis Chapel
22 Tomb of Mgr de Quélen
23 Tomb of Cardinal du Belloy
24 St-Georges Chapel
25 Tomb of Mge Darboy
26 Mausoleum of Duc d'Harcourt
27 Tomb of Mgr Sibour
28 Tomb of Mgr Affre
29 Treasury
30 Sacristy

▶ ▶ ▶   **Notre-Dame**
metro: Cité
'Each side, each stone of the venerable monument is a
page not only of the history of the country, but also of
the history of science and of art.' Victor Hugo's words –
written in 1831 as part of his voluminous historical novel
Notre Dame de Paris, which introduced the famous
hunchback, Quasimodo – ring as true as the bells of this
twin-towered cathedral. Notre-Dame occupies a site that
goes back to early Roman times, when *Lutetia* was
concentrated on the Ile de la Cité, the heart of the city.
Further proof of Notre-Dame's importance is the fact
that it is used as point-zero for measuring distances
from Paris.
Soon after the Romanesque abbey of St Denis, just
north of Paris, was completed (1144), Bishop Maurice
de Sully decided that Paris needed its own cathedral,
and construction started in 1163 with foundations laid by
Pope Alexander III. The choir was completed in 1182

and the west front and twin towers between 1200 and 1250. It was only in 1345 that the original plans were realised, thus making it an edifice of transition, between the Romanesque and the Gothic.

As a work of the people, Notre-Dame was built by guilds of carpenters, stonecarvers, iron forgers and glass craftsmen who all laboured in the pure medieval spirit of a communal religious effort. For years it remained a meeting place for trade unions as well as a dormitory for the homeless. Its adjoining cathedral school was renowned throughout Europe and eventually gave birth to the Sorbonne.

Unfortunately, the structure of Notre-Dame suffered over the centuries, and by the time Napoleon came to crown himself emperor in 1804 it was in a sorry state of disrepair. Victor Hugo's vehement criticism in 1831 finally goaded the government into action, led by the architects Lassus and Viollet-le-Duc, who enthusiastically set about remedying the damage of centuries.

According to Hugo the culprits were threefold: time; political and religious evolution; and, worst of all, the vagaries of fashion. He was virulent about the absence of countless statues from both the façade and the interior (many toppled during the Revolution), the clear

One of the classic views of Notre-Dame – from the river

155

glass (Louis XV had decided that stained glass was out of date and replaced most rose windows), the replacement of the old Gothic altar with a heavy marble sarcophagus, and the amputation of the spire in 1787 by an architect of 'good taste'. Much of Hugo's ranting was well headed: the Gallery of Kings was reproduced (some of the originals, were excavated in 1977, and are now at the Cluny) and a 90m spire erected, but it was not until after World War II that the stained-glass windows were remade. Viollet-le-Duc also modestly added a statue of himself amongst the Apostles.

The 7,000 or so pipes of the massive 1730 organ make it one of France's largest, fit to inspire the 6,500 music lovers who flock to free recitals held every Sunday at 17.45hrs.

156

West façade Crowned by two 69m towers are three imposing, asymmetrical portals representing (left to right) the Virgin Mary, the Last Judgement and St Anne, Mary's mother. In the Middle Ages when the statues were painted, these served as a Bible for the illiterate, and it is well worth looking closely at each portal.

Apart from the lintels of the central portal, the sculptures of the tympanums and arches are all original. On the left the Coronation of the Virgin dominates the Resurrection and the Assumption, surrounded by kings, angels, prophets and zodiac signs. The middle of the Last Judgement was much tampered with by Soufflot in 1771, and the statue of Christ is 19th century. The sculptures of St Anne on the right date mostly from 1165–75, showing scenes from her life, the childhood of Christ and, in the tympanum, Mary proffering Jesus to a kneeling King Louis VII (who consecrated the church), seen on the right and the founder, Bishop Sully, on the left.

The towers, originally intended to be surmounted by spires, make a strenuous climb (225 steps to the summit of the north tower, and another 125 to the top of the south tower). In the south tower hangs the famous 13-ton bell 'Emmanuel', recast in 1686, evoking memories of a tormented Quasimodo. The fantastic range of gargoyles – grotesque stone figures of demons, birds and weird beasts – are again the work of Viollet-le-Duc, serving to keep evil spirits at bay.

North and south façades These sides present three distinct, receding storeys with bold flying buttresses. Look at the magnificent north porch, the *portail du cloître*, built in 1250 by Jean de Chelles. The statue of the Virgin is original, and the tympanum relates the story of Theophilius, a monk who, after signing a pact with the devil was saved *in extremis* by the Virgin. Immediately to the east is the red door (*porte rouge*), a superb sculpted work by Pierre de Montreuil (1260), Here the tympanum shows the crowning of the Virgin, and the arches episodes from the Crucifixion and Resurrection of Christ.

Regally facing the Left Bank, the south porch is dedicated to St Stephen and was started by Jean de Chelles in 1258. Most of the arch statues are copies, but the tympanum relating the life of the saint and the medallions of student life are all original. The garden at the back of the cathedral was entirely filled with houses and chapels until the 1831 uprising, which destroyed most of this church property.

Notre-Dame

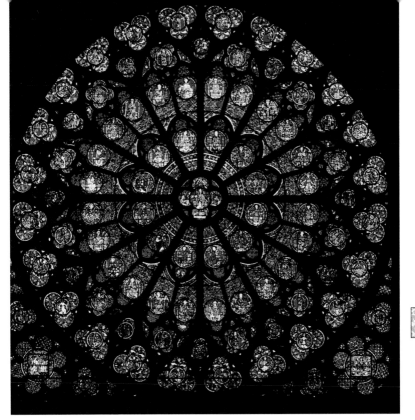

Interior Entering this awesome cathedral, notice the difference in light between the nave, the transept and the chancel – thanks to the gradual cleaning of the interior.

The traditional Gothic layout consists of a nave of 10 bays flanked by double aisles which continue around the choir. The walls are line with 37 chapels altogether, added during the 13th and 14th centuries. Amongst the traditional annual offerings by the goldsmiths' guild are those adorning the first two chapels to the right, by Le Brun, and in the transept, by Le Sueur.

At the crossing of the transept you can admire the three rose windows, to the north depicting Old Testament figures surrounding Mary (almost totally original glass) and, to the south, Christ in a crowd of angels and saints. The choir, much altered under Louis XIV, also atttracted Viollet-le-Duc's untiring attention: over half the original stalls remain, as well as some bronze angels (1711). Numerous tombs of bishops lie below the choir and around the ambulatory. The sacristy, on the south side of the choir, houses the treasure of Notre Dame (*open:* 10.00–18.00hrs, Sundays 14,00–18.00hrs), which consists of medieval manuscripts, ecclesiastical plate and reliquaries. The famous crown of thorns and piece of the True Cross are brought out on Good Friday.

Big ceremonial moments are, of course, at Easter and on Christmas Eve, but the cathedral, this 'vast symphony in stone', radiates an extraordinary power at any time.

The southern Rose Window, depicting Christ surrounded by saints and angels

A 3,300-year-old needle: the Obelisk, in the place de la Concorde

▶▶▶ **Obelisk**

place de la Concorde, 75001
metro: Concorde

Like Cleopatra's Needle in London, the Obelisk is the city's oldest monument – about 3,300 years old. For once it is not a result of colonial grabbing, as it was actually donated in 1831 to King Louis-Philippe by Mohammed Ali Pasha, Viceroy of Egypt. The place de la Concorde has been a central symbol since the removal of Louis XV's equestrian statue during the Revolution, and the 230-tonne pink granite Obelisk, after a lengthy journey from Luxor, ended the ongoing polemics.

▶▶▶ **Olympia**

28 boulevard des Capucines, 75009
metro: Opéra

Still a favourite venue for solo performers of variety, old-time pop or sometimes jazz since the days of Piaf, Aznavour, Charles Trenet and Yves Montand, the Olympia possesses that rare quality in an old concert hall – comfort. Check out its varied programme.

▶▶▶ **Opéra Bastille**

120 rue de Lyon, 75012
metro: Bastille

This prestigious architectural operation, instigated by President Mitterrand, was a case of 'watch the controversy grow'. From day one, when a design by an unknown and relatively inexperienced architect (Carlos Ott) was inadvertently selected, all hell broke loose. Heavily criticised for its ungainly volume and exorbitant cost, the Opéra Bastille finally overcame most teething problems (including last-minute changes in musical director) and by 1990 creaked into operatic action. Technically sophisticated and highly flexible, with about 3,000 seats in the main auditorium and a smaller downstairs hall, it is still proving its worth.

▶▶▶ **Opéra Comique**

5 rue Favart, 75002
metro: Richelieu-Drouot

This strangely oriented theatre is tucked down a side street with its back firmly turned to the boulevard des Italiens. Originally built in 1780 (and rebuilt since after several major fires) to house the Comédie-Italienne, it was constructed in this way to distinguish it from the numerous 'popular' theatres springing up along the boulevard. Often called the Salle Favart, the Opéra Comique long specialised in Italian opera and operetta and recently extended to classical music concerts and, occasionally, ballet.

▶▶▶ **Opéra de Paris**

8 rue Scribe, 75009 Paris
metro: Opéra

The sumptuous and prestigious Opéra Garnier was inaugurated in 1875, 15 years after the 35-year-old Charles Garnier's riotous design had been officially accepted. A fittingly lavish epitaph to the manic architectural activities of the Second Empire, it was once the largest theatre in the world (11,000sq m).

Since the opening of the Opéra Bastille, the Opéra Garnier has become exclusively devoted to ballet. Although the quality of the Ballet de l'Opéra de Paris is internationally renowned, its repertoire tends to remain on the traditional side of contemporary dance. Previously directed by the fiery Rudolf Nureyev, who disappeared in 1990 in a cloud of controversy, the company is now enthusiastically run by the youthful *danseur étoile* Patrick Dupond.

Even if you don't see a performance here, make sure you look at Garnier's breathtaking marble and gilt Grand staircase and the equally baroque Grand Foyer. Outside, keep an eye open for Carrier-Belleuse's provocative lamp-bearing statue and the copy of Carpeaux's sculpted group *La Danse* to the right of the front arcade: the original is now at the Musée d'Orsay.

▶ ▶ ▶ L'Orangerie

place de la Concorde, 75001
metro: Concorde

Echoing the Second Empire architecture of the Jeu de Paume, its Tuileries twin, the Orangerie was originally the greenhouse for the Tuileries Palace, before becoming an exhibition centre in the early 20th century. Home to the extensive Walter-Guillaume collection, which ranges from the Impressionists to the 1920s (Cézanne, Renoir, Sisley, Rousseau, Derain, Matisse, Soutine, Modigliani, Picasso, Van Dongen) it offers a pleasant, uncrowded art tour. Although airily displayed, the 144 works are patchy in quality and do not always represent the best of these masters. However, the high point is Monet's eight gigantic panels of *Water Lilies*, painted for the Orangerie's two oval basement rooms, which were presented to the museum in 1927, a year after his death. Go to Giverny to see his original inspiration, but make sure you see these glorious reflections and the depth of their multiple tones.
Open: Wednesday to Monday, 09.45–17.15hrs.

The Opéra de Paris' immense stage can accommodate 450 performers, watched by 2,200 spectators under a domed ceiling painted by Chagall (1964).

L'Orangerie

MUSEE D'ORSAY

GROUND FLOOR

UPPER LEVEL

MIDDLE LEVEL

▓	Painting
░	Sculpture
░	Architecture
☐	Decorative Arts

▓	Art Nouveau
▓	Photo and Cinema
▓	Special Exhibitions

A Main Entrance
B Bookshop
C Impressionism before 1870
D Realism and the Barbizon School
E Symbolism before 1870
F Academism, Romanticism and
  Classicism 1848-1870
G Sculpture 1848-1870
H Salle de l'Opéra
I Architecture and Town Planning
  1850-1900
J Decorative Arts 1850-1880

K Galerie des Hauteurs-
  Impressionism after 1870
L Les Salles d'Angles-
  Neo-impressionism and
  Pastels
M Galerie Bellechasse-
  Pont-Aven school and
  the Nabis
N Café des Hau

O Painting and Sculpture
  of the Third Republic
P Symbolism and Naturalism
  1870-1914
Q Early 20th century painting
R Sculpture 1870-1914
S Art Nouveau in France
  and Belgium
T International Art Nouveau
U Restaurant

▶▶▶ Musée d'Orsay

1 rue de Bellechasse, 75007

metro: Solférino

Yet another example of Parisian metamorphosis, this building was originally a palace and subsequently a hotel and railway station. Now it is a rewarding, accessible museum of the fine and applied arts, 1848–1914.

Ground floor: to the right of a central sculpture passage are paintings by Ingres, Gérôme, Delacroix and the academics of the period. Symbolism is represented by Puvis de Chavannes, and Gustave Moreau, along with early works by Degas. The galleries on the other side present the pre-1870 teething days of Impressionism in Manet's superb *Olympia, Le Balcon* and *Déjeuner sur l'Herbe*, Bazille, Renoir, Fantin Latour, Whistler's *La Mère* and several seminal works by Monet. Towards the front of this floor are grouped realist works.

Top floor: to follow the collection chronologically go straight to the top floor using the front escalators. Here you move into the Ecole de Pont-Aven (Gauguin, Emile Bernard, Sérusier), the Nabis (Maurice Denis, Bonnard, Vuillard, Vallotton), the mysterious world evoked in Odilon Redon's pastels, Toulouse-Lautrec's, Henri Rousseau, and finally Seurat. Then starts the heart of the Impressionist collection, devoted to Cézanne, Van Gogh, Monet, Renoir, Degas, Sisley and Pissarro.

Middle level: overlooking the entrance below, the middle level concentrates on the sculpture and painting of the late 19th century until 1914. In the superbly renovated ballroom are paintings by Bouguereau, *La naissance de Vénus* and Gérôme's *Tanagra* alongside monumental sculptures. Through naturalism (Dalou, Cormon) discover more symbolist works with foreign parallels such as Burne-Jones and Böcklin. Most striking here are Rodin's sculptures (the powerful *Balzac,* busts, *The Thinker)* and his followers Camille Claudel, Rosso, Bourdelle, Bernard and the familiar rounded forms of Maillol. In the galleries to the right are the beginnings of modernism with the Fauves (Derain, Braque, Van Dongen) and Bonnard, Matisse and Rousseau. This floor also displays some superb applied arts, concentrating on art nouveau furniture and objects.

Open: Tuesday to Sunday, 10.00–18.00hrs (Thursday till 21.45hrs).

The original hotel and railway station comprising what is now the Musée d'Orsay were erected in an astonishing two years to be completed for the Exposition Universelle in 1900. Victor Laloux was the architect responsible for its soaring glass and iron roof, together with a wildly ornate Belle Epoque restaurant and ballroom, all still intact.

The striking Café des Hauteurs, on the top floor of the Musée d'Orsay, has an unusual view across Paris through the face of the enormous station clock.

Space and style in the Musée d'Orsay

The Panthéon was Louis XV's way of thanking Ste Geneviève, patron saint of Paris, for his recovery from gout.

The interior of the Panthéon's soaring dome was used in 1849 by the scientist Foucault to prove, with a pendulum, the rotative movement of the earth.

▶ ▷ ▷ Panthéon

place du Panthéon, 75005
metro: Cardinal-Lemoine

Necropolis for the atheist citizens of France, the Panthéon shelters luminaries such as Voltaire, Rousseau, Victor Hugo, Zola, Louis Braille (inventor of braille), Jean Jaurès and the Resistance martyr Jean Moulin, as well as a shrine containing the heart of left-wing hero Gambetta. Originally commissioned by Louis XV in 1744, the Panthéon was only completed at the Revolution.

By this time its architect, Soufflot, had died and his neo-classical edifice, based on the form of a Greek cross, was subsequently finished by one of his students. In 1791 its windows were bricked up and its function changed from that of church to Temple of Fame. In 1885 it again changed to become the lay temple it remains today.

The austerity of this monument is slightly alleviated by late 19th-century paintings, the most famous being those by the Symbolist Puvis de Chavannes, depicting the life of Ste Geneviève.

▶ ▶ ▷ Pavillon de l'Arsenal

21 boulevard Morland, 75004
metro: Sully-Morland

Inaugurated in 1988 as a window on the city's architectural evolution, the Pavillon de l'Arsenal is proof of Paris' growing awareness of its museum-like role. A permanent exhibition on the ground floor, *Paris, la ville et ses projets*, retraces through drawings and photographs the historic projects which have etched the face of the city. These are arranged around a spectacular 50sq m laser-activated scale model. Temporary exhibitions on the upper mezzanines of this luminous, sky-lit building cover architectural projects and competitions, often in an international context. All in all it is well worth a detour.

Open: Tuesday to Saturday, 10.30–18.30hrs, Sunday 11.00–19.00hrs.

▶ ▶ ▷ Père Lachaise

boulevard de Ménilmontant, 75020
metro: Gambetta, Père Lachaise

The strange fascination of this vast cemetery stems partly from its illustrious incumbents and partly from the fantastic variety of tomb designs. Laid out in 1803 on the slopes of a hill in Ménilmontant to echo a peaceful English-style garden, the cemetery is full of twisting paths, unexpected views, swaying trees and, above all, some ornate sculpture, altogether making it far from lugubrious.

Pay homage at the Mur des Fédérés to the 147 last defenders of the 1870 Commune, who were gunned down here and buried in a common grave, or to any number of political or cultural figures. An essential investment is the plan sold at both entrances, which will lead you to the tombs of Abelard and Héloise, Chopin, Haussmann, Modigliani, Edith Piaf, Proust, Delacroix, Oscar Wilde, Alice B Toklas and Jim Morrison.

Open: daily, 08.00–17.30hrs.

Petit Palais

avenue Winston-Churchill, 75008
metro: Champs-Elysées-Clémenceau
When you tire of the aggressive sights of the Champs Elysées, this is where to take refuge. Rarely crowded, unless a popular exhibition is on, the museum offers an exceptional patchwork collection of mainly 19th-century French works: Delacroix, Ingres, Courbet, Carpeaux, the Impressionists and Post-Impressionists. Examples of the Dutch school and two private donations complete this eclecticism.
Open: Tuesday to Sunday, 10.00–17.40hrs.

 Photographie, Centre National de la

13 avenue du Président Wilson 75016
metro: Iéna
Symmetrical to the Musée d'Art Moderne, the lofty rooms of this former museum now present temporary exhibitions of photography, historical and contemporary, usually comprehensive and of a high quality. Extensive renovation currently under way will lead to the centre's gradual mutation into the Palais de l'Image et du Son, thus centralising under one generous roof a number of audio-visual organisations. An auditorium is already used for film projections, so it may be worth checking their programme.
Open: Wednesday to Sunday, 09.45–17.00hrs.

Like its twin, the Grand Palais, the Petit Palais' glass and iron domed building was constructed for the 1900 Universal Exhibition, not as a permanent fixture.

Nineteenth-century works are displayed in the Petit Palais

GAZETTEER A-Z

The Jardin des Plantes was set up in the 17th century to cultivate medicinal plants for Louis XIII.

When set up in 1795 the 'people's democratic zoo' displayed survivors from the royal menagerie at Versailles. Although popular throughout the 19th century, with exotic animals donated from far afield, it was obvious prey for hungry citizens in the 1870-1 Prussian siege. For months, better connected Parisians regaled themselves with the equivalent of *éléphant bourguignon* or *blanquette de girafe*.

Buste d'une femme (1931), part of the excellent collection housed in the Musée Picasso

▶▶▶   Picasso, Musée

Hôtel Salé, 5 rue de Thorigny, 75003
metro: Chemin-Vert, St Paul

The grand opening of this museum in 1985 signalled the end of 11 years of legal wrangling over Picasso's potentially astronomical death duties. The difficulty for the French government lay in establishing just how much work he had hoarded away: he had an annoying habit of shutting one château and moving on to the next when it was full. Finally, one quarter of his collection was accepted from his heirs in lieu of death duties. Thus this superb, expensively renovated 17th-century mansion with fixtures designed by Diego Giacometti contains over 200 paintings, 158 sculptures, 1,500 drawings and numerous other creations, as well as 60 or so works by mentors and contemporaries such as Cézanne, Miro, Braque, Matisse.

A must for anyone remotely interested in 20th-century art, it is arranged chronologically, taking the visitor from Picasso's youthful turn-of-the-century Classicism through years of Cubist experiments with Braque to the high points of the 1930s and beyond. The many women in his life figure strongly – including Dora Maar, Françoise Gilot, and Jacqueline, who survived him but eventually committed suicide. But above all the collection gives a strong sense of the freshness and inventiveness which permeated every medium he touched – and they were many – throughout his long and creative life.

Open: Wednesday to Monday, 09.15–17.15hrs (Wednesday till 22.00hrs).

▶▶▶   Pigalle

metro: Pigalle

The mere name sets many a bell ringing. Renowned quartier of the low-life since the last century, when local painters Renoir and Toulouse Lautrec would scout around the place Pigalle looking for models among the dancers, it now flourishes in a blatant sex trade. Lining the boulevard Rochechouart and surrounding streets are sleazy bars, sex shops, peep shows, 'live sex' and far more. Pimps, hookers, transvestites all ply their trade here and rows of tourist buses ensure the right balance of payments. But don't be put off by the sleaze, as the area also has some of the hippest night-clubs and bars in town, frequented by respectable trendies who enjoy the early hour downhill crawl home (see pages 230–3).

▶▶▶   Plantes, Jardin des

metros: Gare d'Austerlitz, Jussieu, Monge

This spacious garden, which runs down to the Seine from the Montagne Ste-Geneviève, is composed of a mosaic of carefully tended horticultural experiments. Presiding over this botanical paradise is the gigantic **Muséum d'Histoire Naturelle** (*open*: Wednesday to Monday, 10.00–17.00hrs) and some ageing tropical greenhouses.

On the Jussieu side, France's oldest public zoo still survives, although conditions are unfortunately rather pathetic.

Open: daily, 07.30hrs–sunset.

The Ateliers

■ **Few other cities in the world have embraced the visual arts in the same way as Paris. The countless artists attracted to the city have left an unusual heritage of custom-built artists' studios and new ones are still being built. Although one of the most famous, Le Bateau Lavoir, went up in smoke, many other historic *ateliers* remain, peaceful islands in a city increasingly prone to gentrification and less and less accessible to 'bohemians'. .....■**

Even before the Revolution artists were pandered to and some were given studios in the Louvre Palace; ironically they were booted out so that the museum could be installed. The 19th century saw a rapid increase in the artist population and many of Haussmann's boulevards in Montparnasse, Montmartre and around Monceau incorporate studios, their high windows north-facing to benefit from the unchanging light.

Creation to conservation Some of the more bourgeois artists' studios have since become museums: the **Musée Henner** (43 avenue de Villiers, 17th); the **Musée Gustave Moreau** (14 rue de La Rochefoucauld, 9th); the **Musée Delacroix** (see page 112); **Musée Bourdelle** (see page 152); and the **Musée Bouchard** (25 rue de l'Yvette, 16th). Meanwhile the likes of Rousseau, Degas and Van Gogh moved from one miserable garret to the next, proof that creation is not dependent on comfort.

Working studios Most of the community studio complexes which flourished at the turn of the century are still inhabited, so if visiting them be discreet. Most famous is **La Rûche**, in the Passage Dantzig, south of Montparnasse, where Soutine, Chagall, Léger and Diego Rivera gathered in the 1920s, heating themselves with vodka and using a communal water-pump in the garden. Conditions were rough, but from this emerged *l'Ecole de Paris*. Equally verdant, the **Cité Fleurie** in the boulevard Arago is the queen of

studio communities and recently only just escaped redevelopment.

<< Celebrated paintings of the atelier include *Hommage à Manet* (Fantin-Latour, 1869), showing many of the artist's contemporaries, and *Atelier du peinture* (Courbet, 1858). >>

Survivors At no 31 rue Campagne Première in Montparnasse stands an exceptional block of *ateliers* built in 1911, while further south around the Parc Montsouris, the creative hub of the 1920s survives in the **Villa Seurat**, adjoining rue Gauguet and rue Braque. Here struggled no lesser figures than Salvador Dali, De Staël, Le Corbusier, Braque, Derain, Foujita and, recording it all for posterity, Henry Miller.

The Musée Delacroix is a former atelier in the place Furstemberg

GAZETTEER A-Z

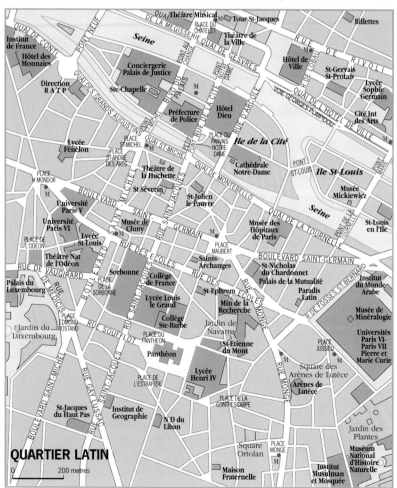

▶▶▷ **Quartier Latin**

For centuries Paris' intellectual heart, the Latin Quarter, still thrives on its literary and artistic reputation. As you wander past Roman ruins (above all the Cluny) along its boulevards and side-streets, you will experience a distinctly relaxed and youthful atmosphere compared with the Right Bank's frenetic, business-oriented pace. Here, the cliché of artists and students lingering for hours in cafés is actually true. No other area of Paris claims so many bookshops or schools, while historic churches, cinemas, jazz-clubs and narrow streets peppered with a cosmopolitan range of restaurants prevent any terminal tedium.

The university The founding of the university in 1253 (the Sorbonne) led to an animated influx of European students and professors; labelled 'Latin' because students all spoke Latin, even outside classes, the area formed a Papal city within a city right up until the Revolution. In the 15th century its intellectual life was

QUAI/Théâtre Musical

Tour St-Jacques

Billettes

QUAI DE LA MEGISSERIE

PLACE DU CHÂTELET

Théâtre de la Ville

RUE DE LIBAN

RUE DE RIVOLI

Seine

QUAI DE LA CONTI

Institut de France

Hôtel des Monnaies

PONT NEUF

Conciergerie
Palais de Justice

QUAI AU CHANGE

QUAI DE GESVRES

Hôtel de Ville

St-Gervais
St-Protais

VOIE GEORGES POMPIDOU

Lycée
Sophie
Germain

QUAI DE L'HÔTEL DE VILLE

Direction
RATP

QUAI DES GRANDS AUGUSTINS

BD DU PALAIS

PONT NOTRE-DAME

RUE D'ARCOLE

Ste-Chapelle

Préfecture
de Police

PETIT PONT

RUE DE LA CITÉ

Hôtel
Dieu

Cité Int
des Arts

Lycée
Fénélon

PLACE
ST-MICHEL

BD ST-MICHEL

QUAI ST-MICHEL

PLACE DU PARVIS NOTRE-DAME

Île de la Cité

PONT ST-LOUIS

Île St-Louis

PLACE
ST-ANDRÉ
DES ARTS

Cathédrale
Notre-Dame

QUAI DE MONTEBELLO

PLACE
H MONDOR

Théâtre de
la Huchette

BOULEVARD SAINT-MICHEL

St-Séverin

St-Julien
le Pauvre

Musée
Mickiewicz

Seine

St-Louis
en l'Île

PONT DE LA TOURNELLE

Université
Paris V

Université
Paris VI

PLACE DE
L'ODÉON

Lycée
St-Louis

Musée de
Cluny

RUE SAINT-JACQUES

SAINT-GERMAIN

RUE DES ÉCOLES

PLACE
MAUBERT

Musée des
Hôpitaux
de Paris

QUAI DE LA TOURNELLE

Théâtre Nat
de l'Odéon

RUE DE VAUGIRARD

Palais du
Luxembourg

RUE DE MÉDICIS

Sorbonne

PLACE DE
LA SORBONNE

Collège
de France

Lycée Louis
le Grand

RUE DES
ÉCOLES

RUE DE FOSSES ST-BERNARD

Saints-
Archanges

St-Nicholas
du Chardonnet

BOULEVARD SAINT-GERMAIN

Institut
du Monde
Arabe

St-Ephrem

Palais de la Mutualité

Paradis
Latin

Min de la
Recherche

Musée de
Minéralogie

PLACE
EDMOND
ROSTAND

RUE SOUFFLOT

Collège
Ste-Barbe

Jardin de
Navarre

Jardin du
Luxembourg

PLACE DU
PANTHÉON

St-Étienne
du Mont

RUE MONGE

PLACE
JUSSIEU

Universités
Paris VI-
Paris VII
Pierre et
Marie Curie

Panthéon

Lycée
Henri IV

Square des
Arènes de Lutèce

Arènes de
Lutèce

PLACE DE
L'ESTRAPADE

BOULEVARD SAINT-MICHEL

RUE GAY-LUSSAC

RUE SAINT-JACQUES

St-Jacques
du Haut Pas

Institut de
Geographie

N D du
Liban

PLACE DE LA
CONTRESCARPE

Jardin des
Plantes

QUARTIER LATIN

0 ___ 200 metres

Square
Ortolan

PLACE
MONGE

Maison
Fraternelle

Institut
Musulman
et Mosquée

Muséum
National
d'Histoire
Naturelle

further extended by the proliferation of printing presses, which soon made the rue St-Jacques France's publishing headquarters.

Wild reputation However, the area fast acquired a reputation for its undisciplined and bohemian inhabitants, making it fertile soil for the Revolution. Nearly 200 years later, the same characteristics of the Latin Quarter again hit the headlines in May 1968, when the students took to the streets, raised barricades and gave the riot police hell. Demands for university reforms combined with a general refusal of consumer society values with such vehemence that the government was brought down and De Gaulle forced to resign.

Out with the old Unfortunately, much of the authentic Latin Quarter has disappeared behind the interchangeable façades and interiors of Greek restaurants, which have a particularly high profile between the **rue de la Huchette** and the **rue de la Harpe**. This is tourist land *par excellence*, although highlights such as the neighbouring **Square René Viviani** with **St Julien le Pauvre** and **St Sévérin**, are not far. Keep heading east into the side streets off the quais and you'll discover a wonderland of small specialist shops along streets reeking pleasantly of the Middle Ages, as well as President Mitterrand's firmly guarded private home in the **rue de Bièvre**. Further south, off the rue des Ecoles and within spitting distance of the **Sorbonne** and the **Collège de France**, you can plunge into the heart of academia and probably find a café once frequented by Latin Quarter intelligentsia such as Verlaine, Sartre or Camus.

In the Latin Quarter people really do discuss life and the universe in cafés and brasseries

Map of the Latin Quarter showing: CARREFOUR DE BUCI, RUE ST-ANDRE DES ARTS, RUE DE L'ANCIENNE COMEDIE, Cour de Rohan, Lycée Fénelon, PLACE ST-ANDRE DES ARTS, QUAI DES GRANDS AUGUSTINS, PONT ST-MICHEL, Pref de Police, QUAI DU MARCHE NEUF, PONT NEUF, PLACE DU PARVIS N D, Ile de la Cité, BOULEVARD, Café Procope, PLACE H MONDOR, Statue du Danton, CARREFOUR DE L'ODEON, SAINT-GERMAIN, PLACE ST-MICHEL, QUAI ST-MICHEL, RUE DE LA HUCHETTE, Théâtre de la Huchette, Square René Viviani, Cathédrale Notre-Dame, Seine, MONTEBELLO, St-Séverin, St Julien le Pauvre, RUE DE LA HARPE, RUE DE LA PARCHEMINERIE, Université René Descartes-Paris V, RUE DE L'ECOLE DE MEDECINE, BOULEVARD SAINT-MICHEL, BOULEVARD SAINT-GERMAIN, RUE DANTE, RUE DE LA GRANGE, RUE DE BIEVRE, Université Paris VI, Musée de Cluny, RACINE, RUE DE L'ODEON, RUE DE CONDE, RUE M LE PRINCE, RUE A DUBOIS, PLACE DE L'ODEON, Palais du Luxembourg, Théâtre National, Lycée St-Louis, Sorbonne, RUE DES ECOLES, RUE ST-JACQUES, Ecole Speciale des Travaux Publics, Saints-Archanges, Collège de France, Musée de la Pref de Police, PLACE MAUBERT, St Nicholas de Chardonnet, RUE MONGE, PLACE PAUL CLAUDEL, 100, 200 m

Walk Tracing the Latin Quarter's streets

Start at the place St-Michel and turn down the rue de la Huchette. Cross the rue St-Jacques and continue straight on to the square René Viviani.
Honoured by an acacia tree reputed to be the oldest in Paris, this square is the setting for the partly Gothic church of St Julien le Pauvre.

Circle back to the rue St-Jacques, passing St-Sévérin. Cut through the narrow rue de la Parcheminerie to reach the medieval rue de la Harpe, which, to the left, leads to the boulevard St-Germain. Walk up the boulevard Saint-Michel to the rue de

l'Ecole de Médecine on your right. The radical Marat was stabbed in his bath by Charlotte Corday in this street.

Turn left up the rue André Dubois to reach the rue Monsieur le Prince. The rue **Monsieur le Prince** closely follows Philippe-Auguste's city wall; sections are embedded in nos 41 to 47. Today it is packed with cheap restaurants, including the historic Polidor at no 41.

Go uphill and turn into the rue Racine leading to the place Paul Claudel. The 18th century **Théâtre National de l'Odéon** dominates this area.

Meander down the rue de l'Odéon to reach Odéon metro. Across the boulevard St-Germain is the rue de l'Ancienne Comédie. Pass Paris' oldest café, **Le Procope**, now a restaurant, on your right before you reach the Buci crossroads.
At the crossroads turn sharp right into the rue St André des Arts, This street is thick with pizzerias, buskers and cafés.

This leads you back to St-Michel.

The square René Viviani

▷▷▷ Raynouard, rue

This long street running parallel to the Seine takes you through the residential heart of Passy towards Auteuil. Apart from Balzac, who lived at no 47 (see page 71), other illustrious inhabitants included the philosopher Jean-Jacques Rousseau, the poet Béranger and Benjamin Franklin. Numbers 51 to 55 are the work of architect brothers Auguste and Gustave Perret who, after Le Corbusier had broken with their 'classical' conceptions, built this block for their agency and apartments (1929) before turning to the astonishing Musée des Travaux Publics, place d'Iéna.

▶▷▷ Rivoli, rue de

It's easy to forget that Rivoli is an Italian town, scene of an almighty Napoleonic thrashing of the Austrians in 1797. In homage to this victory the long, colonnaded street was designed by the Emperor's official architects, Percier and Fontaine in 1811, but only completed in 1835. Today its gracious arcades shelter rows of tacky tourist shops interspersed with one or two smarter joints such as the **Hôtel Meurice**, the *salon de thé* **Angélina** and the bookshop **Galignani** (next door to each other). On its south side are the **Tuileries gardens**,

The first lightning conductor ever seen in France was erected by Benjamin Franklin on the roof of his house in rue Raynouard.

Elegant apartments in the heart of Passy

the **Musée des Arts de la Mode**, the **Musée des Arts Décoratifs** and, finally, the **Louvre**.

▶▶▷ Rohan, Hôtel de

87 rue Vieille du Temple, 75003
metro: Chemin Vert

Yet another Marais mansion enlisted to house the extensive Archives Nationales, the Hôtel de Rohan can only be seen during temporary exhibitions. Designed by Delamair in 1704 for the son of the Prince of Soubise, whose neighbouring Hôtel (see page 126) was built at the same time, it was inhabited by a string of fast-living cardinals. Their apartments are examples of the ornate yet delicate mid-18th-century style.

▶▶▶ Rodin, Musée

Hôtel Biron, 77 rue de Varenne, 75007
metro: Varenne

Even if not invited to the Elysée Palace or the Hôtel

Jo Goldenberg's, the most famous delicatessen and restaurant on the rue des Rosiers, was the tragic scene in 1982 of a terrorist attack, when gunmen killed six customers.

Musée Rodin

Matignon, at least you can experience the pleasures of Paris' third largest private garden, which surrounds the Hôtel Biron. Originally built for a prosperous wig maker in 1730, the harmonious mansion of columns and pediments was bought in 1753 by a dedicated horticulturalist, the maréchal de Biron, who proceeded to indulge his gardening passion until dragged off to the guillotine.

Changing faces Subsequently a dance hall, convent and school, the Hôtel Biron was in 1908 yet again transformed, this time into artists' studios. In moved the redoubtable Rodin, who stayed until his death in 1917, paying his rent with works. His fellow inmates included Rainer Maria Rilke (working as Rodin's secretary), Isadora Duncan, Cocteau and Matisse. On Rodin's death the house became the Musée Rodin.

The gardens The blissful rose gardens are one of Paris' greatest hidden treasures, containing several of Rodin's most important pieces: *Le Penseur*, permanently meditating, *la Porte de l'Enfer*, and *les Bourgeois de Calais* eternally dragging their chains. A former chapel housing temporary sculpture exhibitions and an outdoor café, open during the summer months, complete its attractions.

The house Inside the elegant, airy house you can follow Rodin's evolution chronologically, from his early academic sketches and paintings to his vigorous water colours. His lyrical power and technical breadth are as apparent in the passionate white marble *Kiss*, the nude *John the Baptist*, the spiritual *Main de Dieu* or *Eve* and *L'Age d'Airan*, each of which is displayed in the rotundas. Busts of contemporaries such as Puvis de Chavannes, Mahler, Carrier-Belleuse, Lady Sackville-West or the suffragette Eve Fairfax reveal his penetrating approach to humanity, particularly evident in his paunchy nude studies of Balzac on the first floor. Works by contemporaries include his tragic model, muse and mistress, Camille Claudel, Eugène Carrière, Munch, Renoir, Monet and Van Gogh.
Open: Tuesday to Sunday 10.00–17.45hrs (to 17.00hrs in winter).

▶ ▶ ▶ Rosiers, rue des
This ancient street runs the length of Philippe-Auguste's famous city wall and some remnants remain, hidden behind recent façades. It was already known in 1230 under its present name, probably thanks to numerous rose gardens, but today street odours tend more towards Middle-Eastern falafel. Heart of the Jewish quarter, the street houses a noisy, animated community with numerous take-away Mediterranean specialities and Jewish shops.

▶ ▶ ▶ Royal, Palais
metro: Palais Royal
From heaven to hell, the Palais Royal has run the full gamut of social status. Designed by Lemercier for the wily Cardinal Richelieu, who died there in 1642, the

palace became royal when the Regent Anne of Austria moved in with her young son Louis XIV. His horizons being wider, Louis XIV eventually settled into the more spacious Versailles, leaving the Palais Royal to his brother, Philippe d'Orléans, who turned it into a lively meeting place for the wits and fashion victims of the day. The houses and galleries surrounding the gardens were added in the 1780s and soon sheltered gambling dens, cafés and brothels; one visitor described it as possessing 'every kind of luxury, dirt and magnificence imaginable.' Since the police were banned, its cafés became a fermenting ground for revolutionary ideas.

Current occupation Today the magnificent palace buildings are occupied by the Ministry of Culture and the Conseil d'Etat, while the shops display a bizarre mixture, from stamps and medals to contemporary design, antique porcelain and books. The garden remains resolutely formal and its restaurants, *salons de thé* and benches are notorious summer crowd-pullers. A recent landmark is Buren's columns, which, in their black and white striped splendour, with underground waterways and nocturnal airport lighting, invaded the courtyard.

▶ ▶ ▶ Royale, rue
metro: Madeleine, Concorde
Haunt of luxury goods-hunters, the 18th-century rue Royale joins the Concorde to the Madeleine. Its most famous establishment must be **Maxim's**, at no 3, where high society flocked during the Belle Epoque, while at no 21 once stood the famous literary café, the **Café Weber.**

▶ ▶ ▶ Sacré-Coeur
metros: Abbesses, Anvers
It is often forgotten but the Sacré-Coeur was commissioned as atonement for the 58,000 dead of the 1870/71 Franco-Prussian war. Even today priests work in relays to keep the prayers going 24 hours a day. This extraordinary neo-Romanesque-Byzantine edifice has a strong tourist pull, mainly for its hill-top site overlooking Paris. Climb the dome *(open*: daily, 09.15–18.30hrs) at dawn or dusk for one of Paris' most spectacular views.

Sacré-Coeur

Auguste Rodin (1840–1917) Rodin supported himself for years moulding and chiselling before creating a scandal with *L'Age d'Airan*, in 1877. By 1900 he was established in the official cultural community and enjoyed a public fame greater than any of his contemporaries. His works often caused violent quarrels among the critics; he despised outward 'finish' and was mistakenly categorised with the Impressionists.

A public subscription was opened to finance the Sacré-Coeur, a method which contributed to its lengthy construction period – 35 years.

Spectacular stained glass in Sainte-Chapelle

During the Revolution St Louis' ornate and valuable reliquary was melted down and the chapel itself narrowly escaped demolition, but the relics were saved and today they are kept in Notre Dame, brought out only on Good Friday.

► ► ►   **Sainte-Chapelle**
boulevard du Palais, 75004
metros: Cité, St-Michel
Despite being one of Paris' oldest and most significant monuments, the Sainte-Chapelle is hidden in a courtyard behind the Palais de Justice, modestly holding back its charms. Built in under three years, its spire soars 75m above ground, unimpeded by flying buttresses – a daring architectural feat for the time. Proof of the intelligence of its design is that nothing has cracked over its 700-year existence, although there was a serious fire in 1630. But the most astonishing feature of this chapel is the ambitious range, colour and intricacy of its stained-glass windows; 1,134 biblical scenes are illustrated, so don't forget your binoculars.

Simple style Most castle chapels of the early Middle Ages were as architecturally straightforward as the fortifications themselves and built on two floors, to accommodate the master and his family above, with retainers banished to the lower floor. In France the real development of castle chapels came with Louis IX (later canonised), who employed Pierre de Montreuil to build the Sainte-Chapelle, his private chapel, completed in 1248. St Louis' aim was to have a shrine worthy of various relics acquired during the Crusades, including what was reputed to be the Crown of Thorns, pieces of the cross and drops of Christ's blood. These he had obtained, at an exorbitant cost, from the Emperor of Constantinople.
The front of the chapel is given relief by two porches,

above which rises an immense rose window, rebuilt under Charles VIII in 1485, surmounted by a *fleur de lys* balustrade. Entrance through the portal takes you into the sombre lower chapel. The decorative paintwork here is a product of the mid-19th century, when attempts were made to reproduce the medieval style. It was badly damaged during the Revolution, when it was used as a flour warehouse, and Haussmann's medievalists (in particular Viollet-le-Duc) were only too happy to go to town on this exceptional monument.

The upper chapel A narrow spiral staircase leads to the upper royal chapel: here a visual shock awaits you. Instead of walls you have luminous, unmitigated colour – the concentrated effect of 618sq m of the oldest stained-glass windows in Paris. Surmounted by delicately sculpted gables, the structure of the vaults unfortunately recedes behind more 19th-century paint; however, the main interest lies in the windows. Starting immediately to your left, you can follow the biblical narrative from Genesis through the Crucifixion to the Apocalypse (the rose window), taking in St Louis himself on the way. Each window should be read left to right, bottom to top, apart from certain scenes in the choir apse.

Features to look out for include the niches reserved for the royal family on both sides of the chapel in the fourth bays, and St Louis' oratory. Their escape route back to the adjoining palace was via a gallery leading off from the second bay.

The windows Starting with the first bay these are the main themes:

1. Genesis, Adam and Eve, Noah, Jacob
2. Exodus, Moses on Mount Sinaï
3. Exodus, the Law of Moses
4. Deuteronomy, Joshua, Ruth and Boaz
5. The Judges, Gideon, Samson
6. Isaiah, the Tree of Jesse
7. St John, the Virgin, Christ's childhood
8. Christ's passion
9. St John the Baptist, Daniel
10. Ezekiel
11. Jeremiah, Tobias
12. Judith, Job
13. Esther
14. Kings, Samuel, David, Solomon
15. St Helena and the True Cross, St Louis and the Relics
16. The Apocalypse – a rose divided into 86 panels

Leaning against each pillar is a statue of an apostle but few are originals, and all are heavily restored. Damaged originals are displayed at the Cluny.

In front of the altar stands a wooden canopied platform which once displayed the famous relics. The open spiral stairs leading to it (only the left-hand one is original) were often used by St Louis in a ceremonial inspection of his treasure.

Acoustic advantages Concerts are regularly held in the chapel, taking advantage of its fantastic acoustics, but as these are in the evening you will not have an opportunity to admire the stained-glass windows.

Open: daily, 10.00–17.00hrs (winter); 09.30–18.30hrs (summer).

Across the moat outside the Cité des Sciences et de l'Industrie stands the spherical Géode cinema, which programmes special wide-angle films in its hemispherical interior (booking essential; tel: 42 95 50 50).

▶ ▷ ▷ St-Denis, rue

This idiosyncratic street was named after the martyr St-Denis, who apparently accomplished the astonishing feat of staggering headless from where he was decapitated in Montmartre to the site of the future basilica of St-Denis. The long Roman rue St-Denis was once the processional route for French royalty arriving for coronation and departing for burial; today it presents a very different face, one of prostitutes, sex shops and, at the Les Halles end, fast food joints. Despite this sleazy appearance there are a few picturesque old-world bars squeezed between the new-world tack and a wander north towards the ornamental 1672 **Porte St-Denis** can be amusing.

St-Germain see pages 176–7

▶ ▷ ▷ St-Honoré, rue

Like the rue St-Denis it runs off the central area of Les Halles, yet the rue St-Honoré is quite a different, well-mannered world. Lined with respectable clothes, food and antique shops it is also one of Paris' oldest roads: Jeanne d'Arc was wounded here, Molière was born here and Marie-Antoinette was transported to the guillotine along it. It takes in the baroque **Eglise St-Roch**, skirts around the **Comédie Française** and crosses the **place du Palais-Royal** behind the massive **Louvre des Antiquaires**, a costly antique market. On the western side of the rue Royale it becomes the Faubourg St-Honoré which, along with the avenue Montaigne, provides the greatest concentration of luxury clothes shops in the capital.

▷ ▷ ▷ St-Jacques, rue

Apart from its status as Paris' oldest street (another Roman feat), the steep rue St-Jacques at last makes clear the origin of those delicious *coquilles St-Jacques* so common in Parisian restaurants. With a street named after the crusader St Jacques, Paris became the starting point for pilgrims trekking south to his shrine in Spain who set off attired in the saint's symbol, a scallop shell.

▶ ▷ ▷ St-Jacques, Tour

metro: Châtelet

The flamboyant Gothic tower still standing in this square dates from the early 16th century, once part of the church of St-Jacques-La-Boucherie, which was demolished in 1797. It is now a meteorological station.

▶ ▶ ▷ St-Sulpice, Eglise de

metro: St-Sulpice

Apart from housing one of the world's largest organs, St-Sulpice is a remarkable example of a public edifice, that took 134 years to build and was left with two strangely asymmetrical towers. Don't miss Delacroix's murals in the first chapel on the right as you enter, and look out for a bronze meridian line in the transept which, at winter solstice and equinoxes, reflects sunbeams onto an obelisk and then onto the cross – a true tribute to France's 19th-century scientific spirit.

Open: 07.30–19.30hrs and during services on Sunday.

The Sewers (*egouts*), Pont de l'Alma, Quai d'Orsay (tel: 47 05 10 29) have, for some bizarre reason, become a popular tourist destination. One of Haussmann's greatest accomplishments, this vast 2,100km underground network – which also contains telephone wires and electricity cables – can be seen on a guided tour which includes a film and photographic display. *Open*: Saturday to Wednesday, 11.00–16.00hrs.

▶▶▷ Sciences et de l'Industrie, Cité des

30 avenue Corentin Cariou, 75019
metro: Porte de la Villette

Set in the far-flung northeast of Paris in the expanding Parc de la Villette, the futuristic Cité des Sciences attracts crowds of young visitors to participate in its spectacular displays of science and technology. Life is never the same again after visiting their 'inventorium' or 'Explora', which whisks you through 30,000 sq m of 'space, life, matter and communication', the very spacey Planetarium or the *Cité des Enfants*.

Open: Tuesday to Sunday, 10.00–18.00hrs.

▶▶▶ Sens, Hôtel de

1 rue du Figuier, 75004
metro: St-Paul

It is well worth a special trip to see this mansion overlooking the Seine, Le Marais' greatest medieval building dating from 1475 to 1507. Built for the archbishops of Sens, it was later inhabited by Henri IV's first wife, Queen Margot. Her taste for young lovers created deadly rivalries, culminating in her ordering the beheading of one unfortunate victim on the mansion steps. Today, less dramatically, the building is used as an applied arts library, the Bibliothèque Forney, and sometimes organises related exhibitions.

Open: Tuesday to Saturday 13.30–20.30hrs.

▷▶▷ Sèvres, Musée de la Céramique de

place de la Manufacture, 92310 Sèvres
metro: Pont de Sèvres

A leading name in world porcelain, this rich collection covers several centuries of Sèvres production, as well as European pottery of the Middle Ages, Islamic and Chinese ceramics and Italian Majolica.

Open: Wednesday to Monday, 10.00–17.15hrs.

▶ ▶ ▶ **St-Germain**

Tranquilly cradled at the heart of Paris, St-Germain remains eternally magnetic for the visitor and resident alike. Modern incursions are rare and the atmosphere still has something of the Paris of history, literature and cinema. The pace seems more leisurely than on the other side of the river, cafés still play their traditional role and backstreet bistros whisk diners back half a century or so. Aproned waiters and waitresses scold as they are reputed to, and the residents still include a fair share of eccentrics and/or intelligentsia.

Origins Symbol of its genesis, the **Eglise St-Germain-des-Prés** dates from the late 10th century, when it was part of a Benedictine monastery which replaced a 6th-century abbey. By the 14th century it was surrounded by a fortified wall, which disappeared with the age of enlightenment to make way for housing — and the new nobles of the Faubourg St-Germain to the west. Badly

ST-GERMAIN DES PRES
0   100   200 mètres

The Eglise St-Germain-des-Prés: inside...

...and outside, where the pace is relaxed and leisurely

damaged during the Revolution, only one of its original three towers remains but the massive flying buttresses of the choir (12th-century), among the oldest in France, remain intact. As usual, the 19th century brought much retouching and both the nave and the choir contain murals by Flandrin from that period.

The living heart of St-Germain is, of course, the **boulevard**, which runs west from the Latin Quarter to join the staid government buildings and bourgeois mansions of the 7th *arrondissement.* North of the boulevard, towards the Seine, remains an essentially arty district, crowded with small cinemas, galleries, antique shops, the national art school (see page 79) and the Mint (see page 147). In the shadows of its narrow streets you can make your own discoveries of shops, restaurants or hidden courtyards, all finished with a veneer of affluence. It's a *quartier* in limbo, which cannot decide whether it is part of Mitterrand's shiny new capital or clinging to its pre-war intellectual days.

South of the boulevard the streets widen and the atmosphere changes. From the church of **St-Sulpice** to the **Jardin du Luxembourg**, through the shopping streets of the **rue Bonaparte, rue de Sèvres** and **rue de Grenelle**, this is the St-Germain of fashion and publishing. Chic bars replace crowded cafés and furniture design shops line the **boulevard Raspail**, leading up to the crossroads of Sèvres-Babylone, which is dominated by the renovated art deco **Hôtel Lutetia** and Paris' first department store, **Les Trois Quartiers.**

Seat of learning: La
Sorbonne

 La Sorbonne
45–7 rue des Ecoles, 75005
metro: Cluny
Symbol of France's great spirit of learning, the Sorbonne
was founded in 1253 and for centuries maintained an
independent attitude to the state, recognising the
English Henry V as King of France, condemning Joan of
Arc, later fiercely opposing Protestants (Henri IV) and the
18th-century 'philosophers'. The student revolts in 1968
gave the state its first opportunity to allow police to
enter these premises. Richelieu was responsible for the
rebuilding of the dilapidated college in 1642, although
Lemercier's domed chapel, where the Cardinal lies in
splendour, is all that remains: today's amphitheatres and
endless corridors all date from the late 19th century. You
can enter the imposing courtyard off the rue de la
Sorbonne and ask for permission to see Puvis de
Chavannes' mural in the 'Grand Amphitheatre'.

 Sully, Hôtel de
62 rue St-Antoine, 75004
metro: St-Paul
All was not sweetness and light in the heyday of Le
Marais, as the gambling owner of this superb 1630
mansion is said to have lost his fortune overnight. He
left a richly decorated home which was soon bought by
Henri IV's former minister, the Duc de Sully. The
courtyard is a particularly impressive example of Louis
XII, and the recently restored interior boasts some
ornate ceilings and panelling. In the garden an Orangerie
is used for temporary exhibitions and the bookshop of
the Caisse Nationale des Monuments Historiques at the
entrance has useful information on guided tours and
monuments.
Open: guided tour only Saturday or Sunday, 15.00hrs.

 Synagogue
metro: St-Paul
Although the architect Hector Guimard is best
remembered for his fanlighted *Metropolitain* entrances,
he was also prolific between 1895 and 1910. The
synagogue in the heart of the Jewish quarter in Le
Marais was one of his later designs, built in 1913.
Distressed by the rise of fascism, Guimard later
emigrated to the US, where he died in 1942.

▶▶ Techniques, Musée National des
292 rue Saint-Martin, 75003
metro: Arts et Métiers
This extraordinary and much overlooked museum was set up under the Revolutionary government of 1794, based on a foresighted idea of Descartes' who, a century earlier, had seen the need for conserving and exhibiting artisan machinery. Installed in a medieval priory, the museum encompasses a 13th-century church, and a section of wall is still crowned by two original towers of the same period.

Cars and curios The enlightening collection includes models and examples of early transport (what other church nave accommodates parked Peugeots, Foucault's pendulum and Blériot's first flying machines?), astronomical equipment, clocks (including a decimal example for the Revolutionary calendar), automats (mostly 18th-century rococo), energy, acoustics, glass (Daum, Lalique, Gallé, Murano), photography and broadcasting. Modern inventions include an antiquated 1938 wooden washing machine and the first mass-manufactured car, made by Ford in 1908. Unfortunately, renovation is changing the museum's Victorian atmosphere.
Open: Tuesday to Sunday, 10.00–17.30hrs.

▶▶▶ Tristan Tzara, Maison
15 avenue Junot, 75018
metro: Abbesses
In one of Montmartre's select streets stands the only house in Paris designed by the Austrian architect Adolf Loos. Opponent of the 'decorative' art nouveau and defender of a pure rationalist style, Loos settled in Paris in 1923 and soon designed this house for the monocled writer Tristan Tzara, at the time deeply involved in bringing about the death-rattle of Dadaism.

▶▶ Trocadéro, place du
metro: Trocadéro
Another landmark Parisian square, Trocadéro is actually laid out in a semi-circle facing the wings of the **Palais de Chaillot** and beyond that, in a direct line, the **Eiffel Tower**. Named after an Andalusian fort occupied by the French in 1823, it was not given its present shape until 1858, when a first **Palais de Chaillot** was built. The 1937 Exposition Internationale replaced the palace with the present monumental buildings, which house several museums (see pages 91 smf 94). Around the area are well frequented cafés and restaurants, including the *salon de thé* **Carette**, a regular on the Passy agenda.

▶▶▶ Tuileries, Jardins des
metro: Tuileries
The famous Tuileries gardens were originally laid out Italian-style to complement the palace built for Catherine de Médicis in 1564. Corneille described them as 'the land of the beautiful people and of gallantry', where balls, concerts and fireworks provided constant animation. In 1649 Louis XIV stepped onto the scene with his minister Colbert and commissioned major

The Palais de Chaillot, in the place du Trocadéro

Jardins des Tuileries

Messing about with boats in the Jardins des Tuileries

changes by his favourite landscape gardener, the prodigious André Le Nôtre (also responsible for the immaculate gardens at Versailles, Chantilly and Vaux le Vicomte). Two lateral esplanades were built up and the central alley which led away from the château laid out. At the time the garden was considered one of the best kept in Europe and was a fashionable promenading area. Although the royal residence went up in serious smoke at the hands of the Communards in 1871, the gardens survived, changing their appearance little over the next century.

Mark of time Yet years of neglect and pollution have left their mark. Today the carefully aligned fountains, ponds, terraces, lawns, flower beds and statues are undergoing renovation, as official light has been thrown on the sorry state of the vegetation and particularly the sick, badly pruned trees. A five year plan has been drawn up to ensure that the Tuileries gardens will be as sparkling as the Louvre when its extension and renovations are completed in 1996.

Regained role Opposite the Pyramid the Arc du Carrousel will regain its original role as a gate to the garden, a canal will be built and lined with Maillol's famous statues, which used to be dotted all over the lawns, and a terrace built up to improve the view looking across the gardens towards the Concorde. The main area will keep its basic form but with numerous improved facilities (children's playgrounds, bowling areas) and a vastly regenerated and replanted vegetation. Whatever immediate improvements are visible, a quarter century is estimated as necessary for the full impact of new plantations.

■ **If caught in Paris on one of its rare rainy days – March showers being the rule – head for the 2nd and 9th *arrondissements*, where a network of covered passages creates a sheltered itinerary full of surprises. Relics of pre-department store days, these passages were the fashionable shopping malls of early 19th-century Paris. .....■**

Almost 30 survive out of the original 140 passages: many have been heavily restored, others are dusty, partly derelict reminders of an age past, but all have traders in the strangest of domains.

Start with one of the most picturesque, hardly touched since it was built in 1822, the **Galerie Véro-Dodat**, which runs between the rue Jean-Jacques Rousseau and the rue Croix des Petits Champs. Named after two butchers, it was one of Paris' first streets to be illuminated by gas. Today its black and white tiled floor, window boxes and carved wood mouldings make a shadowy, harmonious setting for an old-world restaurant, antique shops and galleries, including a wonderful antique doll shop.

High fashion A few streets away, beyond the place des Victoires, is the **Galerie Vivienne**, perhaps the most fashionable of these passages, built in 1828. Home to one of Paris' best wine-merchants, Legrand, the now legendary *enfant terrible* of fashion, Jean-Paul Gaultier, an extraordinary toy-shop, a unique bookshop and a chic *salon de thé*, whose tables spill out under the lofty skylights, the Galerie Vivienne should not be missed. Running parallel and off it is the over-restored **Galerie Colbert**, which houses some interesting shops and galleries, all belonging to the Bibliothèque Nationale, as well as a brasserie, the Grand Café Colbert.

Head north up the rue Vivienne past the Bourse and you will find a passage with a strange past: the **Passage des Panoramas**. It was built in 1800 by an American who came to France to propose various

The Galerie Vivienne

inventions to the new Directoire, among which were a torpedo and a submarine. To earn a few bucks while waiting, he built two towers containing panoramas at the boulevard end of his passage. Today the passage is a mass of specialist shops (look for the card-engraver, Stern) with some unusual eating places, including a tea shop installed on the site of an old chocolate factory and an Italian trattoria which could be straight out of Rome.

Other options Across the boulevard Montmartre the passages continue (Passages Jouffroy and Verdeau), each one revealing its own unique character to the inquisitive visitor with time to explore them.

Notable residents of the place Vendôme have included Chopin, who died at no 12, and Anton Mesmer, the inventor of mesmerism, whoheld experiments at no 16. The Ritz guest-book includes Proust, Barbara Hutton, Chanel and others worth their financial salt.

182

Juliette Drouet became Victor Hugo's devoted mistress and accompanied him on his self-imposed exile to Guernsey (in furious reaction to Napoleon III's *coup d'état*), where they remained from 1848 to 1870.

Maison de Victor Hugo: the Salle à Manger Chinoise

▶ ▶▶ Vendôme, place

metro: Opéra, Tuileries

Supreme symbol of Parisian chic, the place Vendôme is densely populated by jewellery shops and anything else that can approach the same level of quality and price tags. The **Ritz Hotel**, for example. The square's façades were designed in 1685 by Hardouin-Mansart as an aptly gracious setting for an equestrian statue of Louis XIV by Girardon. This effigy did not outlast the energies of the mob during the Revolution and it was duly felled, to be replaced by the present bronze column. This was initially crowned by a figure of Napoleon; in 1814 a statue of Henri IV took over but after several more changes, including the toppling of the column by the Communards, a copy of Napoleon's original statue resumed its post. The bronze itself came from canons captured at the Battle of Austerlitz.

▶ ▶▶ Vert Galant, Square du

metro: Pont-Neuf

The pointed western tip of the Ile de la Cité is named after Henri IV, Paris' first regal town planner, who commissioned both the Pont-Neuf and the place Dauphine immediately across from his fine equestrian statue. This little garden has a wonderful view west along the Seine. Boat trips leave from the quay here.

Versailles see pages 210–13.

▶ ▶▶ Victor Hugo, Maison de

6 place des Vosges, 75004
metro: Bastille

This is one of Paris' most characteristic museums, giving a rounded view of the great writer's many talents and his changing residences, which included the second floor of this town house from 1832 to 1848. Displayed on the first floor are numerous pen and ink drawings by Victor Hugo, alongside occasional temporary exhibitions. Upstairs the rooms are laid out to give the atmosphere of his diverse abodes and include a surprising *salon chinois* and furniture from actress Juliette Drouet's room in Guernsey, all carved and/or decorated by the writer himself. Other Hugo memorabilia include a bust of him by Rodin, portraits of his wife and mistress, photographs and a few family souvenirs.

Open: Tuesday to Sunday, 10.00–17.40hrs.

Vidéothèque de Paris

Forum des Halles, Porte St-Eustache, 2 Grande Galerie, 75001

metro: Les Halles

Another underground destination of Les Halles, the Vidéothèque is a must for anyone interested in both film and Paris. Since opening in 1988, this municipal video library has built up a stock of over 3,500 videotapes covering anything that has ever been put on celluloid concerning the capital – from the Lumière brothers in 1896 to the present – including TV documentaries, commercials and feature films. You can either watch the excellent thematic programmes shown daily on the large screen or use an individual monitor to view your own choice of film(s). Entrance costs less than a cinema seat. *Open*: Tuesday to Sunday, 12.30–20.30hrs.

▶ ▶ La Villette, Parc de

metro: Porte de la Villette, Porte de Pantin

Nearing completion, the multi-purpose Parc de la Villette is one of Paris' most important cultural projects of the last decade. Stretching around the northeastern perimeter of the city, the 55-hectare park has been developed since 1979 by architect Bernard Tschumi to offer a concentrated range of cultural and leisure activities.

High points in Vincennes' history include La Fayette heroically saving it from destruction by the mob in 1791, the Duc d'Enghien savouring his last dinner in the splendour of the Pavillon du Roi before facing Napoleon's firing squad at midnight, the peglegged General Daumesnil refusing to surrender the castle to the Allies in 1814 with the cry 'First give me back my leg' (he had lost it at the Battle of Wagram) and the execution of the tantalising spy Mata Hari in 1917.

Facilities and follies A major integral part of the project, the **Cité des Sciences et de l'Industrie** (see page 175), sits in its moat beside the canal, faced by a spherical cinema, **La Géode** (both designed by Fainsilber), but many of the surrounding walkway structures and red metal 'follies' are cumbersome and apparently aimless. A survivor from 1867 is the original slaughterhouse, **La Grande Halle**, which in a renovated form now accommodates temporary events, from trade fairs to exhibitions to concerts. In front, dominating the Porte de Pantin park entrance, is the recently completed **Cité de la Musique**, designed by Portzamparc in a neo-1930s style, which gives music students modern facilities and a superb public concert hall. Another concert hall, **Le Zénith**, conceived specifically for rock concerts, stands on the northern edge of the park. Scattered between these landmarks are numerous children's facilities, cafés, gardens, a submarine and the Inventorium, where you can 'build' a house or programme a computer.

Parc de la Villette

The Château de Vincennes

▶▶▶ **Vincennes, Château and Bois de**

metro: Château de Vincennes, Porte Dorée

Before its many reincarnations, the sturdy medieval castle commanding the east of Paris arose in the 14th century and was completed under Charles V. The symmetrical Pavillon du Roi and Pavillon de la Reine were added to the southern end by Le Vau while Cardinal Mazarin ruled the roost in 1652, but were badly damaged in 1944 when the Germans were abandoning Paris.

Although Louis XIV spent his honeymoon here, Vincennes was soon supplanted by Versailles (completed in 1680) and thus started its string of transformations. Successively a prison, a porcelain factory (which then moved west to become the famous Manufacture de Sèvres), a military school, an arms factory and, under Napoleon, an arsenal, Vincennes became a fortress under Louis-Philippe in the 1850s and an ammunition depot during the German Occupation. For over a century, starting with the fanatical medievalist Viollet-le-Duc, intermittent restoration has been carried out.

Entrance to the château (*open*: daily, 10.00–16.15hrs, in summer till 18.15hrs) is through the Tour du Village, a powerful 42m-high tower which leads into the central courtyard. On your left is a strange museum, with even stranger opening hours (tel: 49 57 32 00) dedicated to the history of shoes. Entrance to the dungeons is with guided tours, in French only.

The chapel The royal chapel dominating the courtyard, although in 14th-century Gothic style with a superb rose window, was completed in 1552 under Henri II, and its gracefully vaulted interior is well worth entering. The stained-glass windows in the choir are unusually toned Renaissance scenes of the Apocalypse, much restored in the late 19th century.

The dungeons Opposite the chapel, the dungeons are in a walled area surmounted by a square turreted tower, one of the finest in France. Inside, the ground floor once housed the kitchen and has now gained a door rescued from the Temple prison, where Louis XVI was imprisoned. A spiral staircase leads to the upper floors, where resident royalty, including Henry V of England and Charles IX, and later prisoners of state, enjoyed a panoramic view of Paris.

The royal courtyard, accessible through another gateway and closed at the southern end by the monumental Tour du Bois, is flanked by the royal pavilions, closed to the public apart from a small section containing yet another idiosyncratic museum, the Musée des Insignes. Le Vau's Classical structure was inhabited by various minor royalty, as well as Cardinal Mazarin, who died there.

Bois Landscaped at the same time as the Bois de Boulogne by Baron Haussmann, the Bois de Vincennes traditionally served the working-class population of eastern Paris. It possesses no fewer than three lakes, the Parc Floral, a race-course, a zoo, a tropical garden, a Buddhist centre, a theatre complex and, at the Porte Dorée entrance, the Musée des Arts Africains et Océaniens (see page 63). Like Boulogne, it too was once rich royal hunting-ground, sectioned off by another of Philippe-Auguste's walls in the 12th century. By Louis XV's reign it had become a popular promenading area and the woods were replanted.

The Zoo Near the Lac Daumesnil, France's largest zoo (*open*: 09.00–17.30hrs) houses over 600 mammals and 200 species of birds in a fairly natural, spacious environment. The best time is had by mountain goats, careering up and down their 70m-high artificial rock. Avoid Wednesday afternoons and weekends, particularly in summer, as queues are long.

Nearer the château, the **Parc Floral** (*open*: 09.30–18.30hrs) provides an exceptional floral display renewed every season. Special sections exist for dahlias, water lilies, medicinal plants, iris, orchids, tulips, rhododendrons and azaleas, and there is also an exhibition hall and a children's playground. Rowing boats and bicycles can be hired at the lakes. Vincennes also houses, adjacent to the Parc Floral, the famous collective theatre, the **Théâtre du Soleil** at La Cartoucherie (an abandoned munitions factory), founded by Ariane Mnouchkine in the late '60s.

Macabre legend has it that on his death Henry V's body, rotten with dysentery, was boiled in the château kitchens.

Contemplating life as residents of the Bois de Vincennes zoo

Staying chic

■ **Parisians seem to have an innate knack of staying chic. Even though 66 per cent of French women now work full-time and often cope with children too, they seem never to have a hair out of place or an uncoordinated accessory. Not to speak of the men who swing along the boulevards or stub out their Gitanes with a flourish that is unmistakably Gallic. .....■**

Wine can be ordered and delivered from any of the Nicolas chain of shops

So what's their eternal and annoying secret? Self respect (sometimes called egocentricity) is one good reason. And this means taking good care of oneself, pampering one's ego and one's outer shell.

Body beautiful Alexandre de Paris (3 avenue Matignon, 8e, tel: 42 25 57 90) is perhaps Paris' most famous hairdresser for men and women and also offers massages and facials. Service is suitably syncophantic and meals are also served during what can be lengthy treatments. **Carita** (11 rue du Faubourg St-Honoré, 8e, tel: 42 65 79 00) now specialises in both sexes, and their three floors of clinical-looking individual booths cater for manicures, pedicures, massages, facials and (the speciality), hair treatments. Phones and snacks are all part of the service. Now you will understand how Catherine Deneuve remains eternally youthful.

For skin care only, it is hard to beat the time-honoured **Guerlain** (68 Champs-Elysées, 8e, tel: 47 89 71 80, and 29 rue de Sèvres, 6e, tel: 42 22 46 60). Elegant private salons in their original 1828 premises contrast with the frayed Champs Elysées outside. In a similar vein the **Institut Payot** (10 rue de Castiglione, 1e, tel: 42 60 32 87), founded by a Russian émigrée in 1919, has a timeless salon that specialises in body massages and, above all, facial care using its own excellent products. You can also buy the Institut's Pavlova perfume created for the great ballerina.

If the pores of your body really need liberating, head for the Hammam at the Mosquée where the steam and dry baths will cure any ills (see page 125).

Clothes beautiful Impeccable turnout is another criterion for Parisian chicness. For clothes alterations or perfect mending go to **Mermoz Retouches** (21 rue Jean Mermoz, 8e, tel: 42 25 73 36); prices and quality are both high. Most dry cleaners also offer mending services, and you could do worse than have your *foie-gras*-stained jackets cleaned and delivered to your door by **Allo Pressing** (tel: 48 30 56 95); the prices and time are hardly more than your local dry cleaner. However, if it's a question of your *haute-couture* evening dress, opt for **Delaporte Star** (62 rue François I, 8e, tel: 43 59 82 11), much used by neighbouring boutiques such as Dior and Balmain. Prices are monstrous but service is excellent. For really top-class old-fashioned laundering, make for **Vendôme** (24 rue du Mont Thabor, 1e, tel: 42 60 74 38), which starches and irons collars for the

Presidential minions of the Elysée. Deliveries are part of the friendly service.

Down at the heel? Then make sure you see a *cordonnier*. There are plenty of old-fashioned cobblers in every neighbourhood, but you can always rely on the delivery service of **Claraso** (34 rue Godot-de-Mauroy, 9e, tel: 47 42 49 79). Repairs take at least a week.

Missing a tuxedo or a chic cocktail dress for an occasion you didn't anticipate? Then go to **Beral** (2 rue Caulaincourt, 18e, tel: 43 87 72 37) for the former and **Latreille** for the latter (62 rue St André-des-Arts, 6e, tel: 43 29 44 10).

Be chic to others How to thank your Parisian dinner hostess without arriving under a veritable forest of flowers? The answer is have said forest delivered, and by the best. **Lachaume** (10 rue Royale, 8e, tel: 42 60 57 26) remains the incontestable king, established in 1845. Although prices are astronomical, your hostess will appreciate the label. **Les Jardins d'Anaïs** (52 rue Montorgueil, 2e, tel: 42 33 14 81), although a more modest establishment, creates the most imaginative, artistic bouquets.

Bottles clanking up the stairs never create a suave entrance, so why not have some of your chosen elixir delivered in advance? Any branch of the long-established (1822) wine shop chain **Nicolas** (tel: 42 27 22 07) will take phone orders and deliver; the minimum order is 200FF.

Finally, a discreet box of fine chocolates never goes amiss, but again make sure it has the right label: choose from specilaists **Christian Constant**, **Debauve et Gallais** or **Dalloyau**.

Debauve et Gallais: chocolates with a chic label

Hot chocolate was served three times a week to the Sun King at Versailles. The first chocolate shop opened in Paris in 1659 and Voltaire was reported to drink 12 cups a day in his old age. In the early 19th century Debauve et Gallais opened their shop, still in the rue des Saintes-Péres today, to promote chocolate's therapeutic qualities.

Itineraries

Week's Itinerary

Day one
St-Germain-des-Prés. Besides the church, explore the art galleries, cafés and antique shops along the rue Jacob, rue Bonaparte, rue de Seine and the **rue de Buci** street market.
Visit the church on the **place St-Sulpice**; then continue to the **Jardin du Luxembourg**. By the river go to the **Musée d'Orsay**. Cross the bridge and walk through the Tuileries to finish at the **Orangerie**.

Day two
Saint-Honoré. Start at the **Louvre**, not missing the **Cour Carrée**; cross to the **Palais Royal**, entering the gardens beside the **Comédie Française**. Explore this area and see the **Bibliotheque Nationale** before continuing to the **Opéra**.
Walk through the **place Vendôme**, past the **Ritz**, to the **rue de Rivoli**. Visit the **Jeu de Paume** and walk around the **place de la Concorde** to the gardens of the **Champs-Elysées**.

Day three
Le Marais/Bastille. Start exploring the islands, **Notre Dame** and **Sainte-Chapelle**. Pass the **Hôtel de Ville** and go to **Beaubourg** then walk through **Le Marais.** Visit the **Hôtel de Soubise**, the **Musée Picasso**, walk through the **place des Vosges** to the **Bastille**. Walk up the rue de la Roquette or take a bus to **Père Lachaise** at the top.
Dine in **Belleville.**

Day four
Trocadéro. Start at the **Tour Eiffel**. Cross the bridge to the **Palais de Chaillot** and museums. Go to the Porte de la Muette, the **Jardin de Ranelagh** and the **Musée Marmottan** then head for the **Arc de Triomphe**. Take the RER to **La Défense** and visit **La Grande Arche**.

Day five
Spend the day in **Versailles**. Or drive to **Fontainebleau** and **Vaux-le-Vicomte.**
Dine in **Montparnasse.**

Day six
Latin Quarter. Start at the **rue Mouffetard** market and nearby streets.
Tea at the **Mosquée**, a stroll in the **Jardin des Plantes**, then to the Roman **Arènes de Lutèce** and the **Institut du Monde Arabe**.
Follow the *quais* to **Saint Séverin** and finish at the **Cluny** museum.

Day seven
Montmartre. If Saturday or Sunday, start at the **Marche aux Puces**, Porte de Clignancourt. Explore Montmartre, climb **Sacré Coeur**. Metro from **Pigalle** to **Monceau**; stroll in the park and visit the **Musée Nissim de Camondo**.
Buy presents at **Galeries Lafayette!**

Weekend's Itinerary

The following is designed for visitors on their first trip to Paris.

Day one

Start at the **Louvre**, at 09.00hrs. On leaving don't miss the **Cour Carrée** behind the pyramid. Then stroll along the rue de Rivoli to **Angélina's** tea room or the adjoining luxury **Hôtel Meurice** for a drink. Turn right along rue Castiglione to the **place Vendôme** and the **Ritz**, past the glitziest jewellers. At the place de l'Opéra take the rue Auber past the **Opéra** to the RER express metro. Take line A to **La Défense**. From the roof of **La Grande Arche** survey Paris.

Return by RER to **Les Halles** for lunch. Walk due east to the **Centre Pompidou (Beaubourg)** then enter **Le Marais** following the rue des Francs Bourgeois. A short detour takes you to the **Musée Picasso**; alternatively, go straight to the **Musée Victor Hugo** on the **place des Vosges**, a good spot for a coffee. Cross the rue St-Antoine and take the rue St-Paul through the antique market, the **Village St-Paul,** towards the **Hôtel de Sens**. Cross the Pont Marie, explore the lower *quais* and spend your evening on the **Ile St Louis**.

Day two

Start in **Montmartre**, exploring the back streets, and **Sacré Coeur**. Return to the boulevard below by taking the lively market street, the rue Lepic. The **Moulin Rouge** is to your right at the bottom. Take the metro from **place Clichy** to Varennes and the **Musée Rodin** with its pleasant café and gardens. Walk or take a taxi past **Les Invalides** to the **Champ-de-Mars** dominated by the **Tour Eiffel**.

Continue the afternoon in the **Latin Quarter**, going first to the **Cluny** museum. Explore the surrounding narrow streets before crossing to the **Ile de la Cité** to see the dazzling **Sainte-Chapelle**. Finish at **Notre-Dame** (free Sunday concerts at 17.45hrs). Return to the Left Bank, following the *quai* to the **Hôtel de la Monnaie**. Turn into the mass of streets leading to the charming **place de Furstenberg,** past the church of **St-Germain-des-Prés** and start your evening at the elegant **Café de Flore**.

PARIS - EXCURSIONS

▶▶▶ **Cartier, Fondation**

3 rue de la Manufacture, 78350 Jolly-en-Josas

By car: take the autoroute to Chartres from the Porte de St-Cloud, exit at Bièvres.

By train: from the Gare d'Austerlitz, or via Versailles.

This interesting experiment in corporate sponsorship has given Parisian art groupies an idyllic exhibition centre outside the metropolis. Trademark promotion is increasingly channelled into sponsorship these days, an eminently more subtle form of advertising. Since it opened in the mid-1980s, the Fondation Cartier has no doubt enhanced the sales figures of luxury watches as much as it has the well-being of the living artists it promotes.

Set in a lush green park graced with centennial trees and a small château, the art centre itself is composed of a concrete 'bunker' (once used by Nazis during World War II, now an art gallery) and charming entrance buildings, which function as a café, artists' studios and more exhibition spaces.

Outdoor sculpture If no special exhibition is on when you visit, go for a wander anyway in the sculpture park and discover wonders of contemporary creativity – from Arman's incredible pile of compressed cars (their real metal carcasses sandwiched with concrete into a towering wrecker's yard) to Barry Flanagan's bronze boxing hares, César's giant thumb or some more discreet and often extremely enigmatic sculptures

Traffic jam at the Fondation Cartier

nestling in the trees at the back of the park.
During the summer months the Fondation can be relied upon to produce a blockbuster exhibition, often combining several art forms under one theme and inventively exhibited so that even children will enjoy the visit.

When to go Aim to coincide with lunchtime so that you can snack on the sunny terrrace of the café, which turns out some suitably arty salads. In this way you may have a chance to meet one of the resident foreign artists or critics and even visit their temporary studios to see what new masterpieces are being produced.

Environs The surrounding rolling green Bièvres valley makes a pretty drive if you are in the Versailles area, but this destination should only be seriously followed up if you are genuinely interested in contemporary art – and need a break from the dust of the châteaux.
Open: Tuesday–Sunday, 11.00 to 18.00hrs.

The 19th-century version of the Château de Chantilly

▶ ▶ ▷   Chantilly

Musée Condé, 60500 Chantilly

By car: Autoroute du Nord, A1 to Survilliers exit.

By train: from Gare du Nord to Senlis, then bus shuttle to Chantilly.

Due north of Paris is the classy epicentre of French horses and riding fanatics. Over 3,000 trusty steeds are stabled in the forested area surrounding Chantilly, and anything horsey is a semi-permanent talk of the town; both the local horse museum and the racecourse attract the relevant crowds. The 19th-century château contains a stunning art collection, and the surrounding canal-crossed park is a pleasure to explore.

Chantilly was originally founded by a Roman named Cantilius, but it was the famous head of the French army, the constable Anne de Montmorency, who in 1528 built a Renaissance château on the present site on his return from valiant battles in Italy. Montmorency brought in some of the greatest artists of the period: François Clouet, Bernard Palissy and Jean Goujon all participated. Soon after, the architect Jean Bullant was commissioned to build a small neighbouring château, the Capitainerie, which still survives today.

Change of hands After the Montmorencys the château passed into the hands of the Condé family, powerful nobles who from 1643 to the 1830s made Chantilly their family seat. The prince known as the Grand Condé soon called in the great landscape designer Le Nôtre; he transformed the gardens and added lakes and canals, helping to make Chantilly one of the era's favourite partying places. Famous literati invited to the fashionable gatherings included La Fontaine, Fénélon, Bossuet, Racine and Molière. It was also during this period that the resident chef, invented *crème chantilly*.

During the 18th century the magnificent stables were erected, intended to accommodate 240 horses and over 400 hounds for stag and boar hunts. (Today these stables are devoted to a horse museum and dressage displays.) The Revolution, however, soon left its inevitable mark: most of the château was pillaged and demolished – except for the Capitainerie. Around 1840 the last of the Condé family bequeathed the property to the Duc d'Aumale. This was the man responsible for undertaking the rebuilding of the château, (1876–83), which produced the Renaissance pastiche that we can visit today.

The main château On the ground floor the Musée Condé displays some magnificent works and furnishings, from the Italian and French Renaissance through to the 19th century. The *pièce de résistance* is the illuminated medieval manuscript *Très Riches Heures du Duc de Berry* (only its reproduction is displayed). Look out for Poussin, Delacroix, Raphael, Van Dyck, Corot and the remarkable Cabinet Clouet, which displays 16th-century portraits painted by the Clouet brothers. The same fraternity designed the stained-glass windows in the nearby Galerie de Psyche, made in 1542 for the Château d'Ecouen. In Le Sanctuario are exhibited major works such as Raphael's *Trois Grâces*, Filippo Lippi's *Esther et Asséurus* and Jean Fouquet's 1455 miniatures for a book of hours. The Cabinet des Gemmes exhibits further miniature portraits, porcelain, a rare collection of fans and a copy of the famous *Diamant Rose*. A large octagonal room called the Tribune houses masterpieces by Watteau, Delacroix, Ingres and Philippe de Champaigne.

A guided tour of the apartments leads to the Capitainerie, which, apart from its superb restaurant (tel: 44 57 15 89), contains some fascinating features such as panels painted by Huet in the main bedroom and the superb carved wood panelling of the music room. The balustrade of the main staircase leading to the chapel took 30 craftsmen a year to complete. Gobelins and Beauvais tapestries, inlaid furniture, a room entirely decorated with paintings of monkeys – Chantilly is not short of interest.

Park Allow an hour or so to wander around. Take in the Hameau, an aristocratic version of rustic living built in 1774, similar to that used by Marie-Antoinette at Versailles. Follow Le Nôtre's canals, in particular La Manche, which leads you to an amphitheatre-shaped lawn on either side of which are the *allées des philosophes*, where the thinkers of the day cogitated in bucolic surroundings. Finish by going through the English-style garden with its temple, island and waterfall.

Open: Wednesday to Monday, 10.30–17.00hrs (till 18.00hrs in summer).
Musée Vivant du Cheval 13.00–17.00 Wednesday to Monday, 13.00–17.00hrs (open all day in summer).

Detail from the Château de Chantilly

EXCURSIONS

Notre Dame de Chartres

Even before the Christian era, Chartres was famous for its Druid temple, and many scholars believe it was actually the Druid capital of the Carnutes described in the famous Latin text, Caesar's 'Gallic Wars'.

▶ ▶ ◻ **Chartres**

By car: take the A10 from the Porte de St-Cloud.
By train: from Montparnasse.
Rising above the wheat fields of Beauce are the two extraordinary mismatched spires of Chartres cathedral, 'the very idea of the Middle Ages rendered visible' (Emile Male).
Notre Dame de Chartres is the Virgin Mary's cathedral *par excellence*, built to house the precious relic of her *sacra camisia* (her tunic), still displayed in the Treasury in only slightly frayed form after 2,000 years. King Charles the Bald donated the valuable relic in the late 9th century and it rapidly attracted streams of fervent pilgrims (many come on foot from Paris even today). Fires burned no fewer than five successive churches on the site, culminating in the devastating flames of 1194. Miraculously, Mary's tunic survived unsinged, which led to a revival of religious fervour and a strong motivation for rebuilding. From the king to the lowliest farm worker, everyone offered money or physical labour, and the new cathedral was erected in a record 25 years.

Chartres today Centuries later, Chartres remains a remarkably homogeneous example of the transition from Gothic to Romanesque. The lower half of the façade, surviving from the earlier church, is pure 11th-century Romanesque. Its main entrance, the *Portail Royal*, illustrates the life of Christ, and the central tympanum shows him surrounded by the Evangelists and the Apostles. The door to the right is dedicated to

Mary. The left-hand door focuses on the Ascension.

The right-hand octagonal spire, which crowns the 105m south tower, is original, but the north tower was decapitated by lightning and rebuilt in the early 16th century. The latter can be climbed, but be prepared for 378 steps. From the outside, admire the flying buttresses, the two magnificently sculpted porches and the 14th-century chapel in the garden at the back.

The 176 stained-glass windows cover an area of 2,500 sq m: the three crowning the façade escaped the 1194 fire, while most others are 13th-century. The three rose windows represent the Apocalypse, the Virgin Mary and the Last Judgement; *Notre Dame de la Belle Verrière*, in the south choir, is reputedly the oldest window.

The circular labyrinth on the nave floor is a unique medieval survivor symbolising good and evil with its centre representing paradise. Pilgrims used to crawl around all 280m of its pattern on their knees. The choir, one of the widest in Europe, is surrounded by a magnificent lace like wall of stone sculpture incorporating 200 statues. Behind the choir is the staircase leading to the Treasury in the Chapelle Saint-Piat. Below the cathedral is the impressive 9th-century crypt; guided tour start from the Maison des Clercs.

Chartres makes a charming spot for a day's wandering, as the lower part of the town boasts more historic churches. The river provides a picturesque backdrop for old public washhouses and drying lofts, while in Vieux Chartres some fabulous architectural features await discovery.

For a touching and astonishing spiritual monument go to the Maison Picassiette (22 rue du Repos, tel: 37 34 10 78). In a nondescript suburb a local street sweeper, Raymond Isidore, spent his entire life decorating his house with fragments of china and glass, starting in 1938 on the interior and finishing his garden tomb in 1962. Not even his wife's sewing machine escaped his mania.

CHARTRES CATHEDRAL

1 Portail Royal
2 Stained glass windows
3 Old Bell Tower
4 Vendôme Chapel
5 Organ
6 Portail Sud
7 St-Fulberts window
8 Parclose screen
9 Notre-Dame de la Belle-Verrière
10 Crypt entrance
11 St-Piat Chapel
12 Sacristy
13 Vierge du Pilier
14 Window of Peace
15 Portail Nord
16 Access to New Bell Tower
17 Clock Pavilion
18 New Bell Tower

EXCURSIONS

▶ ▷ ▷ **Euro Disney Resort**

Espace Euro Disney
Central Reservations Office/ BP 105, 77777 Marne-la-Vallée
By train: RER line A.
By car: autoroute A4.

Euro Disney Resort, a mega-project started in 1988 and opened in 1992, is situated 32km east of Paris in the bleak countryside of Marne-la-Vallée. The fourth of its kind in the world after California, Florida and Tokyo, this sprawling resort will eventually cover an area of nearly 2,000 hectares, one-fifth the size of Paris, giving visitors a seemingly endless variety of Disney-related activities.

Some concessions to French culture have been made, notably an area of the park called Discoveryland, inspired by Jules Verne's visions of the future. Yet the project budget – $4.2 billion – is more than comparable to even the greatest of Louis XIV's extravagances in Versailles. For this vast operation to break even financially and be completed as planned, it will have to attract 11 million visitors annually – no mean crowd.

For those who wish to immerse themselves in the Disney experience five hotels are grouped around an artificial lake, each one corresponding to a different American regional style and visitor's budget, while a sixth, the Magic Kingdom Hotel, leads the way into the heart of Euro Disneyland. Noted American architects such as Michael Graves and Frank Gehry were used to give at least some semblance of an established culture other than the Donald Duck variety.

The Euro Disney Resort includes a wooded camping site (remember Davy Crockett?), restaurants, shops, an entertainment centre with a lake for motorboating, and an 18-hole golf course. To be included in a later phase of the project (reaching far into 2017) are Disney film production studios (due to open in 1995), a second golf course and a water park. The managers of this massive theme park like to quote Jules Verne's words: 'What man can conceive, man can achieve' – which seems a fair assessment of the scope and ambition of the undertaking.

As the somewhat disoriented visitors stagger around wondering which continent or planet they have landed on, they can't help encountering some of the 12,000 beaming 'cast members', employed from all over Europe to aid visitors and maintain the squeaky-clean image. To be found at every corner, their Disney smiles are their only common denominator, as when not disguised as Disney characters they wear period clothes to blend in with the different areas of the Magic Kingdom.

Magic Kingdom It is in the Magic Kingdom, of course, where your offspring can at last meet all those characters previously reserved for the cinema or television screen – Mickey, Minnie, Goofy, Pluto and diverse fairy-tale comrades. Divided into five distinct areas or 'lands', it has as its centrepiece the elaborately turreted Snow White's Castle. On entering the Kingdom visitors find themselves projected into an idealised turn-of-the-century America on Main Street, with ragtime

Sleeping Beauty Castle, Euro Disney

piano tunes, horse-drawn trolley cars and 'ye olde' shops and houses. Steam trains and boats leave here for a trip through Frontierland, with its fake canyons, gold mines and rivers.

Fantasyland Inside the 15-storey castle you enter Fantasyland, where Disney classics and European folklore are relived, with Sleeping Beauty the out-and-out winner. Make-believe becomes reality and young children squeal approval. Adventureland, on the other hand, is geared more to a slightly older age group as here swashbuckling adventurers fight it out in a tropical setting. A 28m-high 'tree' created to be climbed brings visitors to the rustic dwelling of the Robinsons, while the island of the hidden treasure is ferociously guarded by Long John Silver and Captain Hook look-a-likes.

Discoveryland This final stopover, is completely inspired by Jules Verne's and other visionaries' images of the future. Boasting its spectacular Star Tours – a flight simulator that whisks visitors onto an interplanetary journey – it also projects a circular film, *Circle-Vision 360*, which draws visitors into themes of the future. Meanwhile, Starjets whizz above during the day and fireworks light up the sky at night.

You never know who might be joining you on a Euro Disney ride

EXCURSIONS

▶ ▶ ▶   Fontainebleau, Château de

77300 Fontainebleau

By car: Take A6 or N7 from the Porte d'Orléans.

By train: from the Gare de Lyon.

A magnificent vast forest of 17,000 hectares, once royal hunting ground, surrounds the marshy terrain of the château, number two in the French royal domain stakes after Versailles. Apart from touring the imposing palace, visitors can indulge in horse-riding, cycling, rock-climbing or simply walking in the forest. Only a few kilometres to the north lies Barbizon, famous for its mid-19th century school of landscape painters.

A former hunting lodge dating from the 12th century, the château was transformed into a major royal residence by François I in the 16th century; he brought the best of Italy's Renaissance artists and craftsmen to decorate its lofty interior and laid out the garden with lakes and canals. Le Nôtre stepped in during the mid-17th century to redesign the garden, and the palace

The Château de Fontainebleau, once a hunting lodge and a palace, now draws crowds of tourists

198

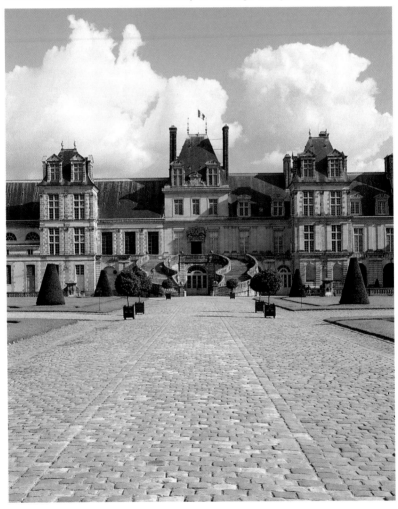

itself underwent numerous modifications and additions over the years before being finally adopted by Napoleon as a suitably majestic base.

The Château Entrance is through the famous Cour des Adieux, where the emperor bade farewell to his Imperial Guard in 1814 before being exiled on Elba. The famous horseshoe-shaped staircase was built by Du Cerceau for Louis XIII in 1634. In the Galerie François I, the original Renaissance frescos painted by the Florentine Rosso remained hidden behind other paintings, only coming to light in the 19th century. More Renaissance glories decorate the staircase of honour.

The highlight of the interior, however, is the **Salle de Bal**, the ceremonial ballroom which hosted many a glittering occasion. Dazzlingly furnished and decorated with original frescos and wood panelling, it was commenced under François I, the last elegant gilt touches being added under his successor Henri II.

Napoleon's apartments occupy the second storey of a wing built under Louis XVI, overlooking both the Jardin de Diane and the carp pond. His bedroom idiosyncratically contains a camp bed and some richly inlaid Boulle commodes. The **Salle du Trône**, created by Napoleon in 1808, is a decorative mixture of Louis XIII, XIV and XV in the same way as the Queen's Apartments, the Chambre de la Reine, reveal the passage of every queen from Marie de Médicis to the Empress Eugénie. Adjoining this is the **Salon du Jeu de la Reine**, beautifully decorated thanks mainly to the luckless Marie-Antoinette, who commissioned Rousseau to paint its murals.

The most brilliant of 18th-century decoration can be seen in the **Salle du Conseil**, built under François I but entirely reworked under Louis XV, who commissioned the fabulous ceiling paintings by Boucher.

Further apartments can be toured but only with guides; enquire at the ticket desk. Otherwise, head outside to the gardens and the Tiber – the square central pond in Le Nôtre's formal Grand Jardin. Facing the Cour de la Fontaine is the fountain of Ulysees, which in its turn fronts the peaceful expanse of a carp pond. On the other side of this aquatic area, immediately to the right of the Cour des Adieux, stretches the English-style garden relandscaped by Hurtault in 1812.

Open: Wednesday to Monday, 09.30–12.30hrs and 14.00–18.00hrs (till 17.00hrs in winter). Gardens open sunrise to sunset.

Barbizon The illustrious village of Barbizon is now characterised by up-market restaurants and tourist galleries. Between 1825 and 1870 it attracted a group of painters who were the first to practise outdoor painting, creating their own movement, the Ecole de Barbizon, and paving the way for the Impressionists. Corot, Millet, Rousseau and Daubigny all worked here, spending their days dabbling on canvas and their evenings at the Auberge du Père Ganne. The inn exhibits some touching memorabilia, as do the houses of Millet and Rousseau (both situated on Grande Rue). Don't be surprised to encounter traffic jams of tourist coaches here.

If the forest surrounding Fontainebleau is beckoning, go to the Office de Tourisme (31 place Napoléon Bonaparte, tel: 64 22 25 68) for information on horse-riding or bicycle hire. If you come by train, you can hire fairly basic bicycles at the station. If you have a car, then the 9km to the village of Barbizon will be easy.

199

Barbizon, where art moved away from the studio

Giverny

The sleek, low-lying building along the road from Monet's house is the Musée Americain, which aims to show US work inspired by the Impressionists.

▶ ▶ ▶ Giverny

Fondation Claude Monet, 27620 Giverny
By car: autoroute A13, exit at Vernon, take D5 to Giverny.
By train: from St Lazare to Vernon, then taxi or bus.
Situated on the banks of the Seine as it flows northwest through Normandy, Giverny is famous for only one reason – Claude Monet. This charming village was where the painter lived from 1883 until his death in 1926, tending his famous garden which became as important to him as the works it inspired. Each month is characterised by a dominant colour, but the most striking is perhaps May/June, when apple trees blossom, rhododendrons flower around the lily pond, and the wisteria tumbles over the Japanese bridge. However, any of the summer months will provide a ravishing vision of a discreetly controlled, colour-coordinated Nature.

Entrance is through the vast studio that Monet had built, which now unfortunately only houses reproductions of his works and a souvenir shop. Monet's simple two-storey house dominates the gardens, which slope down to the Japanese section. The pink house with its green shutters is pure delight for the colours of its interior, extensively restored in the late 1970s after decades of neglect. Deep blue dominates the kitchen, brilliant yellow the dining room, while Monet's vast Japanese print collection is hung throughout the house exactly as it was in his time. Upstairs his bedroom has a superb view extending across the garden and beyond to the valley.

Oriental influence The opening up of Japan to the West in the late 19th century stimulated artists' imaginations, and Monet was no exception: his Japanese garden stands as proof and memorial. When prospering finances allowed him to purchase this plot of land, Monet set about diverting the River Epte to create a pond. This was soon crossed by an arched bridge and surrounded by bamboo and other vegetation reminiscent of the Orient. Monet spent the rest of his life capturing in canvas the essence of its shadows and light, mottled tones, wisteria and water lilies.
Open: April to October, Tuesday to Sunday 10.00–12.00hrs/14.00–18.00hrs; gardens open all year.

Claude Monet (1840–1926) Brought up in Normandy, the youthful Monet soon moved to Paris to study painting. Here he met Bazille, Lepic, Renoir and Sisley, with whom he associated at the Brasserie des Martyrs. Monet and Bazille spent Easter near Barbizon, painting like Millet and Daubigny in that open air; the same year, Monet discovered Manet. By 1870 he was following the fate of a *peintre maudit*, with his work refused by the official Salon.

After a trip to London where he discovered the works of Turner, Monet returned to Paris and settled in Argenteuil, on the Seine just north of Paris. Here, like Daubigny, he installed his studio on a boat, capturing the changing light of the river as he travelled. Artistically Monet always remained faithful to water, from his origins on the Channel coast to the banks of the Seine and eventually, of course Giverny. In 1874 the Impressionist group was finally able to exhibit together, and it was Monet's 1872 painting entitled *Impression: soleil levant* that gave the group their identity. Success, however, did not come easily, and Monet's dire financial straits were only alleviated by friends like Manet who bought his paintings.

In 1879 Monet's wife died, just a few years before he finally achieved recognition as the high priest of a radically new movement in painting. By 1882 critics were at last favourable, and the following year he moved to 'Le Pressoir' in Giverny, together with his two sons, his mistress Alice Hoschedé (whom he later married) and her six children. Other Impressionists such as Renoir, Sisley and Degas all visited him there over the years, and Cézanne actually moved into the local inn for a period.

In 1897, with the maturing of the adjoining Japanese garden, Monet started on his water lily series. He later had a studio built in the garden to accommodate his large-scale. When Clémenceau asked him for a gift to the nation, Monet, by then in his 80s, set about painting a series of panels for the Orangerie, which he completed just before his death.

Monet's Japanese garden was the inspiration for his water lily paintings

201

EXCURSIONS

Right next door to Malmaison stands the late 17th-century Château de Bois-Préau, bought by Josephine in 1809 to house her doctor, ladies-in-waiting and guests (avenue de l'Impératrice Joséphine, 92500 Rueil-Malmaison; tel: 47 49 20 07). Today it is a memorial museum for Napoleon. Souvenirs ranging from the grandly kitsch to the absurdly intimate include portraits of Napoleon on his deathbed in St Helena, his campaign bed, boots, hairbrushes, marble busts and his death mask. *Open*: Wednesday to Monday, 10.30–12.30hrs and 13.30–17.00hrs.

▶ ▶ ▷ **Malmaison, Château de**
avenue du Château de Malmaison, 92500 Rueil-Malmaison.
By car: N13 from La Défense.
By train: RER line A to La Défense. Bus 158A.
This 17th-century manor with its unassuming front is the most elegant and luxurious surviving example of Napoleonic (Empire) decoration in France. Bought by the young general in 1799 as a present for his bride Josephine – Paris' most celebrated, though hardly most virtuous, beauty of the time – it was from the start more her domain than his. When Napoleon divorced Josephine in 1809 to marry Marie-Louise of Austria, he magnanimously allowed Josephine to keep the château, along with her imperial title and retinue.

Little was done to the exterior by Napoleon's architects, who merely added a canopied entrance in the form of a Roman tent, but the interior was entirely remodelled. The columned vestibule recalls a Roman atrium, its style perfectly reflecting Napoleon's love of grandeur and his imperial ambitions. Haughty busts of the Bonaparte family now line the walls. To the right are the billiard room, the *salon doré* and the music room. The wall colours and hangings, are a faithful recreation of the original décor, while the furnishings and bronze candelabra are Empire originals from Malmaison itself or other imperial palaces. In the music room, which in Josephine's time had a picture gallery extension, were once displayed some of the greatest pictures in Europe, from Rembrandt to Rubens, many looted by Napoleon's armies in Italy.

On the left of the entrance hall is the dining room which contains a remarkable 125-piece gilded silver service. The delicate wall paintings of muses and 'Greek' motifs recall the decoration of ancient Pompeii. In Napoleon's council room next door the walls and ceiling in striped silk create the illusion of a Roman military tent. The emperor's library boasts the most elaborate wall paintings as well as his famous mechanical desk brimming with secret drawers.

Upstairs are the emperor's bedroom, dressing room and sitting room decorated with portraits of the family. The central rooms are devoted to painting and memorabilia: David's celebrated *Napoleon Crossing the Alps*, Napoleon's toilet case, swords and captured weapons from the Egyptian campaign and a rare Sèvres porcelain tea set with Egyptian motifs. An album of hand painted flower prints by Redouté evokes Josephine's passion for exotic flowers, once extended to the Malmaison hothouses and gardens, the richest in Europe, which boasted plants and also animals specially imported from South America, Africa and Asia.

Beyond lies Josephine's private apartment. In her 'official' bedroom the magnificent canopied bed decorated with gilded swans is the centrepiece of the room. This glamorous 'imperial' style was redecorated the year of Josephine's divorce as a gesture of defiance to the new empress Marie-Louise. Next door is Josephine's smaller, more modest real bedroom painted in subtle colours. The exquisitely painted boudoir has a much lower ceiling and two fireplaces, making it the warmest room in Malmaison. This was where Josephine retreated in winter, her childhood in Martinique having left her with a lifelong aversion to cold weather.

In the attic rooms are Josephine's wardrobe and that of her daughter Hortense. Always coquettish, Josephine – much to Napoleon's annoyance – spent fortunes on clothes and jewellery and was easily the most luxuriously and best-dressed woman of her time. The dozens of pairs of shoes, parasols, day and court dresses with richly embroidered trains testify to this passion. Paintings and other memorabilia in these rooms illustrate the appearance of the Malmaison gardens and park under Josephine and trace the history of her descendants by Napoleon, including the future emperor, Napoleon's great-nephew Napoleon III.

The Château de Malmaison

Malmaison forest

Louis XIV's place of birth at St-Germain-en-Laye

▶ ▶ ▶ **Saint-Germain-en-Laye**

By car: Autoroute de l'Ouest (N13), exit at Versailles-Nord.

By train: take the RER line A1.

In under half an hour you can reach this rather chic suburb, once the home of kings of France, from François I to Louis XIV. Its popularity and clean air were such that in 1847 the Baron de Rothschild personally financed a connecting railway line with Paris. Often overlooked by tourists, it is nevertheless a continuing favourite with Parisians. The atmosphere is unlikely to project you into provincial France, and on Sunday mornings most shops are open to accommodate the day-trippers – so be warned.

The main attraction remains the formidable fortress originally erected in 1122 to protect the west of Paris but substantially rebuilt by François I in the 16th century. One of its splendours is the Sainte-Chapelle, a 13th century Gothic masterpiece, 10 years older than its Parisian counterpart, although minus the stained glass, and with its rose window unfortunately obstructed by one of François I's constructions. Notice the sculpted heads crowning each arch, which are portraits of St Louis and his family.

Sun King's setting It was in this château that Louis XIV was born, took refuge during the popular uprising known as the Fronde (1648–53), and altogether spent more time than at Versailles later in his life. Once Versailles was fit to move into, he graciously left the use of St-Germain-en-Laye to the exiled James II of England, who died there in 1701 (his mausoleum stands in the church across the square from the château).

Le Nôtre, created the impressive esplanade high above the Seine; a stroll along here and back to base covers 5km. The view from the terrace across the valley of the Seine inspired the Impressionist painter Sisley.

Since 1867 the château has housed the **Musée des Antiquités Nationales** (*open* Wednesday to Monday, 09.45–12.00hrs and 13.30–17.15hrs). This unique and fascinating archaeological collection ranges from prehistory to the Middle Ages. Superb examples of silver and gold Merovingian jewellery, weapons and glass are displayed alongside Gallo-Roman ceramics, images of Celtic and Roman divinities and funerary objects. The most astounding exhibit, going back 24,000 years, is the first known representation of a woman's face, **La Dame de Brassempouy**. Somewhat younger is the superb Bronze Age helmet with an engraved gold band from Amfreville. An entire room is devoted to a replica of the wall paintings of bulls from Lascaux's caves in the Dordogne.

The other landmark to head for in St-Germain-en-Laye, the **Musée du Prieuré**, is a short walk away (go past the church opposite the château and turn left down the rue au Pain, until you reach the rue Maurice Denis). A former 17th-century hospital, this building is devoted to the painter Maurice Denis, who died in St-Germain-en- Laye (*open:* Wednesday to Sunday, 10.30–17.30hrs). Symbolism, the Nabis and Post-impressionism are the movements represented in the posters, paintings and sculpture of his contemporaries Bonnard, Vuillard, Vallotton, Maillol and Paul Sérusier. Denis tried to revive the tradition of sacred art; one example of his efforts is the chapel decorated by him, which adjoins the museum.

Maurice Denis (1870–1943) When still a precocious art student aged 18, Denis was already helping to form the group of Nabis. Sérusier, who had just spent the summer in the company of Gauguin at Pont-Aven in Brittany, shared the new theories with Denis and showed him the *Talisman*, an arrangement of pure colours on a wooden box lid painted under Gauguin's guidance. By 1890 Denis had published a manifesto of what he called neo-traditionalism, outlining the formula that subsequently influenced much modern painting, a vindication of pure and autonomous painting: 'Remember that a picture before becoming a warhorse, a nude woman or any kind of anecdote, is essentially a flat surface covered with colours arranged in a certain order.'

While borrowing certain elements from Impressionism, the Nabis were also interested in contemporary influences such as the newly popular Japanese print, equally visible in Gauguin's use of flat colour. Their art was intimate, an art of domestic interiors such as in Vuillard's and Bonnard's works. Denis was the main exponent of its spiritual qualities, which he linked with nostalgia for the primitive and for nature.

Don't miss the Pavillon Henri IV in the gardens, where the Sun King was born and Alexandre Dumas wrote *Les Trois Mousquetaires*. It is now a rather exclusive hotel-restaurant and the only remaining element of the *château neuf* which the future Charles X gaily started to demolish in 1777.

The Grande Terrace, Château de St-Germain-en-Laye

EXCURSIONS

A tapestry workshop was set up in nearby Maincy to produce the necessary hangings for the château. This later became the celebrated Manufacture des Gobelins.

▶ ▶ ▶   Vaux-le-Vicomte, Domaine de

77950 Maincy

By car: Autoroute A6, exit at Melun-Sénart.

By train: from Gare de Lyon to Melun, then bus or taxi.

Near Melun, 46km southeast of Paris, lies Vaux-le-Vicomte, one of France's great baroque châteaux. Its colourful history, apart from its face, is so extraordinary that it needs to be known beforehand.

The land itself was bought in 1641 by Louis XIV's power-hungry Minister of Finance. Regent of France until Louis XIV came of age, Fouquet was also a great patron of the arts and passed on some of his immense fortune to the likes of Molière, La Fontaine and Madame de Sévigné. His family motto *Quo non ascendet?* (roughly, 'the sky's the limit') was particularly relevant to his tastes in decoration.

In 1656, he assembled the most talented artists and craftsmen of the time to create the ultimate symbol of his power and what was to become the first example of the Louis XIV style. Thus Louis Le Vau was appointed architect, the painter Le Brun brought in for the interiors, and André Le Nôtre for the landscaping of the enormous park. For five years an army of 18,000 workers slaved away to construct a château whose proportions were equalled only by the rate of embezzling Fouquet was reputed to have indulged in to pay his bills.

The party Finally, on a warm summer night in 1661, Fouquet threw a legendary house-warming party. The famous chef Vatel supervised the ovens, La Fontaine and Molière the cultural entertainment. Dishes of solid gold crowned dozens of buffet tables set out in the garden, while jewel-studded elephants lined the alleys of orange trees and Chinese fireworks were shot off from the ponds (there were over 1,000 fountains and waterspouts). Never had Parisian society seen a social event quite so extravagant. Nor had the 23-year-old Louis XIV, who had recently come of age to rule in his own right. Two weeks later Fouquet was arrested by the famous D'Artagnan, imprisoned, his possessions confiscated, and at his trial found guilty of embezzlement. Thus his dream ended in a dank cell, where he remained until his death. Meanwhile, his talented craftsmen found new employment working on the king's new residence at Versailles – directly inspired by Vaux-le-Vicomte.

Although spared during the Revolution, the château nevertheless fell on hard times. Only seven paintings, six statues and two tables remained when a wealthy industrialist, Alfred Sommier, bought it in 1875. Today the interior and the grounds have been magnificently restored by his descendants, while installed in the stables is a Musée des Equipages (horse-drawn carriages and accessories). Its historic collection includes the carriage Charles X used to escape from Paris in 1830.

The interior In the château itself, after entering through the hall with its 12 doric columns, don't miss the Salon des Muses, with Le Brun's painted ceilings illustrating nine different muses. Here Molière and his troupe acted

L'Ecole des Maris for the first time, with Queen Henrietta-Maria of England and Fouquet as audience. The intimately scaled Cabinet des Jeux possesses another Le Brun masterpiece on its ceiling, this time *Le Sommeil*. It is hardly surprising that the artist spent two years closeted in the château accomplishing his marvels, which continue in the Salle des Buffets and upstairs in Fouquet's bedroom. Another highlight is the Chambre du Roi – which of course never hosted the King – used as a model for Versailles and subsequently imitated throughout Europe. Try to tour the château during one of its breathtaking candlelit evenings: over 1,000 candles flicker away, conveying the atmosphere of Fouquet's time (every Saturday from May to September, 20.30–23.00hrs).

The monumental gardens of Vaux-le-Vicomte are Le Nôtre's first masterpiece. A succession of terraces, lawns, fountains and ponds, lined with statues and neatly sculpted bushes, lead away from the château down towards an impressive canal, hidden until your footsteps bring you to its edge. You can continue into the woods on the other side.

Open: April to October 10.00–18.00hrs; winter, 11.00–17.00hrs daily. Fountain displays April to October, second and last Saturday of the month, 15.00–18.00hrs.

Vaux-le-Vicomte

Drive Parks and châteaux

Leave Paris from the Porte Maillot, taking the N185 through the Bois de Boulogne and across the Seine towards Suresnes. Follow it through St-Cloud and into the park.

A perfect combination of water and forest, the **Parc de St-Cloud** was laid out by Le Nôtre, although the château was burned down during the 1870 Franco-Prussian War.

Continue along the N185 through Ville d'Avray to Versailles.

Stop to visit this remarkable architectural and landscaping feat. The town itself has some charm, particularly the small quartier of **St-Louis**, near the royal kitchen garden.

Take the N10 and soon, at a rather complex series of intersections, turn onto the N12, leading to Neauphle-le-Château. Follow this road through a mixture of rolling countryside and far-flung suburban developments to the village of Pontchartrain.

Here there stands a pink and white 17th-century château, now a school

of agriculture, in a perfectly composed perspective. Although it is not open to the public, drive down through the curtain of trees to enjoy its setting. Continue through the village of **Neauphle-le-Vieux**, with its 13th-century church, once part of a Benedictine monastery.

Follow the D11 past the Forest of Beynes to Thoiry.

This is the perfect destination to appease restless young spirits, as the château (not open to the public), is set in a zoological park (*open: daily 10.00–17.00hrs*).

Immediately beyond the park on the D11 the road forks: turn left towards Villiers, where you pass another private château, and continue south to Garancières. At Millemont take the D197 and then the D199, turning right through Grosrouvre; a detour to the Château la Couarde is possible en route.

The **Château de la Mormaire** soon appears in this pretty agricultural

The President's retreat: the Château de Rambouillet, once a royal residence

landscape, where you join the D112 towards **Montfort-l'Amaury,** one of the most charming towns in the region. Once home to the powerful counts of Montfort (the 13th-century Simon de Montfort being the most notorious), the ruined castle remains at the top of the hill, as well as elements of former fortified walls. Don't miss the Gothic-Renaissance cemetery in the village centre, which belongs to the church of St-Pierre.

Leave Montfort by the D138 to St-Léger-en-Yvelines, a village built up around a 12th-century church. Near by stands an ancient menhir, a kilometre's walk from the village.

Taking the D936, you soon come to the harmonious town of Rambouillet. The château of **Rambouillet,** once favoured by kings and aristocrats, is now the President's official weekend and summer retreat. When he is not in residence it is open to the public; don't miss the extensive grounds. This *parc à l'anglaise*, with its follies, canals and islands, was bought by Louis XVI for Marie-Antoinette and a dairy was built to keep her amused. The château was mainly rebuilt in the early 18th century and its superb

woodwork is only rivalled by Versailles. The bulky Tour François I testifies to the Renaissance king's presence here; this is where he died.

Leave Rambouillet by the N306, turning immediately right along the D27, which takes you through the forested Vallée de Chevreuse to Rochefort-en-Yvelines and joins the A10 motorway leading back to Paris.

Stained-glass windows in St-Pierre church, Montfort-l'Amaury

EXCURSIONS

The Château de Versailles, seen from the south Parterre

▶ ▶ ▶ **Versailles, Château de**

By car: take autoroute A13, then A12.

By train: RER line C to Versailles Rive-Gauche (closest) or main line from Saint Lazare to Versailles Rive Droite.

More than a palace, the Château of Versailles, Louis XIV's greatest creation, was conceived as a world unto itself. Seat of government, permanent residence of the royal family and the cream of French nobility, it also functioned as a permanent exhibition of French grandeur and sophistication. The endless grounds were tamed into a geometry so perfect that even nature seemed to obey the Sun King's commands. Surrounding the palace and its formal gardens were the largest kitchen gardens in the kingdom, the only zoo, the largest artificial lake, acres of game-filled forest, a new town catering to the needs of the court, and two weekend retreats with their own grounds, the Trianons.

The original château, built by Louis XIII in 1631, was a modest hunting lodge. In 1661 Louis XIV announced his intention of moving his court to this deserted swamp 17km southwest of Paris, an astute way of isolating the nobility and his ministers while keeping an eye on his not-too-distant capital. Building hardly stopped until the king's death in 1715.

Three majestic avenues lined with trees and mansions converge on the great place d'Armes in front of the courtyard. Facing the square are the monumental stables built by Jules Hardouin Mansart, the second Versailles architect.

The first architect, Louis Le Vau, built around the original lodge on three sides, tarting up the old brick front in the centre of the courtyard with urns, busts and a wrought-iron balcony for the king's bedroom. Louis XIV's last addition to the palace was the magnificent baroque chapel behind the north courtyard block, finished in 1710.

Garden façade It is the garden façade that best epitomises the Sun King's ambitions. Faced in stone, lined with Ionic columns and capped by an ornamental balustrade and carved trophies, the central section is part of the original 'envelope' designed by Le Vau. In 1678 Mansart filled in the terrace to create the Hall of Mirrors and added two lengthy blocks to the north and south, which make the garden front of Versailles the longest (570m) in Europe.

Royal apartments The central royal apartments are divided into two sections. Access to the Grands Appartements is from entrance A next to the chapel in the courtyard. The Petits Appartements (guided tour only) are reached from the south side of the courtyard. The Grands Appartements, laid out in the 1670s by the king's chief painter, Charles Le Brun, were the public rooms. Grand, luxurious and draughty, they were used for official court assemblies and lavish entertainments.

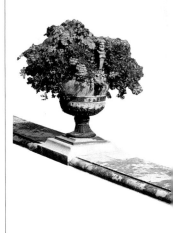

Preceding the apartments is the king's private entrance to the chapel, laid out on two levels, the upper for the royal family and highest nobility, the ground floor for the rest of the court. The vaulted ceilings are painted in the illusionist Italian manner.

The **Grands Appartements** themselves are dominated by coloured marble, gilded bronze, sculpture, illusionist painting, velvet and silk. Each salon is dedicated to an Olympian deity symbolising a royal virtue or duty. Apollo, closely linked to the cult of the Sun King, lends his name to the throne room.

What most visitors come to see is the Hall of Mirrors. Flanked on either side by the ornate salons of War and Peace, it is the largest, most magnificent and last to be completed. It once boasted – apart from the 17 great mirrors – crystal chandeliers, precious furniture and vases, gilded candelabra, damask curtains, potted orange trees and a silver throne. The painted ceilings, Le Brun's masterpiece, depict the King himself. It was here that Bismarck proclaimed the unification of Germany in 1871 and that the Treaty of Versailles, ending World War I, was signed in 1919.

From the Hall of Mirrors you enter the queen's official apartment. Hard to miss is the queen's bedroom, with the famous feather-canopied bed where all the royal babies were born in public view. Redecorated for Marie Leszinska, wife of Louis XV, the panelling is in the delicate rococo style, a welcome relief from the monumental grandeur of the Louis XIV salons.

Beyond the queen's apartment begin a series of dull picture galleries devoted 'to the glories of France'. Undoubtedly the greatest picture is David's huge *Distribution of the Eagle Standards* and a copy of his *Coronation of Josephine* (in the Louvre), both painted for Napoleon.

The **Petits Appartements** were the living quarters of the royal family and, of course, the king's mistresses. Built around dark inner courtyards, they aimed for privacy and an escape from court etiquette. They provide the finest and most priceless examples in France of 18th-century panelling and decoration.

212

Versailles was the ultimate symbol of royal grandeur, from the symmetry of its façade...

...to the Apollo Fountain, a story of divinity for a king who believed in his own glory

The gardens The 100-hectare Versailles grounds, the largest palace gardens in Europe, are the epitome of the French formal style. Laid out by Le Nôtre along a central axis leading to the great canal in the park, the severe symmetry is relieved by hundreds of statues, follies and fountains. The most stunning are those of Latona and Apollo illustrating the story of the Sun King's favourite god. The monumental Orangerie south of the palace is by Mansart. From the great Neptune fountain on the north side, stroll back to the centre and past the Apollo fountain till you reach the canal, where rowboats and bicycles can be hired and a pleasure boat or mini-train taken to the Trianons.

The Trianons The Grand Trianon was built for Louis XIV as a love nest and an escape from palace routine. Its delicate pink marbled architecture is a welcome contrast to the official grandeur of the palace. The garden, planted with flowers all year round (a million pots), was the most luxurious in France.

The Petit Trianon, built for Louis XV's mistress, Madame du Barry, was later presented to Marie-Antoinette by Louis XVI. Often described as the absolute jewel of French neo-classical architecture, its grounds were entirely transformed by her into a romantic 'English' park with a make-believe village (Hameau), where the Queen could lead the 'simple' life away from the despised duties of the court.

Open: State apartments Tuesday to Sunday, 09.45–17.00 hrs; Grand Trianon 09.45–12.00, 14.00–17.00hrs; Petit Trianon 14.00–17.00hrs. The park is open daily from sunrise to sunset. Go on the first or third Sunday of the month (May to September) to see the spectacular fountains functioning.

Don't miss the gastronomic tour of the recently restored Potager du Roi (the royal kitchen garden). Open from May to mid-November, this delightful garden of Eden can be toured with the resident experts, tasting vegetables and jams, at the end. Tours start at 14.00hrs (daily except Tuesday) at the gate, 6 rue Hardy.

VERSAILLES - LE PARC

Whether *foie gras* or shoes, Parisian goods just beckon customers, and totting up small fortunes on credit card bills. But that is part of what this city is about, and nobody should leave with empty hands. Lovers of clothes and stylish accessories should window-shop in streets like rue des Francs-Bourgeois (affordable shoes, accessories, clothes), rue de Grenelle (designer clothes and shoes), rue Etienne Marcel (the mecca of young designers), place des Victoires (successful designers) or Faubourg St-Honoré (luxury). Both the rue de Rennes and boulevard St-Germain are good stretches for reasonably priced boutiques. For gourmets the choice is similarly enticing, and for everything one of the greatest pleasures is the perfect packaging, making even a modest purchase look royal.

Accessories

Annick Goutal, 14 rue de Castiglione, 75001 (tel: 42 60 52 82), metro: Concorde. Delicate, sensuous scents, oils and lotions, beautifully packaged, make a pleasant change from the usual mass-produced couture perfumes.

Charles Kammer, 14 rue de Grenelle, 75007 (tel: 42 22 91 19), metro: St-Germain. Branch off place des Victoires. Smart shoe designs with imaginative details and almost possible prices.

Fabrice, 33 and 54 rue Bonaparte, 75006 (tel: 43 26 57 95), metro: St-Germain. Very Rive Gauche accessory shop: colourful jewellery, decorative headbands. Certainly not understated.

Lancel, 8 place de l'Opéra, 75009 (tel: 47 42 37 29), metro: Opéra. Branches all over Paris. Classic, good-quality bags, wallets, luggage.

Madeleine Gély, 218 boulevard St-Germain, 75007 (tel: 42 22 63 35), metro: rue du Bac. Astonishing selection of over 400 walking sticks (cigarette-holder canes, watchcanes) and umbrellas of all shapes, designs and sizes.

Marie Mercié, 56 rue Tiquetonne, 75002 (tel: 40 26 60 68), metro: Etienne-Marcel. Also at 23 rue Saint-Sulpice, 75006. Paris' whackiest hat designer who also produces some seductive, very wearable designs. Look for the bargain bin in this tiny, very feminine boutique.

La Maroquinerie Parisienne, 30 rue Tronchet, 75009 (tel: 47 42 83 40), metro: Madeleine. Vast choice of cut-price leather goods and luggage. Some top brands are available here.

Réciproque, 95 rue de la Pompe, 75016 (tel: 47 04 30 28), metro: Pompe, Victor-Hugo. Not strictly accessories but an excellent address for picking up second-hand couture and designer clothes abandoned by fickle ladies of the 16th *arrondissement*. Large accessory department stocks some real finds.

Sacha, 50 rue de Turbigo, 75002 (tel: 45 08 13 15), metro: Etienne-Marcel. Branches all over Paris. Young, fun shoes at accessible prices.

Stephane Kélian, 6 place des Victoires, 75002 (tel: 42 61 60 74), metro: Bourse. Branches in the Marais and Champs Elysées. Some sensational designs (matched by prices) at one of Paris' top shoe designers. Beautifully made, last for ever.

Books, Records
Fnac Librairie Internationale, 71 boulevard St-Germain, 75005 (tel: 44 41 31 50), Other branches at Forum-des-Halles, rue de Rennes and avenue Wagram. Part of Fnac chain of low price stores, also stocking camera, computer and hi-fi equipment. This branch specialises in international publications from UK to China.
Galignani, 224 rue de Rivoli, 75001 (tel: 42 60 76 07), metro: Tuileries.
Well-stocked, old-fashioned bookshop. Helpful bilingual service. Range of English-language books.**Virgin Megastore,** 52 Champs Elysées, 75008 (tel: 40 74 06 48), metro: Franklin-Roosevelt. The Parisian record shop. Track down records by French teeny-boppers' hero Patrick Bruel or latest British groups.

Children
Agnès B Lolita, 3 rue du Jour, 75001 (tel: 45 08 49 89), metro: Les Halles. Ineffably Parisian, simple and stylish cotton-knit and jersey clothes that don't come particularly cheap.
Au Nain Bleu, 406/410 rue St-Honoré, 75008 (tel: 42 60 39 01), metro: Concorde. The oldest toy store, illustrious, magical, unforgettable with toy soldiers galore, puzzles, dolls and their houses, soft toys.
Jacadi, 38 place du Marché St-Honoré, 75001 (tel: 40 20 97 05), metro: Pyramides, l'Opéra. Branches all over Paris. Good quality and value chain offering up-to-minute clothes for babies to early teens.
Jouets & Cie, 11 boulevard de Sébastopol, 75001 (tel: 42 33 67 67), metro: Châtelet. Gigantic labyrinth stocking every toy and game currently available.
Pom d'Api, 13 rue du Jour, 75001 (tel: 42 36 08 87), metro: Les Halles. Also at 28 rue du Four. Adorable hip miniature footwear. Doc Martens for toddlers made in France.
Si Tu Veux, 68 Galerie Vivienne, 75002 (tel: 42 60 59 97), metro: Bourse. Charming, affordable toy shop with teddy bear branch and party dressing-up/games department.

Department Stores
Au Bon Marché, 38 rue de Sèvres, 75007 (tel: 42 60 33 45), metro: Sèvres-Babylone. Founded in 1852, the oldest in Paris and the only Rive Gauche department store. Less crowded than the boulevard Haussmann stores, more genteel, more courteous. Good for household goods, lingerie and children's wear. Basement bookstore is excellent.
Au Printemps, 64 boulevard Haussmann, 75009 (tel: 42 82 50 00), metro: Havre-Caumartin. An old classic. Wide-ranging clothes and accessories, good household and furniture departments – watch out for own-range Primavera. Quality not always up to its neighbouring rival (Galeries Lafayette) but prices often lower. Own-label goods, Sélection Printemps, are good value.
BHV (Bazar de l'Hôtel de Ville), 52 rue de Rivoli, 75004 (tel: 42 74 90 00), metro: Hôtel-de-Ville. For kings and queens of do-it-yourself. The basement is a paradise of every imaginable tool, gadget, hardware, etc. Forget the fashion and stick to paint stripping; materials on 4th

France produces more varieties of cheese than any other country in the world. From Normandy to the Alps, cows', goats' and lambs' milk is syphoned off to create those miraculous odorous objects displayed in Parisian cheese shops – just a few kilos of the 160,000 tons produced annually. The French consume 21kg per year (the Americans a mere 10kg).

215

A treasure-house of consumer goods: the Galeries Lafayette

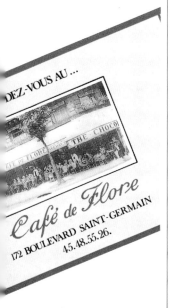

floor. Assistants are employed by brand names, so are supremely unhelpful.

Galeries Lafayette, 40 boulevard Haussmann, 75009 (tel: 42 82 34 56), metro: Chaussée d'Antin. Spectacular glass-domed store, luxurious, often pricey but also stocks more economical, own-label goods. Two floors devoted to fashion. Every top designer has an outlet here selling latest designs. Comparisons are easier and hours of window-shopping saved. Ground-floor accessory department is excellent for presents. There is a smaller branch of Galeries Lafayette at Montparnasse at the base of the tower.

La Samaritaine, rue de la Monnaie, 75001 (tel: 40 41 20 20), metro: Pont-Neuf. Labyrinthine multi-building department store which sells everything if you can find it. Usually helpful service. Most useful is Magasin 2 for *perfumerie,* do-it-yourself, household goods, furnishings and, surprisingly, some designer clothes. La Samaritaine is not as crowded as BHV (see page 215). Rooftop tearoom.

Marks & Spencer, 35 boulevard Haussmann, 75009 (tel: 47 42 42 91), metro: Havre-Caumartin. British chain store, clothing and well-stocked quality food department, now a favourite with chic Parisians. No concessions to French taste.

Food and wine
Cheese

Androuet, 41 rue d'Amsterdam, 75008 (tel: 48 74 26 90), metro: Liège. Encyclopaedic range of aromatic French cheeses, perfectly ripened. Famous old restaurant and shop, delivery in Paris.

La Maison du Fromage, 62 rue de Sèvres, 75007 (tel: 47 34 33 45), metro: Sèvres-Babylone. This where the five-star Lucas-Carton restaurant orders its cheeses. Sublime selection.

Tachon, 38 rue de Richelieu, 75001 (tel: 42 96 08 66), metro: Palais-Royal. Fabulous range of goat's cheeses, not forgetting the cow's, in atmospheric old shop. Friendly professional advice.

Gourmet Groceries

A la Mère de Famille, 35 rue du Faubourg-Montmartre, 75009 (tel: 47 70 83 69) metro: Le Peletier. Superb 18th-century grocery with shelves of ornate and colourful sweets, biscuits, jams. Friendly, old-fashioned service.

Fauchon, 26 place de la Madeleine, 75008 (tel: 47 42 60 11), metro: Madeleine. Over 20,000 exotic and luxury products from spices to fruit, tea, *charcuterie*, cakes. Too famous for good service. Outrageous prices.

Hédiard, 21 place de la Madeleine, 75008 (tel: 42 66 44 36), metro: Madeleine. Fauchon's main rival has branches all over Paris. Freshly roasted coffee, spices, expensive wines.

Izraël, 30 rue François Miron, 75004 (tel: 42 72 66 23) metro: St-Paul. Colourful souk of North African and Oriental products. Sacks of grains, bottles of spices, piles of African baskets.

La Maison du Miel, 24 rue Vignon, 75009 (tel: 47 42 26 70), metro: Madeleine. Offers countless types of honey (tasting possible) in pretty tiled interior. Established in 1908.

Legrand Filles et Fils, 1 rue de la Banque, 75002 (tel: 42 60 07 12), metro: Bourse. Renowned wine and fine grocery shop founded in 1890. Unbeatable range of wines, helpful service. Situated in the delightful Galerie Vivienne.

Paul Corcellet, 46 rue des Petits-Champs, 75002 (tel: 42 96 51 82), metro: Pyramides. Wonderful old emporium stocking delicious own products: sauces, mustards, vinegars. Also jams, sweets, alcohols.

Robert Labeyrie, 6 rue Montmartre, 75001 (tel: 45 08

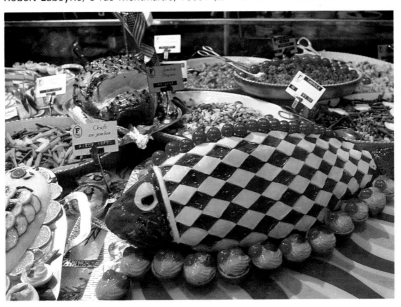

A feast for the eyes and the taste buds: Fauchon, place de la Madeleine

95 26) metro: Les Halles. Famous shop selling products from Landes. Raw goose and duck livers, truffles, dried cêpe mushrooms, *foie gras*.

Soleil de Provence, 6 rue du Cherche-Midi, 75006. tel: 45 48 15 02. metro: Sèvres-Babylone. Quality Provençal products: olive oil, olives, honey, herbs, natural soaps.

Pâtisseries and chocolates

Brocco, 180 rue du Temple, 75003 (tel: 42 72 19 81), metro: République. One of Paris' top pâtisserie shops/tearooms. Delicious *Cérisette* or Brazilian mocha cakes.

Christian Constant, 26 rue du Bac, 75007 (tel: 42 96 53 53), metro: rue du Bac. Tantalising fruit tarts and rich cakes like Macao, Kalinka or Pont Royal.

Debauve et Gallais, 30 rue des Saint-Pères, 75007 (tel: 45 48 54 67), metro: St-Germain. Ask for Marie-Antoinette's chocolates! Original 18th-century shop selling tea, coffee, divine chocolates and vanilla.

Dalloyau, 99/101 rue du Faubourg St-Honoré, 75008 (tel: 43 59 18 10). metro: St-Philippe-du-Roule. Pastry-maker for Napoleon. Exquisite macaroons and Mogador cake. Branches in 6th and 15th.

Lenôtre, 44 rue du Bac, 75007 (tel: 42 22 39 39), metro: rue du Bac. World-famous desserts, cakes, chocolates and ice creams. Try an *opéra* or a *concorde*. Main branch in 16th.

Fashion
Designer clothes (women's)

Agnès B, 6 rue du Jour, 750091 (tel: 45 08 56 56), metro: Les Halles. A young Parisian classic. Smart, sporty clothes at reasonable prices. Branches all over the world.

Anne-Marie Beretta, 24 rue St-Sulpice, 75006 (tel: 43 26 99 30), metro: St-Sulpice. Feminine, elegant clothes, often with original details.

Azzedine Alaïa, 17 rue du Parc-Royal, 75004 (tel: 42 72 19 19), metro: St-Paul. The inventor of the much-copied skin-tight dress. Follow Grace Jones' example if you can afford it.

Barbara Bui, 23 rue Etienne Marcel, 75001 (tel: 40 26 43 65), metro: Etienne-Marcel. Gossamer silk fabrics, drapey designs. Up-to-the-minute femininity. Expensive.

Cacharel, 3 place des Victoires, 75001 (tel: 42 33 29 88), metro: Bourse. Good-quality designs for middle-of-the-road tastes. Last year's collection is sold off at Stock, 114 rue d'Alésia, 75014 (tel: 45 42 53 04).

Chantal Thomass, 11 rue Madame, 75006 (tel: 45 44 60 11), metro: St-Sulpice. Quality sexy designs from lingerie to gabardine suits. Romantic, imaginative, pricey.

Emmanuelle Khanh, 2 rue de Tournon, 75006 (tel: 46 33 41 03), metro: Odéon. Very Rive Gauche style, sharp yet fluid cuts, superb blouses. Rummage in her stock shop in Les Halles for a bargain from last year's designs: 6 rue Pierre-Lescot (1st floor).

Irié, 8 rue du Pré-aux-Clercs, 75007 (tel: 42 61 18 28), metro: rue du Bac. Cheerful, brightly coloured designs in supple, inventive fabrics. A former designer with Kenzo. Reasonable prices.

Issey Miyake, 3 place des Vosges, 75004 (tel: 48 87 01 86), metro: St-Paul. Other boutiques on Left Bank, but this one is stunning. Now legendary sculptural designs beautifully displayed.

Jean-Paul Gaultier, 6 rue Vivienne, 75002 (tel: 42 86 05 05), metro: Bourse. Witty, irreverent clothes in a soaring futuristic boutique. Questionable prices.

Kenzo, 3 place des Victoires, 75001 (tel: 42 36 81 41), metro: Bourse. King of zappy fun clothes. Huge boutique displayscollection and accessories at high prices.

Scooter, 10 rue de Turbigo, 75001 (tel: 45 08 89 31), metro: Etienne Marcel. Wildly trendy, latest '60s revivals in clothes and accessories.

Tehen, 5 bis rue des Rosiers, 75004 (tel: 40 27 97 37), metro: St-Paul. Stylish but comfortable jersey and knitwear coordinates in wide range of colours. Reasonable prices.

Un Après-Midi de Chien, 10 rue du Jour, 75001 (tel: 40 26 92 78), metro: Les Halles. Teeny-retro styles, embroidered cotton blouses, pastel colours. Reasonable

Menswear

Autour du Monde, 12 rue des Francs Bourgeois, 75003 (tel: 42 77 16 18), metro: St-Paul. Safari image copied from surplus clothing. Timeless, ageless, good prices.

Daniel Hechter, 146 boulevard St-Germain, 75006 (tel: 43 26 96 36), metro: Odéon, Mabillon. Branches all over Paris. Relaxed classicism, well cut, beautifully colour-coordinated range. Not cheap, but not outrageous either. Women's range too.

Façonnable, 25 rue Royale, 75008 (tel: 47 42 72 60), metro: Madeleine. Parisian view of British style at astronomical prices, but you can always stick to the silk boxer shorts.

Island, 4 rue Vide Gousset, 75001 (tel: 42 61 77 77), metro: Bourse. Casual sportswear and accessories, well displayed, not over priced.

Loft Design By, 12 rue du Faubourg St-Honoré, 75008 (tel: 42 65 59 65), metro: Concorde. Revamped tweedy jackets, oilskins and casual separates at very reasonable prices.

Household

Collection Orient Express, 15 rue Boissy-d'Anglas, 75008 (tel: 47 42 24 45), metro: Madeleine. For nostalgic travellers, an old-fashioned shop selling reproductions of crystal, china, tableware, etc, that was designed for the famous luxury train.

Dehillerin, 18 rue Coquillière, 75001 (tel: 42 36 53 13), metro: Les Halles. Gigantic copper pans, hundreds of sharp knives, *bain maries*, skewers, sieves etc. The foodie's paradise, and where every self-respecting Parisian chef stocks up.

Etamine, 63 rue du Bac, 75007 (tel: 42 22 03 16), metro: rue du Bac. Vast home design shop, superb objects and fabrics imported from all over world, but always with a Parisian stamp of taste. Own fabric range.

Soleiad, 78 rue de Seine, 75006 (tel: 43 54 62 25), metro: Mabillon, Odéon. Cheerful range of fabrics beaming out Provençal warmth. Traditional designs made into napkins, tablecloths, cushions etc.

219

Food and Drink

Although Napoleon apparently proudly claimed to complete his meals in under 18 minutes, you will rarely be able to do this in Paris and nor will you want to. Although trends towards more efficient eating have reduced traditionally endless lunches to more sprightly affairs, often wolfed down at the counters of bars and bistros, Parisians still enjoy their fodder, and still give it a lot of their time and money. Equally important is the liquid refreshment which over the last decade has given rise to a growing number of *bars à vins* (wine bars), where numerous nectars are served by the glass and, accompanied by very reasonable *plats du jour.*

Restaurants In Paris lunch is generally served from 12.00 till 14.00 or 14.30hrs, after which you should head for a brasserie which serves all day. Dinner is usually served from 19.30hrs, although no self-respecting Parisian dines before at least 21.00hrs, and orders usually stop between 22.00 and 23.00hrs, after which diners will happily linger into the small hours. For avid post-midnight eaters the area to head for is **Les Halles**, where old favourites such as **Au Pied de Cochon, Au Chien qui Fume** or **La Poule au Pot** remain open very, very late (the first all night and the last till 06.00). Near by, in the rue des Lombards, **Au Duc des Lombards** and **Le Sunset** continue the local tradition but with updated décors and music. Booking is essential in more select restaurants, even if it is made in the afternoon for the evening.

Beware of Sundays, a favourite closing day, which leaves some *quartiers* deserted and recovering from the excesses of Saturday night. However as Paris is Paris, you will not starve: head for one of the popular brasseries or the famous and chic **Café Drouant** near the Opéra, where the annual literary prize, the Prix Goncourt, is awarded. If in the 16th, go to the bustling **Brasserie Stella**; in the 7th, indulge in the rich

Food is a form of art in the French capital

specialities of the southwest at **Thoumieux**. Near the Arc de Triomphe? Walk downhill to **Le Boeuf sur le Toit** in the rue du Colisée and join the fun. On the islands? Go to **Nos Ancêtres les Gaulois**, which, despite being a favourite tourist haunt, makes a warm, boisterous retreat on a winter Sunday evening. Want a change from French cooking (unlikely)? **Darkoum** in the rue Ste-Anne, has a spectacular Moorish interior, impeccable service and delectable couscous and tajines.

Budget eating Choosing where you eat in Paris depends very much on budget, although if this is relatively unimportant the city is at your feet. Without going to the ruinous top restaurants such as **Taillevent, Joël Robuchon, Lucas-Carton** or **La Tour d'Argent**, you can still dine divinely in a growing number of serious restaurants which now propose a 'menu' in the evening. Previously this budgeting method (an all-in three-course meal at a fixed price, wine excluded) was only available at lunchtime, but, many chic destinations are now using it to drum up more evening business.

Even if your pocket does not stretch to *haute cuisine*, you can try the more affordable bistros of top chefs Michel Rostang (**Le Bistrot d'à côté**) or Guy Savoy (**Bistrot de l'Etoile**), both of whom opened these more affordable establishments as an alternative to their renowned temples of gastronomy near by. The 17th *arrondissement* running into the 8th, is the heart of Parisian gastronomy, with a heavy concentration of celebrated chefs and their restaurants. Booking sometimes has to be made months ahead but if you want to spend anything approaching 1000 FF for one admittedly divine dinner, it is worth thinking ahead.

If you are looking for a more intimate tête-à-tête at a price that will allow you a taxi back afterwards, then head for **Le Marais** whose back streets are full of surprises. The rue des Rosiers, the Jewish quarter, specialises in both North African and Eastern European restaurants – the classic being **Goldenberg**. Surrounding streets such as the **rue des Ecouffes** (try the chic yet relaxed **Myrtho**), **rue des Francs-Bourgeois, rue Vieille du Temple** and the rue **Ste-Croix de la Brétonnerie** all harbour an interesting selection. The junction of the latter two streets specialises in gay bars.

For more classic cuisine, go to the place des Vosges, where **Ma Bourgogne** reigns supreme on summer nights with tables spilling out under the arcades. Although there is nothing special about its basic dishes, prices are reasonable and the setting is unique. As this *quartier* thrives, the number of restaurants grows, and it is worth investigating the nearby **rue des Tournelles** (try the intimate **Gaspard de la Nuit**) and the **rue de Birague**, without forgetting a charming little square, the place du **Marché Ste-Catherine**, which has several reasonably priced restaurants. Back towards St-Paul, the **rue François Miron** has some old favourites, while the **rue du Pont Louis-Philippe** will take you down to a string of interesting restaurants lining the quai by the Seine. Here **Le Trumilou** serves basic fish dishes in an unpretentious atmosphere.

Many restaurants offer palatial settings which make the food seem irrelevant. Le Grand Véfour, in the Palais-Royal, is a magnificent example of sumptuous decoration from the 1820s, although the establishment itself dates from before the Revolution. On the rue de Rivoli the salon de thé Angélina is unrivalled for its early 1900s classical style, complete with mediterranean landscape murals. Art deco reaches its zenith at La Coupole in Montparnasse; and the most over-the-top example of turn-of-the-century opulence is to be found in the extraordinary restaurant at the Gare de Lyon overlooking the platforms, Le Train Bleu.

221

FOOD AND DRINK

Le Pub Renault, on the Champs Elysées, adds French style to a British institution

Couscous restaurants can be found in every *quartier*. The word 'couscous' refers to the cornmeal grain (semolina) which, ideally, is heaped in a moist, buttery pile and mixed with a fresh vegetable stew. Completing the dish is the meat you have chosen; the best bet is nearly always *brochettes d'agneau* (lamb kebabs) or *méchoui* (a piece of roasted lamb). The other mainstay of Moroccan, Algerian and Tunisian cuisine is the tajine. Baked in a clay dish, tajine is basically a meat stew but with a combination of exotic ingredients – olives, almonds, prunes, conserved lemons – and cooked slowly to create a delicious sauce.

St-Germain Similar in style and budget are numerous restaurants crowded into the narrow side streets of **St-Germain**. Streets leading south from the metro Mabillon towards St-Sulpice are packed with intriguing places, from Brazilian extravaganzas (**Guy**), where you munch to live samba, to family-run pizzerias or haunts papered with old film posters. Perfect for budgeting too, St-Germain claims old favourites along the **rue Monsieur-le-Prince (Le Polidor)** or tiny little places lining the very narrow **rue de l'Echaudé**. This is not the haunt of high gastronomy (although **L'Echaude St-Germain** comes high in the candlelit dinner stakes), but you will emerge well fed without feeling totally fleeced. Continuing in the same direction, the **rue Dauphine** claims some reasonably priced, reliable restaurants, culminating at the bottom in one of Paris' best Indian restaurants, **Yugaraj**.

In the summer months this area is a delight to wander around. Try **Le Bistrot de Paris**, a sign of a return to traditional bourgeois cuisine, or the pricey but elegant fish restaurant, **La Méditerrannée** opposite the Théâtre de l'Odéon. One of the city's best Vietnamese restaurants, **Tan Dinh**, is situated beyond the rue du Bac towards the Musée d'Orsay, and has a particularly impressive wine list. Some of Paris' best shellfish are to be had at a new combination of the old classics, **Le Petit Zinc** and **Le Muniche**, in the rue St-Benoît. Finally, the ultimate in conditions for a *dîner à deux* can be found at **Laperouse**, which still has ornately mirrored turn-of-the-century private rooms upstairs – although its cuisine is not what it used to be.

Wine bars *Bars à vins* are increasingly popular as relaxed lunchtime spots where quality wine accompanies a basic hot dish or even more copious 'menu'. Friendly, bustling places where some clients eat at the counter and others squeeze around small tables, they epitomise the Parisian character: fast, no frills and with a quick patter. Those which come closer in style to bistros are open in the evenings, but the purist *bar à vin* usually closes around 21.00hrs. The 1st and 2nd *arrondissements* where businessmen are thick on the ground have a wide choice, but try and go either before 12.30 or just after 14.00 if you want to get a table. An old favourite is **Le Rubis**, where plates of charcuterie or cheese help absorb varying amounts of wine. **Willie's Wine Bar**, opened and run by an Englishman, and its brother, **Juveniles**, both serve thirsty stockbrokers from the nearby Bourse. In the same *quartier*, **La Côte** is becoming justifiably popular, while **Aux Bons Crus**, overlooking the Palais Royal at the back, is packed with ravenous bankers and business people.

In Le Marais, don't miss **Le Coude-Fou**, a narrow bistro often peopled by local eccentrics. **La Tartine** on the rue de Rivoli, is yet another old-timer, where nothing seems to have changed for at least 40 years. Beyond the Bastille, near the place d'Aligre market, is the traditional old favourite, **Le Baron Rouge**, where locals fill their bottles from the wine-barrels. The atmosphere is particularly lively on a Sunday morning. Another Parisian monument, even further afield, is **Jacques Mélac's** famous wine-bar. The jovial moustachioed owner produces his own Parisian vintage, resulting in a rowdy wine-picking festival every September. During the rest of the year his bistro overflows with enthusiasts of the heavier end of French cuisine.

St-Germain has its famous **Chai de l'Abbaye**, a popular but rather soulless wine-bar near the rue de Buci market, but is better represented by **Chez Georges** in the rue des Canettes. Popular with the local fashion crowd is **Au Sauvignon**, which has a well oriented terrace for improving summer tans. The chain of **L'Ecluse** wine bars (on the Quai des Grands Augustins, in Les Halles or at the Madeleine) is excellent for sampling smooth Bordeaux, but their dishes are mainly cold platters.

Bastille Outside the tourist centre, wine bars gain even more character, generally because of a faithful crowd of regular customers. Near the Bastille, go to **Au Limonaire** or finish your long day or evening in style at **La Nuit des Rois**, which specialises in champagne.

The spread of trendiness is only a recent phenomenon around the Bastille. Squeezed between the latest 'in' places are numerous local restaurants serving basic fare, and many of the hotspots serve ethnic food. Here you can dine on Thai cuisine among low-flying parrots at the **Blue Elephant**, or dive into a mountain of couscous at the reputable **Chez Léon**.

Go for Lebanese specialities to **Ishtar** (order the *mezze*, a selection of mixed hors d'eouvres), for once at a very reasonable price. A favourite with young trendies is the **China Club**, a vast red-laquered restaurant and bar, more recommended for its cocktails than its fairly standard Chinese dishes.

In the same street, the rue de Charenton, but nearer the Opéra-Bastille, is a theatrical Italian restaurant serving regional specialities, **Sipario,** while between the two is a variety of young and friendly eating places. Slip down a side-street here and you can try out a longstanding classic bistro, **Chez Marcel**. Across the place de la

Bastille, go to **La Mousson** if you really like people-watching: the cuisine is so-so exotico-colonial, as is the décor, but it can be a good place for an early evening cocktail.

Chic eating Further east of the Bastille, towards Faidherbe, is a new epicentre for trendy eating. Go to the fashionable and chic Moroccan **Le Mansouria** or, in the rue Chanzy, a decidedly camp, operatic Italian bistro, **La Magnani**. Visitors determined to remain firmly within the limits of Gallic cuisine should go a few steps further to **Chardenoux**, an unpretentious Belle Epoque restaurant serving the best of traditional bistro food. Back in the heart of the Bastille in the rue de Charonne is a firm favourite with locals and visitors alike, **Chez Paul**, where booking is necessary despite its relaxed appearance.

Still in the Gallic home cooking mood, but situated in the uninspiring district around the Gare de Lyon, is a justifiably famous bistro, the elegant **Au Trou Gascon**, where fish is treated in unusually full-flavoured ways and hot *foie gras* is dished up with asparagus.

If you find yourself up at **La Villette**, don't hesitate to

224

There is still plenty of scope for serious foodies, despite the increase of fast-food eateries

stay there for lunch or dinner. On the main avenue **Jean-Jaurès** is a traditional Parisian restaurant complete with red benches and lace curtains, **Au Cochon d'Or,** where generous portions of grilled meat dishes are served – at a price. For those more interested in fish, the next-door restaurant, **Dagorno,** is a local institution and its decorative Belle Epoque setting creates an elegant background.

Eating with a view Finally, for lunching or dining in bucolic splendour, the **Parc Montsouris**, the **Parc des Buttes-Chaumont** and the **Bois de Boulogne** all oblige, each with reputable, chic and rather costly establishments. The greenhouse-styled **Pavillon Montsouris** now has an affordable menu and the view over the park will make up for any frustrations over service. **Au Pavillon Puebla** is in fact, a Napoleon III pavilion, and its decorative style is suitably theatrical: here the cuisine is an astute mixture of traditional and new, served in a vast room overlooking the hillocky park. Queen of them all is **Le Pré Catalan**, housed in a small palace hidden in the verdant Bois de Boulogne. Here you can sample exquisite lobster, crab or tender young

Le Train Bleu restaurant in the Gare de Lyon

rabbit, followed by divine desserts. If the weather is fine, few pleasures are greater than eating in this peaceful, romantic setting.

Ethnic eating Increasingly cosmopolitan, Paris now offers a vast selection of ethnic restaurants. Although St-Germain is traditionally strong, and the streets near the Opéra such as the rue **Ste-Anne** now cater almost exclusively for a growing Japanese business community, much enjoyment can be had by venturing out of the centre to further-flung *arrondissements*. Home to communities of French Asiatics, North Africans or West Indians, *quartiers* such as **Belleville** or the 13th (**Chinatown**) offer a wide spectrum. Good for tight budgets too, many of the Chinese/Vietnamese restaurants are excellent value, proof being the custom generated by Asiatic families. The Royal Belleville, an enormous establishment, **Le Président** and **Le Nioullaville** all have endless menus, satisfying specialities and rapid service. Around the crossroads of the boulevard de Belleville and the Faubourg du Temple, you cannot go wrong. Venture further up the rue de Belleville and you will find **Tai Yien**, another canteen, this time featuring an enormous carp aquarium. But Paris is immense, so track down your own favourites.

Fish and seafood vocabulary

anguille	eel
bar	sea bass
bouillabaisse	fish and seafood soup
brandade de morue	creamed salted cod
brochet	pike
cabillaud	fresh cod
crabe	crab

coquilles St Jacques	scallops
crevettes	shrimps
daurade	sea bream
écrevisses	crayfish/prawns
hareng	herring
homard	lobster
huîtres	oysters
langouste	spiny lobster
loup	catfish
lotte	angler
maquereau	mackerel
merlan	whiting
morue	cod
moules	mussels
raie	skate
rouget	red mullet
saumon	salmon
sole	sole
thon	tuna
truite	trout

Meat and poultry vocabulary

agneau	lamb
andouillette	blood sausage
boeuf	beef
brochette	kebab
caille	quail
canard /caneton	duck / duckling
cassoulet	meat and bean casserole
chevreuil	venison
choucroute	sauerkraut
contrefilet	loin steak
côte de boeuf	T-bone steak
côtelettes	chops
dinde	turkey
dindonneau	young turkey
foie	liver
gigot	roast leg of lamb
langue	tongue
lapin /lapereau	rabbit
lièvre	hare
oie	goose
perdrix	partridge
pintade	guinea fowl
porc	pork
poulet	chicken
poussin	spring chicken
saucisses	sausages
steak tartare	raw minced beef
veau	veal

227

Paris is a paradise for anyone who has a sweet tooth

Cooking methods

Remember that the French love undercooking meat, so if you want what is considered 'rare' in an anglo-saxon country it is safer to say *à point*.

bleu	very rare
saignant	rare
à point	medium rare
bien cuit	well done (relatively..)

See also pages 276 to 281.

Sports

If you're dying to sweat off some of the extra *foie gras* and Sauternes that your poor body has been assailed with, you can turn to the gymnasiums and swimming pools of the capital. But practising sport in Paris is not easy. Although there are officially 97 gyms, 36 pools and 57 tennis stadiums, the real picture is a different one, with inconvenient opening hours, far-flung locations, members-only policies and overcrowding the norm. Don't forget the big peripheral parks of Boulogne and Vincennes: both have good cycling and boating facilities as well as endless jogging potential. For information on municipal facilities and sporting events, contact **Allo-Sports** (tel:42 76 54 54).

Cycling The excellent SNCF system of 'Train + vélo' combines a train trip with hiring a bike from the station at your destination, a perfect way to discover forests, châteaux and villages. A list of stations is available at any mainline SNCF station. Otherwise you can hire them in Paris for confronting merciless city traffic.
La Maison du Vélo: 11 rue Fénélon, 75010 (tel: 42 81 24 72).
Paris-Vélo: 2 rue du Fer-à-Moulin, 75005 (tel: 53 37 59 22).
Calf muscles fading? Then hire a scooter.
Scoot-heure: 6 rue d'Arras, 75005 (tel: 43 25 69 25).

Gymnasiums Private chains have taken the lead over municipal gyms, which remain rather dusty, under-equipped affairs in comparison. It is usually possible to have a day pass or a book of 10 passes at a reasonable rate.
Garden Gym has seven gyms over Paris. Phone to find out the nearest branch (tel: 40 20 03 03).
Gymnase Club is the biggest on the market and ever expanding; more expensive than the above. Call for details (tel: 45 62 99 76).
Vitatop has two more exclusive, sophisticated gyms on the outskirts (tel: 40 68 00 21). The branch on the roof of the Sofitel Hotel offers a spectacular Parisian skyline from your jacuzzi.
Lastly, for those who have really overdone it in the restaurants, a vast and extravagant new multisports complex could be the answer.
Aquaboulevard, 4 rue Louis-Armand, 75015 (tel: 40 60 10 00). Artificial nature brought to the *périphérique* of Paris. As well as a gym, there are indoor putting greens, a wave pool, tennis and squash courts, and water sports. *Open:* late and day pass available.

Swimming Of the 36 pools in Paris, most are municipal, therefore affordable. But avoid, if you can, Wednesdays and weekends when local school kids take over. Opening times are complicated, so phone direct or check *Pariscope* for details. Below are the more central pools.
Piscine des Amiraux, 13 rue des Amiraux, 75018 (tel: 46 06 46 47). An architectural landmark in the north of Paris, built in 1924. Renovated recently; 33m pool.
Piscine Buttes-aux-Cailles, 5 place Paul-Verlaine, 75013 (tel: 45 89 60 05). A tiled art deco gem of a 33m pool,

The loneliness of the long-distance jogger

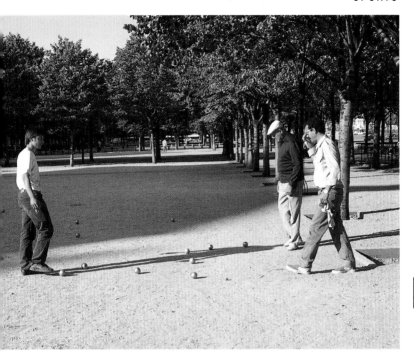

another one outdoors, open in summer.

Piscine Déligny, 5 Quai Anatole France, 75007 (tel: 45 51 72 15). A Parisian institution floating on the Seine since 1840. The outdoor 50m pool and tanning deck is the chic place to get your summer tan.

Piscine des Halles, Porte du Jour, Forum-des-Halles, 75001 (tel: 42 36 98 44), 50m underground pool, clean and bright with 'tropical' garden.

Piscine Jean Taris, 16 rue Thouin, 75005 (tel: 43 25 54 03). Two 25m pools, favourites with local students, and one toddlers pool. Built in 1978; water cleaned electronically, so no chlorine!

Piscine du Marché Saint-Germain, 7 rue Clément, 75006 (tel: 43 29 08 15). Hidden beneath the St-Germain market complex is a 25m pool with special diving section.

Piscine Quartier Latin, 19 rue de Pontoise, 75005 (tel: 43 54 06 23). A 33m pool with a distinct 1930s air. Solarium, squash courts and sauna.

Piscine Saint-Merri, 18 rue du Renard, 75004 (tel: 42 72 29 45). Right next to Beaubourg, small indoor 25m pool with solarium.

Tennis Your best bet is in the Bois de Vincennes, where 24 courts huddle in the Plaine de la Faluère, a gigantic sports complex. The desirable, much-coveted public courts in the Jardin du Luxembourg are more central, but require booking through a municipal club. For details on joining local clubs contact **Allo-Sports** (tel: 42 76 54 54). Numerous private clubs exist, mainly at the *portes* of Paris, but membership is costly and only worthwhile if you are staying for a long period.

Boules is a less strenuous sporting option, but it's taken just as seriously as any other

Nightlife

Where the trendies go: Fickle as ever, Parisian *branchés* (plugged in, hip) float from one club to the next, making and breaking the fortunes of barmen. Pigalle neon and fun tackiness remains a favourite: try Le Moloko for drinks, La Locomotive for a dance floor twirl or La Cigale for a rock concert. The Bastille is now firmly established, and the rue de Lappe never sleeps. Revel in the kitsch splendour of Le Balajo or join the crowd at La Casbah. Other streets like rue de Charenton or rue de Charonne are burgeoning with bars too. Les Halles and in particular the rue des Lombards are good for late drinks and music, but to really rub shoulders with Paris jet-setters head for Les Bains.

Alight for the night: the boulevard de Clichy...

Parisian nightlife changes fashion as the proverbial snake does its skin. Old favourites are few and far between, often handed over to the destiny of tourist buses, while others sink in the wake of youth's fickleness. But a vast choice remains, and you will never find yourself at a loss for a drink or a swing round the dance floor in the wee hours.

One warning: drinks in clubs can be astronomical, so if quantities of alcohol are essential, stick to regular bars (though after 22.00hrs prices are uncontrolled everywhere).

Opening hours Action starts in the nightclubs well after midnight, continuing till 05.00hrs or so, while some of the jazz bars also carry on late. All clubs are closed on Mondays, and jazz is tricky, though not impossible, on both Sundays and Mondays.

Check the listings published in the weekly *Pariscope*, 7 à Paris or *L'Officiel des Spectacles* for detailed programmes.

Feather Clubs

Many visitors come to Paris for just that: the renowned cabaret shows that seem straight out of a time-warped Hollywood. All are virtually monopolised by ogling tourist parties. You can unload a small fortune on exhorbitantly priced drinks.

If this is the kind of evening out you're looking for, the following seletion might be useful.

Crazy Horse Saloon, 12 avenue George V, 75008 (tel: 47 23 32 32), metro: George V. Bare-breasted girls strut through their erotic routines, assuming seemingly impossible postures. Reputed to be the most professional.

Folies-Bergère, 32 rue Richer, 75009 (tel: 42 46 77 11), metro: Cadet, rue Montmartre. Renowned for diamanté, feathers, more breasts and glitter. Not what it used to be, but the vast setting is historic and admission relatively reasonable.

Le Lido, 116 Champs Elysées, 75008 (tel: 45 63 11 61), metro: George V. Fantastic special effects alleviate an otherwise predictable show. The Bluebell Girls dance to a sea of regimented tourists.

Moulin Rouge, 82 boulevard de Clichy, 75018 (tel: 46 06 00 19), metro: Blanche. A thousand costumes, 100 girls, singers and acrobats, an aquarium, crocodiles. What is this? Just the delirium of a spectacular show in the classic venue.

Paradis Latin, 28 rue Cardinal Lemoine, 75005 (tel: 43 25 28 08), metro: Cardinal Lemoine. Not in the same league as the above, but a shimmering floor show.

Jazz Bars

Au Duc des Lombards, 42 rue des Lombards, 75001 (tel: 42 33 22 88), metro: Châtelet. Comfortable, dark jazz lounge with average to good musicians. Nightly.

Baiser Salé, 58 rue des Lombards, 75001 (tel: 42 33 37 71), metro: Châtelet. Blues, funky or jazz, with cocktails till 04.00hrs.

Les Bouchons, 19 rue des Halles, 75001 (tel: 42 33 28 73), metro: Châtelet. Relaxed American-style bar in restaurant basement with live groups.

Café de la Plage, 59 rue de Charonne, 75011 (tel: 47 00 91 60), metro: Ledru-Rollin, Bastille. Till the early hours, a Bastille hot spot for mixed fauna. Good soul, rap, salsa.

Café Rive Droite, 2 rue Berger, 75001 (tel: 42 33 81 62). High-decibel sounds by local musicians till dawn.

Caveau de la Huchette, 5 rue de la Huchette, 75005 (tel: 43 26 65 05), metro: St-Michel. An old classic.

Smoky, crowded basement bar and dancing for students and tourists.

Meridien, 81 boulevard Gouvion St-Cyr, 75017 (tel: 40 68 34 34), metro: Porte Maillot. Rather staid hotel bar, but good jazz classics play here.

Montana, 28 rue St-Benoît, 75006 (tel: 45 48 93 08), metro: St-Germain. Up-market American-style jazz bar and restaurant for local tourists.

New Morning, 7–9, rue des Petites Ecuries, 75010 (tel: 45 23 51 41). metro: Château d'Eau. Paris' best. Excellent programme of international jazz concerts.

Petit Journal St-Michel, 71 boulevard St Michel, 75005 (tel: 43 26 28 59), metro: Luxembourg. New Orleans style jazz till 02.00hrs in this favourite, though cramped, old venue. Restaurant/bar.

Le Petit Opportun, 15 rue des Lavandières-Ste-Opportun, 75001 (tel: 42 36 01 36). Well-established bar, good French jazz programme in crowded basement.

Le Sunset, 60 rue des Lombards, 75001 (tel: 40 26 46 60), metro: Châtelet. Funky jazz cellar for Les Halles late-nighters. Restaurant and bar.

La Villa, 29 rue Jacob, 75006 (tel: 43 26 60 00), metro: St-Germain. New jazz bar in designer-hotel.

Late-Night Bars

Ascot, 66 rue Pierre-Charron, 75008 (tel: 43 59 28 15), metro: F-D Roosevelt. Established piano-bar for smart set off Champs Elysées.

Bar Romain, 6 rue Caumartin, 75009 (tel: 47 42 98 04), metro: Havre-Caumartin. Original 1905 décor of neo-Pompeii frescoes makes background for choice of over 200 cocktails. Popular with showbiz crowd.

Bilboquet, 13 rue Saint-Benoît, 75006 (tel: 45 48 81 84), metro: St-Germain. Classic, straight-laced atmosphere. Restaurant and bar with live jazz.

Birdland Club, 20 rue Princesse, 75006 (tel: 43 26 97 59), metro: Mabillon. Friendly, late. Golden-oldie jazz records set the laid-back tone.

La Casbah, 18/20 rue de la Forge-Royal, 75011 (tel: 43 71 71 89), metro: Faidherbe-Chaligny. Vast, imaginative mauresque-art deco cocktail bar with dancing downstairs. Video screen and a team of fancy barmen/women.

China Club, 50 rue de Charenton, 75012 (tel: 43 43 82 02), metro: Ledru-Rollin. Vast, shady, red-laquered bar/restaurant with discreet upstairs cocktail lounge. Hip, crowded, buzzy. Near Bastille.

L'Entrepots, 14 rue de Charonne, 75011 (tel: 48 06 57 04), metro: Bastille. Cheerful, popular cocktail bar guarded by bouncer. Smoky billiard room downstairs.

Harry's Bar, 5 rue Daunou, 75002 (tel: 42 61 71 14), metro: Opéra.Old favourite. Pub atmosphere stimulating enough for Gershwin to compose *American in Paris*. Mature, tanked-up crowd.

Kitty O'Shea's, 10 rue des Capucines, 75002 (tel: 40 15 08 08), metro: Opéra. Warm, pub atmosphere frequented by sonorous Irish expatriates and business people revving up.

La Luna, 28 rue Keller, 75011 (tel: 40 21 90 91), metro: Bastille, Ledru-Rollin. Two very gay high-tech floors for Bastille troopers.

American in Paris: Harry's bar, on the rue Daunou

Mayflower, 49 rue Descartes, 75005 (tel: 43 54 56 47), metro: Cardinal-Lemoine. Lively all-night pub. Stagger out at dawn for breakfast on the place de la Contrescarpe.

Moloko, 26 rue Fontaine, 75009, metro: Blanche. Newly 'in' late-night bar for Pigalle clubbers and Party crowd.

Rosebud, 11 bis rue Delambre, 75014 (tel: 43 35 38 54), metro: Vavin. Shady Montparnasse bar, intimate atmosphere for discreet tête-à-têtes.

Night Clubs/Discos

Les Bains, 7 rue du Bourg l'Abbé, 75003 (tel: 48 87 01 80), metro: Etienne-Marcel. Still top, still sniffish at the door, but a nocturnal landmark for fashion, showbiz and media personalities. Go late. Restaurant.

Le Balajo, 9 rue de Lappe, 75011 (tel: 47 00 07 87), metro: Bastille. A survivor of the 1930s, incomparably ritzy décor for hip young things. Monday and Thursday nights are best.

Le Boy, 6 rue Caumartin, 75009 (tel: 47 42 68 05), metro: Havre-Caumartin. High kitsch gay haunt though not exclusive. Dancers groove till 09.00hrs.

Bus Palladium, 6 rue Fontaine, 75009 (tel: 48 74 54 99), metro: Pigalle. Young, upwardly mobile rockers bop away to real pop.

Castel's, 15 rue Princesse, 75006 (tel: 43 26 90 22), metro: Odéon. Members' club for monied, older generation. Bar upstairs and dance floor downstairs. Twinkle a diamond cufflink and you may get in.

Le Central, 102 Champs Elysées, 75008 (tel: 42 89 31 41), metro: George V. Unusually hip for quartier. Latest sounds and mixed trendy habitués, models and rockers.

La Locomotive, 90 boulevard de Clichy, 75018 (tel: 42 57 37 37), metro: Blanche. Ambitiously scaled, three-tiered basement club below Moulin Rouge. Latest hip sounds sprinkled with '60s nostalgia. Concerts too.

Nouvelle Eve, 25 rue Fontaine, 75009 (tel: 48 74 69 25), metro: Pigalle. Gilded theatre changes from cabaret to nightclub on stroke of midnight. Good DJs.

Olivia Valère, 40 rue du Colisée, 75008 (tel: 42 25 11 68), You don't come here by metro. Very up-market, more mature business/glamour crowd. Restaurant.

Le Palace, 8 rue du Faubourg Montmartre, 75009 (tel: 42 46 10 87), metro: rue Montmartre. Once unique in Paris; opened in 1977 in a barely renovated 19th-century theatre. Now lost its eccentric decadence and style to rough bikers. Restaurant in Le Privilège downstairs.

Régine, 49 rue de Ponthieu, 75008 (tel: 43 59 21 60). Careful grooming necessary to get in. Flashy, mature crowd similar to Castel's bops night away.

Rex Club, 5 boulevard Poissonière, 75002 (tel: 42 36 83 98), metro: Bonne Nouvelle. Part of gigantic art deco concert hall and cinema. Different DJ every night from house to rap, rock, disco, salsa. Good concerts.

Sheherazade, 3 rue de Liège, 75009 (tel: 48 74 41 68), metro: Liège. 1,001 nights oriento-exotico décor. Changing nightly style of rap, house, rock, etc.

Le Tango, 13 rue au Maire, 75003 (tel: 48 87 54 78), metro: Arts-et-Métiers. Hot-blooded Afro-Latin rhythms, tango, salsa, reggae keep this unpretentious club boogeying.

Where the rich and famous go: The Champs-Elysées area still attracts those with true glitter, so try Olivia Valère or Régine's where you might trip over the toes of French showbiz personalities or just plain rich folk. Everything is a question of generation so you are more likely to find youthful successes (media, photographers, designers etc) at Les Bains, whose reputation never wanes. Finally, the long standing Castel's, theoretically a members-only club, is where you're most likely to sit next to mature French film stars accompanied by their latest bottle-blonde.

Eating out on the Champs Elysées

Accommodation

In 1990 Paris police handed out 7,994,846 tickets; 7,506,419 of these were parking tickets.

With 1,500 or so hotels and an annual average of 18 million tourists spread between them, Parisian accommodation caters for all tastes and budgets. This is one of the rare European capitals which offers quite acceptable and affordable accommodation in central areas, often family-run in idiosyncratic fashion.

At the top end of the spectrum are the luxury hotels, straight out of another epoch, which cater for countless well-heeled travellers or business people. Their prices, on a one-off basis, are very high, but some make discount arrangements with travel agents abroad, so it is often worth enquiring at home well in advance of your trip.

The season The Paris 'season' is a strange one and is worth bearing in mind if you want good value. May, June, September and October are the hardest months to find rooms and prices often go down in July and August, particularly in the 3-star establishments, which are sorely missing their business clientèle at that time. Remember that check-out time is midday. On arrival, make sure you check in before 18.00hrs as after this time the hotel has the right to give the room to someone else, even if they hold a deposit from you. Breakfasts are always continental-style (coffee or tea and rolls or croissants plus a fruit juice if you are lucky). Only 3-star hotels upwards are obliged to offer service in the rooms, otherwise you will have to head for the dining room. Not all 1-star hotels offer breakfast. No hotel can charge you for breakfast unless you have ordered it, and you may prefer to join in the city bustle outside for better coffee at a lower price.

If you come to Paris by car remember that you will undoubtedly encounter parking problems. Hotels that have car parks are generally the uninspiring modern blocks to be found outside the centre: many are, however, located close to public car parks.

Finding a base Choosing your base *quartier* is tricky. Every part of Paris has its advantages and disadvantages, its charms and its horrors. For the heart of luxury go straight to the 8th *arrondissement* (Champs Elysées, avenue George V, avenue Montaigne, Faubourg St-Honoré and surrounding streets). Here is the highest concentration of luxury, and 4-star establishments, and this is where to stay if you need to pop out for a fitting at Dior's, pick up some presents at Hermès or impress your business acquaintances. Even if your budget does not stretch to these palaces of refinement, at least drop in for a drink at the bar to soak up some of its features – call-girls included. Although everyone has heard of the Ritz, the Crillon, the Bristol, the Plaza-Athénée or the George V, not everyone knows the less monumental establishments, such as the **Hôtel de la Trémoille**, the **Raphaël**, or the **San Régis**, favourites with the more discreet variety of wealthy travellers.

Following closely in the luxury stakes is the 1st *arrondissement* (Tuileries, Louvre, place Vendôme), convenient for high-class jewellery and culture, yet whose side streets have a good sprinkling of 2- and 3-star hotels. Preening themselves in old world splendour here are the **Ritz** and the **Meurice**, both of which have remarkable interiors and are wonderful for an early evening drink. Closer to most people's budgets are places such as **Le Molière**, the **Hôtel des Tuileries** or the **Hôtel Saint-Roch**. Immediately north is the 2nd *arrondissement*, which, despite its small size, has a large number of 2 and 3-star hotels, catering mainly for the business community centred around the banks and the Bourse. **Timhotel La Bourse** is one of a chain of fairly reasonable hotels, usually extremely well situated, and in this case is particularly convenient for doing raids on all the designer boutiques in and around the place des Victoires.

Budget choice The adjacent 9th *arrondissement* (Opéra, Grands Boulevards, Faubourg Montmartre) has the densest concentration of hotels of any Parisian *arrondissement*, and over half of them are budget 2-star establishments. The Faubourg Montmartre and its side streets claims the majority; many of these are used by tour operators, giving a rather un-Parisian feel to this otherwise interesting neighbourhood. One of Paris' most popular nightclubs, Le Palace, is situated here, and the Folies-Bergère is just round the corner in an area full of ethnic restaurants (kosher, Turkish, North African). Try the **Corona**, a 1930s establishment in an interesting back street lined with hotels, or the **Bergère**, now completely modernised and part of the Best Western chain.

If you do decide to give these places a wide berth then head further north towards Pigalle and Montmartre, where a number of characteristic family-run hotels can be tracked down. Near the delightful place St-Georges, try the **Hôtel de la Tour d'Auvergne**, an atmospheric, renovated 3-star place, which boasts four-poster beds in every room.

Paris atmosphere The area most visitors head for with alacrity is the Rive Gauche, the 5th, 6th and even 7th *arrondissements*. Less business-oriented in atmosphere and more *vieux Paris*, the Quartier Latin and St-Germain des Prés provide all the ingredients for a classic holiday in Paris. Throughout this district is a host of reasonably priced 1-, 2- and 3-star hotels whose prices are generally lower than their equivalents across the Seine. In the same area you can find fairly basic student hotels and restaurants, gathered around the rue Mouffetard, the place de la Contrescarpe and the rue des Ecoles, and the slightly more up-market **Hôtel du Collège de France**. Here, in a quiet side street, simple but pleasant rooms rise up to the sixth floor, from where you can glimpse the spires of Notre Dame. Similarly quaint in spirit, although recently renovated, is **Le Jardin des Plantes**, whose freshly decorated rooms look out over the park of the same name. Rock-bottom prices can be had at the tiny **Hôtel des Carmes**, situated in an atmospheric side street off the boulevard St-Germain. With its strong student population, due to the proximity of various colleges and the university, this lively part of the Rive Gauche is particularly recommended for those on a budget. Within easy reach of numerous

235

In the more up-market establishments receptionists are usually bilingual, and any hotel with two or more stars must by law have a receptionist speaking a second language.

ACCOMMODATION

France has the smallest minimum legal size in Europe for hotel bedrooms and bathrooms, and in Paris, where real estate does not come cheap, many hoteliers exploit this to the full. Thus the so-called bathroom is more than likely to be chopped out of the corner of the bedroom. When booking a room make sure you distinguish between a *salle d'eau* (shower-room) and a *salle de bains* (bathroom).

The place de l'Opéra, set in the 9th arrondissement, where hotels are plentiful and often inexpensive

monuments and museums, it has an easy-going atmosphere and caters well for young travellers.

Higher prices St-Germain harbours a wide selection of good 3-star hotels, but prices can rocket here. The **Hôtel de l'Abbaye** is justifiably pricey within its category, but service is impeccable and the rooms are perfectly appointed, if limited in size (this is medieval Paris, after all). The delightful **Hôtel des Marroniers** is tucked away in its pretty courtyard in the heart of the antique district, and here the prices are more reasonable if you can get a room. The area of the rue Jacob, the rue de l'Université and the rue de Seine is thick with small family-run hotels, and it is a chic and pleasant part of town. If you must overlook the river try the **Hôtel du Quai Voltaire**, a rambling old place where Baudelaire once stayed. A sure favourite for its location and price is the **Hôtel Michelet-Odéon**, on the place de l'Odéon, just a few steps from the Luxembourg Gardens.

Montparnasse makes a good base to stay: transport is easy and the bars of the boulevard stay open late. Here you could try squeezing into the tiny **Hôtel Danemark**, renovated from a charming old flowery-wallpaper establishment into a more chic and elegant place. Near by, in the arty rue de la Grande-Chaumière, is a small family-run hotel, excellent for low budgets: the **Hôtel des Académies**. Further east and across the boulevard is the **Hôtel Istria**, part of the Montparnasse cultural legend, and reasonable value. Still following the artists' trail, go as far south as you can in Paris – almost – to the **Hôtel du Parc Montsouris**, a simple establishment but with all the necessary comforts and straight across the road from the park. In this charming, peaceful neighbourhood are many of the artists' custom-built studios from the 1920s.

Le Marais This is a *quartier* not to be forgotten if you want up-to-the-minute Parisian life. Numerous hotels, old and new, pepper this animated district and you are more likely to find peace and quiet here than anywhere else on the Rive Droite. Although these are mainly 2- and 3-star establishments, the occasional budget hotel can still be found such as the minute **Hôtel Sainte-Elisabeth** or the **Grand Hôtel Malher**. In the middle category, try the **Hôtel de la place des Vosges** or the **Jeanne d'Arc**, deservedly popular. Once for low budgets, now with an extra star rising is the characteristic **Hôtel Saint-Merri**, perfectly located for avid visitors to Beaubourg. And for those seeking discreet refinement, the **Pavillon de la Reine** is the *crème de la crème*, modestly set back from the place des Vosges behind a pretty little garden.

See also pages 274 to 276.

■ **It's hard to generalise about 2 million people, but as a rule the best way to communicate with Parisians is by using their language. The tourist who relentlessly speaks loud English is much less welcome than the visitor who squeaks out *s'il vous plaît*, however poorly pronounced. .....■**

Could it be that old devil flattery at work? Whatever, once you have initiated contact, you then run the risk of hearing in return a slew of unintelligible noises, impossible to decipher. To this you simply reply *Parlez-vous anglais?*. If the answer is a brusque *non*, do not despair. An increasing proportion of the younger generation (officially 59 per cent of all age groups and 89 per cent of the 15- to 19-year-olds) speak a foreign language and willingly help foreign visitors. So keep your eyes open for some bright-eyed teenager.

Forms of address For those who speak some remnants of French, it is worth bearing in mind other practical rules. Addressing people with a *Madame* or *Monsieur* tacked on the end is a sign of politeness that is appropriate no matter what the person's social status. It can work wonders in persuasive tactics. With strangers always stick to *vous*, and with acquaintances only use *tu* once they do. The younger generation is less rigid about this now, but the best rule is to play it safe.

As in many Latin countries, you will be pigeon-holed according to the way you dress. Keep in mind that a certain sober elegance will break through most barriers and what seems to an Anglo-Saxon to be 'dressing up' is actually normal daily wear for a Parisian. It is almost impossible to overdress unless you go completely overboard, whereas a sloppy appearance will definitely lose you precious points.

Talking as tourists Because of its incredible popularity among visitors (16 to 20 million annually), Paris has its fair share of locals who believe that tourists equal money, and that is the end of it. Yet they love to hear foreigners praise their city, and waiters and waitresses are only too pleased to hear that the food and/or wine they are serving is good. Humour will also take you a long way – contrary to general belief, the Parisians are actually blessed with a subtle sense of irony and love to share it. Waiters will change from surly monsters to cheerful fellow humans if your French is up to this kind of exchange. Otherwise, a friendly smile never goes amiss.

Although there is no traditional drinking hour in French cafés to facilitate striking up conversations, curiously enough the restaurants can oblige. Bistros and brasseries – those bustling, old-fashioned dining halls where tables are squeezed in and customers barely have enough room to raise their fork – are ideal meeting places. Mealtimes are the moment when the French at last drop their guard and relax, and many a conversation has been started over the label of a bottle of wine or the relative merits of an unusual dish.

Points of etiquette If you manage to break down the barriers and get to know a French person, a number of rules should be remembered. Two men always shake hands when greeting each other and on leaving, even when they know each other. Members of the opposite sex kiss each other on the cheek, usually twice, though suburbanites and people from the provinces actually go through this procedure four times. The 'Continental Kiss' may seem strange, but it is truly commonplace for ordinary, non-professional encounters, even when you've only met the person an hour earlier.

When entering a room full of strangers, it is usual practice to do the rounds of each person, shaking hands and giving your name, as they do theirs. When you leave, you have to go through the same ritual as you say *au revoir*, shaking hands or giving the *bise* (kiss), depending how much communication has taken place.

Lastly, a universal piece of advice holds equally true for Parisians: if you are invited to someone's home for dinner, make an effort to take flowers, chocolates or a good bottle of wine. It always works wonders.

239

Striking up a conversation over a drink or a meal is an ideal way of breaking the ice

TRAVEL FACTS

Arriving

Visas EC nationals can enter with an official identity card or passport. Visas are needed by Australian and New Zealand nationals, but not by Americans or Canadians. Apply to your local French consulate for details well in advance.

Air Paris is served by two airports: Orly in the south and Roissy (Charles-de-Gaulle) in the north. Most northern European and American flights now arrive at the expanding Roissy Airport, while Spain, Portugal, Africa, South America and certain Middle Eastern airlines are relegated to the less slick Orly-Sud. Orly-Ouest terminal is monopolised by internal French flights. The ageing airport of Beauvais is still used by certain European student charters, and an-hour's bus journey into Paris should be included in the ticket. There are no airport taxes paid on arrival or departure.

Both Orly and Roissy have extensive international airline facilities including car hire, duty-free shops, restaurants, post offices, hotels in the proximity and ground transport into the city centre. Air France and airport staff are, on the whole,

The Gare de Lyon. Trains leave here for southeast France and Italy

helpful and always speak English.

Transport to and from Roissy: Two possibilities exist apart from a rather costly taxi ride (150-200FF) covering the 23km. The easiest is the Air France airport bus, which leaves every 20 minutes (05.40–23.00hrs) and in 30 minutes whisks you straight into the central Arc de Triomphe (Etoile) or the nearby Porte Maillot. Taxis usually await the bus, and the metro station is a few yards away. On leaving, pick it up again at Etoile, avenue Carnot.

The budget transport system is the RATP shuttle, which links with Roissy-Rail (RER line B). If you have a lot of baggage, it's not so easy heaving cases on and off the bus and then down escalators to the RER express train, but it will take you directly into the Gare du Nord or Châtelet-Les Halles. Allow 30–40 minutes. Trains run from 05.30–23.00hrs every 15 minutes.

Transport to and from Orly: Only 14km from the centre, Orly is more feasible by taxi, but it also has more transport possibilities. The Air France bus goes to Invalides but will drop you off, if requested, at Porte d'Orléans or Duroc metro. Allow 30 minutes. Much cheaper but less plush is the RATP bus number 215, called Orlybus, which arrives at the RER and metro station of Denfert-

Rochereau in south Paris. You can also take the RER line C, called Orly-Rail, from St-Michel, but the shuttle connection is not as well organised as at Roissy. Similarly, a new system christened Orly-Val connects a shuttle with the RER line B. Passenger information is available at both airports (tel: 48 62 22 80).

Rail Paris has six mainline railway stations, each serving a different geographical area. Trains arriving from Britain and northern Europe terminate at the Gare du Nord, though certain cross-channel connections arrive at the Gare St-Lazare. Trains for southeast France and Italy leave from the Gare de Lyon; for southwest France, Spain and Portugal from the Gare d'Austerlitz. The Gare de l'Est serves Germany, Austria and beyond, while the Gare Montparnasse covers Brittany. Passenger information: tel: 45 82 50 50; bookings on 45 65 60 60. All stations are central and have good metro and bus connections.

Camping

There are altogether 90 campsites scattered throughout the Ile-de-France, many of which are situated in or near the forests. Rating, like hotels, ranges from 1-star to 4-star; those at the top end usually have a swimming pool or are close to a swimmable lake or river.

Useful guidebooks can be obtained from the **Fédération Française de Camping Caravaning** (a campers' association), 78 rue de Rivoli, 75004 Paris (tel: 42 72 84 08). Listing 9,000 campsites throughout France, the book can be ordered by mail (about 90FF).

Many Parisians park their camping vans all year round on a site just outside Paris and use it as a weekend retreat. This is why, although the high season runs from April to September, it is not too difficult to find a pitch in July or August when the Parisians have taken off. It also explains why the 3-star campsite in the **Bois de Boulogne** (between Longchamp rececourse and the Seine) is strictly reserved for non-Parisians (tel: 45 24

30 00). Otherwise head for **Versailles** (tel: 39 51 23 61), **Rambouillet** (tel: 30 41 07 34) or **St-Quentin-en-Yvelines** (tel: 30 58 56 20) – three countrified sites that have excellent transport connections into Paris. Always beware of school holidays (Easter, Pentecost).

For on-site rental, check the guidebook published by the Federation: each campsite offers different facilities.

As a general rule, municipal campsites, though up to reasonable standards, are not particularly dynamic in their upkeep and equipment. However, if you aim for 4-star sites such as at **L'Isle-Adam**, situated beside the biggest river beach in France (tel: 34 69 08 80), or **Ormoy-la-Rivière** (tel: 64 94 21 39), you should be well installed.

The best shop for camping equipment in Paris is **Au Vieux Campeur**, 48 rue des Ecoles, 75005 (tel: 43 29 12 32).

Children

Children can fit in well with visiting Paris. Restaurants do not generally turn up their noses at the sight of a push-chair, and Parisians are on the whole tolerant of their presence. Hotels obviously vary in terms of the services they can provide, but all will provide extra beds, sometimes cots, in a double room at little more than the usual room price. The Novotel chain even allows up to two children under 15 to stay free in their parents' room. Other chains offer good deals, particularly in July and August when there are no business customers. Squares and parks all have specific areas with slides, sandpits and more set aside for children. River trips, science museums and certain parks (see pages 26–7) are always favourites.

English-speaking babysitters can be found through **Ababa**, a private service that also arranges day trips and tea parties; *open*: daily (tel: 45 49 46 46). Qualified babysitters or nannies can also be obtained through **Kid's Service** (tel: 47 66 00 52). **Inter-Service Parents** (tel: 43 48 28 28) is a free telephone advisory service giving details of babysitting

TRAVEL FACTS

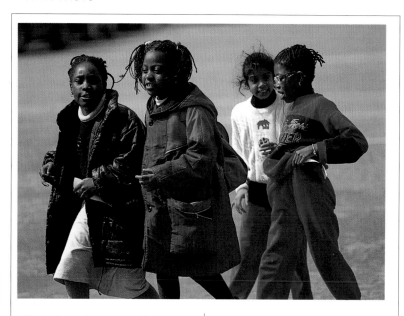

Paris has plenty to offer young people and children

agencies and children's activities all over Paris.

When dining out with children, aim for family-style bistros where staff are generally more helpful. The more elegant, up-market restaurants are obviously less enthusiastic about dealing with un-chic push-chairs and juvenile voices.

Climate
Cool but gloriously sunny days often surprise the population in October and late February, whereas the old cliché of 'Paris in the spring' does

PARIS

July & August

May · August

mm | °C
150— | —30
125— | —25
100— | —20
75— | —15
50— | —10
25— | —5
0— | —0

J F M A M J J A S O N D

not usually apply until well into May. Rarely stifling in midsummer, Paris does tend to get very muggy after a few consecutive days of sun. This is when a good percentage of the population heads down to the *quais* beside the Seine for a fresher breeze and a chance to sunbathe. Blessed with a reasonably low rainfall overall, Paris nevertheless commonly sees showers, above all during March and April as well as November (possibly the least inspiring month climatically, along with chilly January).

Crime
Street crime varies from *arrondissement* to *arrondissement*. Generally speaking, if you stick to the more touristy inner areas you are safe – except for pickpockets. Followers of this pursuit are particularly prevalent on public transport. *Never* keep your wallet in a back pocket, and ladies should make sure their bags are firmly closed and held on to. Be careful, too, in crowded cafés, flea markets, restaurants and cinemas. If you lose something, the first step is to make a declaration at the local police station, which you will need in case of claiming insurance. Ask for the nearest *commissariat*. Stolen credit cards should be reported

immediately to any of the following 24-hour services: American Express (tel: 47 77 72 00); Diners Club (tel: 47 62 75 75); Visa (tel: 42 77 11 90).

You will need to follow this up with written confirmation and a copy of your police declaration. If using travellers' cheques, make sure you keep a separate note of their numbers, along with the relevant phone number to contact in case of theft.

If your car is stolen (unlikely) or broken into (more likely), you will need to follow the same procedure at the commissariat and should contact your insurance office as soon as possible.

The police lost-property office does not deal with phone enquiries but is open Monday to Friday, 09.00–18.00hrs, at 36 rue des Morillons, 75015, metro: Convention. It is worth checking here several days after any theft, as most thieves are only interested in cash and credit cards and so dump the rest. In fact, there is a notable rise in 'gentlemen thieves' who actually return the unwanted contents of wallets to owners' addresses.

Victims of more serious crimes should call SOS Help, an English crisis hotline, *open* daily 15.00–23.00hrs (tel: 47 23 80 80). There is free rape crisis hotline, *open* weekdays (tel: 05 05 95 95).

<< Serious crime (armed robbery, muggings) in Paris dropped between 1990 and 1991, but burglaries and car thefts are on the increase, as are fake identity papers, bouncing cheques and graffiti. >>

Customs Regulations

When arriving in France from another EC country, you are allowed to bring in one batch of the following (non-EC countries in brackets): 300 cigarettes (200), 150 cigarillos ((100), 75 cigars ((50), 400g (250) tobacco. 5 litres (2) of wine or 1.5 (1) litres of spirits. Small amounts of perfume, coffee, tea and prescribed medicines

(sufficient for your stay) are allowed, as well as other goods not exceeding 2,800FF in value. Personal belongings, including sports equipment, are allowed withno formalities.

Specific regulations are applied to bringing in animal products, plants, pets (no quarantine), medicines, firearms and works of art. For any of these, make enquiries at your local French consulate before leaving. Importing and exporting currency, in whatever form, is allowed up to 50,000FF. Above that amount you should declare it to Customs.

No formalities are required for vehicles, caravans, motorbikes etc. For further details on specific items, call the customs information centre (tel: 42 60 35 50).

VAT reclaims (*détaxe*) can be made on purchases from France over the 2,000FF limit. These are worth making. Ask at time of purchase for the relevant forms, which have to be completed and stamped by the trader. These you present to Customs on leaving France, and a refund is either credited to your bank account, sent by cheque or kept at the shop for your next visit.

EC nationals can only claim on individual goods worth over 2,000FF per article, whereas non-EC citizens can spread their 2,000FF minimum over several articles as long as they have been bought at the same shop. Department stores are particularly well-organised for this procedure, as you can imagine. Refunds vary, starting at 13 per cent and rising per VAT category. Remember that you may have to show the goods to Customs on leaving, so keep them within easy reach.

Disabled Travellers

The national organisation for the disabled is **CNFLRH**, 38 boulevard Raspail, 75007 (tel: 45 48 90 13). It publishes two free brochures aimed specifically at disabled travellers in Paris and in France, *Touristes quand-même!*. Clearly laid out with diagrams, the Paris guide shows by *arrondissement* all the facilities available as well as listing museums, theatres and shopping centres with

PARIS BANLIEUE lignes

— RER LIGNE A
— RER LIGNE B
— RER LIGNE C
— RER LIGNE D
✈ Aeroport
◉ Correspondance avec Metro lignes
○ Correspondance avec autre lignes

©TCS   User No. 9C/02/117

easy access. The offices are open Monday to Friday, 09.00–12.000hrs and 14.00–18.00hrs; they will provide advice on all relevant matters.

Buses are not suitable for wheelchairs, but certain metros and the express RER have access. A leaflet listing stations equipped with lifts, and showing which connections are feasible, is published by the Paris transport system, the **RATP**, 53 ter, Quai des Grands Augustins, 75006 (tel: 43 46 14 14).

The RATP also offers a free service, called *Voyage accompagne*, specifically for people with mobility problems (except those in wheelchairs). Phone the RATP number above at least a day in advance to book one of their staff, who will accompany you on your trip round Paris between 08.00 and 20.00hrs for no extra fee.

The RER express train, being more modern, is better equipped for wheelchairs, and certain SNCF trains are now specifically designed for them, but you should enquire with the information service in advance (tel: 45 82 50 50). All Parisian mainline stations have wheelchair access, special toilets and phones, while assistance can be asked for at

Marne-la-Vallée / Chessy
EURO-DISNEY
A4
Roissy-Aéroport Charles de Gaulle
B3
Gare Ouest
Parc des Expositions
Villepinte
Violenne
Collégien
Vert Galant
Mitry-Claye
Sevran-Livry Villeparisis B5
Torcy (Marne-la-Vallée)
Mesnil
Lognes
Noisiel
Noisy-Champs
Noisy Le Grand-Mont d'Est
Bry Sur Marne
Neuilly-Plaisance
Val de Fontenay
Nation Vincennes
Boulevard Masséna
Fontenay Sous Bois
Ivry sur Seine
Nogent Sur Marne
Joinville Le Pont
Vitry sur Seine
St Maur-Créteil
Les Ardoines
Le Parc de St Maur
Champigny
Choisy le Roi
La Varenne-Chennevières
Les Saules Villeneuve Le Roi
Ablon
Sucy-Bonneuil
Athis-Mons
A2
Juvisy
Boissy St Léger
de Rungis Savigny sur Orge
Épinay sur Orge
Saint Geneviève des Bois
rnelle Saint Michel sur Orge
rville St Germain Les Arpajon Brétigny sur Orge
Arpajon Marolles en Hurepoix
Bouray
Egly
itel Lardy
Chamarande
Étréchy
Étampes
Saint Martin d'Étampes

PARIS SUBURBAN lines

━━━ RER LINE A   ✈ Airport
━━━ RER LINE B   ◉ Connection with Metro lines
━━━ RER LINE C   ○ Connection with other lines
━━━ RER LINE D

the *accueil* in each station. Both Orly and Roissy airports are well-equipped for disabled people. For more specific information contact the Département Relations Publiques, Aéroports de Paris, 291 boulevard Raspail, 75014 (tel: 43 35 70 00). It publishes a brochure, *Guide des personnes handicapées* describing facilities available. A specially equipped shuttle exists between the terminals at Roissy for passengers in transit, but there is nothing between Orly and Roissy. For getting to Orly Sud or Ouest, contact **Serval** (tel: 47 26 45 00). Parisian taxis must by law accept

The Arc de Triomphe and the Champs Elysées

disabled clients. There is no longer a specific service for the disabled, but minibuses can be hired through a number of non-profit organisations. Try **Handibus** (tel: 42 03 61 67). For hiring wheelchairs, the very central **Pharmacie Canonne**, 88–90 boulevard Sébastopol, 75003 (tel: 42 72 83 08) will oblige, while specially equipped cars can be hired from **Inter Touring Service**, 117 boulevard Auguste Blanqui, 75013 (tel: 45 88 52 37).

Hotels (particularly the budget category) are not always easily accessible, but the red Michelin hotel and restaurant guide shows which ones are, as does the list published by the Office de Tourisme de Paris. The Paris branch of the **Association des Paralysés de France**, 22 rue du Père-Guérin, 75013 (tel: 45 80 82 40) publishes *Où ferons-nous étape?*, a guide listing specially equipped hotels and motels throughout France.

Although Paris is not an easy city for disabled people (kerbs are high, ramps are few and lifts sometimes too small), facilities are improving and awareness of needs is growing. All renovated and newly constructed buildings are now well-equipped.

Driving

Drivers in Paris should be 18 or over, have valid car registration papers, a driving licence and car insurance. France follows international road signs and regulations, but for British and other left-side drivers the French 'priority to the right' can be a surprise. You may be hurtling along what appears to be a main road but be caught short when a car turns in front of you from the right. All road signs are those of the international code except one: *Vous n'avez pas la priority* (you do not have priority). Parisian streets are regularly resurfaced. August is the peak month for any kind of road works; this is also when driving is most

Driving up the avenue: a bird's-eye view of the Champs Elysées

pleasurable, as the capital is relatively empty. For the rest of the year, you will find a car more of a hindrance than a help, and Parisian traffic manners need getting used to. Nobody waits or watches out for anyone else, cars move fast when possible, pedestrians dive across streets risking life and limb. However dangerous all this may seem, drivers do have fast reactions and are used to getting out of unexpected situations. Several main north-south and east-west axes have now been declared *axes rouges*, which means parking or even stopping is absolutely forbidden.

Accidents/Breakdown 24-hour breakdown services can be obtained through the garages listed below. Others are listed in the yellow pages phone-book under *Dépannages et remorquages:*

Aleveque 166 rue de la Convention, 15e (tel: 48 28 12 00).
Allô-Assistance 4 rue Nicolas-Charlet, 15e (tel: 43 06 39 16).
Alfauto 4 avenue Bartraux, 18e (tel: 45 31 61 18).
Garage Emile 40 rue Trousseau, 11e (tel: 43 55 62 05).
Paris Dépannage Assistance 34 avenue des Champs Elysées, 8e (tel: 40 12 07 96).

Car/ motorcycle/ camper rental If you really must hire a car in Paris (you must be over 21), try any of the following. Their rates are similar, though Hertz and Avis usually cost the most. Larger rental firms allow you to drop off the car in a city other than where it was hired. Weekend deals are often worth asking about and should include unlimited mileage and third-party insurance. Personal insurance is optional.

Cars/vans
Avis 5 rue Bixio, 75007 (tel: 45 50 32 31).
Budget 4 avenue du Président Roosevelt, 75008 (tel: 42 25 79 89).
Citer 40 cours de Vincennes, 75012 (tel: 43 41 05 50).
Europcar (central booking, tel: 30 43 82 82).
Hertz (central booking, tel: 47 88 51 51).

Motorcycles are available for hire at several outlets – and can be the object of admiration...

Rent-a-Car 79 rue de Bercy, 75012 (tel: 43 45 98 99).
Rual 23 rue du Départ, 75014 (tel: 43 21 56 50).
Valem 41 boulevard Richard Lenoir, 75011 (tel: 43 55 81 83).
Chauffeur-driven cars
Air Limousine Aéroport Le Bourget (tel: 48 35 93 57). Bilingual chauffers.
Carey Limousine 25 rue Astorg, 75008 (tel: 42 65 54 20).
Motorcycles/ bikes
Choppers Rent 180 boulevard Voltaire, 75011 (tel: 43 79 25 35).
Mondial Scooter Location 20 bis avenue Charles-de-Gaulle, 92200 Neuilly (tel: 46 24 63 64).
Monneret Location Motos 3 rue Brunel, 75017 (tel: 47 63 68 22).
Paris Vélo 2 rue du Fer-à-Moulin, 75005 (tel: 43 37 59 22).
Paris By Cycle 99 rue de la Jonquière, 75017 (tel: 42 63 36 63).
Mountain Bike Trip 13 rue St-Ambroise, 75011 (tel: 40 21 90 51).
Campers
Avis Car-Away 60 rue de Caen, 92400 Courbevoie (tel: 43 34 15 81).
Mobiloc 189 rue d'Aubervilliers, 75018 (tel: 40 36 01 79).
Le Monde du Camping-Car 54 avenue Division Leclerc, RN20, 91160 Ballainvilliers (tel: 64 49 01 87).

Fuel Super, *sans plomb* (lead free) and gas-oil (diesel) are the three types of fuel available. Fuel pumps are located above ground as well as in car parks. There are several 24-hour pumps:

249

corner Champs Elysées/avenue
Georges V, 8e
1 boulevard de la Chapelle, 10e
avenue de la Porte de Chatillon, 14e
6 avenue de la Porte de Clichy, 17e
avenue de la Porte de Saint-Ouen,
18e

>> Of all major European cities
Paris has the highest rates of
lead and carbon-monoxide
pollution. Cars are responsible
for 75 per cent of city polution,
and 59 per cent of Parisians
favour a limitation of traffic in the
centre. >>

Headlights France has now adopted
EC regulations and uniform white
headlights.

Motoring organisations Auto-
Camping et Caravaning Club de
France 37 rue d'Hauteville, 75010
(tel: 47 70 29 81).
Automobile Club National 9 rue
Anatole de la Forge, 75017 (tel: 42
27 82 00).

Parking This is Paris' perennial
problem. Most central streets are
now metered, a system that costs
residents considerably less than
visitors. Meters are situated at
intervals along streets: put in the
coins corresponding to the length of
time you want to park, press the
button, collect the ticket and put it
inside your car visible on the
dashboard.
More and more underground parking
lots are being constructed to meet
the growing demand, and these can
be spotted by their blue signs
marked with a large 'P'. If you decide
to park your car for a few days and
visit Paris in a more leisurely fashion,
the cheapest 24-hour parking
facilities are situated on the
perimeter (Porte de Saint-Ouen,
Porte de Clignancourt, Porte d'Italie).
Otherwise, central underground
parking costs considerably more.
Clamps and car pounds (*fourrière*):
Although clamps are not as abundant
as in, say, London, they do appear,
so avoid parking illegally (pedestrian

crossings, loading zones, bus lanes,
axes rouges, etc). You may be towed
away to one of the six Parisian car
pounds which cover all Parisian
arrondissements. Contact the local
police station to find out where you
have to go. It is a costly business,
whatever.

>> 1,300,000 vehicles circulate
in Paris daily – four times as
many as 20 years ago. About 85
per cent of traffic jams in France
are to be found in and around
Paris. >>

Speed limits 50km/h (30mph) in
cities; 80km/h (50mph) on the
périphérique (ring road); 130km/h
(80mph) on motorways (110km/h
(68mph) on dual carriageways).

Electricity
Voltage is 220 V, and sockets take
two round pins.

Embassies and Consulates
Always check opening hours by
phone in advance: many consulates
are only open in the morning and
close for both French public holidays
and those of their own country. In

The Panthéon

general the consulate deals with day-to-day problems facing their citizens or travellers to the country, whereas the embassy is for more official business. Many nations have both the embassy and the consulate located under the same roof. Embassies which are not listed below are in the phone book under *Ambassades*.

Australia Embassy: 4 rue Jean Rey, 75015 (tel: 40 59 33 00); visa section (tel: 40 59 33 07), metro: Bir-Hakeim.

Canada Embassy: 35 avenue Montaigne, 75008 (tel: 47 23 01 01); visa section (tel: 47 23 52 20), metro: Franklin-D-Roosevelt.

Ireland Embassy: 4 rue Rude, 75016 (tel: 45 00 20 87), metro: Etoile.

New Zealand Embassy: 7 ter rue Léonard de Vinci, 75016 (tel: 45 00 24 11), metro: Victor-Hugo.

UK Embassy: 35 rue du Faubourg St-Honoré, 75008 (tel: 42 66 91 42), metro: Concorde. Consulate:16 rue d'Anjou, 75008 (tel: 42 66 91 42), metro: Courcelles.

US Embassy: 2 avenue Gabriel, 75008 (tel: 42 96 12 02), metro: Champs Elysée-Clémenceau. Consulate/visas: 2 rue St-Florentin, 75001 (tel: 42 96 14 88), metro: Concorde.

Emergency Phone Numbers
Ambulance (Samu) 15 (or 45 67 50 50)
Fire 18
Police 17
Anti-poison 40 37 04 04
Doctor (SOS Médecins) 47 07 77 77. Emergency house calls only. Ask for an English-speaking doctor or contact **The American Hospital,** 63 boulevard Victor Hugo, Neuilly (tel: 46 41 25 25), which has a 24-hour emergency service – at a price. **The Hertford British Hospital,** 3 rue Barbes, Levallois-Perret (tel: 47 58 13 12) provides a similar emergency service.

For burns go to the **Hôpital St-Antoine,** 184 rue du Faubourg St-Antoine, 75012 (tel: 43 44 33 33). Emergency treatment for children can be obtained at the **Hôpital Necker**, 149 rue de Sèvres, 75015 (tel: 42 73 80 80).

Dentist (SOS Dentistes), (tel: 43 37 51 00). Emergency house calls only.

Motorway and road information (tel: 48 49 33 33).

SOS Help (tel: 47 23 80 80) is an emergency crisis line for English-speakers.

Making contact in a restaurant on the Left Bank

Etiquette

French etiquette is hardly different from that of Anglo-Saxon countries; just more formal, although that is disappearing with the younger generations. Hand-shaking is more prevalent when meeting someone, even when you have already been introduced. You can feel justifiably proud when the local barman or restaurant owner proffers his hand on your arrival. This is a sign of respect and acceptance. Do not use Christian names unless you yourself have been addressed in this way. Smoking is more widespread than in Anglo-Saxon countries but is completely banned in cinemas and inside Parisian buses and metros. Taxis will display a no-smoking sign when drivers are averse to it; but if you as a non-smoker find yourself with a smoking taxi driver, there is little you can do. A new law will soon be responsible for creating no-smoking sections in the Gauloise-fume-filled cafés and restaurants.

Health

There are no inoculations necessary to enter France, but if you plan on staying more than three months a medical check-up is required for non-EC nationals.

France offers no more health risks than any other European country (apart from the effects of over eating and drinking, so bring a stock of Alka-Seltzers with you). Tap water in Paris is perfectly drinkable, though you may prefer the taste of mineral water.

The French national health system is complex. Any salaried person can have treatment by a doctor or public hospital and be reimbursed roughly 70 per cent. Reciprocal agreements exist with EC countries; UK visitors should take form E111 (available from British post offices). Otherwise, make sure you take out a private health insurance before you leave home. For a modest amount you will be sure that any treatment costs are completely reimbursed.

Hospitals Public hospitals can be found all over Paris (listed in phone book under *Hôpital*), the most central being the Hôtel Dieu right outside Nôtre Dame. All have a 24-hour emergency service *(urgences)* as well as specialist doctors in every field. Payment is made on the spot for any kind of consultation, but if for any reason you are hospitalised ask to see the *assistante sociale* to arrange reimbursement directly through your own insurance. By law any emergency case must be treated and, once out of danger, foreign patients are flown home.

Private hospitals are a lot more expensive and treatment is not necessarily better, but for linguistic reasons you may prefer one of the following:

American Hospital 63 boulevard Victor Hugo, Neuilly (tel: 45 41 25 25).

Hertford British Hospital 3 rue Barbes, Levallois-Perret (tel: 47 58 13 12).

Local doctors can be found by asking at a nearby *pharmacie*.

Appointments are usually made in advance, but very few will refuse to see an emergency case. House calls can be arranged by calling **SOS Médecins** (tel: 47 07 77 77). A similar dental service exists (tel: 43 37 51 00).

Specific problems   AIDS advice (in English): **FAACTS** (Free Anglo American Counselling Treatment Support), The American Church, 65 Quai d'Orsay, 75007 (tel: 45 50 26 49).

SIDA AP (AIDS hotline) (tel: 45 82 93 39). *Open:* 09.00–17.00hrs weekdays and Saturday mornings.

Poison centre (tel: 40 37 04 04).

Burns centre (tel: 42 34 17 58).

Drug crisis (tel: 05 05 88 88).

VD clinic Institut Vernes, 36 rue d'Assas, 75006 (tel: 45 44 38 94), metro: Rennes. Free consultations, no appointment.

SOS Help English Hotline (tel: 47 23 80 80).

Hitch-hiking

Hitching in France is legal except on motorways. As in any city, hitching inside Paris will get you nowhere unless there is a general transport strike. However, if heading out of the capital to the rest of France, the best places are at the relevant Portes leading to the main motorways – but do not stand where traffic is already travelling at speed. Firstly, it is dangerous and, secondly, nobody will stop.

At the Porte d'Orléans there is usually a queue of hopeful hitchers on the slip road leading down to the southbound autoroute du Soleil, and a similar crowd of optimists gathers at the Porte de la Chapelle for the Autoroute du Nord. For those heading west, go to the Porte d'Auteuil, while for eastern destinations go to the Porte de Bercy. It is a good idea to have a sign declaring your destination, but do make sure you are standing where cars can pull in safely without stopping the traffic flow, otherwise the local *gendarmes* will pick you up instead.

A much safer and surer method is to contact a hitch-hiking service. This links up drivers with potential passengers, who contribute to fuel costs: **Allostop**, 84 Passage Brady, 75010 (tel: 42 46 00 66), metro: Strasbourg-St Denis. It has existed for over 15 years and is reliable.

253

Insurance

Travel insurance should be taken out before leaving home. Travel agents usually have information, and certain credit cards provide cardholders' insurance if tickets are purchased with their card. **Europ-assistance** is one of the most universally known travel insurance companies and is reliable.

Language
Numbers

1	un/une
2	deux
3	trois
4	quatre
5	cinq
6	six
7	sept
8	huit
9	neuf
10	dix
11	onze
12	douze
13	treize
14	quatorze
15	quinze
16	seize
17	dix-sept
18	dix-huit
19	dix-neuf
20	vingt

TRAVEL FACTS

30	trente
40	quarante
50	cinquante
60	soixante
70	soixante-dix
80	quatre-vingt
90	quatre-vingt-dix
100	cent
1000	mille

Days of the Week

Monday	lundi
Tuesday	mardi
Wednesday	mercredi
Thursday	jeudi
Friday	vendredi
Saturday	samedi
Sunday	dimanche

Basic Phrases

Yes/no	oui/non
Please	s'il vous plaît
Thank you	merci
Excuse me	excusez-moi
I'm sorry	Je suis désolé
Hello	bonjour
Goodbye	au revoir
How are you?	comment allez-vous?
Very well, thanks	Très bien, merci
Do you speak English?	Parlez-vous anglais?
I don't understand	Je ne comprends pas
why?	pourquoi?
who?	qui?
what?	quel?
when?	quand?
how?	comment?
how much?	combien?
today	aujourd'hui
yesterday	hier
tomorrow	demain
this morning	ce matin
this afternoon	cet après-midi
tonight	ce soir

Directions

where is...	Où est...
the nearest metro	le métro le plus proche
the telephone	le téléphone
the bus stop	l'arrêt de bus
the bank	la banque
the bookshop	la librairie
where are the toilets?	Où sont les toilettes?
in the basement	au sous-sol
on the first floor	au premier étage
turn right/left	tournez à droite/gauche
go straight on	allez tout droit
the first street	la première rue
before the crossroads	avant le carrefour
after the roundabout	après le rondpoint
at the traffic lights	aux feux rouges

Hotels

do you have...?	avez-vous...?
a double room	une chambre double
with bathroom	avec salle de bains
with shower room	avec salle d'eau
a single room	une chambre simple
we need an extra bed	nous avons besoin d'un lit supplé-mentaire
what time is breakfast?	quelle heure est le petit déjeuner?
do you accept credit cards?	prenez-vous les cartes de crédit?
we leave tomorrow	nous partons demain
please prepare our bill	s'il vous plaît préparez la note

Restaurants

waiter! waitress!	Monsieur! Madame!
we want to book a table for 9 o'clock	nous voulons réserver une table pour neuf heures.
do you have a fixed price menu?	avez-vous un menu?
I am a vegetarian	je suis

	végétarian
a bottle of ...	une bouteille de ...
a glass of ...	un verre de...
can I have the menu please?	
	donnez-moi la carte, s'il vous plaît
the bill	l'addition
breakfast	le petit déjeuner
lunch	le déjeuner
dinner	le dîner

Lost Property

The central lost property office for anything handed to the police is at 36 rue des Morillons, 75015, metro: Convention. No information is given over the phone.
Open: Monday, Wednesday, Friday 08.30–17.00hrs; Tuesday and Thursday 08.30–20.00hrs.

Maps

The Office du Tourisme – at 127 avenue des Champs Elysées, 75008 (tel: 47 23 61 72), metro: George V – is open daily 09.00–20.00hrs and provides extensive free information. City maps can also be found free in most hotels, while metro stations and some buses have free transport maps. If you are staying for a longer period, it is worth investing 40FF or so in a *Paris par Arrondissement*, a small publication with road index and *arrondissement* maps.

Media

Parisian Press Reading habits in France are very different from those of both the UK and the US. Parisians do not spend their Sundays perusing bulky supplements to catch up on the week's news. This role is filled by weekly magazines (similar to *Time* or *Newsweek*), all published on Thursdays. Covering the political spectrum, they range from *Le Nouvel Observateur* and *L'Evénement du Jeudi* (broadly left-wing) to *L'Express* (centre) and *Le Point* (centre-right). *Paris-Match* still deals in society gossip or disaster-related scoops, while political scandals are dug up in the investigative satirical weekly newspaper, *Le Canard Enchaîné*.

CONVERSION CHARTS

FROM	TO	MULTIPLY BY
Inches	Centimetres	2.54
Centimetres	Inches	0.3937
Feet	Metres	0.3048
Metres	Feet	3.2810
Yards	Metres	0.9144
Metres	Yards	1.0940
Miles	Kilometres	1.6090
Kilometres	Miles	0.6214
Acres	Hectares	0.4047
Hectares	Acres	2.4710
Gallons	Litres	4.5460
Litres	Gallons	0.2200
Ounces	Grams	28.35
Grams	Ounces	0.0353
Pounds	Grams	453.6
Grams	Pounds	0.0022
Pounds	Kilograms	0.4536
Kilograms	Pounds	2.205
Tons	Tonnes	1.0160
Tonnes	Tons	0.9842

MEN'S SUITS

UK	36	38	40	42	44	46	48
Rest of Europe	46	48	50	52	54	56	58
US	36	38	40	42	44	46	48

DRESS SIZES

UK	8	10	12	14	16	18
France	36	38	40	42	44	46
Italy	38	40	42	44	46	48
Rest of Europe	34	36	38	40	42	44
US	6	8	10	12	14	16

MEN'S SHIRTS

UK	14	14.5	15	15.5	16	16.5	17
Rest of Europe	36	37	38	39/40	41	42	43
US	14	14.5	15	15.5	16	16.5	17

MEN'S SHOES

UK	7	7.5	8.5	9.5	10.5	11
Rest of Europe	41	42	43	44	45	46
US	8	8.5	9.5	10.5	11.5	12

WOMEN'S SHOES

UK	4.5	5	5.5	6	6.5	7
Rest of Europe	38	38	39	39	40	41
US	6	6.5	7	7.5	8	8.5

255

Numerous monthly magazines exist, two of the most interesting being *Actuel*, a young glossy socio-cultural mag, and *L'Autre Journal*, a recent arrival in a similar field.

There are seven main daily newspapers, none of which has an enormous circulation. Most respected intellectually, although sometimes tough to read, is *Le Monde*, which you can purchase from 14.30hrs daily except Sunday and remains on sale till the following day. Its entertainment supplement, published on Wednesday afternoon, gives a useful overview of the best current shows and exhibitions. The other afternoon newspaper, *France Soir*, is lightweight, concentrating more on consumer affairs, sports and entertainment.

The Parisian daily par excellence is *Libération*, a young, witty daily carrying on much of the 1968 radical thought, although many of its readers are now affluent and middle-aged. Its coverage of the arts is excellent.

Le Figaro, historically the most established (since 1866), veers from being ultra-conservative to providing a useful anti-government voice, while its classified ads constitute the bible of property and job-seekers.

On the far right of the political spectrum stands *Le Quotidien de Paris*, while swimming along beside it is *Le Parisien*, a tabloid that only seems to be read free of charge in cafés.

L'Humanité, the anachronistic Communist Party newspaper, creaks along with a faithful hardcore readership.

Foreign Press Central newspaper kiosks usually carry a fairly reasonable selection of European dailies, and you can always pick up the European edition of the *International Herald Tribune*, which is published in Paris.

For a wide range of European and American press and magazines, go to one of the NMPP bookshops, (52 rue Jacques Hillairet, 75012, or 93 rue Montmartre, 75002). This is the central distribution organisation for all press in France and so carries the gamut of the extensive French regional press too.

Entertainment magazines All three come out on Wednesdays, the day new films are released. Take your pick from the old mainstay *Pariscope*, *L'Officiel des Spectacles* (less easy to follow the latter's classifications, but pocket-sized like *Pariscope*) or the irreverent, pun-loving magazine, *7 à Paris*, *Le Figaro* also enters the fray on Wednesdays with a well-listed entertainments supplement, *Figaroscope*.

Radio If you tune in to FM in Paris, you will be amazed at what bounces off the crowded and varied airwaves. No longer the bonanza that it was in the early 1980s, when anybody and everybody jumped on the free-radio bandwagon, the number of stations is now – thankfully – controlled. Minority tastes are catered for, from **Fréquence Juive** (94.8 MHz) to **Radio Notre Dame** (100.7 MHz) for Christians, or **France Maghreb** (94.2 MHz) for the North African community. **Tropic FM** (92.6 MHz) takes you even further, specialising in African and Caribbean sounds. **Fréquence Gaie** (94.4 MHz) is aimed at the gay community. News is broadcast round the clock on France Infos (105.5 MHz), while the latest on Parisian traffic jams interjects a mixed music programme on **FIP** (90.4 MHz).

Classical music fans should tune in to **France Musique** (91.3 MHz), though presenters tend to chat, whereas **Radio Classique** (101MHz) provides virtually non-stop music. Not as influential as they were, but still powerful, are current afairs and variety stations such as **France Inter** (87.8MHz), **RTL** (104.3MHz), **Radio Monte Carlo** (103.1MHz) and **Europe 1** (104.7MHz).

For unadulterated rap/rock/House/world music, your best bet is to tune in to **Radio Nova** (101.5 MHz) or **NRJ** (100.3 MHz).

The **BBC World Service** can be found on medium wave, 648 KHz.

Television The two main state channels, **Antenne 2** and **FR3**, still have a long way to go in the quality of their programmes, but the recently privatised **TF1** is even worse. Addicted to trite panel discussions, variety shows, reruns of 'family' films and dubbed American cops series, none has a clear identity. Antenne 2 occasionally rises out of mediocrity with a good

documentary and, like FR3, gives cultural events reasonable coverage. **Canal Plus,** a private subscribers' channel launched in 1983, has been very successful in its rotation of recent films, good documentaries, sports events and children's programmes. It starts the day at 07.00hrs with the CBS evening news. However, **Le Cinq**, largely financed by Italian TV magnate Berlusconi, narrowly escaped disaster in 1991 but has now finally disappeared. On the other hand, the sixth channel (M6), created in 1987, is increasingly popular. Mixing music videos with movies, it also programmes some excellent BBC documentaries and TV films (dubbed). Finally, the French satellite channel, **La Sept**, is devoted to cultural and minority interests for those who have the necessary decoders, although some of its programmes are broadcast on FR3. Satellite TV can be picked up easily, and most big hotels are linked up.

Money Matters
The French currency is the franc (symbolised by FF) which is divided into 100 centimes. Coins come as 5, 10, 20 and 50 centimes; 1, 2, 5 and 10 francs. Bank notes start at 20FF, continue with 50FF, 100FF, 200FF and end at 500FF. The latter are hard to change in taxis and small shops, so try to avoid being given them when you change money. Foreigners can bring in currency, up to the generous limit of 50,00FF, in any form: cash, travellers' cheques, Eurocheques etc.

Banks Most Parisian Banks are open 09.00–16.30hrs Monday to Friday, but shut at noon the day before any public holiday (see below). They usually have a foreign exchange counter, which charges a small commission on any operation. If you are confronted with a choice, BNP is likely to offer the best rates and lowest commission. Banks that display credit card symbols outside will also advance cash on the basis of your card. Remember to have your passport on you for any transaction. Cash distributors outside

257

<< Although central Paris represents only 0.022per cent of the total French territory with 4 per cent of its population, it possesses 96 per cent of bank head offices, 70 per cent of insurance company head offices, 39 per cent of all professional people and furnishes 45 per cent of income tax revenue. **>>**

any bank take Visa, sometimes Diners Club and Mastercard, and often give instructions in English. For emergency exchange at the weekend, go to the Champs Elysées, where the CCF (103 Champs Elysées, metro: George V) remains open daily except Sunday till 20.00hrs. The cash machine at the BRED (66 Champs Elysées, metro: George V) exchanges foreign currency notes (dollars, pounds, marks, lire) into francs 24 hours a day. If you have large amounts of cash to change, it may be worthwhile going to the rue Vivienne near the Stock Exchange (metro: Bourse), where numerous private money-changers give good rates and charge no commission. Some are open till 19.00hrs.

If you're truly desperate, it's 20.30hrs, the exchange machine on the Champs Elysées has run out of notes and you have no credit cards – well then, you have no other choice than to go to a bureau de change at one of the main stations (*open*: 08.00–21.00hrs daily at the Gare du Nord and the Gare de Lyon; Monday to Saturday at the Gare St-Lazare and Austerlitz). Exchange bureaux at Orly and Roissy airports are open 07.00–23.00hrs daily.

Foreign banks American Express is at 11 rue Scribe, 75009 (tel: 42 66 09 99), metro: Opéra. Here you can cash personal cheques if you are a cardholder, as well as having funds rapidly transferred from the US but with a high commission.
Barclays (main branch), 33 rue du Quatre-Septembre, 75002 (tel: 40 06 85 85), metro: Opéra. There is also a branch at St-Germain-des-Prés.

Citibank 17 avenue Montaigne, 75008 (tel: 40 70 00 80), metro: FD Roosevelt.
Lloyds 15 avenue d'Iéna, 75783 (tel: 42 61 51 25), metro: Opéra.
National Westminster 18 place Vendôme, 75001 (tel: 42 60 37 40).
Credit cards are now widely accepted anywhere from supermarkets to restaurants. Top of the popularity list is any card linked to the Visa network, including Mastercard (Access), but always check before making assumptions. American Express is less popular due to the relatively high percentage the trader loses on any transaction. Bring a combination of cash, travellers' cheques (in French called simply *travellers'* with a heavy Chevalier accent) and credit cards, and you can't go wrong. Travellers' cheques are not accepted in place of currency and need to be changed at banks. Avoid changing large amounts in hotels, as rates are considerably worse. Eurocheques are not as widely accepted as the banks at home make them out to be.

National Holidays
The many public and religious holidays in France are known as *jours fériés*. Transport timetables change, banks, most museums and shops close, even newspapers do not come out. So bear this in mind when booking your holiday. Parisians make a habit of stretching a public holiday to bridge with a weekend, commonly known as *le pont*, which gives them a four- or five-day holiday. This is particularly visible in May, when there are no fewer than three public holidays. The following are the official one-day *jours fériés*:

1 January	New Year's Day
	Easter Monday
1 May	Fête du Travail (Labour Day)
8 May	Armistice (WWII)
Last week in May	
	Ascension
Early June	Whit Monday
14 July	Bastille day
15 August	Assumption
1 November	Toussaint (All Saints)

11 November Armistice (WWI)
25 December Christmas
The most steadfastly respected of the above are 1 January, 1 May, 1 November, 11 November and 25 December, when nearly everything is closed. Always check with museums and monuments to see if they remain open on the public holidays. Some smaller ones even shut up shop for all of August. Whatever the cultural potential is, you will, however, never starve. Restaurants do a good trade on these days, as do certain local grocery shops, but public transport slows down considerably, so do not try to venture far afield.

Hotels are notoriously difficult to book in May, June, September and October, when trade fairs and fashion shows abound, attracting thousands of business visitors. July and August are, surprisingly, not particularly booked up, as no self-respecting Frenchman would be seen in the capital at this time of year.

Opening Hours

Banks respect to the letter every public holiday and tack on the preceding afternoon, so beware! Otherwise their hours are generally 09.00–16.30hrs, although smaller branches may close for lunch and remain open an hour longer.

Shops Most shops open at 09.00hrs and close at 19.00hrs, although many fashion boutiques wait till 10.00hrs or even later. Few large food shops in central Paris close for the lunch hour, although small specialist traders may take a one- or two-hour break. Department stores, supermarkets and central boutiques all remain open. Saturday is a major trading day. Sunday – apart from food markets and the odd local grocer (who often remains open daily till 22.00hrs) – is definitively closed, while Monday provides a balance between the two.

Galeries Lafayette, queen of department stores

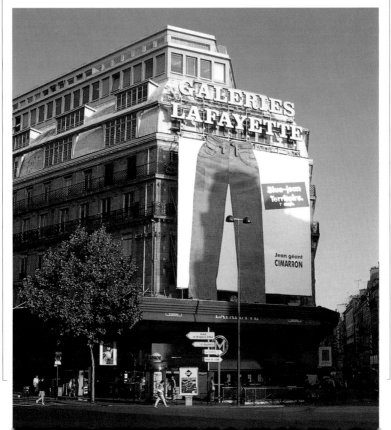

Museums These, too, vary. On the whole, the golden rule is the larger the museum the less likely it is to close for lunch, but watch out for the common closing days of Monday and Tuesday. National museums close on Tuesdays (except the Musée d'Orsay, which opts for Monday), while municipally financed museums close on Mondays. Most remain open on Sunday, when entrance fees are reduced or waived. Opening hours vary. The more traditional museums stick to about 09.30–17.00hrs while certain avant-garde art museums (centre Pompidou, Jeu de Paume, Arts Décoratifs, Arts de la Mode) don't open their doors till past noon. The important museums usually have a late-night opening (*nocturne*), and this is often a good opportunity to avoid queues (for example the Musée d'Art Moderne de la Ville de Paris and the Grand Palais all remain open late on Wednesdays). Always check small museums in advance; their habits can be idiosyncratic, and the renovation craze has not helped.

Organised Tours
Bicycle tours
Paris by Cycle, 99 rue de la Jonquière, 75017 (tel: 42 63 36 63)

organises tours of Paris by bike.

Boat trips
One of Paris' greatest pleasures is the Seine, so make sure you see some of the monuments from this perspective.
The enormous glass-roofed Bateaux-Mouches leave every half-hour from the Pont de l'Alma (Right Bank), take you east to beyond the Ile-Saint-Louis, then circle back. The entire trip takes over an hour and commentaries are given in five languages.
In summer, trips start at 10.00hrs and the last one at night leaves at 23.30hrs. In winter (mid-November to mid-March) departures are less frequent but are guaranteed at 11.00, 14.30, 16.00 and 21.00hrs. Try the extra-long lunch trip or even longer dinner trip – a spectacular way to see the monuments (leaving at 13.00 and 20.30hrs respectively). Reductions for children under 12 (tel: 42 25 96 10/42 25 22 55).
Very similar, but more central and easier to get to, is the flotilla of Vedettes du Pont-Neuf (tel: 46 33 98

A detail from the Grand Palais – one of the museums with late-night opening on Wednesdays

One of the great riverside sights of Paris: the Louvre

38), which leaves from the tip of the Ile-de-la-Cité at Pont-Neuf. These boats accomplish a 1-hour trip round the islands and down to the Eiffel Tower, but have the advantage of dropping you back in central Paris. Also covering five languages, the slightly more expensive summer departures start at 10.00hrs, running almost every half-hour through to the last boat at 22.30hrs. The evening tours do not include dinner. The winter service is more limited. Reductions for children under 10.
The **Bateaux Parisiens-Tour Eiffel** leave from the Left Bank side of the Pont d'Iéna and provide an almost identical service to the Bateaux-Mouches (tel: 47 05 50 00).

Canal St-Martin
Paris Canal Croisières organises 3-hour boat trips that take you along the Seine from the Musée d'Orsay to the Canal St-Martin and north to the Parc de la Villette. Commentaries are in French and English. This is a more unusual trip, perfect for a sunny afternoon, and will take you through parts of Paris you have probably never seen. Departures are at 09.30 and 14.15hrs from the Musée d'Orsay and 09.45 and 14.30hrs from La Villette. Booking by phone is essential (tel: 42 40 96 97). Prices are reasonable for the length of the trip, and children under 11 get a reduction.

Trips along the Canal St-Martin with **Canauxrama** between the Bastille and La Villette leave at 09.15hrs from 5 bis Quai de la Loire, 75019 (metro: Jean-Jaurès) or 09.45hrs from the Port de l'Arsenal opposite 50 boulevard de la Bastille (metro: Bastille). Departures in the other direction leave at 14.45 and 14.30, respectively. The same company organises a delightful one-day trip through canals out into very pretty countryside. Commentaries are in French and English. Reductions for children under 12. Booking is essential (tel: 42 39 15 00)

Coach trips
For first-time visitors without much time, a coach trip is ideal to orient yourself if you don't mind the group-style travel. All these tours are in comfortable double-decker buses, with a live or recorded commentary (in whatever language you want) and last two to three and a half hours.

Inside-out architecture at the Centre Georges Pompidou

Two companies, **Paris Vision** and **Cityrama**, monopolise the field; their services are virtually identical, although **Cityrama** is slightly cheaper. Both organise thematic tours (Paris by Night, Artistic Paris, Erotic Paris, Cabarets) as well as excursions to Versailles, Fontainebleau, Chartres and the Loire Valley.

Brochures are available and bookings can be made through the Office du Tourisme, 127 Champs Elysées (tel: 47 23 61 72), metro: George V. **Paris Vision** (terminus), 214 rue de Rivoli, 75001 (tel: 42 60 31 25), metro: Tuileries. Tours start at 09.30 and leave hourly till 14.30hrs. Arrive at least 15 minutes in advance.

Cityrama (terminus), 4 place de Pyramides, 75001 (tel: 42 60 30 14), metro: Tuileries, Palais-Royal. The same conditions apply as above.

A third company, **Parisbus**, has recently entered the field with red double-decker buses and a system leaving you free to get on and off their buses at any of the nine stops. Buses leave from the place du Trocadéro at 10.15hrs and the Eiffel Tower at 10.30hrs. It is cheaper than the above two companies, the ticket is valid for 24 hours, and commentaries are in French and English. The negative point is that they only have six departures a day, leaving you a lot of time to fill in between buses.

Walking tours

An excellent daily programme of walking tours of Paris covering specific areas or themes (often with entrance to monuments closed to the general public) is organised by the **Caisse Nationale des Monuments Historiques**, Hôtel de Sully, 62 rue St-Antoine, 75004 (tel: 42 74 22 22). Many walking tours are listed in the weekly entertainment magazines (under Conférences), and you can simply turn up at the appointed time and place. The only problem is that the guides speak only French but the accessibility of unusual sites may outweigh this.

Pharmacies

The hundreds of pharmacies in Paris are identified by large illuminated green crosses in front of their entrances. Most are open Monday to Saturday 09.00–19.00 or 20.00hrs. When closed, they always provide on the door a list of other local pharmacies that are open. Authorised to supply medication under prescriptions, they also have a monopoly on the sale of certain beauty and health products. Generally helpful, pharmacists also give immediate first aid (bad cuts, etc), and you will probably find that there is at least one who speaks English. They can also direct you to local doctors and specialists. For ordinary items (soap, toothbrushes, razors etc) it is cheaper to go to a supermarket. All health needs are available in pharmacies, from aspirin to condoms to tampons or baby requisites.

Late-night pharmacies:

Caillaud 6 boulevard des Capucines, 75009 (tel: 42 65 88 29), metro: Opéra. *Open*: Monday to Saturday 08.00–00.30hrs, Sunday 20.00–00.30hrs.

Cariglioli 10 boulevard Sébastopol, 75004 (tel: 42 72 03 23), metro: Châtelet. *Open* : 09.00hrs to midnight Monday to Saturday.

Delaitre 149 boulevard St-Germain, 75006 (tel: 42 22 80 00), metro: St-Germain. *Open* : Monday to Saturday 09.00–02.00hrs, Sunday 10.00–02.00hrs.

Dhéry 84 avenue des Champs Elysées, 75008 (tel: 45 62 02 41), metro: George V. *Open* : 24hours daily.

> **<<** Only about 50 of the 300 churches which stood in 18th-century Paris remain today. A further 150 have been built since World War II. **>>**

Places of Worship
Worshippers of any religion should be able to find the appropriate church or temple in Paris, although Catholics obviously get the most choice. Below is a selection.

Anglican Protestant
American Cathedral 23 avenue George V, 75008 (tel: 47 20 17 92), metro: Alma-Marceau.
American Church 65 Quai d'Orsay, 75007 (tel: 47 05 07 99), metro: Invalides.

The Eglise St-Germain-des-Prés dates back to the 10th century

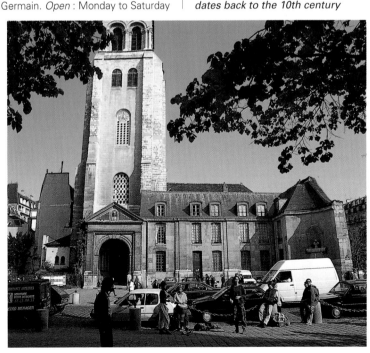

Church of Scotland 17 rue Bayard, 75008 (tel: 47 20 90 49), metro: F-D Roosevelt.

St George's English Church 7 rue Auguste Vacquerie, 75016 (tel: 47 20 22 51), metro: Etoile.

St Michael's Church of England 5 rue d'Aguesseau, 75008 (tel: 47 42 70 88), metro: Madeleine.

Buddhist

Centre Bouddhiste de Kagyu Dzong route circulaire du Lac Daumesnil, 75012 (tel: 43 41 86 48), metro: Porte Dorée.

Institut National de Bouddhisme 20 Cité Moynet, 75012 (tel: 43 40 91 61), metro: Reuilly-Diderot.

Catholic

See pages 140-141. Every *arrondissement* has at least four or five.

Sacré-Coeur has hourly services every morning, and evening mass

Jewish

Synagogue 8 rue Pavée, 75004 (tel: 42 77 81 51), metro: St-Paul.

Synagogue Nazareth 15 rue Notre Dame de Nazareth, 75003 (tel: 42 78 00 30), metro: République.

Synagogue 44 rue de la Victoire, 75009 (tel: 45 26 90 15), metro: Notre Dame de Lorette.

Orthodox

Eglise Grecque Orthodoxe 2 bis rue Laferrière, 75009 (tel: 48 78 35 53), metro: St-Georges.

Saint Alexandre de la Néva (Russian Orthodox), 12 rue Daru, 75008 (tel: 42 27 37 34), metro: Courcelles.

Police

No longer those familiar figures sporting *képis*, Parisian police now look like any other national police force and wear flat caps. There are over 16,000 uniformed policemen and women scattered round the police stations and streets of central Paris. The fire brigade is loosely attached and will deal with immediate first aid, lost cats, victims of accidents, gas leaks etc, apart from dealing with fires.

Each *arrondissement* has several police stations, including a main one open 24 hours a day which is often integrated into the *arrondissement* town hall. They will help with most problems (finding a plumber, local vet, doctor etc) as well as administrative matters, drug problems and, of course, crime.

1e	place du Marché St-Honoré (tel: 42 61 09 19)
2e	place des Petits Pères (tel: 42 60 96 87)
3e	5 rue Perrée (tel: 42 78 40 00)
4e	place Baudoyer (tel: 42 77 67 21)
5e	4 rue Montagne Ste-Geneviève (tel: 43 29 21 57)
6e	78 rue Bonaparte (tel: 43 29 76 10)
7e	116 rue de Grenelle (tel: 45 55 40 81)
8e	1 avenue du Général Eisenhower (tel: 42 25 88 80)
9e	14 bis rue Chauchat (tel: 42 46 30 26)
10e	26 rue Louis-Blanc (tel: 46 07 57 77)

11e place Léon-Blum (tel: 43 79 39 51)

12e 5 rue Bignon (tel: 46 28 26 85)

13e 144 boulevard de l'Hôpital (tel: 43 37 11 99)

14e 16 avenue du Maine (tel: 43 20 14 80)

15e 154 rue Lecourbe (tel: 45 31 14 40)

16e 62 avenue Mozart (tel: 45 27 03 78)

17e 19 rue Truffaut (tel: 42 93 05 50)

18e 77 ter rue du Mont-Cénis (tel: 46 06 43 84)

19e 2 rue André Dubois (tel: 42 40 10 39)

20e 6 place Gambetta (tel: 46 36 06 10)

The central Préfecture de Police on the Ile de la Cité deals with driving licences, residence and work permits, licences for various activities, etc (tel: 43 29 21 55). Another section of the police force is the river police, which controls crime and administrative matters on the Seine. Parking fines are usually dished out by a separate section, generally female and dressed in cornflower blue uniforms. The CRS are the military-looking, shield-bearing riot police, who hang around in vans near any demonstration, ready for action.

Emergency calls:
Police 17
Firemen *(pompiers)* 18
Hotline for drug problems 05 14 21 52

Post Offices
French post offices are known as la poste, officially the PTT, and in Paris they are signposted in the street. Many have outside cash dispensers that accept Visa cards.
Opening hours are:
Monday to Friday 08.00–19.00hrs, Saturday 08.00–12.00hrs. Avoid lunch hours and late afternoon when office workers dealing with business mail create endless queues. Most have phone booths, photocopiers, fax *(télécopieur)* and free access to the Minitel directory service. Express post facilities (called *Chronopost*) for

within France and abroad are also available.

Stamps can also be bought at *tabacs* (tobacco shops) and yellow postboxes are situated immediately outside.

The central post and sorting office of the Louvre is open 24 hours a day, but at night this is only for sending mail and poste restante.

PTT, 52 rue du Louvre, 75001 (tel: 40 28 20 00), metro: Louvre.

Poste Restante Use the Louvre post office for convenience; it is central and you can pick up mail at any time. Otherwise every post office provides this service as long as the full address is given. American Express (see Banks) also has a poste restante service.

Other central post offices
PTT Paris Archives, 67 rue des Archives, 75003.
PTT Hôtel de Ville, 9 place de l'Hôtel de Ville, 75004.
PTT Paris Bastille, 12 rue Castex, 75004.
PTT Paris Sorbonne, 13 rue Cujas, 75005.
PTT Paris St-Germain-des-Prés, 53 rue de Rennes, 75006.
PTT Paris Pigalle, 47 boulevard de Clichy, 75009.
PTT Paris Champs Elysées, 75008.

Public Transport
Parisian public transport is one of the best systems in the world, so use it! Metro/RER and bus maps are available free from any metro station and from some hotels. Bus routes are clearly marked at every bus stop and again inside the bus, so don't be afraid to use this as an excellent and cheap sightseeing service. As in every big city, avoid the morning and evening rush hours, when travel can become unbearable (roughly 08.30–09.30hrs and 17.00–19.00hrs).

Buses Buses should be hailed from bus stops. Use one or more metro tickets (depending on length of journey), which you punch in a machine beside the driver. It is possible to buy a single ticket on the bus, but it costs more this way. Most routes operate from

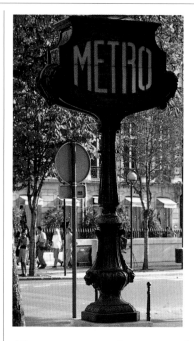

The metro: a convenient means of transport and a work of art

06.00–20.30hrs, with a few exceptions carrying on till midnight. Night buses (*noctambus*) radiate out hourly from Châtelet between 01.30 and 05.00hrs.

Metros Identified by a large 'M' in a circle, metro stations are easily spotted. The network of lines covers central Paris, and every station has clear indications, so you are unlikely to need help. Lines are identified by their end station; only two have branches, which means checking the destination on the front of the train. Doors open easily: lift the handle or press the button, and they shut automatically. Connections are called *correspondances*, and an orange sign on the platform indicates directions to your connecting line. Blue signs marked *sortie* indicate the exits.

<< Opened in 1900, the Metro's 15 lines measure 198km placed end to end and have 366 stations. The RER has added a further 102km. **>>**

One ticket is valid for every uninterrupted journey. After braving the automatic barriers, keep the ticket on you until you end your journey in case of inspectors. There is no longer a first-class carriage service.

First metros start at 05.30hrs, last around 00.30hrs.

Radio taxis

Alpha-taxis:	45 85 85 85
Taxis Bleu:	49 36 10 10
Taxi Etoile:	42 70 41 41
G7	47 39 47 39

All the above take advance bookings for travel to airports.

RER This express train system runs underground in the city centre and stretches far out into the suburbs. It can be a good time-saver if you are going from one side of Paris to the other, but access to platforms is often long and complicated, so it is not often worth it for a short trip. Metro tickets can be used for trips in central Paris; otherwise buy a ticket from a machjne. Keep it on you, as you have to slot it into a ticket machine on exiting as well as on entering the train.

Taxis These can be hailed in the street (when the roof light is switched on completely), picked up from taxi ranks or ordered by phone. Not the most open-minded of species, some taxi drivers are also accompanied by a faithful, slavering hound. Few accept more than three passengers. Fares (displayed on a meter) are reasonable compared with other European cities, and it is normal to add a 10–15 per cent tip.

Tickets/Travel passes Various formulae exist for travel passes, but

267

The Gare de Lyon

even if you don't use one of them make sure you buy a *carnet* of 10 tickets (metro/RER/bus) rather than the more costly individual tickets. A special tourist pass called *Paris Visite* gives you unlimited travel for three or five days. You can choose how many travel zones it covers (from two to four, plus the suburbs and airports). Formule I is a one-day pass, also valid on metro, RER and bus, with a similar choice of zones. Parisians themselves rely on monthly passes (*carte orange*) or weekly passes (*coupon hebdomadaire*), but for both of these you need a photo to have a special pass made on the spot. They are valid from the first day of the month or, for weekly passes, from Monday.

Senior Citizens
If you can prove with your passport that you are over 60, you will be given reduced-rate entry to museums and monuments. There is no reduction on Parisian public transport. Internal flights with Air Inter are available at reduced rates, again for those over 60.

Sport
Unless you are staying for a lengthy period in Paris, this is probably not the reason that brought you to the City of Light. However, if desperate, there are some possibilities, notably swimming pools, gyms and cycling round parks (see pages 228–9). Check the weekly entertainment magazine *Pariscope* in the *Sports et*

> **<<** Over 45 billion francs are spent annually between the national lottery, Loto, horse-racing and casino-gambling. This represents 12 billion francs for the government. **>>**

Loisirs section for a list of bowling alleys, skating rinks, squash and tennis clubs. For more specific information contact the Hôtel de Ville phoneline that specialises in municipal sports facilities and sporting events in the Paris area: **Allô-Sports**, 25 boulevard de

Bourdon, 75004 (tel: 42 76 54 54), metro: Bastille.
Golf enthusiasts who want to keep their wrists supple should contact: **Fédération Française de Golf**, 69 avenue Victor-Hugo, 75016 (tel: 45 02 13 55), metro: Victor-Hugo. The Federation provides a list of golf courses in France, but remember that most of them are out in the suburbs.

Spectator Sports
Palais Omnisport Paris-Bercy 8 boulevard de Bercy, 75012 (tel: 43 46 12 21), metro: Gare de Lyon. A vast, modern structure holding up to 17,000 spectators for cycling races, horse jumping, motocross or hockey championships.
Parc des Princes 24 rue du Commandant-Guilbaud, 75016 (tel: 42 88 02 76), metro: Porte de St-Cloud. The king of Parisian stadiums holds 50,000 spectators and is home to two Parisian soccer teams: Paris St-Germain and Racing Paris 1. It also hosts major rugby matches.

Roland-Garros 2 avenue Gordon-Bennett, 75016 (tel: 47 43 00 47), metro: Porte d'Auteuil. Home to the French Tennis Open held in late May, Roland-Garros is increasingly popular, but many of the tickets are in the hands of black-marketeers charging exorbitant prices at the gates.

Book seats in advance, asking for a reservation form (by February) – contact:

FFT Service Réservation BP 333-16, 75767 Paris Cedex 16.

Race courses

Hippodrome d'Auteuil Bois de Boulogne, 75016 (tel: 42 24 47 04), metro: Porte d'Auteuil. closed during July and August. Mainly hurdle racing.

Hippodrome de Longchamp Bois de boulogne, 75016 (tel: 42 24 13 29), metro: Porte d'Auteuil, then shuttle bus. Closed for part of summer. One of the world's most famous flat races, the Prix de l'Arc de Triomphe, is held here.

Hippodrome de Vincennes Bois de Vincennes, 75012 (tel: 43 68 35 39), metro: Porte de Vincennes, then shuttle bus. Mainly sulky racing, a colourful treat to watch. The big race is the Prix d'Amérique.

Student and Youth Travel

If you have a valid International Student Identity Card, it will give you numerous reductions (museums, cinemas, air and rail travel). Being a student city, Paris has endless facilities aimed specifically at the student population. The following organisations will set you in the right direction.

AJF (Accueil des Jeunes en France), 119 rue St-Martin, 75004 (tel: 42 77 87 80), metro: Châtelet, Rambuteau. *Open*: Monday to Saturday 09.30–19.00hrs. Help and information for accommodation, discount train tickets etc, for foreign students. It also runs some centrally located youth hostels. Another branch is at 139 boulevard St-Michel, 75005 (tel: 43 54 95 86).

CIDJ (Centre d'Information et de Documentation Jeunesse), 101 Quai Branly, 75015 (tel: 45 67 35 85), metro: Bir-Hakeim. *Open*: Monday to Friday, 09.00–18.00hrs. Excellent information centre for young people looking for jobs, courses, sports etc.

CROUS 39 avenue Georges Bernanos, 75005 (tel: 40 51 36 00), metro: Port-Royal. *Open:* Monday to Friday, 09.00–17.00hrs. Useful student organisation which runs university restaurants, organises sporting and cultural events and can provide information on jobs and accommodation.

Youth Hostels

UCRIF 4 rue Jean-Jacques Rousseau, 75001 (tel: 42 60 42 40), metro: Louvre. Open: Monday to Friday, 10.00–18.00hrs. Operates several cheap hostels in Paris as well as social events and language courses for foreigners.

Cité Universitaire 19 boulevard Jourdan, 75014 (tel: 45 89 13 37), RER: Cité Universitaire. During the summer months, rooms are available in the student residences for anyone with an International Student Card.

Student travel agencies

Council 51 rue Dauphine, 75006 (tel: 43 26 79 65), or 16 rue de Vaugirard, 75006 (tel: 40 51 84 88). Two

The Latin Quarter

agencies of the Council network specialising in cheap airfares, tours and charters to the US.

Jeunes Sans Frontières (Wasteels), 5 rue de la Banque, 75002 (tel: 42 61 53 21). Cheap flights and train fares.

USIT Voyage 6 rue de Vaugirard (tel: 43 29 85 00). Student charters.

SNCF and Air Inter

Both give up to 50 per cent reductions on standard fares to students under 27 or any youth under 26. These must be used during low-peak periods. The French Rail Pass must be purchased before leaving for France. The same goes for the Eurail Pass and Eurail Youthpass (only available to non-Europeans). Ask at your local French Tourist or French Railway office.

Telephones

Repairs: 13

Directory enquiries
(national): 12; (international): 19 33 12 + country prefix

Telegrams
(national): 36 55; (international): 05 33 44 11.

All numbers in France now have eight digits. For calling a number in the Ile de France, you do not need any prefix. For numbers outside the region but within France, you need to first dial 16, await the tone, then dial the main number. For phoning

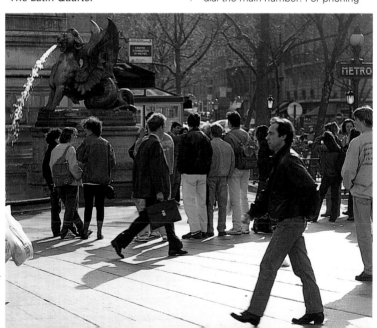

Paris from the provinces, dial 16+1, then the eight-figure number. For phoning abroad, dial 19, then your country code, then dial your number (omitting the area code's initial 0).

International calling Dial 19 33 + country prefix and you will reach an international operator. Otherwise the following countries provide a free direct service with their operators:

Australia	19 00 61
Canada	19 00 16
New Zealand	19 00 64
UK	19 00 44
US	19 00 11 (AT&T)

International prefixes:

Australia	19 + 61	+ town code
Canada	19 + 1	+ town code
Ireland	19 + 353	+ town code
New Zealand	19 + 64	+ town code
UK	19 + 44	+ town code
US	19 + 1	+ area code

Public phones Most Parisian public phones now function with phonecards (télécarte). These can be bought at post offices or tabacs for 50 or 120 units. Public phones in cafés and restaurants either use phonecards, coins or have to be switched on by staff, in which case you pay after the call (ask which system it is beforehand). For coin phones lift the receiver, insert a 1F or 2F piece, await the dialling tone, then dial.
Avoid using hotel phones for long-distance calls, as they are usually far more expensive.

Reduced rates For calls within France the cheapest times are at night, 22.30–06.00hrs. Next cheapest rate is after 21.30hrs on weekdays, after 13.30hrs on Saturday and all day Sunday. Lunchtime (12.30–13.30hrs) and early evening (18.00–21.30hrs) periods are 30 per cent cheaper than peak daytime rates.
International off-peak rates depend on the destination, but are generally 30 per cent or so less than normal rates.
Australia and New Zealand: weekdays 21.30–08.00hrs and Sunday all day.
Europe (EC) 21.30–08.00hrs

weekdays, 14.00–20.00hrs Saturdays and all day Sundays.
US and Canada: cheapest is daily, 02.00hrs to noon. Medium rate is noon to 14.00hrs and 20.00hrs Sunday.
Any public holiday has the same rates as Sunday.

Time
As the world has not yet agreed on the exact start and finish of winter time and summer time, there is often a floating period in spring and autumn when the winter time differences given below are incorrect for a week or so. However, for most of the year these apply. France changes her clocks in late September (back one hour) and late March (forward one hour). Her winter time is the same as that of Western Europe (except Portugal, which goes along with the UK).

Australia	
Perth	+ 7 hours
Sydney/Melbourne	+ 9 hours
Canada	
Montreal	– 6 hours
Vancouver	– 9 hours
Ireland	– 1 hour
New Zealand	+ 11 hours
UK	– 1 hour
US	
New York	– 6 hours
Los Angeles	– 9 hours

Tipping
Tipping in France is a complex affair, varying from service to service. In hotels, restaurants and cafés, service is included (up to 15 per cent), but it is usual to leave a small extra tip if you are satisfied, ranging from 50 centimes for a coffee to 10 or 20FF at a restaurant.
Theatre ushers look for tips (5 or 10FF) and cinema attendants depend on them for a living, so slip them 2FF when they tear your ticket. Taxi drivers expect 10–15 per cent, as do hairdressers.
Hotel porters and bellboys should be given 10FF or so per bag (going up with class of hotel) and chambermaids a bank note at the end of your stay. Room service also appreciates at least 10FF. If the hotel

concierge has achieved the impossible for you, he too will appreciate a solid tip.
Any tour guide should be tipped roughly 10–15 per cent.

Toilets
Public toilets can be found all over the city. Large off-white plastic affairs, they function with 1FF pieces, have automatic flushing and disinfecting systems, and are usually well-maintained. Every café has a toilet, ranging from the old smelly squatters to pristine affairs reeking of chlorine. These are designed for customers only, so don't tempt fate by marching in off the street to use one without first ordering a drink. They are nearly always situated in the basement. A small number are coin-operated. Some metro stations still house relics from the old days of public toilets, those at Madeleine being particularly remarkable.

Tourist Offices
L'Office de Tourisme de Paris 127 avenue des Champs Elysées, 75008 (tel: 47 23 61 72), metro: George V. *Open*: daily 09.00–20.00hrs. Drop by here to pick up free maps and leaflets about museums, tours, châteaux in and around Paris. They will find you accommodation and are generally extremely helpful.
Other smaller tourist offices are situated in the main railway stations (Gare du Nord, de l'Est, Austerlitz, de Lyon), and in the summer the Eiffel Tower claims its own branch. The station offices can be very useful in getting last-minute accommodation; in summer they open till 22.00hrs. Each French region has its own tourist office in Paris and can be a useful source of information if you are travelling round the rest of the country after Paris. The Maison de la France, 8 avenue de l'Opéra, 75001 (tel: 42 96 10 23) regroups information from all of them, but in less detail. Below is a selection of regional tourist offices.
Maison Alpes Dauphiné 2 place **André Malraux**, 75001 (tel: 42 96 08 43).
Maison d'Alsace 39 avenue des **Champs Elysées**, 75008 (tel: 42 56

15 94).
Maison de la Bretagne 17 rue de l'Arrivée, 75015 (tel: 45 38 73 15).
Maison des Hautes Alpes 4 avenue de l'Opéra, 75001 (tel: 42 96 05 08).
Maison du Nord-Pas de Calais 18 boulevard Haussmann, 75008 (tel: 47 70 59 62).
Maison du Périgord 30 rue Louis-le-Grand, 75002 (tel: 47 42 09 15).
Maison de Poitou-Charentes 68 rue du Cherche-Midi, 75006 (tel: 42 22 83 74).
Maison des Pyrénées 15 rue St-Augustin, 75002 (tel: 42 61 58 18).
Maison de Savoie 31 avenue de l'Opéra, 75001 (tel: 42 61 74 73).

Local French Tourist Offices
Australia: BNP Building/12th floor, 12 Castlereagh Street, Sydney, NSW 2000 (tel: (2) 231 5244, fax: (2) 233 4576).
Canada: 1981 avenue McGill College, Suite 490, Montréal, Québec H3A 2W9 (tel: (514) 288 4264, fax: (514) 845 4868).
1 Dundas Street West, Suite 2405, Box 8, Toronto, Ontario (tel: (416) 593 4722, fax: (416) 878 7087).
Ireland: 35 Lower Abbey Street, Dublin 1 (tel: (1) 77 18 71, fax: (1) 74 73 24).
UK 178 Piccadilly, London W1V 0AL (tel: (071) 491 7622, fax: (071) 493 6594).
US 610 Fifth Avenue, Suite 222, New York, NY 10020–2452 (tel: (212) 757 1125, fax: (212) 247 6468).
645 North Michigan Avenue, Chicago, IL 60611–2836 (tel: (312) 337 6301, fax: (312) 337 6339).
9454 Wilshire Boulevard, Beverly Hills, CA 90912–2967 (tel: (213) 271 7838, fax: (213) 276 2835).
2305 Cedar Springs Road, Suite 205, Dallas, TX 75201 (tel: (214) 720 4010, fax: (214) 720 0250).

Valeting / Laundry
For general laundry go to a launderette *laverie automatique*, although these are not as common as dry cleaners. Dry cleaners *(pressing)* can be found all over Paris but do not come cheap. Some have an economy service, but this is not recommended for your best silk jacket.

DIRECTORY

DIRECTORY

Accommodation

Expensive

L'Hôtel 13 rue des Beaux Arts, 75006 (tel: 43 25 27 22). A Parisian legend that doesn't come cheap. Antiques galore, elegance and memories of Oscar Wilde. Much-frequented basement restaurant and piano bar.

Hôtel Lutetia 45 boulevard Raspail 75007 (tel: 45 44 38 10). Huge, historic, a masterpiece of art deco architecture. Renovated and restyled by Sonia Rykiel in 1989. Elegant, well-located between St-Germain and Montparnasse. Good brasserie.

Hôtel du Pont Royal 7 rue de Montalembert, 75007 (tel: 45 44 38 27). A favourite venue for affluent antique dealers, best-selling authors and international publishers. Comfortably appointed, efficient service and a famous basement bar.

Hôtel San-Régis 12 rue Jean Goujon, 75008 (tel: 43 59 41 90). Elaborately redecorated a few years ago, a favourite with American film stars.

Personalised style for each room. All top 4-star facilities.

Hôtel de la Trémoille 14 rue de la Trémoille, 75008 (tel: 47 23 34 20). Down a chic side street off the fashion hub of the avenue Montaigne, a discreet luxury hotel with all the comforts and consequently high prices.

Pavillon de la Reine 28 place des Vosges, 75004 (tel: 42 77 96 40). A historic setting for a discreetly luxurious hotel. Flowery courtyard, and tasteful period decoration.

Regent's Garden 6 rue Pierre-Demours, 75017 (tel: 45 74 07 30). Elegant townhouse with magnificent garden, huge rooms decorated in period or provincial style. Excellent amenities, though no restaurant.

Le Warwick 5 rue de Berri, 75008 (tel: 45 63 14 11). Suitable for incognito VIPs, a modern luxury hotel off the Champs Elysées.

Moderate

Hôtel de l'Abbaye 10 rue Cassette, 75006 (tel: 45 44 38 11). A very up-market but affordable hotel in a former monastery. Flowery, cobbled courtyard, elegant salons, terraced duplex rooms, smiling staff.

Hôtel Agora 7 rue de la Cossonerie, 75001 (tel: 42 33 46 02). Bang in the middle of Les Halles in a 12th-century street. Part modern, part provincial in atmosphere; reasonable value. Branch in St-Germain.

Hôtel Banville 166 boulevard Berthier, 75017 (tel: 42 67 70 16). Elegant, well-decorated, small hotel. Not central, but excellent value.

Hôtel Bergère Best Western 34 rue Bergère, 75009 (tel: 47 70 34 34). Reliable service and comforts in this chain-owned hotel. Close to the *Grands Boulevards*. Some rather tacky haunts surround the neighbouring nightclub, Le Palace.

Hôtel Bradford 10 rue St-Philippe-du-Roule, 75008 (tel: 43 59 24 20). Old-fashioned chic, period furnishings. Impeccable service, large rooms. Consequently pricey, but worth it.

Hôtel Chopin 46 passage Jouffroy, 75009 (tel: 47 70 58 10). A remarkable setting in a 19th-century shopping arcade for this modest 2-star hotel.

Hôtel du Collège de France 7 rue Thénard, 75005 (tel: 43 26 78 36).
Simple, quiet bed and breakfast establishment in a tiny street off boulevard St-Germain.

Hôtel Corona 8 Cité Bergère, 75009 (tel: 47 70 52 96). A large, well appointed hotel favoured by tour operators. Comfortable rooms, a *quartier* that stays awake late. Parking available.

Hôtel Danemark 21 rue Vavin, 75006 (tel: 43 26 93 78). Well spruced up, a small friendly family-run hotel near the high spots of Montparnasse.

Hôtel des Deux Iles 59 rue St-Louis-en-l'Isle, 75004 (tel: 43 26 13 35). Chintz-covered comfort, at the hub of the island. A charming patio and vaulted breakfast room add to its attraction.

Hôtel Esmeralda 4 rue St-Julien-le-Pauvre, 75005 (tel: 43 54 19 20). Bang opposite Notre-Dame, so some rooms have great views. Dolls-house atmosphere and scale with characteristic 19th-century furniture and *objets d'art*.

Hôtel des Grandes Ecoles 75 rue du Cardinal-Lemoine, 75005 (tel: 43 26 79 23). Well-kept rooms overlooking the garden of this picturesque country-house hotel in a verdant corner of the Latin Quarter. Advisable to book well ahead.

Hôtel Istria 29 rue Campagne Première, 75014 (tel: 43 20 91 82). Follow Montparnasse legends such as Rilke, Duchamp, Man Ray and Aragon to this friendly, comfortable hotel.

Hôtel Lenox 9 rue de

l'Université, 75007 (tel: 42 96 10 95). A favourite with the design and fashion world. Chase TS Eliot's ghost and enjoy the restored, stylish 1930s bar. Make sure you book well ahead.

Hôtel des Marroniers 21 rue Jacob, 75006 (tel: 43 25 30 60). Its fame has spread. Book well in advance to enjoy this gracious country-house atmosphere (see page 147).

Hôtel Mayflower 3 rue du Châteaubriand, 75008 (tel: 45 62 57 46). Near the Etoile, a well-run, relaxed English-style hotel with pretty, peaceful bedrooms. Prices vary according to size of room.

Hôtel Michelet-Odéon 6 place de l'Odéon, 75006 (tel: 46 34 27 80). Extremely reasonable rates for superb, quiet location near the Luxembourg Gardens. Modernised interior, no frills.

Hôtel Opal 19 rue Tronchet, 75008 (tel: 42 65 77 97). Tiny rooms but well located behind the Madeleine. Convenient for forays into the nearby department stores.

Hôtel du Parc Montsouris 4 rue du Parc Montsouris, 75014 (tel: 45 89 09 72). Very reasonable 2-star establishment outside the centre and located across the road from a delightful park.

Hôtel de la place des Vosges 12 rue de Birague, 75004 (tel: 42 72 60 46). Charming 17th-century townhouse with modernised rooms. Quiet, well-maintained, a few steps from the place des Vosges.

Hôtel du Quai Voltaire 19 Quai Voltaire, 75007 (tel: 42 61 50 91). Dusty 18th-century setting, but unbeatable location overlooking Seine opposite Louvre. Baudelaire and Wagner stayed there in their day.

Hôtel Riboutté-Lafayette 5 rue Riboutté, 75009 (tel: 47 70 62 36). Close to Opéra and Grands Boulevards.

Peaceful, small, place, very reasonably priced.

Hôtel Saint-Louis 75 rue St-Louis-en-l'Isle, 75004 (tel: 46 34 04 80). Tasteful, comfortable hotel with well-equipped, though small rooms right in centre of Ile St-Louis.

Hôtel Saint-Merri 78 rue de la Verrerie, 75004 (tel: 42 78 14 15). Eccentric, neo-Gothic style, attached to a church. Rather boxy rooms but extremely central and quiet.

Hôtel Saint-Roch 25 rue Saint-Roch, 75001 (tel: 42 60 17 91). Good value 2-star hotel near the Tuileries on an interesting street. Disregard the entrance.

Hôtel Spéria 1 rue de la Bastille, 75004 (tel: 42 72 04 01). Convenient for Bastille nights and Marais days. Reasonable value; unpretentious renovated interior.

Hôtel de la Tour d'Auvergne 10 rue de la Tour d'Auvergne, 75009 (tel: 48 78 61 60). A small, well maintained 3-star hotel in a relatively undiscovered area between the *Grands Boulevards* and Pigalle.

Hôtel des Tuileries 10 rue St-Hyacinthe, 75001 (tel: 42 61 04 17). Renovated 18th-century style, comfortable and quiet but with small rooms.

Hôtel du Vieux Marais 8 rue du Plâtre, 75004 (tel: 42 78 47 22). Floral wallpaper territory in heart of Marais. Friendly hotel and reasonably priced.

Le Jardin des Plantes 5 rue Linne, 75005 (tel: 47 07 06 20). Still reasonably priced for the facilities it offers – including a sun terrace and views over the botanical gardens.

Le Molière 21 rue Molière, 75001 (tel: 42 96 22 01). Convenient for central monuments, on a quiet street which is near the Louvre and Opéra. Reasonable rates and well equipped rooms.

La Résidence Montmartre 10 rue Burq, 75018 (tel: 46 06 45 28). Well-situated, attractive hotel. Smart though small rooms.

Excellent value for the facilities provided.

Timhotel La Bourse 3 rue de la Banque, 75002 (tel: 42 61 53 90). Small, friendly chain hotel with billiards room. Well located near the place des Victoires.

Budget

Grand Hôtel des Arts et Métiers 4 rue Borda, 75003 (tel: 48 87 73 89). Tucked away just north of Marais. Small, friendly hotel, very reasonable rates.

Grand Hôtel Malher 5 rue Malher, 75004 (tel: 42 72 60 92). In a quiet side street near St-Paul, a tiny nine-room hotel for very thin wallets: no credit cards taken.

Hôtel des Académies 15 rue de la Grande-Chaumière, 75006 (tel: 43 26 66 44). A historic street for artists in Montparnasse. Family-run hotel with some basic 1950s-style garrets. Good value.

Hôtel Andréa 3 rue Saint-Bon, 75004 (tel: 42 78 43 93). Friendly, well-maintained hotel in quiet street behind rue de Rivoli. Good value, so popular.

Hôtel André Gill 4 rue André

DIRECTORY

Gill, 75018 (tel: 42 62 48 48).
Very reasonable, pleasant
rooms and charming
courtyard setting, round the
corner from less
picturesque Pigalle.
Hôtel des Carmes 5 rue des
Carmes, 75005 (tel: 43 29 78
40). In a narrow street of the
Latin Quarter, a very
reasonable 2-star hotel.
Limited facilities.
**Hôtel les Degrés de Notre
Dame** 10 rue des Grands-
Degrés, 75005 (tel: 43 25 88
38). Choose between view
of Notre Dame at the front
or tranquillity at the back in
a very pleasant, well-kept
hotel.
Hôtel Esmeralda 4 rue St-
Julien-le-Pauvre, 75005 (tel:
43 54 19 20). Dolls' house
hotel in one of the most
hectic parts of the Latin
Quarter. Charmingly
furnished, reasonable rates.
Hôtel Henri IV 25 place
Dauphine, 75001 (tel: 43 54
44 53). Extremely basic. One
communal bathroom per
floor, but a rare old-world
atmosphere on one of
Paris' most delightful
squares. Advance booking
essential.
Hôtel le Home Latin 15/17
rue Sommerard, 75005 (tel:
43 26 25 21). Basic but clean
and at heart of Latin
Quarter. Some rooms have
showers, others not, but all
are quiet.
Hôtel Jeanne d'Arc 3 rue
Jarente. 75004 (tel: 48 87 62
11). Charming, provincial-
style hotel in heart of
Marais, clean and quiet, so
well booked-up.
Hôtel Lion d'Or 5 rue de la
Sourdière, 75001 (tel: 42 60
79 04). Excellent location
near Louvre, modernised
but fairly basic amenities.
Hôtel de la Loire 39 bis rue
du Moulin-Vert 75014 (tel:
45 40 66 88). For a taste of
the provinces near the Parc
Montsouris, a small,
charming hotel with garden
and range of room prices.
Hôtel Montpensier 12 rue
de Richelieu, 75001 (tel: 42
96 28 50). Once the
residence of one of Louis
XV's mistresses, a hotel
with a difference and
remarkably cheap. Next to

the Palais Royal.
Hôtel de la Nouvelle France
23 rue des Messageries,
75010 (tel: 48 24 70 74).
Good value, roomy and
clean, although in a rather
uninspiring neighbourhood.
Hôtel de Rouen 42 rue
Croix-des-Petits-Champs,
75001 (tel: 42 61 38 21).
Small, basic hotel. Well
situated for Louvre and Les
Halles.
Hôtel St-André-des-Arts 66
rue St-André-des-Arts,
75005 (tel: 43 26 96 16). A
17th-century Latin Quarter
classic, usually packed.
Lively but noisy.
Hôtel Sainte-Elisabeth 10
rue Sainte-Elisabeth, 75003
(tel: 42 72 01 66). Very basic
1-star hotel for very limited
budgets only. Conveniently
located in the north of
Marais.
Hôtel Sévigné 2 rue Malher,
75004 (tel: 42 72 76 17).
Near the Jewish quarter in
the Marais, a pleasant,
relaxed, well run place,
excellent value.
Hôtel du Vieux Paris 9 rue
Gît-le-Coeur, 75006 (tel: 43
54 41 66). Near action of St-
Michel, the original 'beat'
hotel frequented by
Burroughs, Ginsberg and
the like. Relaxed
atmosphere, tiny rooms.
Plaisant Hôtel 50 rue des
Bernardins, 75005 (tel: 43 54
74 57). Good location close
to rue Monge, very
reasonable, well-maintained
hotel with range of room
amenities and prices.
Tim Hôtel 11 rue Ravignan,
75018 (tel: 42 55 74 79).
Near the famous Bateau
Lavoir in Montmartre, a
chain hotel, well maintained
and friendly.
Welcome Hôtel 5 Impasse
Royer-Collard, 75005 (tel: 43
54 09 63). Quiet, central
location near gardens.
Friendly and very good
value.

Restaurants

Expensive
Au Chien qui Fume 33 rue
du Pont-Neuf, 75001 (tel: 42
36 07 42). Classic seafood
brasserie from way back.
Au Cochon d'Or 192 avenue

Jean-Jaurès, 75019 (tel: 42
45 46 46). A wordly Parisian
crowd pours in here for its
famed grilled meat dishes
and gigantic steaks.
Au Pavillon Puebla Parc des
Buttes-Chaumont, 75019
(tel: 42 08 92 62). In the
incomparable setting of this
landscaped park, an elegant
restaurant serving
imaginative cuisine
influenced by its Catalan
owner.
Au Quai des Ormes 72 Quai
de l'Hôtel-de-Ville, 75004
(tel: 42 74 72 22). Inimitable
architecture and setting
facing Ile Saint-Louis. Fresh
dishes culminating in
delicious desserts. Terrace
in summer.
Au Trou Gascon 40 rue
Taine, 75012 (tel: 43 44 34
26). Lost in the 12th, a
monument to the rich
cooking of southwest
France. Divine cassoulets,
imaginative fish
preparations and emphatic
cheeses.
Beauvilliers 52 rue Lamarck,
75018 (tel: 42 54 54 42).
Elegant 19th-century
setting. Delicious *nouvelle
cuisine* dishes, menu
changes weekly.
Le Bélier l'Hôtel, 13 rue des
Beaux Arts, 75006 (tel: 43 25
27 22). Romantic restaurant
in basement of elegant
hotel. Fountain, flowers and
sophisticated cuisine.
Café Drouant 18 rue Gaillon,
75002 (tel: 42 65 15 16).
Illustrious old literary
sanctuary, superb décor.
Expensive specialities but
reasonable *menu* offered in
evenings.
Chez Pauline 5 rue Villedo,
75001 (tel: 42 96 20 70). One
of Paris' prettiest bistros.
Successful combination of
traditional and modern
dishes. Pricey.
Chez Georges 1 rue du Mail,
75002 (tel: 42 60 07 11).
Thronging with clients day
and night, ruled by brusque
matrons. Character and
classic French cuisine.
Le Closdenis 57 rue
Caulaincourt, 75018 (tel: 46
06 20 26). Discreet, tiny
restaurant serving fresh
specialities of southwest
France.

276

L'Escargot 38 rue Montorgueil, 75001 (tel: 42 36 83 51). Famous old restaurant, elegant setting. Sophisticated cuisine and prices; the speciality is snails.

La Fermette du Sud-Ouest 31 rue Coquillière, 75001 (tel: 42 36 73 55). Famous for home-made southwest France specialities, meaty fare.

La Fermette Marbeuf 5 rue Marbeuf, 75008 (tel: 47 20 63 53). Stunning setting. Imaginative, seasonal dishes. Elegant , stylish clientèle.

Jules Verne Tour Eiffel, 75007 (tel: 45 55 61 44). For a spectacular, memorable treat overlooking Paris. Book several weeks ahead.

Lapérouse 51 Quai des Grands-Augustins, 75006 (tel: 43 26 68 04). No longer renowned for its cuisine, but remains a typical *fin de siècle* setting.

Le Grand Véfour 17 rue de Beaujolais, 75001 (tel: 42 96 56 27). For a memorable dinner in historic splendour next to the ghosts of Colette, Cocteau, Sartre and Napoleon.

La Marlotte 55 rue du Cherche-Midi, 75006 (tel: 45 48 86 79). Exquisite cuisine in sophisticated, candlelit setting. Not excessive prices but restaurant is closed at weekends.

La Méditerranée 2 place de l'Odéon, 75006 (tel: 43 26 36 72). Chic expanse of tables opposite the theatre. Exquisite seafood specialities.

Olympe 8 rue Nicolas-Charlet, 75015 (tel: 47 34 86 08). Smiling lady chef serves up some of Paris' best, most aromatic cuisine.

Pavillon Montsouris 20 rue Gazan, 75014 (tel: 45 88 38 52). Paris' most deliciously bucolic setting in the Parc Montsouris. Go for a discreet summer lunch if you want to enjoy adventurous dishes in this 1900 pavilion.

Le Petit Riche 25 rue Le Peletier, 75009 (tel: 47 70 68 68). Superb, ornate 1880s interior. Delicious bourgeois cuisine, impeccable service. Favourite for business lunches.

La Poste 34 rue Duperré, 75009 (tel: 42 80 66 16). Superb historic setting, offering elegance and trendiness combined. Late bar, *nouvelle cuisine* menu in the restaurant, dance section.

Le Pré Catalan route de Suresnes, Bois de Boulogne, 75016 (tel: 45 24 55 58). Very expensive, but if you must dine in a Parisian rose-garden, this is it. Don't skip Lenôtre's desserts.

Le Procope 13 rue de l'Ancienne Comédie, 75006 (tel: 43 26 99 20). Claims to be Paris' first café, dating from 1686. Touristy but spectacular, renovated décor and good seafood dishes.

Taillevent 15 rue Lamennais, 75008 (tel: 45 61 12 90). Book months ahead, save years in advance. One of Paris' top gourmet restaurants.

Tan Dinh 60 rue de Verneuil, 75007 (tel: 45 44 04 84). Exquisite personalised Vietnamese cuisine served with equal delicacy. Renowned wine list. Chic oriental décor.

Le Train Bleu Gare de Lyon, 75012 (tel: 43 43 09 06). A stunning Belle Epoque décor overpowers the Lyonnais cuisine; choose simple dishes and revel in the setting.

Yugaraj 14 rue Dauphoine, 75006 (tel: 43 26 44 91). One of Paris' best Indian restaurants. Charming and friendly Sri Lankan service, in a very discreet atmosphere.

Moderate

Androuet 41 rue d'Amsterdam, 75008 (tel: 48 74 26 93). Famous old cheese restaurant, over 200 varieties. Recently renovated.

Angélina 226 rue de Rivoli, 75001 (tel: 42 60 82 00). One of Paris's classic *salons de thé*, on the tourist trail. Proustian setting, delectable

DIRECTORY

cakes, light lunches.
Daytime only.

Arthus 36 rue Vivienne,
75002 (tel: 40 39 09 45).
Stylish new restaurant;
inventive, seasonal cuisine
offered in glamorous
setting.

Astier 44 rue Jean-Pierre
Timbaud, 75011 (tel: 43 57
16 35). No hidden surprises
in Astier's copious,
reasonable menu, fantastic
cheeses. Friendly,
unpretentious local spot.

Au Gourmet de l'Ile 42 rue
Saint-Louis-en-l'Ile, 75004
(tel: 43 54 79 62), metro:
Pont-Marie. Reasonably
priced menu with simple,
bourgeois dishes;
unpretentious, old-
fashioned décor.

Au Pied du Cochon 6 rue
Coquillière, 75001 (tel: 42 36
11 75). An old classic from
market days of Les Halles.
Open non-stop, good place
for pig's trotters at 05.00hrs.

Aux Lyonnais 32 rue Saint-
Marc, 75002 (tel: 42 96 65
04). Old-fashioned,
straightlaced bistro serving
classic dishes, a favourite
for after the opera. Very

reasonable.

Baalbeck 16 rue de
Mazagran, 75010 (tel: 47 70
70 02). Popular with Paris'
Lebanese community.
Delicious Middle Eastern
cuisine, with belly-dancers
after 22.00hrs.

Le Balzar 49 rue des Ecoles,
75005 (tel: 43 54 13 67).
Fashionable brasserie near
the Sorbonne. Classic fare
and service, but quite
pricey.

Bar des Théâtres 6 avenue
Montaigne, 75008 (tel: 47 23
34 63). Sophisticated,
animated bar/restaurant
opposite famous theatre.
Actors and chic audience
mix in here for reliable
dishes.

La Belle France Tour Eiffel,
75007 (tel: 45 55 20 04).
Belle Epoque setting,
unique views, very fair fare,
considering.

Bilboquet 13 rue St-Benoît,
75006 (tel: 45 48 81 84).
Favourite with jazz
enthusiasts, good
atmosphere.

Bistro d'à Côté 10 rue
Gustave Flaubert, 75017 (tel:
42 67 05 81). For those who
can't afford chef Michel
Rostang's 5-star affair round
the corner, his bistro fare is
excellent. Not cheap.

Bistrot de l'Etoile 75 avenue
Niel, 75017 (tel: 42 27 88 44).
Top chef Guy Savoy has
also opened this middle-
market branch down the
road. Succulent and chic
dishes.

Le Bistrot de Paris 33 rue de
Lille, 75007 (tel: 42 61 16
83). Bourgeois cuisine at its
best in a sleek, very Parisian
setting.

Bistrot sur le Toit 34 rue du
Colisée, 75008 (tel: 43 59 83
80). Not the original but a
huge, glittery replacement.
Open late for seafood and
classic brasserie fare.

Brasserie dè l'Ile Saint-Louis
55 Quai de Bourbon, 75004
(tel: 43 54 02 59). Noisy,
crowded, fun brasserie on
tip of island. Sunny terrace,
reasonable prices.

Blue Elephant 43 rue de la
Roquette, 75011 (tel: 47 00
42 00). Over-the-top décor
for a trendy Thai restaurant
serving spicy specialities.

Le Boeuf sur le Toit 34 rue
du Colisée, 75008 (tel: 43 59
83 80). Part of Paris' famous
chain of brasseries,
reopened in 1985.
Spectacular 1920s setting
for a good sprinkling of rich
and famous. Fabulous
seafood and *foie gras*.

Brasserie Stella 133 avenue
Victor-Hugo, 75016 (tel: 47
27 60 54). Original 1950s
décor. Large, animated, up-
market brasserie with
classic seafood.

Café Max 7 avenue de la
Motte-Piquet, 75007 (tel: 47
05 57 66). Popular with local
yuppies. Typical old bistro
proposes classic reliable
dishes.

Le Caméléon 6 rue de
Chevreuse, 75006 (tel: 43 20
63 43). Great, imaginative
bistro food in slightly run-
down but characteristic
setting.

Chardenoux 1 rue Jules-
Vallès, 75011 (tel: 43 71 49
52). Charming 1900s bistro
setting. Adventurous,
dependable cuisine. Pricey.

La Chaumière en l'Ile 4 rue
Jean-Bellay, 75004 (tel: 43
54 27 34). Pleasant,
atmospheric 19th-century
setting on Ile Saint-Louis.
Rich specialities from
southwest.

Chez André 12 rue Marbeuf,
75008 (tel: 47 20 59 57). Chic
lady shoppers and
businessmen congregate
here for lunch: game,
seafood or bistro cuisine.

Chez Léon 11 boulevard
Beaumarchais, 75011 (tel:
42 78 42 55). Classic
couscous. Rather plasticised
interior but popular.

Chez Maître Paul 12 rue
Monsieur-le-Prince, 75006
(tel: 43 54 74 59). Friendly
little bistro, delicious
specialities from eastern
France.

Chez Marcel rue Saint-
Nicolas, 75012 (tel: 43 43 49
40). Charming, old-
fashioned bistro with a
faithful clientèle keen on
Beaujolais. Closes early.

Chez Paul 13 rue de
Charonne, 75011 (tel: 47 00
34 57). Favourite with local
gallery owners, artists and
clients. Revamped old bistro
with traditional dishes.

Booking essential.

Chez Ribe 15 avenue de Suffren, 75007 (tel: 45 66 53 79). In shadow of Eiffel Tower, a plush, discreet bistro amiably serving reliable fare. Terrace in summer.

Chez Toutoune 5 rue de Pontoise, 75005 (tel: 43 26 56 81). Fashionable, busy restaurant with fresh, hearty cooking. Service slow, quite expensive.

La Closerie des Lilas 171 boulevard du Montparnasse, 75006 (tel: 43 26 70 50). Famous old Montparnasse bar/brasserie/restaurant. Piano tinkles in background; sophisticated, bustling atmosphere.

Coup de Coeur 19 rue St-Augustin, 75002 (tel: 47 03 45 70). Slick and sleek interior, delicate inventive cuisine. Reasonable menu.

La Coupole 102 boulevard du Montparnasse, 75014 (tel: 43 20 14 20). A Montparnasse institution. Restored art deco interior, still magnificent. Vast, noisy, trendy. Tourists and regulars. Classic seafood and brasserie fare.

Dagorno 190 avenue Jean-Jaurès, 75019 (tel: 40 40 09 39). Another spectacular 1900 setting for a variety of seafood and traditional meat dishes in La Villette, an area once dominated by the abattoirs.

Da Graziano 83 rue Lepic, 75018 (tel: 46 06 84 77). Topped by one of Montmartre's last windmills. Copious Italian cuisine in bright, theatrical surroundings.

Darkoum 44 rue Ste-Anne, 75002 (tel: 42 96 83 76). Spectacular Moorish interior for delectable couscous, tajine and pastilla.

L'Echaudé St-Germain 21 rue de l'Echaudé, 75006 (tel: 43 54 79 02). Romantic St-Germain ambience; reliable cuisine.

L'Ecluse 15 place de la Madeleine, 75008 (tel: 42 65 34 69). One of a small chain of wine bars. Bordeaux by the glass, cold snacks.

Fashionable clientèle.

Le Flamboyant 11 rue Boyer-Barret, 75014 (tel: 45 41 00 22). Reasonable value for one of Paris' best *antillais* restaurants. Spicy *accras*, stuffed crab, turtle kebab.

La Fontaine de Mars 129 rue Saint-Dominique, 75007 (tel: 47 05 46 44). Closed weekends. Friendly local bistro offering tasty, simple cuisine.

La Galoche 41 rue de Lappe, 75011 (tel: 47 00 77 15). Rare survivor in hub of trendiness. Robust, central France in old-fashioned clog-lined setting.

Gaspard de la Nuit 6 rue des Tournelles, 75004 (tel: 42 77 90 53). Calm, comfortable atmosphere for classic bourgeois cuisine.

Le Grand Colbert 4 rue Vivienne, 75002 (tel: 42 86 87 88). Recently restored Belle Epoque brasserie serving classic dishes and seafood till late.

Guy 6 rue Mabillon, 75006 (tel: 43 54 87 61). Lively Brazilian restaurant serving the speciality *feijoada*. Samba and salsa background sounds.

Jacque Mélac 42 rue Léon-Frot, 75011 (tel: 43 70 59 27). An exuberant patron keeps the bistro overflowing with clients and wine. Good for daytime sustenance and Tuesday and Thursday evenings only!

Joe Allen 30 rue Pierre-Lescot, 75001 (tel: 42 36 70 13). Faithful hamburger branch for more mature crowd. Predictable but enjoyable classic.

Le Lance-Roquette 53 rue de la Roquette, 75011 (tel: 47 00 14 42). Modern restaurant for local Bastille trendies. Interesting clientèle and reliable food.

La Magnani 21 rue Chanzy, 75011 (tel: 43 71 27 48). Theatrical Italians feed satisfied locals with a wide range of their specialities.

Le Mansouria 11 rue Faidherbe, 75011 (tel: 43 71 00 16). Fashionable Moroccan restaurant with elegant décor and delicate tajines.

Mexico Café 1 place de Mexico, 75016 (tel: 47 27 96 98). Fashionable haunt. International cuisine, quite chic.

La Mousson 9 rue de la Bastille, 75004 (tel: 42 71 85 20). One of the Bastille's first trendsetters, now a little past it. Cocktail bar downstairs and neo-ethnic cuisine upstairs.

Le Muniche 22 rue Guillaume Apollinaire, 75006 (tel: 46 33 62 09). Majestic new setting for favourite seafood brasserie.

Myrtho 10 rue des Ecouffes, 75004 (tel: 42 77 00 36). Relaxed elegance, smartly designed interior, inventive French cuisine.

Natacha 17 bis rue Campagne Première, 75014 (tel: 43 20 79 27). For showbiz star-gazing, not cuisine. Copious bourgeois cooking in elegant setting. Pretentious, very Parisian.

Nioullaville 32/34 rue de l'Orillon, 75011 (tel: 43 38 30 44). Hong Kong comes to Paris, or Belleville. Vast kitsch Chinese restaurant with endless menu and passing trolleys for sampling.

Nos Ancêtres les Gaulois 39 rue St-Louis-en-l'Ile, 75004 (tel: 46 33 66 07). Unlimited wine...rowdy, fun atmosphere in pseudo-medieval setting.

La Nuit des Rois 3 rue des Pasteur-Wagner, 75011 (tel: 48 07 15 22). Comfortable, quite elegant retreat for sipping champagne late into the night.

Pharamond 24 rue de la Grande Truanderie, 75001 (tel: 42 33 06 72). Pretty, ceramic-tiled old bistro. Increasingly trendy clientèle. Quite pricey classic dishes.

Le Poète Ivre 8 rue Leopold Bellan, 75002 (tel: 40 26 26 46). Eccentric décor and proprietor, but good spicy Thai cuisine.

La Potée des Halles 3 rue Etienne-Marcel, 75001 (tel: 42 36 18 68). Robust regional cooking served up in superb Belle Epoque tiled setting.

La Poule au Pot 9 rue

DIRECTORY

Vauvilliers, 75001 (tel: 42 36 32 96). Open till 06.00hrs. Spend all night here sampling traditional dishes in a very animated atmosphere.

404 69 rue des Gravilliers, 75003 (tel: 42 74 57 81). Low seats, low lighting, high ceilings. Popular Moroccan restaurant with lively young crowd.

Restaurant Curieux 14 rue Saint-Merri, 75004 (tel: 42 72 75 97). Curiouser and curiouser. Eccentric baroque interior, clients regimented by strict, buttoned-up waitresses, but excellent choice of classic cuisine.

Sipario 69 rue de Charenton, 75011 (tel: 43 45 70 26). Classy Italian cuisine and theatrical restaurant. Near Bastille Opera.

Thoumieux 79 rue Saint-Dominique, 75007 (tel: 47 05 49 75). Part bistro, part brasserie, a fashionable, friendly, animated place serving southwest specialities.

Vagenende 142 boulevard St-Germain, 75006 (tel: 43 26 68 18). Art nouveau setting and classic cuisine.

Willi's Wine Bar 13 rue des Petit-Champs, 75001 (tel: 42 61 05 09). Cheerful, British-run restaurant/wine bar. Stylish with good, fresh cuisine.

Budget
A la Cloche des Halles 28 rue Coquillière, 75001 (tel: 42 36 93 89). Typical animated local wine bar. Good for lunch; closes at 21.00hrs and at weekends.

L'As du Fallafel 34 rue des Rosiers, 75004 (tel: 48 87 63 60). Good kosher food shop with delicious fallafels to eat on the spot or take away.

Au Bistrot de la Sorbonne 4 rue Toullier, 75005 (tel: 43 54 41 49). Crowded with students, noisy, friendly. Very basic dishes and prices.

Au Limonaire 88 rue de Charenton, 75011 (tel: 43 43 49 14). Classic, friendly bistro specialising in Côtes-du-Rhône. Local crowd comes for *plats du jour* and

occasional spontaneous live music.

Au Petit Prince 3 rue Monsieur-le-Prince, 75006 (tel: 43 29 74 92). Gothic shadows reign. Attentive service and imaginative, seasonal dishes. Slightly up-market.

Au Sauvignon 80 rue des Saint-Père, 75007 (tel: 45 48 49 02). Good for a quick snack if shopping in St-Germain. Small, popular wine bar with much frequented terrace in summer.

Aux Artistes 63 rue Falguière, 75015 (tel: 43 22 05 39). Rock-bottom prices, but avoid the carafe wine. Otherwise copious, hearty menu. Crowded, not for *tête-à-têtes*.

Aux Bons Crus 7 rue des Petits Champs, 75001 (tel: 42 60 06 45). Popular wine bar serving hot lunches. Barrels tower over tiny tables packed with locals.

Aux Savoyards 14 rue des Boulangers, 75005 (tel: 46 33 53 78). Generous menu, shared tables. Animated, crowded, friendly.

Le Baron Rouge 1 rue Théophile-Roussel, 75012 (tel: 43 43 14 32). A classic bistro selling wine from its barrels and serving delicious little platters. Closes early.

Batifol 14 rue Mondétour, 75001 (tel: 42 36 85 50). Part of chain but lively, friendly café-bistro attracting gregarious youth.

Bistro de la Gare 59 boulevard du Montparnasse, 75006 (tel: 42 22 22 55). Also part of a chain but good value meat dishes, superb turn-of-the-century décor.

Le Bistrot d'Asie 16 rue de Belleville, 75020 (tel: 46 36 23 97). In a row of comparable Asian restaurants. Thai, Laotian and Chinese specialities.

Casa Miguel 48 rue St-Georges, 75009 (tel: 42 81 09 61). World-famous soup kitchen. Rock-bottom prices; queues are endless: 12.00–13.00hrs and 19.00–20.00hrs only.

Chai de l'Abbaye 26 rue de

Buci, 75006 (tel: 43 26 68 26). Good lunchtime spot. Wine by the glass, reasonable salads and *plats du jour* in heart of market street.

Chartier 7 rue du Faubourg-Montmartre, 75009 (tel: 47 70 86 29). Famous food institution popular with tourists but still a must. 1900s setting, shared tables, speedy waiters.

Chez Georges 11 rue des Canettes, 75006 (tel: 43 26 79 15). A rowdy Left Bank institution, much loved by intellectual drinkers. Open till 02.00hrs.

Chez Pépita 21 rue Bayard, 75008 (tel: 47 23 58 49). A rarity in this area: traditional cuisine in provincial-style bistro.

Le Citoyen 22 rue Daguerre, 75014 (tel: 43 22 53 53). Fresh dishes and home-made desserts, delightful summer terrace in animated market street.

Le Cochon à l'Oreille 15 rue Montmartre, 75001 (tel: 42 36 07 56). Open 04.00–15.00hrs. Old-time Les Halles classic bar, good for early risers and late-nighters. Delicious hot dishes and lunchtime. Crowded.

La Côte 77 rue de Richelieu, 75002 (tel: 42 97 40 68). Quick, bustling wine bar, a favourite with local businessmen at lunchtime.

Les Deux Saules 91 rue St-Denis, 75001 (tel: 42 36 46 57). Visitors love the authentic tiled Belle Epoque interior. Small, popular; onion soup speciality. Terrace.

Dilan 13 rue Mandar, 75002 (tel: 42 21 46 38). Friendly, large tables, basic setting, Kurdish and Turkish specialities.

Le Drouot 103 rue de Richelieu, 75002 (tel: 42 96 68 23). Large canteen style similar to Chartiers but less fancy. Basic cuisine, cheap and cheerful.

Le Duc des Lombards 21 boulevard de Sébastopol, 75001 (tel: 42 33 22 88). Reasonably priced menu in young, friendly setting with late jazz-bar on ground

280

floor.

L'Ecluse 15 Quai des Grands-Augustins, 75006 (tel: 46 33 58 74). Bordeaux by the glass, cold platters, small relaxed wine bar.

La Ferme 40 rue de la Montagne-Ste-Geneviève, 75005 (tel: 43 54 49 85). Relaxed, rustic atmosphere. Good value, popular with local students.

La Frégate 1 rue du Bac, 75007 (tel: 42 61 23 77). Unbelievable value for a chic quartier beside Musée d'Orsay. Old-fashioned, stilted brasserie (quite cheap) and restaurant (pricier).

Le Grand Bistrot 7 rue Saint-Séverin, 75005 (tel: 43 25 94 21). Serves late. Noisy, friendly atmosphere with reasonably priced menus. Make sure you try the snails.

La Gueuze 19 rue Soufflot, 75005 (tel: 43 54 63 00). A beer-lovers' paradise. Belgian specialities, lengthy list of beers.

Hawaï avenue d'Ivry, 75013 (tel: 45 86 91 90). Huge, animated canteen-like restaurant in Chinatown. Generous soups and Vietnamese specialities on offer.

L'Incroyable 26 rue de Richelieu, 75001 (tel: 42 96 24 64). Tiny, friendly, tucked away in atmospheric passage. Closes early.

Ishtar 17 rue Paul Bert, 75011 (tel: 43 73 08 32). Friendly restaurant serving classic choice of Lebanese cuisine.

Juveniles 47 rue de Richelieu, 75001 (tel: 42 97 46 49). Tapas-style snacks and salads served with wine by glass. Small, crowded, hard to squeeze in. Go early!

Osteria del Passepartout 20 rue de l'Hirondelle, 75006 (tel: 46 34 14 54).Simple Italian restaurant down miniscule alley. Inventive pasta dishes for reasonable prices.

Le Petit Machon 158 rue St-Honoré, 75001 (tel: 42 60 23 37). Close to Louvre. Simple bistro food with accent on Lyon-style meat-based

dishes.

Le Petit Saint-Benoît 4 rue Saint-Benoît, 75006 (tel: 42 60 27 92). A favourite cheap restaurant, its waitreses and décor unchanged since the 1930s.

La Petite Chaise 36 rue de Grenelle, 75007 (tel: 42 22 13 35). Founded in 1680. Copious all-in menu. Smart, popular, fun place.

Polidor 41 rue Monsieur-le-Prince, 75006 (tel: 43 26 95 34). In every guide book but still good value. Cheerful, open late and tasty basic dishes. Service can be brusque.

Relais de la Butte 12 rue Ravignan, 75018 (tel: 42 23 94 64). Heavily laid-on Montmartre atmosphere, but excellent value nevertheless.

Le Relais Savoyard 13 rue Rodier, 75009 (tel: 45 26 17 48). Family-run neighbourhood bistro. Good bourgeois fare.

Restaurant des Beaux Arts 11 rue Bonaparte, 75006 (tel: 43 26 92 64). Popular meeting place for art students and impoverished philosophers. Inspiring décor and classic family cuisine.

Rose de Kashmire 66 Passage Brady, 75010 (tel: 42 46 23 75). Indian and Pakistani dishes in dilapidated covered passage, monopolised by Asian restaurants.

Le Royal Belleville 19 rue Louis-Bonnet, 75011 (tel: 43 38 22 72). Vast, canteen-like Chinese restaurant with endless menu of fine specialities. On the first floor with a different entrance is Le Président, which is slightly more up-market.

Le Rubis 10 rue du Marché St-Honoré, 75001 (tel: 42 61 03 34). Time-honoured wine by the glass and platters of cheese or *charcuterie* in jovial atmosphere.

Le Sunset 60 rue des Lombards, 75001 (tel: 40 26 46 60). Open till early hours, for jazz fanatics only. Traditional French food on the menu.

Tai Yien 5 rue de Belleville,

75019 (tel: 42 41 44 16). Another Belleville institution, popular with the local Asiatic community. Wonderful soups and dim sum specialities.

La Tartine 24 rue de Rivoli, 75004 (tel: 42 72 76 85). Popular old wine bar, good for lunchtime snacks, a glass of wine and smoky atmosphere.

Le Temps des Cérises 31 rue de la Cérisaie, 75004 (tel: 42 72 08 63). Closed in the evening. Popular 1900s bistro. Excellent value lunches.

Thuy Huong 15 avenue de Choisy, 75013 (tel: 45 86 87 07). Extraordinary concrete jungle environment for pavilion restaurants. Delicious Cambodian and Vietnamese specialities on the menu.

La Tourelle 5 rue Hautefeuille, 75006 (tel: 46 33 12 47). Unpretentious restaurant in historic building. Local favourite; fast service, reliable simple dishes.

Le Volcan 10 rue Thouin, 75005 (tel: 46 33 38 33). Dependable old favourite with choice of menus, international dishes.

Index

A

INDEX/ACKNOWLEDGEMENTS

ACKNOWLEDGEMENTS

Acknowledgements

The Automobile Association would like to thank the following photographers, libraries and associations for their assistance in the preparation of this book.

ALL SPORT (UK) LTD 95a (Gerard Vandy Stadt)

FULTON PICTURE LIBRARY 14, 46/7

MARY EVANS PICTURE LIBRARY 30b, 31a, 33, 36a, 37a, 37b, 38a, 38b, 39a, 40, 42b, 43a, 48b, 49, 112

MUSEE BACCARAL 79

MUSEE DE CLUNY 105a, 140a

PHILIPPE COVETTE 84

POPPOFOTO 115

TOPHAM PICTURE SOURCE 19

© WALT DISNEY COMPANY 196, 197a, 197b

ZEFA PICTURE LIBRARY 82, 83

The following photographs were taken by BERTRAND REIGER and from the Automobile Association's picture library (© AA Photo Library).

P ENTICNAP 3, 56b, 114, 134/5, 137a, 137b, 171

E MEACHER 24c, 181b

D NOBLE 29a, 35, 61a, 192a, 193, 194, 198, 199, 202/3, 204, 205, 209a, 209b, 210, 211, 212a, 212b

K PATERSON 2, 5, 6, 12, 13, 16, 20a, 21, 23, 26/7, 41, 46a, 52, 55a, 56, 69b, 71b, 76a, 87a, 88a, 89b, 91a, 93a, 94a, 98a, 101a, 101b, 106, 110a, 116a, 120b, 122a, 139, 140b, 166, 172, 177a, 177b, 184, 185, 186a, 186b, 187, 216, 226, 227, 232, 238, 244, 248, 249, 250/1, 256, 262, 263, 268/9, 270, 273, 277

B REIGER 4, 7, 9, 14, 20b, 22, 26, 29, 30, 32, 34, 44a, 48a, 54, 58a, 59a, 59b, 60a, 63, 66, 66/7, 68, 69a, 70, 71a, 73a, 73b, 75a, 75b, 76b, 77, 81, 87b, 88b, 89a, 92a, 92b, 93b, 95b, 96a, 96b, 97a, 97b, 98b, 99a, 102, 107a, 107b, 109a, 109b, 111a, 113a, 113b, 117a, 118, 119a, 119b, 120a, 123a, 124, 125, 126, 127, 128a, 128b, 130a, 130b, 134, 136, 143, 144a, 144b, 146, 148, 149a, 149b, 150, 151a, 158, 163, 165b, 170, 173, 178a, 180a, 181a, 182a, 188, 191, 192b, 203, 207, 217, 218, 219, 220, 222, 223, 225, 228, 236/7, 239b, 242, 247, 260a, 261, 264, 267, 274, 275, 278, 281

C SAWYER 200, 201

B SMITH 237

A SOUTER 8, 17, 18, 24a, 36b, 42a, 45a, 61b, 64, 82a, 85b, 100a, 121a, 132a, 138a, 145, 156, 159, 161, 164, 165a, 168, 169, 174, 175, 179a, 179b, 224, 229, 230, 231, 233, 239, 252, 259, 265, 266